A FORTIFIED SEA

MARITIME CURRENTS: HISTORY AND ARCHAEOLOGY

SERIES EDITOR

Gene Allen Smith

EDITORIAL ADVISORY BOARD

John F. Beeler
Alicia Caporaso
Annalies Corbin
Ben Ford
Ingo K. Heidbrink
Susan B. M. Langley
Nancy Shoemaker
Joshua M. Smith
William H. Thiesen

A FORTIFIED SEA

THE DEFENSE OF THE ANGLO-SPANISH CARIBBEAN IN THE EIGHTEENTH CENTURY

Edited by
Pedro Luengo and Gene Allen Smith

THE UNIVERSITY OF ALABAMA PRESS
Tuscaloosa

The University of Alabama Press
Tuscaloosa, Alabama 35487–0380
uapress.ua.edu

Copyright © 2024 by the University of Alabama Press
All rights reserved.

Inquiries about reproducing material from this work should be addressed to the University of Alabama Press.

Typeface: Alegreya

Cover image: San Juan de Ulúa fort, Mexico; photograph courtesy of Pedro Luengo
Cover design: Sandy Turner Jr.

Pedro Luengo acknowledges funding from Spain's *Ministerio de Ciencia e Innovación Arquitecturas del poder* for the project *Arquitecturas del poder. Emulación y pervivencias en América y el sudeste asiático (1746-1808)*. Grant PID2021-122170NB-I00 funded by MICIU/AEI/10.13039/501100011033 and by "ESF Investing in your future."

Cataloging-in-Publication data is available from the Library of Congress.
ISBN: 978–0–8173–2204–5 (cloth)
ISBN: 978–0–8173–6152–5 (paper)
E-ISBN: 978–0–8173–9522–3

Contents

Introduction
Gene Allen Smith and Pedro Luengo
i

Abbreviations
xv

Part I
A Common Background: Early Modern Caribbean and the Training of Military Engineers

Chapter 1
Fortification and Pedagogy: Theoretical Military Engineering and Cartography between Academic Institutional Rigor and Ludic Poliorcetics
Juan Miguel Muñoz Corbalán
13

Chapter 2
Military Engineers and the Real Academia de Bellas Artes de San Fernando's Censure
Jesús María Ruiz Carrasco
28

Part II
The British Plan: Warfare, Intelligence, and Rhetoric of the Empire

Chapter 3
Fortification, Engineering, and Empire in Mid-Eighteenth-Century Jamaica
Aaron Graham
45

Chapter 4

Vernacular Architecture and the Defense of Antigua, 1670–1785

Christopher K. Waters

55

Chapter 5

The English Settlement of Guantánamo, Cuba: Urban and Defensive Features

Pedro Luengo

68

Chapter 6

Fortification Systems Designed to Counter Charles Knowles's
Attacks in Cuba and Saint-Domingue in 1748

Ignacio J. López-Hernández

86

Chapter 7

The Versatility of the Military Engineer Luis Huet:
Engineer, Urban Planner, and Spy

Pedro Cruz Freire

101

Chapter 8

Text and Image: The 1762 Capture of Havana

Alfredo J. Morales

112

Part III
The Spanish Plan: Fortifying the Caribbean Sea

Chapter 9

The Interior Defense of Santiago de Cuba: The Fort of San Francisco

María Mercedes Fernández Martín

129

Chapter 10

Engineering and the Articulation of Territory: Juan de Herrera y Sotomayor and the Canal del Dique Improvement Project in Cartagena de Indias, 1725–1728

Francisco Javier Herrera García

137

Chapter 11

Projects and Defensive Reforms at the End of the Viceregal Cartagena: The Military Engineer Manuel de Anguiano and the Martyrs of Independence

Manuel Gámez Casado

160

Chapter 12

The Fort of San Carlos de Perote: The Historical Context of Its Construction

Mónica Cejudo Collera and Germán Segura García

174

Chapter 13

The Three Defensive Lines Built on the East Front of Puerta de Tierra, San Juan, Puerto Rico

Nuria Hinarejos Martín

185

Chapter 14

The Defense of New Orleans as a Capital of the Government of Louisiana and Western Florida

José Miguel Morales Folguera

198

Chapter 15

"Without Any Fighting or Disturbance": Conquering Spanish Baton Rouge and Mobile

Gene Allen Smith

209

Epilogue

Pedro Luengo and Gene Allen Smith
221

Notes
225

Bibliography
273

List of Contributors
291

Index
295

Introduction

Gene Allen Smith and Pedro Luengo

From the twelfth century onward, the expression that "all roads lead to Rome" has described the centralization of an empire with a capital and roads radiating out to the periphery. Conversely, the expression also describes the periphery from which the roads run and how that entity supports the center. Beginning in the 1960s, this expression's meaning has spurred an ongoing historiographical debate about the "center and periphery dependency model" in defining local, regional, and global interdependency. Many recent historical approaches have expanded the question to explore the importance of imperial marginal spaces as cultural crossroads and the process of how they came to be so. The periphery—spaces usually explained by their distance from power centers—had become the focus and is being studied in its own contexts. For example, Richard White's *The Middle Ground: Indians, Empires, and Republics in the Great Lakes Region, 1650–1815* broadened our understanding of imperial competition on the periphery by looking at accommodation and the search for common meaning in the contested Great Lakes area during the seventeenth and eighteenth centuries. Similarly, Andrew K. Frank and A. Glenn Crothers's more recent collection *Borderland Narratives* contends that geographic expansion on the periphery of North America placed Native Americans and Europeans as full partners in the process and maintains that the concept of borderlands redefined regions. Cultural appropriation, marginalized peoples, and even race have all become central features as scholars attempt to situate the borderlands as a geographical concept defined by political boundaries and as a process in which conflict and interaction define culture, peoples, and empires in liminal regions.[1]

The Caribbean, especially during the eighteenth century, offers a good example of the periphery and a cultural crossroads. Considered the traditional periphery of European western expansion, it has generally been explored or analyzed as part of an empire rather than as a complex scenario on the periphery with multiple contested boundaries. Diverse European colonizers, including

Spaniards, Dutch, English, French, and Danish, converted the Caribbean Sea into a cultural patchwork, forming a palimpsest alongside native traditions. These differing cultural contexts, containing their own internal segmentation, appeared especially evident during regional and national conflicts that took place throughout the eighteenth century, prompting the need for fortifications to protect imperial interests. The emergence of Anglo-American colonies during the eighteenth century and later the United States gradually modified the existing geopolitical balance, redefining the cultural and geopolitical boundaries of the region.[2]

The eighteenth-century wars for empire—the War of the Spanish Succession (1701–14) through the War of Jenkins' Ear/War of Austrian Succession (1739–48) to the Seven Years' War (1753–64) and the American War for Independence (1775–83)—all redefined frontiers, borderlands, and colonial possessions. These conflicts also forced imperial powers to reexamine how they defined their empire, defended their possession, fought future wars, and what military contributions they would expect from their colonial subjects. As imperial boundaries became more rigid, borderlands became contested frontiers in which geographical spaces and human experiences shifted across time and place, but even the rigidity of boundaries and space did not prevent different people from traveling throughout the region. European fortifications constructed to define and defend geopolitical boundaries represented impressive physical sites demonstrating the extent of imperial power on the periphery. Yet they also assumed an important role as occupying cultural borderlands, and their presence exhibited construction techniques defined by geographical context and a theoretical approach unlike any in Europe. Exercising power and building forts in the contested boundaries of the periphery required innovative solutions, which inevitably had to include a knowledge of and adaptation to native traditions.[3]

Local solutions to imperial problems ultimately reached the metropolis as profitable innovations. Their significance is not limited to historical events, because forts became the only surviving remains of imperial heritage in many cases. As such, the history of some local communities can only be explained by examining forts—their construction, operation, and role in local society—that dominated their environment. Forts ultimately explain the history of communities and how local empowerment shaped modern nation-state discourse. This new historical discourse, based on preserved relics of fortifications, reshapes current contested boundaries between Western, native, imperial, local, and enemy as well as between past and present. Forts represent historian Frederick Jackson Turner's frontier coming-to-an-end, as the structures embodied the presence of government, power, and authority on locals, native peoples, and colonial subjects alike. Yet forts also embody historian Herbert Eugene Bolton's conception of borderlands because they initiated a historical process of transformation from contested boundaries to periphery, connected to the metropole.[4]

This broad topic has been addressed by different scholarly traditions during the last half century. Borderland historiography, comparative history, and entangled history is vast and encompasses the Anglo-American and Spanish American worlds. Moreover, the comparative size of the two imperial domains differed drastically, with Spain's American holdings containing significantly more area. First, it is necessary to understand the importance of classic studies by authors such as Jorge Cañizares-Esguerra, J. H. Elliott, and Eliga H. Gould, who all have used the comparative history approach as a method to transcend national frameworks in Anglo-American and Spanish American historiography; the concepts employed by these authors have shaped virtually every chapter of this project.[5] Previous scholarship on fortifications in New Spain has helped create a theoretical framework for this study.[6] Moreover, recent modern interpretative studies about forts in Spain, which reveal a deep and rich array of sources, have become available and also provide the necessary context for understanding this project on fortifications.[7] And along these same lines, UNESCO has published books on American fortifications and their recovery, while several scholars have studied specific monuments or buildings within fortifications in Spanish Cuba and around the Caribbean.[8] Ultimately, the first two decades of the twenty-first century have witnessed a renewed interest on this subject from both sides of the Atlantic.[9]

During the last decade several publications have emerged describing eighteenth-century military engineering and fortifications in Spain.[10] These works have provided an important foundation for understanding the reality of military engineering in Spain, yet the expansion of fortifications into the Americas and Asia still reveals the need for additional research. A recent examination of the drawings of engineers during a three-century period has also shown how their artistic plans and illustrations permitted the Spanish to control and transform cities and territories.[11] In 2016, several important books were published that used case studies to illustrate how military engineers reshaped the physical landscape of the Caribbean and Gulf of Mexico region for imperial reasons and in doing so laid the foundation for colonial development, ultimately broadening our understanding of the military and civil heritage of Hispanic and American cities—military engineer Silvestre Abarca, for example, whose work as a member of the Royal Corps of Military Engineers employed different defensive approaches and theories that were adopted in Spain and in its overseas possessions as well as embraced tactics for territorial control in America,

Europe, and North Africa.[12] While all these important recent studies have provided a solid historiographical foundation, unfortunately they give little attention to the cross-imperial connections or an entangled view of the Caribbean phenomenon.

Fortifications in North America have also been gaining attention from scholars. Several scholars have addressed warfare in North America between the imperial European powers and various Native American tribes. Ian Steele focused on the British surrender to French forces on August 9, 1757, at Fort William Henry; as soldiers, servants, and their families marched south toward Fort Edward they were ambushed and massacred by French-allied Indians, marking the bloodiest day of the French and Indian War. While not only about the building of the fort and the imperial intercontinental competition for North America, the setting also provided the backdrop to James Fenimore Cooper's classic novel, *The Last of the Mohicans*.[13] The French constructed the Vauban-styled Fort Ticonderoga, which commanded the Lake Champlain corridor north to Canada, on the south end of the lake during the Seven Years' War.[14] Fred Anderson's magisterial study highlights the fort's importance to the region during that conflict. Richard Ketcham and James Kirby Martin both highlight the fort's role during the campaigns of the American War of Independence, yet neither deal specifically with the structure itself.[15]

Castillo de San Marcos at St. Augustine, the oldest and most historically important masonry fort in the United States, was constructed by the Spanish to protect their North American empire and provide defense to the Spanish Treasure Galleons exiting the Florida Straits. Using local *coquina* (small shells formed into limestone) as building material and indigenous labor from Spanish missions, it took twenty-three years (from 1672 to 1695) to complete construction of the fort. Yet given the structure's importance, there is no study that details the fort's construction, its history, and its cultural resources impact or legacy. US National Park Service studies and brochures, in addition to archaeological studies, provide information gleaned from years of intellectual labor, but they do not place the information in the context of how forts shaped society or empire. Historian David Weber's important book, *Spanish Frontier in North America*, does show how the fort played into Spain's imperial ambitions, but it does not focus on the fort itself. All told, these important sources also lay a foundation for understanding how forts fit into the picture of empire, but they do not address the topic of this book either.[16]

In this complex but suggestive context, this book presents an original contribution on the role of forts in the greater Caribbean during the long eighteenth century. It defines a trans-imperial dialogue, technical transfer processes and challenges, and how anachronistic physical fort remains can address the ongoing question of heritage. This book has brought together a diverse multinational collection of scholars who employ varied and different approaches and assembles a complementary product on the role of forts in society. On the one hand, this book includes several historiographical traditions—from Spanish to the English—with local research contributions, all portraying the *borderland* as a breakthrough contested cultural, social, economic, and military boundary. At the same time, the book offers visual or war studies approaches as well as architectural and historical contributions, enriching a usually monothematic point of view. Finally, cultural management of the historical remains of forts reveals the last step of the transfer process of historical research, as local communities try to preserve and interpret the role of these structures for their society.

This book addresses the question of forts in three parts. The first two chapters by Juan Miguel Muñoz Corbalán and Jesús María Ruiz Carrasco, respectively, generally define the training of military engineers before reaching America. This part focuses on the Spanish experience, which was similar to that of French engineers and completely unlike the English or Dutch experience. Yet too little is known about the local training of engineers and the native oral traditions that influenced military architecture in the region.

Chapters in part II examine English military plans and settlements in the Caribbean. Three chapters focus on Jamaica (Aaron Graham), Antigua (Christopher K. Waters), and the military camps in Cartagena de Indias or Guantánamo (Pedro Luengo). Other chapters reveal how these efforts were critically linked with other intelligence works (Ignacio J. López Hernández) counterbalanced by the enemy (Pedro Cruz Freire), and later converted into tools for casting public opinion in London (Alfredo J. Morales). Taken together, these chapters reveal how the British planned the defense of their ports and holdings, and how they dealt with the rhetorical image of the empire. Conversely, Spanish defense projects formed the required counterpoint.

In contrast to the scarcity of works focusing on British cases, the chapters in part III clarify the building processes of fortifications in Santiago de Cuba, Cartagena de Indias, Havana, Veracruz, and Portobelo, among others. Rather than merely repeat compilations of known information, these authors have addressed the question from different perspectives. First, they define the context of the seventeenth-century Caribbean (María Mercedes Fernández Martín) and the importance of military engineers in other civic works including fluvial engineering (Francisco Javier Herrera García) and religious buildings. Second, the unique colonial-inspired building techniques illustrate how cultural dialogue was interchanged in the Caribbean. Additionally, some significant fortification reforms of the time, barely known to modern audiences, reveal the contributions to important military positions such as San Juan of Puerto Rico (Nuria

Hinarejos Martín), Perote (Mónica Cejudo Collera and Germán Segura García), Louisiana and Western Florida (José Miguel Morales Folguera), and Cartagena de Indias (Manuel Gámez Casado). Finally, forts at timed played important roles in the shifting imperial geopolitical boundaries, such as when Americans conquered Baton Rouge and Mobile, thereby redefining the contested US-Spanish Florida boundary (Gene Allen Smith).

Hopefully, the approach used here will continue to be applied. After including English, Spanish, and local contributions in a wider perspective, we still need further study on other territories, such as those under French, Dutch, or Danish control and those that may be completely forgotten today. Furthermore, rarely studied fortifications in locations such as modern-day Guatemala, Nicaragua, or Venezuela might offer opportunities for future study. If so, taken together with more detailed information on the exchange of military architectural knowledge across geographic zones, this volume will help to rescue and to resurrect the role and importance of native workers and colonial societies to the empire. Finally, we will have a greater understanding of how forgotten structures can serve as bases for modern interpretations about the colonial past and how they shaped contested imperial holdings and postcolonial discourses.

Abbreviations

AGI—Archivo General de Indias
AGMM—Archivo General Militar de Madrid
AGNM—Archivo General de la Nación de México
AGS—Archivo General de Simancas
AHN—Archivo Histórico Nacional
AHPC—Archivo Histórico Provincial de Cádiz
ANOM—Archives Nationales d'Outre Mer
ARABASF—Asociación de Amigos de la Real Academia de Bellas Artes San
    Fernando
BL—British Library
BNF—Bibliothèque Nationale de France
CGEM—Centro Geográfico del Ejército de Madrid
CSPWI—Calendar of State Papers Colonial, America and West Indies
JA—Jamaica Archives
LC—Library of Congress
MNM—Museo Naval de Madrid
NAAB—National Archives of Antigua and Barbuda
SGE—Servicio Geográfico del Ejército
TNA—The National Archives, Kew, UK

A FORTIFIED SEA

Part I

A Common Background

Early Modern Caribbean and the Training of Military Engineers

1

Fortification and Pedagogy

Theoretical Military Engineering and Cartography between Academic Institutional Rigor and Ludic Poliorcetics

Juan Miguel Muñoz Corbalán

During the eighteenth century, the Caribbean consisted of a complex political scenario in which European nations competed for political hegemony and extended control, and as a result, imperial regimes needed many technically trained professionals to administer and defend their valuable holdings. This competition, along with economic and social challenges, also created the need for continued construction and improvement of public buildings, but more importantly for fortifications to defend the colonial holdings. Between Queen Anne's War (1702–1713) and the independence conflicts of the nineteenth century, the Caribbean gradually emerged as a center of international struggle. As this occurred, military engineers began playing important roles, although not every specialist always had the recommended training; in fact, many were just self-taught volunteers, as Fernández Martín (chapter 9 herein) reveals for the late seventeenth century. To address the general lack of expertise, European powers selected from two different options. On the one hand, the English mainly relied on professionals experienced in military affairs but who often lacked a profound theoretical background or educational foundation, as many chapters in this volume show. On the other hand, other states, such as France or Spain, reopened or inaugurated specialized academies to provide technicians for their possessions in both Europe and overseas. Clarifying the theoretical knowledge offered by these institutions is crucial for understanding the starting point for the cultural dialogue that later developed in many of these Caribbean examples. This dialogue is evident especially in military architecture, but it can also be applied to other American building processes where only the minor influence of the Academia de San Fernando, as addressed in the following chapter, complemented the European architectural impact in the region.

To define the background of these European technicians, this chapter reveals how the fortification of American ports by European powers during the eighteenth century was based on academic training, especially in the French and Spanish empires. Military engineers spent their first years studying mathematics or geometrics through European treatises, allowing them later to direct building works and exchange information with the metropolis from the Caribbean. Alongside this academic approach, these technicians developed other tools, lighter in nature, to consolidate the newly acquired knowledge. This chapter clarifies both perspectives to define the basis of engineers for later technical transfer in America.

This academic approach, specialized for wartime and military architecture, provides a parallel to that of the Royal Academy of Fine Arts, which Ruiz Carrasco addresses in chapter 2. But none of these trained engineers reached the Caribbean before the eighteenth century. Previous fortification experiences were supported by self-taught technicians who usually had little knowledge of the most recent European theories. Yet this situation progressively changed during the eighteenth century, thanks to the efforts of Spanish academies that trained men for the Caribbean. Treatises on mathematics and fortifications were written and published, ensuring somewhat standardized technical training among all those who were taught in military academies, those who joined the Corps of Engineers, or even those who just worked in situ because of their excellent capabilities.[1]

The Academy of Mathematics: The Homogenization of Technical Knowledge

Courses taught at the Academy of Mathematics based their content on the theoretical substrate provided by several authors who had formerly published their own knowledge and about their own experiences. These treaties on poliorcetics and fortification also incorporated other topics that were necessary for the integral training of engineers and artillerymen. In eighteenth-century Spain, mathematics academies were founded in Barcelona, Ceuta, and Oran. The textbooks used there were the normative texts published by European experts who had created the theoretical framework of military engineering from the sixteenth century to the most recent contributions from some prestigious professionals, culminating by the late seventeenth century with Sébastien de Vauban. Spanish authors themselves, including Cristóbal de Rojas and Sebastián Fernández de Medrano, who had managed to locate the Spanish engineering military in a dignified place within the European panorama of the modern era, were also studied alongside some outstanding French, Dutch, and Italian architects. At the Academy of Mathematics of Brussels—one of the leading institutions in Europe for military engineering—director Fernández de Medrano used his own treaties to carry out the corresponding pedagogical work for teaching aspirants who applied to become engineers.[2] The texts taught in the Academy of Barcelona followed the same tradition of the school established in Flanders.[3] But seventeenth-century classics were not the only material to be studied. During the eighteenth century, new works appeared that updated several aspects set by the hegemonic normative proposals that needed to be improved. In the Hispanic case, a work published in 1746 by John Müller—a German who had relocated to Britain—titled *Treatise containing the Practical Part of Fortification, for the use of the Royal Military Academy*, became the primary manual used in academic studies. The 1769 Spanish-language translation by Miguel Sánchez Taramas, who officially oversaw the academy after 1784 after five years of leading it in an interim capacity, eased its access among Barcelona Academy's students.[4] Treatises by Bernard Forest de Bélidor and Benito Bails were also important reference books for the studies in the academy.[5] Throughout the century, this center for mathematical education maintained a well-organized library that included a great number of titles related to subjects taught in its various courses. Another important contribution resulted in the transfer of all the volumes from the library of the Real Sociedad de Matemáticas de Madrid, led by Pedro Lucuze, the general director of artillery and engineers. He was named director of the Academy of Barcelona in 1739, after the dismissal of Mateo Calabro, its first head. Because the Real Sociedad de Matemáticas de Madrid lasted only two years, between 1756 and 1758, when the Conde de Aranda resigned as the commander of engineers, most of its bibliographic material was transferred to Barcelona, while Lucuze continued to lead the Academy of Mathematics of Barcelona during his preparation of *Principios de fortificación*.[6]

Given the authority of such a bibliographic collection and the guidelines proposed by such an excessive number of authors to design each permanent bastioned fortification system from the sixteenth century until the end of the eighteenth century, the 1801 publication of *De l'architecture des forteresses, ou, De l'art de fortifier les places* by Charles-François Mandar, a French engineer and architect, must be highlighted.[7] In it, Mandar inquired into the obsolescence of some systems, even to affirm the absurdity of certain proposals, especially those launched by various eighteenth-century authors. Following the postulates of his master, General of Artillery Marc-René de Montalembert, Mandar became aware of the inevitable change that fortification techniques needed to take at the turn of the century because of a radical evolution made in the defensive concept, newly developed weapons, and a transformation of tactics, mostly directed toward campaign actions. In his comparative exposition, or *"parallèle des systèmes,"* Mandar exposed in a critically objective way the formalist delusions and the obsession with geometry designed by many poliorcetic theorists as an answer to the ineffectiveness of the legacies proposed since the seventeenth century by the normative fortification.

Military engineer Guillaume Le Blond, in the "Fortification" entry of the *Encyclopédie*, already noted that apart from the Count of Pagan, Menno Van Coehoorn, Johann Bernhard von Scheither, and, above all, Sébastien de Vauban, "the other systems can only serve to verify the history of the fortification progress."[8] With this opinion, conceived from the rationalist thought of the Enlightenment, he argued the scarcity of relevant fortification contributions since the seventeenth century. The graphic synopsis in Mandar's treatise showed the creative delirium of the last hundred years, the lack of pragmatism that had already been noted by Le Blond in his encyclopedic article, when he wrote that "since the establishment of the modern fortification, engineers have proposed different ways to fortify, or, what is the same thing, different systems of fortification. Many people still imagine new things every day; but as it is very difficult to propose more advantageous ones, less expensive than those which are in use, most of these new ideas remain in the books, and no one undertakes to have them executed."[9] The *Encyclopédie méthodique*, a work that sought to continue the aims found in the *Encyclopédie*, tried to adapt the limitations of its predecessor to the new times while complementing the knowledge that could have been half-baked, insisting on the obsolescence of most traditional systems of permanently bastioned fortifications.

The acknowledgment of uselessness in the approaches to the design of permanent bastioned fortification systems did not really occur until the end of the eighteenth century, however, when the evidence of their lack of operability led to a profound transformation in the defensive tactics of the territory. Until then, the teachings transmitted in the academies maintained their own inertia, meaning permanently bastioned fortifications were still considered the most appropriate for the technical instruction of all those nascent engineers and artillerymen. The *Ordenanzas* for the regular operation in the academies of mathematics of the Spanish Crown, published in 1739, relied on the cartographic procedures that had progressively been perfected because of the excellence developed by several members of the engineering corps who had assumed responsibilities in those fields.

Regular institutional training consisted of lectures that experienced teachers imparted to their pupils in the classroom. In fact, those lectures were written by the students as an academic copy from selected treatises on poliorcetics, geometry, mathematics, trigonometry, and so on. But this method was not always the best way of learning because of its mechanical methodology. Like at the Royal Academy of Mathematics in Brussels from the end of the seventeenth century onward, the desired aim was to achieve a good level of formation throughout magisterial courses that were literally read by several specialized professors. The purpose was to avoid "the scholastic manners used at the universities and seminars,"[10] but very often this way remained just a simple process of copying theoretical texts, schemes, and graphics.

The *Instrucción* for the creation of the Spanish Corps of Military Engineers, published in 1718, was structured in two parts.[11] The first focused on the design of maps and plans to make a clear, good, and useful product, and the second one dealt with the directives for projecting works, their reparation and their conservation, with a special emphasis on harbors and their maintenance. However, there were no mandates about how to organize an educational structure. Immediately after the end of the War of the Spanish Succession (1701–14), the priority became a practical control of territory and the creation of a solid structure for organizing the kingdom. Even though the Royal Academy of Mathematics in Barcelona began teaching in 1720, it was not until 1739 that a formal curriculum was determined for all the educational centers established in Barcelona, Oran, and Ceuta.[12]

The 1739 *Ordenanza* of academies fixed exactly the pedagogical postulates to be followed in the educational practice: "To achieve teaching, according to this idea, the General Director must choose the most useful treatises of mathematics, ordering them with the corresponding method so as to be profitable for the academics, writing the subjects to be taught and dictated, as his doctrine, which must be whatever explained in the academy, extending in each part so much as he considers convenient; to whom his assistants must support. After being approved by the inspector, the instructors must deliver to the assistants their notebooks with everything each one has explained, according to their respective classes, to which the students must attend and be provided with paper, ink, pencil and whatever else is needed to write the lesson, and every fortnight they will fair-copy it, for their respective teachers can supervise it." One of the main outcomes was the excellent drawing and cartographic work made by the students. The Ordenanzas had some chapters to establish the criteria to reach the adequate objectives that the engineer must achieve with absolute technical control for his later dedication to his professional obligations.[13] In the academy's organizational configuration, the drawing director was a key element of the pedagogical structure. Unfailingly, this position had to be held by an engineer appointed by the Crown, through the secretary of war. The drawing director had the responsibility of leading the terminal semester in the curriculum, which was structured in four courses of nine months each and followed a logical order based on the students' formative needs, from the mathematical, poliorcetic, and fortification theory to its practical application in terms of delineation and graphic representation. The treatment of maps and cartographic material did not occur until the second year. If a pupil passed the exams but did not wish to continue his training by pursuing the final two courses, he had enough knowledge to be able to serve in his corresponding destination. When aspiring to a promotion or new destination, his two first years of meritorious academic studies were his ticket to obtain this promotion.

This graphic training was so special for those second-course students that "by special choice, on one day per week they will be instructed on the size and shape of the Earth, creation and use of terrestrial and celestial globes, and geographic charts; along with the knowledge of plans, in accordance with the various colors with which they are drafted, and what each one means, by which the academics will be fully instructed to carry out the assignments that are given them within the royal service."

During the third course, in addition to other subjects of a more technical nature, the students would be instructed in "the proportion and symmetry of the five orders of architecture, that of the different parts of a building, the description of the levels and their profiles, as well as straight lines as obliques, the formation of the most common vaults and arches, their pressure against the straight bases or walls that hold them up and the strength they must have to resist those forces. . . . In a special course, they will be appraised of the military perspective and of the rigorousness of gnomonics, as well as the creation and use of hydrographic charts, with the aim of solving nautical problems with them."

The real challenge in addressing the difficulties of cartography and drawing occurred during the fourth and final course of the academic studies, under the tutelage of the drawing director. During this course

> the manner of drafting with clarity and applying the colors will be taught, according to practice, for the demonstration of its sections, its distribution and ornamentation, with the finery belonging to all the military buildings, creating their respective plans, profiles, and elevations to this end. . . . They will be instructed in the manner of bringing about specific plans and provincial maps, the means of distinguishing and depicting terrain on paper . . . all with the colors that correspond to them, the decrease and the increase of the plans from greater to lesser, the reduction of scales, and the manner of taking or drafting the view of a plaza or terrain to

depict it on paper according to its natural view, and generally the manner of projecting and extending the projects that are contrived on the plans that are needed, with the profiles, elevations, and views corresponding to the clearest intelligence of thought, the relationships with which should be brought together by rationales that lead to them and the advantages that will follow from their execution.

All this theoretical instruction had to be translated onto paper in a practical way by the students with the help of the drawing director. He had to facilitate their process of comprehension and assimilation by delivering "all the necessary designs, as well as explain them to the students, after they are approved by the Academy's inspector and director general, all of which leads to the end, so that by copying them, and aided by his experienced voice, they will later take charge of the manner by which they should be executed, imitating them punctually through his teaching." The manner of evaluating individuals who tried to achieve their rank as *ingeniero ordinario* was not always the same.[14] Prior to the opening of the Academy of Mathematics in Barcelona, the evaluation system consisted of a face-to-face interview with a competent engineer, usually an *ingeniero director* or an *ingeniero jefe*. In the interview, the applicant was challenged with some theoretical and technical questions he had to resolve positively. Once the Academy of Mathematics was opened, the procedure became more complicated. First, examinations to pass every course were carried out in the school itself. The final exam, also held at the academy, required sufficiency at all required levels to be able to perform the labors of a professional engineer. The *Ordenanza* of 1739 emphasized that the role of both manuscripts and graphic materials the student submitted for examination had to provide: "the director general should take an account of the Logbooks that he gives to his Assistants and the director of drawing, for the explanation of the treatises respective to each class, with the design of the shapes and corresponding plans to come to the clearest knowledge of the manner in which they are being taught to the academics, which he will hand over as quickly as he can, signed by his hand, to the Inspector, so that when he sees these, he will forward them to the custodian for his knowledge."

A New World of Possibilities after the Academy

With the creation in 1737 of the Real Junta de Fortificaciones in Madrid, the students of the mathematics academies who had achieved the corresponding degree satisfactorily also had to undergo an examination before a jury formed by the four engineers who constituted the aforementioned *Junta*.[15] In addition to their competence in theoretical terms, together with all the disciplines studied during the four required years of study, the students had to solve some problems and make a series of drawings related to poliorcetics and fortification, based on certain parameters given to the students by the examiners. This examination incorporated a graphic demonstration of their artistic skills in civil architecture. In the case of the artillerymen, they were also asked to make a design for an artillery piece with its corresponding calculations and explanations.

One of these students, a second lieutenant of the Cantabria Infantry regiment, Antonio Lozano, petitioned the competent authority in 1747 to take the corresponding examination to join the artillery corps, "having entirely completed the course of Mathematics as it has existed at Academy of Barcelona, with the specialty of the regulations of Artillery, in the corps of which he desires to serve."[16] The member of the *Junta de Fortificaciones* Pedro Superviela, who had formerly been for many years one of Jorge Próspero Verboom's draftsmen, agreed with his request, as did Juan del Rey, a representative of the artillery corps. Lieutenant of Infantry and Extraordinary Commissar of Artillery José de Bussa determined on December 10, 1747, that Lozano's examination in Madrid met the expectations for Lozano to join the artillery corps. The detailed report indicated that he

> has proven himself knowledgeable of the Euclidean Elements, lower and higher arithmetic, practical geometry, rectangular trigonometry, royal and campaign, attack, and plaza defense Fortification and especially in the speculation of the Treatise of Artillery and its sections, with sufficient fundamentals in the other treatises, such as Machinery, Statics, Hydraulics, [and] Civil Architecture, which correspond to the duty with which he is entrusted. What has been stated in his exam, in which he has fortified, attacked, and colored the enclosure and attached plan, sliced the profile of his work and terrain, trigonometrically resolved the values of its lines and angles, executed the stereometric calculation of a section of its works and excavations, he has successfully resolved the propositions and has built a corpus of civil architecture as is seen in the attached papers.

Thus, the final aim was to bring together a talented professional staff that would be able to work starting at all stages of the project, from planning to construction, both in time of war and peace.[17] In 1765, Pedro Lucuze and Pedro Martín Zermeño, who became general engineer a few years later, drew up a report on the suitability of conserving or abandoning the *presidios menores* [small presidios] of the African coast. Their reflection showed the desire for clarity and objectivity that they had learned in their formative years at the Academy of Mathematics in Barcelona. The intention was to discern, through a technical and logical analysis, the viability of the Spanish Crown to maintain the possession of these three strategic enclaves for the control and security of the western Mediterranean. Their arguments were honest:

> We do not presently intend to criticize how much is exposed by one part or another but instead simply to relate what seems to us conducive to form the opinion, supporting those maxims that conform to and direct the good of the State in accordance with the advantages and the times.... This is, Your Excellency, how much is offered to us on the controversial point according to the folder's documents and the practical knowledge that we have of these plazas, with the rationale of having served within them. We have tried to make the reflections in the most natural, clearest, and simplest manner, in accordance with such a serious and interesting matter to the monarchy as is this. The discourse lacks erudition and eloquence, because it does not seek ostentation, but instead the knowledge of the truth, by the most secure and well-known pathways of the Prudence of Art and Experience.[18]

In fact, these words affirmed the achievement of the pedagogical objectives pursued by the academic teachings, both in technical aspects, from theory to practice, and in the ethical rectitude that professionals of military engineering must observe in their actions and responsibilities. Pedro Lucuze himself, in his role as former director of the Real Sociedad de Matemáticas de Madrid and director of the Barcelona Academy, showed the need to observe integrity, honesty, and professionalism by all members of the Corps of Engineers in an *Examen de la Verdad* (Test of Truth), where he reported a series of unpleasant circumstances that altered the positive development of professional and personal relationships within that group as a result of the abandonment of functions by Conde de Aranda during his role as general director of artillery and engineers.

The integral formation of the military engineers had a clear teleological purpose, consisting of the practical enforcement of their theoretical knowledge. This is probably the clearest difference between the proposals by the Royal Academy of Fine Arts, studied by Ruiz, and the autodidactic attempts by local engineers, as the example of Císcara examined by Fernández shows. An added factor of pedagogical character appeared when the secretary of war ordered the director engineer in Catalonia, the Frenchman Miguel Marín, to make an atlas with the graphic representation of the kingdom's main strongholds and a collection of scale models of similar characteristics. This initiative, arising under the ministry of the Duque de Montemar, had dual purposes: first, to articulate the Crown's power on paper and through a series of scale models (and, by extension, the aristocratic pride of the war minister), and second, to demonstrate the instrumental function of the material, both in graphic and three-dimensional form, for increased knowledge of the territorial reality and the status of Spanish strongholds, along with their current defensive systems. The training of engineers, so careful in its aesthetic aspects at the highest level, was a key element for the transmission of real data from which other engineers could plan their specific projects. This initiative, unfinished because of its magnitude, was re-attempted under the reign of Charles III, son of Philip V, with the order in the 1770s to engineer Alonso Ximénez to organize the long-awaited collection of scale models. This enterprise, however, was never completed.[19]

Mateo Calabro, first director of the Academy of Mathematics of Barcelona, pointed out the difference between the laborious and the delectable when defining the tasks of graphic representation by the academic students. Facing this apparently contradictory dichotomy, Calabro emphasized the effort of *Science* of drawing in contrast to the pleasure implied by *Art* in coloring plans and maps. The speech manifested his negative prejudices about it, since he considered coloring as something strictly subsidiary and even subversive compared to designing:

> The art of coloring does not have any more basis than that of each individual's fantasy, because this art (which is only accessory to engineers and some others) is not a thing that is applied to the section of the building, machine, and encampment (already designed by the engineer), the colors that make known the materials of which they are composed, knowledge for which little time is needed, although some people require much time to train in the good taste of the application of colors, and others never attain it, regarded as being, as it is said, incidental (as I have experienced it in my students, to whom I have taught coloring after having trained them in the spirit of the parts of mathematics that a good drafter requires). Drafting is a very laborious thing and coloring is a very enjoyable thing, for which I must declare to Your Excellency that it is very beneficial to the service of Your Majesty and to the academics that somebody be established who teaches coloring for those who are quite advanced in the science of drafting, but not for the beginners, in that beginners would easily abandon the difficult for the delightful.

This attitude reflected his personal obsession about the primacy of drawing, as a direct expression of mathematics, over the features that could be qualified as mostly aesthetic. However, both the *Instrucción* of 1718 and the *Ordenanza* of 1739 emphasized the value of the chromatic element in maps and plans, setting the guidelines for its use and the specific instructions for the rigorous accuracy of cartographic information. This unilateral interpretation of the essences of graphic representation, together with other excessively undisciplined behavior by Calabro, led him to be fired and replaced by Pedro Lucuze.

Delectando docere: Recreation and Knowledge

The combination of ludic and pedagogical issues was demonstrated outside the academic environment when making some materials that followed Horacio's aphorism *docere et delectare*. A superb example is the luxurious scale model owned by Philip V that was located in his Cabinet of Antiquities.[20] The piece, made on an ebony board in gilded silver, enamel, and small polychrome figures, was a true three-dimensional study of fortification, which became a real toy of a didactic character. With it, the king and others in the royal household could enjoy its aesthetic attributes while they learned about fortification systems.

This type of object revealed attitudes that went beyond technique and included the aesthetic concerns of their craftsmen. Both in plans conceived as parts of larger cartographic atlas, for instance, the collection of *Planos y Mapas de las Plazas y terrenos de la Península de España*[21] begun by Miguel Marín per the Duque de Montemar's orders, or the *Atlas político y militar del Reyno de Murcia*[22] designed by military engineer Juan José Ordovás, or in scale models or *plansreliefs* like the three-dimensional representation of Cádiz executed by Alonso Ximénez between 1777 and 1779,[23] the engineers who carried out these pieces demonstrated some aesthetic concerns in their conception and execution that transcended their own technical sense of the original intention, which essentially constituted the development of a playful instinct linked to their own intellectual and manual creative act.[24]

Game and pleasure were conceived as an objective in works as exceptional as the *True depiction of the cities, castles and areas, which Excellency the Marquis Ambrosius Spinola, General in the name of the Holy Roman Emperor captured in the Rhineland Palatine in the years 1620 and 1621*, a 1621 engraving by Georg Kress, who designed a board game based on the traditional Game of the Goose, whose track is divided into forty-six spaces and corresponds to the conquests of General Ambrosio Spinola in German territory. More directly related to poliorcetics and fortification, and explicitly based on the Game of the Goose as well, Pablo Minguet e Yrol etched in 1752 *Los Juegos de la Fortificación*, an engraving dedicated to the Caballero de Calatrava José Antonio de Horcasitas y Porras.[25] The board is also structured in a forty-six-spaces track corresponding to the same number of cards of the Spanish and French decks. The road starts from the ace of spades, represented by the "Geometry,—the theoretical basis of the Art of fortification, and ends when reaching the final space, number forty-nine: the 'Conquered Stronghold.'" The capture of the fortress signifies the triumph both in the game board and in poliorcetics. The author indicated in the explanation how to play and learn by having fun, even considering the print as a simple decorative cartographic element: "I have released those two games, because even children know how to play them and they are fond of military mathematics and enjoy themselves with this deck of cards (that also can be played with all the games that are played using ordinary playing cards). The most common fortification terms as well as planning a completed plaza can be learned easily by memory. Finally, those who do not wish to enjoy themselves in these games and have this deck of cards can use them as a decoration in their house, just like any other map" (figure 1.1).

There is another example in which ludic sense and pedagogical attributes reached the popular medium. Military engineer Isidro Próspero Verboom, the eldest son of the general engineer,[26] was commissioned to design and build a fort that displayed exactly the regular morphologies of a modern permanent bastioned fortification. This ludic, but also didactic, ensemble started to be built in a place called Buenavista, on the road between Seville and Dos Hermanas, and was meant to be a place for having fun and learning poliorcetics. In fact, it was a gift by King Philip V for his sons "so that its attack and defense provide instruction and amusement." Works began on this fort on September 21, 1729, but had to be stopped on March 6, 1730. Other true war games required Isidro to be sent to the field of Gibraltar to work on a fortified line in front of the famous rock that looms over the western approach to the Mediterranean. The fort remained unfinished, and soon another wartime campaign, this one on the Italian peninsula, made Isidro forget this unique enterprise.

Diego Saavedra Fajardo, a seventeenth-century Spanish writer and diplomat, understood this conceptual melting pot when thinking about the method by which a prince should be taught both as an individual or as a statesman.[27] In his *Idea de un Príncipe Político Christiano* poliorcetics and fortification appear as two disciplines of great importance in a prince's education if they are planned from a ludic perspective and the exercise of emulation through imitation, which is essentially a gratifying procedure:

> Practice the uses of geometry, measuring distances, heights, and depths with instruments. . . . Learn about fortifications, creating forts and plazas with their hidden entryways, moats, bastions, half-moons and tenailles with some dough, that afterwards you strike with small artillery pieces. And so that those shapes are more fixed in one's memory, they will be

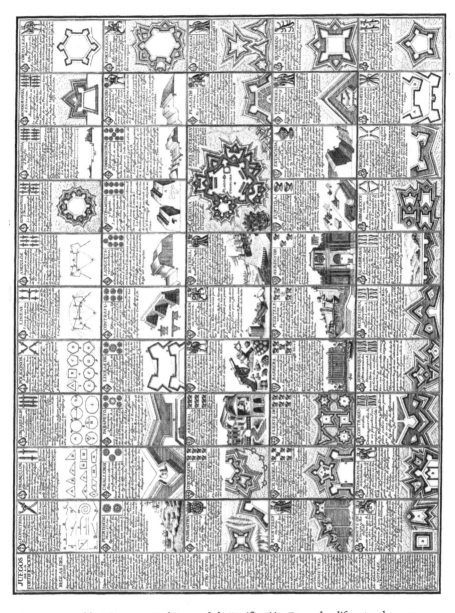

Figure 1.1. Pablo Minguet e Yrol, *Juegos de la Fortificación. En que las diferentes obras que sirven para la defensa de las Plazas, y Campos, están exactamente delineadas según el mas nuevo método, con todas sus definiciones, y una corta, y fácil explicación de los términos, que se usan mas en este Arte* (Games of the Fortification. In that the different works that serve for the defense of the Plazas, and Campos, are exactly delineated according to the newest method, with all its definitions, and a short, and easy explanation of the terms, that are used more in this Art). Madrid, the author, 1752. (National Library of Spain. CC BY-SA 4.0.)

trained in the myrtles and other herbs in the gardens, as is seen in the present work.... Practice commanding, taking metal casts of the all the various types of soldiers, both of cavalry and infantry, that there are in an army, forming with them various squadrons on a table in imitation of some picture card where they are drawn; because the prince should not have either entertainments or games during his adolescence that are not an imitation of what he will do later in life. Thus, he will gently come to love these arts and later, once the light of reason has dawned, he will be able to understand them better with the conversation of learned men, who will elucidate the causes and effects of them, and with his ministers trained in peace and war; because their value is more than the present time, they satisfy doubts, they learn more, and they tire less.[28]

Even the emblem emphasizes the relationship between the labyrinth as a symbolic path toward knowledge and the pentagonal bastioned garden as a citadel to guard a playful wisdom. Game and fortification, pleasure and poliorcetics, all of them shared an interactive sentiment concerning the battlefield, the art

Figure 1.2. Diego de Saavedra Fajardo, "Deleitando enseña" (Delighting teaches), in *Idea de un Príncipe Político Christiano: representada en cien empresas*. (Munich: Nicolao Enrico, 1640, Duke University Libraries.)

of fortification, military engineering, the "Theater of War," cartography, pedagogy. Why not *delectando docere* (figure 1.2)?

In conclusion, it can be said that Spanish academies, together with devices developed by others, were able to provide a skillful generation of military engineers to address the diverse and multiple fortifications challenge in the Americas. Their students were trained to solve problems in critical circumstances, vastly different from the aesthetic discussions supported by academic architects of the Royal Academy in Madrid, as Ruiz Carrasco (chapter 2) explains. The royal initiative of training military engineers must be seen as a significant effort of providing well-trained and avant-garde technicians for an immeasurable new territory. Despite this possibility, their arrival in America was progressive and very limited, as Fernández Martín shows (chapter 9) for the seventeenth century and the other contributors do for later dates. Their technical training was homogenic, allowing for a common design language on both sides of the Atlantic Ocean. This meant that most projects sent from America during the eighteenth century are closely linked, unlike English or French proposals. The Spanish Corp of Engineers provided a common background that unified the strategies of defense as well as provided a common place for global discussions that increasingly included local contributions. The presence of native engineers dislocated the discussion in a different way compared with architects of the Real Academia, which only reached the Americas late and in low numbers. Only through a centralized institution was it possible to manage such a large number of proposals from different ports with different defensive challenges in the metropolis. Furthermore, thanks to this use of the Real Academia, it was easy to diffuse the most recent innovations in military architecture. Despite the lack of field work at this early stage of their lives, most of them acquired it the following years, before crossing the ocean and putting it into action in the Americas. Finally, this academic pattern was also repeated in the American colonies on a smaller scale. Military engineers created smaller, more localized, institutions to teach collaborators and, later, more engineers.

2

Military Engineers and the Real Academia de Bellas Artes de San Fernando's Censure

Jesús María Ruiz Carrasco

The training of military engineers in Spain differed greatly from that of other professionals in construction industries during the eighteenth century, especially during the second half. In this time period, characterized by the growing influence of the Enlightenment on the Hispanic world, the learning of theoretical and practical concepts acquired a mostly new dimension, although it was understood in different ways by engineers and architects. During this period not only were new military academies established, but also other similar educational institutions that, under the auspices of the monarchy, significantly focused their efforts on the dissemination of new constructive norms as well as on the training of a future generation of architects. The most important of these was the Real Academia de Bellas Artes de San Fernando, whose members specialized in the practice and theory of architecture, consisting of an ever- growing collective that not only took charge of projects that had previously been assigned to military engineers but also competed with these engineers in certain instances. This framework established a contrast between both bodies, the engineering and the academic, during the second half of the eighteenth century.

This chapter examines how public works were controlled by the metropole, both through the standards established by the new Royal Academy and through the administrative structure of the Corp of Engineers. This dichotomy is especially important for the Americas because the lack of trained architects in this region required engineers to deal with more than just defensive structures.

Imperial Control of Architecture: The Real Academia de Bellas Artes de San Fernando

In the middle of the eighteenth century, after the founding of the Real Academia de Bellas Artes de San Fernando, an official process began in the lands governed by the Spanish Crown focused on introducing an architectural aesthetic in line with international style. Nonetheless, the social acceptance of the decorative baroque that prevailed throughout the kingdom in the middle of the eighteenth century delayed the implementation of this "New Architecture" until the end of the eighteenth century. Even the dissemination of academic precepts proved ineffective in Hispanic America. Nevertheless, during the final decade of the eighteenth century, the regulatory institution of the arts received several specific projects for the construction of important buildings in different American cities for its evaluation produced by noteworthy military engineers. These professionals' architectural conception differed greatly from the precepts promulgated by the Academia de San Fernando, which thus rejected the plans presented by these men. This public censure, indicated by a series of specific conditions, demonstrated the disjunctions between the architectural concepts and the constructive procedures put into practice by engineers and academics discussed by Juan Miguel Muñoz Corbalán (chapter 1 herein).

Beginning with new Real Academia de San Fernando's provisional creation in 1744 and running through its official recognition and definitive establishment in 1752,[1] its members created a series of guidelines contained in its statutes, drafted in 1751 and published in 1757.[2] These regulations implicitly and explicitly expressed academics' eagerness to control artistic creation throughout the Spanish empire through the teaching of its ideals and the different bureaucratic procedures by which they aspired to administer building under royal patronage.[3] Even so, the aims proposed by these academics could not be carried out in the short term, given the Spanish population's social and cultural characteristics at the time and the shortage of economic, material, and human resources to carry out such an ambitious intent. These difficulties led these academics to act in a positive manner to achieve their interventionist aspirations while progressively increasing the new academics' roster and developing the Enlightenment's artistic values.

Starting in 1768, the Madrid-based academics, in coordination with the members of the brand new Academia de San Carlos de Valencia, intensified their opposition to guilds to achieve the general control of public works definitively, a controversial process that was completed with an appeal the academics addressed to the monarchy on August 23, 1777, titled "Consulta al rey sobre la arquitectura de los Templos."[4] In response to this petition, the Crown published a royal decree, signed November 23 of that year by the Count of Floridablanca,[5] in which it authorized the Real Academia de San Fernando to examine, modify, and approve all architectural projects of a public nature undertaken throughout the kingdom.[6]

Despite the success the promulgation of the 1777 decree brought about, the Academia was unable to exercise royal control over Spanish construction projects. The organization empowered to evaluate these plans was the Academia's *junta ordinaria* (ordinary meeting), which was unable to exercise that role with alacrity and effectiveness, either because of its excessive amount of work or the impracticality of relying on a group of architects in charge of examining the projects received.[7] The board's ineffectiveness resulted in the plans being evaluated slowly and being mostly rejected without alternatives for amendment, which caused most of these projects to be undertaken without the Academia's consent, and fewer and fewer plans were sent to it.[8] This situation occurred mainly in the Spanish Crown's peninsular territories, while in those located in the Americas, the ignorance of the new regulations was absolute. Apart from the difficulties mentioned, the distance to the American territories made the intervention in their public works by the Academia's already overworked *junta ordinaria* almost impossible.

Given this situation, a group of academics proposed the creation of a body sanctioned specifically with the evaluation of the building projects presented to the Academia: the Comisión de Arquitectura, founded on March 22, 1786.[9] The results were almost immediate. The commission examined 973 projects from the year of its founding until 1790, 731 projects between 1790 and 1793, and 393 projects between 1793 and 1796.[10] Among all of these, three projects sent from America developed by different military engineers stood out for their constructive work in that hemisphere. Thus, coinciding with the commission's creation and with the consolidation of a broad group of academic architects on the Iberian Peninsula, the Academia reviewed some of the most important architectural projects of Hispanic America during the final decade of the eighteenth century, interventions whose idiosyncrasies merit a specific analysis.

At this point, it may become obvious that, after having obtained royal authorization, bureaucratic tools, and the appropriate human resources, the Academia beginning in 1786 set about focusing a portion of its efforts on evaluating the plans that concern us. However, their examination was determined by a series of existing or parallel factors that largely explain what happened in this regard, circumstances that determined both the relationship between the Real Cuerpo de Ingenieros and the Real Academia de San Fernando and the reception of the interest level about the referenced building projects.

First, it is worthwhile to note the conceptual and formative differences between the military engineers[11] and the academic architects,[12] evident not only in the formal comparison of their works but also in the aims, priorities, adaptive ability, and knowledge embodied by the members of both groups in their building proposals. This disparity already manifested itself within the Real Academia de San Fernando between 1750 and 1775, when José de Hermosilla (a member of the Academia and a military engineer) disagreed at various times with his academic colleagues over different theoretical and practical questions regarding the construction of public works.[13] These initial discrepancies took place during the Academia's first decades of operation, when the Real Cuerpo de Ingenieros enjoyed both the Crown's confidence and the absence of academic interference to carry out its labors. Nevertheless, on September 12, 1774, by the same royal decree that reorganized the Cuerpo de Ingenieros Militares under the administration of three *directores comandantes* (commanding officers) in charge of three specific departments and that named Francisco Sabatini as the person responsible for the engineers "assigned to roads, bridges, civil architecture buildings, as well as irrigation and navigable canals," the Crown decided that the Cuerpo de Ingenieros must act "without detriment to the establishment and privileges" of the Real Academia de San Fernando with regard to public works of a civil nature. Moreover, for the administration of works that were of the "branch of war," it would be necessary to turn to military engineers.[14] As such, the Real Academia de San Fernando's authority over the Real Cuerpo de Ingenieros regarding the construction of civil architectural works[15] was surprisingly established before the promulgation of the November 23, 1777, royal decree, thus establishing a specific rationale that predates and is in addition to those that brought about the academic evaluation of the projects that are going to be examined here.

Although the sending of architectural plans to the Academia depended on their characteristics and on the will of the Academia's benefactors, during the last two decades of the eighteenth century, the institution began to concern itself with the artistic situation and the architecture in the Hispanic American domains.[16] Despite their remoteness and the focus of academics' efforts on controlling architecture on the peninsula, the founding of the Real Academia de San Carlos of Mexico in 1783 at the expense of its authority[17] induced these academics to monitor the work of the new institution in New Spain and simultaneously to examine more closely the most relevant building projects of the Americas. In particular, the unprecedented involvement of the Madrid-based academics in American art after 1790 asserted, apart from the architectural evaluation on which this chapter focuses, that the Mexican academy was subordinated in certain aspects to the one in San Fernando. For example, it oversaw the opposition to the appointment of the second director of painting of the institution in New Spain between 1792 and 1793,[18] as well as censured various works carried out by members of that institution instructed in the different artistic branches, whose work was rejected harshly by the Madrid-based academics, in 1796.[19] Apparently, the Real Academia de San Fernando's eagerness to oversee the work of the Mexican academy has little to do with the evaluation of the American architectural projects. Even so, taking into account that this attention stems from the academic reaction in light of the breach of its statutes and the insubordination of a new similarly titled body that would compete with it in these territories (two of the Academia de San Fernando's greatest fears, regardless), it was this circumstance that largely explains the interest the Madrid-based academics placed on the art and architecture of these lands.

Finally, it is worth noting that the typology of the plans evaluated corresponds exclusively to the construction of buildings linked to the Crown, which relied on academics to carry out the most relevant projects. As such, while cautioning that if they had not been sent for examination, the Academia would not have been able to exert its influence on them, the plans that concern us deal with the building of a cathedral, a tobacco factory, and a viceroy's palace. These were major projects that, according to everything stated so far, were sent to the Academia to obtain a supposedly favorable opinion about them before their ultimate approval.

American Proposals by Military Engineers

The first and probably most significant of the American projects developed by military engineers and evaluated by the Real Academia de Bellas Artes de San Fernando was Ventura Buceta's proposal for the construction of a new cathedral in Santiago de Cuba. After the earthquake of June 11, 1766, the city was devastated, the original cathedral work was in a "shameful state," and as a result, there was a question about whether to repair it or to undertake construction of a new edifice. After the recommendation of the military engineer Francisco Suárez Calderín[20] favoring the second option, the bishop of the Santiago diocese commissioned Suárez Calderín himself to execute a new proposal, which he delivered in 1772.[21] Although the plan's specific details are unknown, the Crown ruled through a royal decree signed on May 14, 1777, that the construction of a new cathedral would be undertaken, although it considered that, due to the "superficiality and the uselessness" of Suárez Calderín's plan, that new designs that reduce the building's size such that it is "smooth, simple, and beautiful"[22] should be made. As a result, the development of the project was entrusted to master architect Pedro Aguirre, who was replaced as the work's designer by

Ventura Buceta after the rejection of Aguirre's proposal early in 1779.[23]

This engineer, about whom little information is available beyond his work in Cuba,[24] developed an initial plan dated April 15, 1779, in which the floor and the longitudinal and transversal sections were maintained, which presents, in outline, a building of three naves oriented toward the west, side chapels, an ambulatory, a transept and a Doric-style interior elevation.[25] Buceta noted in his plan that the "sequence" employed between the columns would be "Aristotelian following Vitruvio, it being the most suitable for wooden architraves,"[26] which should cover the building despite its stone appearance.[27] Nevertheless, Buceta planned a new project dated February 15, 1784, because of the loss of part of the previous one on its travels to the Council of the Indies,[28] taking advantage of the situation to correct some aspects in the original designs. Particularly, the new plan's changes, from which only the foundation and the longitudinal section are maintained (the rest was within the authority of the Council of the Indies), consisted solely of the fact that the church was to be oriented to the east instead of toward the west and in the elimination of the triglyphs incorporated in the sections of the frieze located above the pillars, except for the four that marked the transept.[29] After the modification of its orientation, the simplification of its ornamentation, Buceta's final plan was approved by the Council of the Indies on April 13, 1785.[30] Despite this, the procedures to begin the work were delayed due to the debate that arose about the desirability of demolishing the old work to build the new building. Thus, Buceta and part of the cathedral chapter, in favor of the destruction, disagreed harshly with the master builders who had to deal with the project, along with another cathedral chapter sector, and the governor of Cuba. The conflict lasted until the beginning of 1790, when, after Buceta's death on December 23, 1789, Governor Juan Bautista Vaillant had to designate a new architect to begin the work, requesting the Council of the Indies to send him the original plans carried out by Buceta.[31]

To comply with the aforementioned request, the governor of the Council of the Indies, Francisco Moñino, entrusted a copy of Buceta's project to Miguel de Hermosilla, also a military engineer, who added a series of modifications to the original plans that he considered indispensable to carry out the edifice's construction.[32] Hermosilla's assessments and modifications (which are unknown) must have created important concerns about the plans from members of the council who, through Moñino, decided to send the already-rectified project to the Comisión de Arquitectura of the Real Academia de Bellas Artes de San Fernando for its evaluation on June 26, 1790.[33] The members of the council sent Buceta's plan, as modified by Hermosilla, to the Academia with the belief that its intervention in the project would contribute an appropriate vision about it and would accelerate the process of its being carried out. However, what the council did not know, probably because this was the first American project examined by the Academia, was the severity with which the Academia evaluated architectural plans from outside its membership as well as the arduous bureaucratic process and the delay that its performance entailed in some cases. These were circumstances that, by a series of extraordinary conditions that are going to be mentioned further on, including the distance between Spain and Cuba, were manifested uniquely during the evaluation of the project under review.[34]

Once the plans developed by Buceta and modified by Hermosilla for the construction of the Santiago de Cuba cathedral were received, the Real Academia de San Fernando's Comisión de Arquitectura examined them in a meeting on September 22, 1790. In this meeting, the academic commissioners determined that Buceta's designs were "unserviceable" as a result of "essential defects in the layout and form." They also cautioned that the changes proposed by Hermosilla, although "they were not so disordered," did not have sufficient "correction and intelligence that would make them worthy to serve for such a costly and unique work to give or to take away credit from the people" who "had supported and approved" it.[35] Therefore, previously noting that it was not "easy to make use of the corrections that have been made without a demonstration well-reflected on paper," the Comisión reckoned that new designs for the work's execution must be carried out.[36] Given that, in this case, the Comisión acted merely as a consultative body, it did not necessarily propose any architect to carry out the work, as was its usual procedure. Nevertheless, on July 15, 1791, the governor of the Council of the Indies communicated to the Real Academia de San Fernando that, by order of the Crown, it was from that moment authorized to undertake the creation of new designs for the construction of Santiago de Cuba's cathedral "in accordance with local circumstances."[37] This warning would determine the future academic project's fate in the same way that the content of a letter that put an end to the nearly year-long process began: with the sending of the Academica's final opinion to Cuba along with Buceta's plans for their communication to the island's governor, the diocese's bishop, and the cathedral's chapter. Thus, since the aforementioned Cuban institutions did not confirm that the work had not been started and did not send a favorable report about the decision to commission the work, a survey of the terrain where the construction was to be carried out, and the original designs to the Council of the Indies, it did not communicate its new task to the Council of the Indies.[38]

In a special meeting on August 7, 1791, the Real Academia de San Fernando decided to put Manuel Martín Rodríguez in charge of creating a new plan for the Santiago de Cuba cathedral; he accepted his new assignment willingly.[39] The designation of Martín Rodríguez, the Academia's director of architecture and one of the most noteworthy members of the Comisión de Arquitectura between

1786 and 1794,[40] shows the importance granted by the academics to the Santiago de Cuba project, the person in charge of which was appointed in an extraordinary manner by the special meeting and not by the Comisión de Arquitectura, generally empowered with such assignments.

Despite this, almost six years after the awarding of the project to Martín Rodríguez, he still had not presented his building proposal. That is why the Council of the Indies sent a letter to the Academia signed March 18, 1797, through its secretary in charge of New Spain's affairs, Francisco Cerdá, reminding it of the delay in the work's planning and communicating the importance of "moving forward" on such "business."[41] Cerdá's petition was dealt with in the Academia's *junta ordinaria* on April 2 of that year, in which it was stated that Martín Rodríguez, although unable to develop the project because of "continuous and urgent occupations" with which he had to deal, he would deliver it "with all brevity."[42] Finally, more than a year later, Martín Rodríguez preliminarily presented the project's drafts, which were praised by the Comisión de Arquitectura in the meeting of June 13, 1798; the six definitive designs were immediately approved "in all their parts" by the academic commissioners on August 31 of that year.[43]

Almost twenty years after the development of Buceta's plan for Santiago de Cuba's cathedral, what should have been presumably the definitive plan for its construction was presented. However, given the height, the dimensions, and the inclusion of a dome in Martín Rodríguez's plan for the cathedral, Bishop Joaquín Antonio Oses de Abía determined the academic architect's approach as unfeasible for the church's construction in 1802.[44] A measure that, even if it was intended to be avoided by means of the sending of the highly regarded academic Pascual de Rezusta to Cuba for the work's management and the failed proposal developed by Antonio Porcel in the name of the Council of the Indies concerning the possible elimination of the dome put forth by Martín Rodriguez (who rejected any modification to his plan) to facilitate the works' execution,[45] led to the putting into practice of a plan devised by the naval lieutenant Agustín de Zabalda during the first decade of the nineteenth century, the administration of which was placed under the direction of the carpenter Pedro Fernández.[46]

In this specific case, this outcome certified the failure of the effort of the Academia to be able to impose the architectural precepts it promulgated on its projects, despite having the support of the Crown and of the Council of the Indies for the work's correction and having discredited Buceta's effort. This episode especially incriminated the extreme rigidity with which its members acted, unaware of the circumstances in the American territories and lacking interest in them. In this sense, the comparison between Ventura Buceta's project and Manuel Martín Rodríguez's project explains to a large extent the reasons for the

Academia's rejection of the former, which, apart from the unknown additions of Hermosilla (whose architectural conception was close to that of the academics),[47] pragmatically exhibited the concerns of the military engineers at the time of their projects' developments: the work's strength and durability. Conversely, cautioning beforehand that, as a basic fact, the Real Academia de San Fernando generally rejected those projects presented by individuals outside its membership, Martín Rodríguez's plan ignored the region's conditions, the architectural knowledge of the masters located in Cuba, and the need to provide stability to the work. He devised a plan, the sole aim of which was to comply with the Academia's precepts, which was unrealizable in the case at hand.

Two Perspectives on an Edifice: Military Engineers and Architects

The disjuncture between the military engineers' pragmatism and the academic architects' idealism is seen in the comparison of Buceta's proposal and Martín Rodríguez's proposal. Although the military engineers were unfamiliar with the new stylistic trends in architecture, in which the academics were well versed, the academics prioritized the formal expression of their precepts over any other facet, ignoring the reasons that led Buceta to propose a building emphasizing the work's stability. Knowledgeable of the characteristics of the terrain where his future work was going to be built and of the effect produced by seismic movements and hurricanes on Cuban architecture, Buceta included the aforementioned wooden structure at the base of the supports within the work's pillars,[48] while he avoided the inclusion of a dome, and he reduced the building's size both vertically and horizontally. In this manner, the engineer introduced an effective solution to resist earthquakes' effects without sacrificing the building's decorum, providing it with both elasticity and stability. In contrast, Martín Rodríguez, who surprisingly respected the foundation designed by Buceta although he reoriented it from west to east (like in the engineer's first plan), proposed a building of larger dimensions, completely of stone, composed of a large barrel vault with lunettes and elegant Doric pillars, with a rather undistinguished dome and a much more robust structure.[49] Formally, the building proposed by Martín Rodríguez fully corresponded with the academic architectural ideal, able to be carried out in any town of the Iberian Peninsula but unfeasible for the place it was proposed to occupy. Thus, the censure exercised by the Comisión de Arquitectura over Buceta's proposal prioritized the Academia's institutional and ideological interests over the work itself, giving rise to an unrealizable project that did not take into account the place of its construction, delaying it, and discrediting the work of a deceased engineer who, although not versed in academic architectural knowledge, put forth a project that took into account the geographic conditions of the island of Cuba that the academics completely ignored.

Our second example concerns the evaluation of military engineer Manuel Agustín Mascaró's[50] plans developed in August 1791 for the Casa de Dirección de la Renta and the Fábrica de Tabacos of México, which were sent by the Count of Floridablanca to the Real Academia de San Fernando on February 21, 1792.[51] Each one of these projects, promoted by the Crown and entrusted to Mascaró by New Spain's viceroy in 1789,[52] were formalized on four levels (elevation, sectional, upper floor, and ground floor) designed by the engineer, who modeled it after the Fábrica de Tabacos of Seville both in its distribution and in its architectural aesthetic.[53] These plans, which were accompanied by another set relating to the future location of both buildings,[54] show two large and irregularly distributed complexes the rectangular floors of which must be established on 200 × 180 varas (167 × 150 meters) in perimeter and 190 varas (159 meters) for each side in the case of the Fábrica and Casa de la Dirección respectively. Likewise, the elevation of both projects shows two long buildings divided on two levels, the main five-sectioned facades of which are marked off by bossage pilasters as well as being characterized by the incorporation of giant pilasters and stylized windows in the Fábrica's case; and a more complex ornamentation based on the conjunction of curved pediments (parted in the case of the crowning), pilasters, blind openings, windows, anthropomorphic figures, and, in the case of the Casa de Dirección, heraldry. As such, Mascaró proposed two projects that, related formally to that carried out by him for the Palacio de Chapultepec in 1787,[55] respond aesthetically and functionally to the official building models of the mid-nineteenth century on the Iberian Peninsula. This was an architectural conception that largely determined the project's future, the evaluation of which was in the hands of the stiff, idealistic, and closed-off academics.

A few days after receipt of Mascaró's two projects, the Comisión de Arquitectura evaluated them in its meeting on March 6, 1792,[56] which, in contrast to the delay in dealing with the plans for the cathedral in Santiago de Cuba, indicates the importance placed on the New Spain building project by the Academia. As has already been stated implicitly in the previous paragraph, the characteristics of Mascaró's building plans demonstrated an architectural conception entirely aesthetically and functionally different from that of the academics, who harshly critiqued both projects. The Comisión labeled the two proposals as "faulty" for three reasons: first, "for a lack of good proportion and location in all its windows and doors"; second, for the defects found in the "the most substantial pieces that are manifested in its cuttings," basically the planning of the arches and their distribution; and, last, for "the arbitrary profusion of decorations of bad taste without the least architectural idea that the main and other facades were overloaded."[57] Consequently, in accord with the Comisión's standard manner of action, it proposed the well-regarded academic and director of architecture of the Real Academia de San Carlos de México, Antonio González Velázquez, as a new planner for both works.[58] González Velázquez must have received the necessary instructions related to the number of offices and general spaces that the separate buildings should have.[59]

At the same time, in June 1792, before the Academia's opinion had arrived in New Spain, Viceroy Juan Vicente de Güemes Pacheco decided to commission the military engineer Miguel Constanzó[60] to scout possible plots to situate the new Fábrica de Tabacos. Constanzó identified three possible locations, which he recommended according to the land's firmness and the suitable supply of water that was previously allocated for in the Jardín Botánico, located "between the Calzada de Chapultepec at noon and the Paseo de Bucarelli from West to the North."[61] As a result, the viceroy decided to carry out the beginnings of the works in the place proposed by Constanzó under his direction, which implied a change of location vis-à-vis Mascaró's project and the undertaking of the architectural group without the Real Academia de San Fernando's consent. Moreover, for unknown reasons, the construction of one edifice for the Fábrica and another for the Casa de la Dirección de la Renta was not proposed at this time, but merely the construction of the former was arranged.

The Academia's decree was received in New Spain in February or March of 1793, when the work was already in the foundation phase under the direction of Constanzó, who, despite everything, was confirmed on March 21 by the Crown in the employment of his duties, in which he must have been aided by Antonio González Velázquez,[62] the architect proposed by the Comisión de Arquitectura, to carry out the project. Thereby, the viceroy's incentive on one hand and the Academia's decree on the other created a complex situation in which Constanzó was the director of the work but González Velázquez must have sent the new plans to the Comisión de Arquitectura, which received them on September 22, 1793, and proceeded to their evaluation on October 2 the same year.[63] Despite the fact that González Velázquez was a well-regarded academic architect and that the project he presented to the Academia was much more normal, ordered, and symmetrical in its distribution, rationale, and was plainer than those proposed by Mascaró, the commissioned academics harshly criticized these new designs. Warning previously that it addressed a project that exceeded 163,700 pesos (Mascaró's, which was 586,077 pesos in total) because of its "greater extension and regularity on the floor," the Comisión expressed its doubts that the designs were the work of González Velázquez, because it found "the expertise and good taste with which he has been reputed" in the Academia incompatible "with the repeated and primary defects that were noticed" in the proposal: "the disgraceful aspect of the *fábrica* from the front," the limited "relationship" between the "exterior walls of the interior walls of the elevation with those of the floor," the faulty "location of the woods" of the flooring and the deficiencies in "interlocking" the interior walls, that are exposed "to collapsing on the exterior side."[64]

Surprisingly, the Comisión de Arquitectura, which disapproved of González Velázquez's designs without proposing any solution in response, figured out that the designs had a second authorship unrelated to its teachings despite being signed by the well-regarded academic. And it is that the designs, which lacked a report that would accompany and explain them, must have been designed together by González Velázquez and Constanzó, or by the former according to the initiatives of the latter, because the Academia's suspicions are connected to the fact that the military engineer at this time already served as director of the work. Thus, there is no doubt that, despite the fact that González Velázquez sent various designs signed by him to the Comisión de Arquitectura (surely with the only objective of complying with the Academia's decree about administrative matters) the person truly responsible for the designs was Constanzó. This theory is even supported by the fact that the building begun in 1792 under the direction of Constanzó, whose works continued until 1807 and are preserved today,[65] does not correspond to the one planned by González Velázquez. All this constitutes a rather unique case in which, despite the Academia's censure and its rejection of one of the designs developed by a military engineer for a future building of such importance in New Spain, its construction finished under the direction of and lead of another engineer, who gave it its current aesthetic: recognizable in its geographic and chronological context as well as against the architectural precepts of the Madrid-based academics.

The final project that concerns us was the one developed by Domingo Esquiaqui[66] for the new viceregal palace in Santa Fé de Bogotá, which Viceroy Francisco Gil Lesmes decided to undertake in 1790 after the fire that ravaged the former seat of the Viceroyalty of New Grenada in May 1786.[67] The designs carried out by Esquiaqui, remitted to the Real Academia de San Fernando by the Council of the Indies in January 1795,[68] were evaluated on February 13 of that year by the Comisión de Arquitectura, which disapproved of them for not finding "in them good distribution, comfort, and beauty, that correspond to a building so worthy for its quality, sumptuousness and magnificence of forms," thus contradicting "the pleasing architectural productions as practiced presently."[69] To this last quotation, which summarizes the vision that the members of the Real Academia de San Fernando had of the architectural labor of the military engineers assigned to the Americas, followed the appreciation of the need for a new, more appropriate and less costly project for the viceregal palace.[70]

The decree was remitted to the Council of the Indies, which communicated to the Academia the acceptance of its decision and the commission of the project to one of its members on December 9, 1797, almost three years after the rejection of the eight designs carried out by Esquiaqui.[71] As a result, the Academia's *junta ordinaria* on January 7, 1798, entrusted the execution of new designs for the building of the viceregal palace in Santa Fé de Bogotá to the architect Juan Pedro Arnal,[72] who, despite the letter sent by the Council of the Indies to the Academia on October 3, 1801, with the aim of bringing up the matter's importance, never presented a project.[73]

Although the designs carried out by Esquiaqui are not known, taking into account his status as military engineer, the formal characteristics of his work, and what happened in the cases previously discussed, that they were rejected by the Academia was to be expected. Once again, we find a case of academic intransigence that resulted in the failure of an important American building enterprise at the end of the eighteenth century, with the aggravating circumstance that on this occasion a building was not built at the expense of the Academia's opinion, but that it was not even undertaken.

Probably this final case, the least complex and the most mysterious of the three for the lack of graphic documents, is the most representative of the censure exercised by the Real Academia de San Fernando on the civil and religious architectural labors of the military engineers assigned in America, given the unsuccessful result that its successive decisions put forth in this regard. This represented a case in which not even the initiative of a viceroy, a bishop, or a governor could prevent the undertaking of the work, clearly dramatizing the ineffectiveness with which the academics acted in each of the matters discussed here. Whether due to ignorance of the place for which the projects were intended, the intransigence of their decisions, the lack of understanding of the circumstances of the works, the distance, the lack of interest on the part of the members of the Comisión de Arquitectura or of the academics in charge of executing the projects, the eagerness to impose their precepts, or the goal of superseding the Real Cuerpo de Ingenieros by discrediting their activity, the Real Academia de Bellas Artes de San Fernando made the execution of the projects difficult. Moreover, it discredited the important work carried out by the military engineers in America, where they were the highest architectural exponents and the greatest experts in the construction techniques most suitable for building solidly in those territories, the complex geographical characteristics of which differed from those existing on the Iberian Peninsula. These engineers were a group that, despite their censure on the part of the Real Academia de San Fernando, offered effective solutions to the problems proposed in the works they developed, as shown by Muñoz Corbalán (chapter 1), in contrast to the unrealistic and utopian projects presented by the academics. This would be crucial in the American framework, where the lack of budget and skillful artisans was a regular feature. Perhaps for this reason, academics were far less common in the Caribbean than engineers, who managed both fortifications and other sort of buildings. This represents a disparity between pragmatism and architectural ideals that, in these three specific cases, created a series of unique conflicts that expose the antagonistic characteristics of the work of these two organizations, protagonists of an onerous dispute that confronted them both in the nineteenth century and that proceeds from what was developed in this chapter.

Part II

The British Plan

Warfare, Intelligence, and Rhetoric of the Empire

3

Fortification, Engineering, and Empire in Mid-Eighteenth-Century Jamaica

Aaron Graham

In a confidential report submitted to the Board of Trade in 1754, the governor of Jamaica, Edward Trelawney, reported on the poor state of the island's fortified places, especially the three main fortifications of Fort Augusta, Fort Charles, and Rock Fort, which protected the town of Kingston on the south coast.[1] "The whole art of engineering seems to have been employed in making them as expensive as they are defenceless," he reported, even though some £60,000 had been spent on them since 1743. After only six years of peace since the conclusion of the War of the Austrian Succession in 1748, Fort Charles was already in a ruinous condition, "so defenceless a work (being very unskillfully designed at first) that it is not worth repairing," while Fort Augusta was in much the same state. A further report by one of Trelawney's successors in 1764 repeated these concerns. Fort Charles had over one hundred guns, but most were so old and worn that their barrels were distorted, "which," the governor reported, "would cause great uncertainty in firing at an object."[2] Fort Augusta had been damaged by the explosion of its powder magazine in 1763 and had not been repaired. Nor had conditions improved by 1781 either. "So much remains yet to be done," noted the governor, "notwithstanding the amazing sums laid out by the country on forts and fortifications, that it is almost difficult to determine which place ought to be attended first."[3] The island's fortifications therefore remained in a poor state throughout the mid-eighteenth century despite the wealth of the island and the threats it faced from both foreign invasion and internal revolt. This chapter argues that this did not reflect problems of engineering, which were mirrored in French and Spanish islands. Instead, it was a product of the particular political constitution of Jamaica and other British islands, which held back funds for maintenance and construction except in wartime, when prices of labor and materials were highest, reducing the success of construction. Any consideration of the fortification of the Caribbean in this period must therefore take account of the wider context in which it occurred, and the differing political challenges that faced imperial regimes dealing with largely the same problems.

Context

Jamaica was captured from Spain in 1655 and rapidly settled by English settlers as a privateering and smuggling base, and then as a plantation colony. By the middle of the eighteenth century, it was the largest, wealthiest, and most politically developed British colony in the West Indies, with some 200,000 whites, free people of color, and enslaved people.[4] British imperial authority was represented by a governor appointed by ministers in London, who also funded and controlled the large garrison of regular troops who protected the island from both foreign invasion and domestic revolt. However, this authority existed alongside and in connection with a colonial assembly elected by white planters in the island, which alone had the power to raise taxes for government. The question of who had the authority and responsibility for building and maintaining fortifications was therefore complex, confused, and contentious. The imperial government had built Fort Charles and provided the island engineer, from the Ordnance Office in Britain, who was under the authority of the governor but was paid a salary by the colonial assembly. A political settlement in 1729 had allotted £8,000 a year out of colonial taxation to support the costs of the imperial government, including £1,250 specifically for maintaining forts and fortifications, but this was increasingly inadequate for the growing needs of the island by the mid-eighteenth century.

Consequently, most of the fortifications, barracks, and other military installations in Jamaica were funded by the legislature or assembly of the island through annual grants of colonial taxation. The assembly also subsidized the imperial garrison in the island and covered several other vital expenses, such as the cost of the "Maroon" parties who hunted down enslaved runaways in the interior after a treaty was concluded with the Maroons in 1739. Taxation and spending rose from about £20,000 per year in the early eighteenth century to double or triple that in the 1740s, and nearly £100,000 per year in 1760, when the island faced a dangerous revolt of enslaved people called Tackey's Revolt. Expenditure rose to similar heights after 1778, with entry of France into the American War of Independence, then Spain in 1779 and the Dutch Republic in 1781, suggested the island was under imminent danger of attack.[5] A French fleet under Comte de Grasse captured other British islands and neared

Jamaica in 1782, the assembly funded an ambitious building program that included repairs to Fort Charles and Fort Augusta, the construction of new barracks at Stoney Hill near Kingston, and a variety of other fortifications.[6] Along with payment to the expanded garrison, taxation in 1782 reached £240,000. The assembly was therefore prepared under some circumstances to vote very large sums for fortification, about 5 percent of total national income, but to retain oversight over expenditure they insisted that the funds be spent through a joint committee, the Commissioners of Forts and Fortifications. Composed of the governor and several representatives from the assembly and the island council, and appointed by the governor, it met to examine reports, approve and audit spending, and to give directions to the island engineer and other contractors.[7] The governor could circumvent the commissioners by drawing on imperial funds to build the forts, but this would get him into trouble with the Treasury in London, who firmly believed that the colonies should pay for their own defense as much as possible.

As in French and Spanish colonies, the fortifications in Jamaica were thus a battleground between imperial and colonial groups, but in Jamaica the two sides had greater political definition than elsewhere, which exacerbated the existing problems of fortification in the Caribbean during this period. The construction of fortifications in the long eighteenth century represented a major and ongoing investment for governments. Military departments had to maintain a large staff of trained engineers and artisans with expertise in the latest advances in artillery and fortification, and required access to large stockpiles of stone, brick, timber, earth, and other essentials, to say nothing of the vast workforces required to construct the massive earthworks modern fortifications required, using only shovels, axes, adzes, and baskets. Islands in the West Indies such as Jamaica lacked many of these vital resources. Brick, stone, and timber were all imported in large amounts in peacetime for the construction of plantations and other buildings, and any fortifications would have to compete with planters for these materials. Labor was likewise at a premium in Jamaica and other British islands during this period, due to the expansion of sugar cultivation, and unlike the French or Spanish islands the number of free people of color was very small. Most of the labor not tied to the plantations was under the control of local slaveowners, who hired out their "gangs" to plantations on a seasonal basis for tasks such as hoeing or cutting cane.[8] Barry Higman estimates that by the 1830s at least 6 percent of enslaved Africans had been trained as carpenters, masons, and other artisans, but these were the enslaved men that planters were least likely to make available for work on fortifications, leaving engineers dependent on a large unskilled labor force.[9]

Supplies

The obvious solution to such problems was for the island to stockpile these resources when prices were low in order to guarantee access as prices increased, by purchasing large stocks of brick, stone, tile, timber, and lime for cement, and by maintaining their own cadre of enslaved people as the core of the workforce. By 1774, there were at least forty of the "King's Negroes" at Fort Augusta and Fort Charles, under the control of the island engineer, who were used to maintain the forts and carry out minor repairs. However, they were a constant source of expense for the island. The commissioners resolved in September 1769 that they would be allowed 3 reales (three-eighths of a dollar) per week for subsistence and 7s 6d per head for clothing, but this still amounted to some £215 per year, plus about £12 for medical care.[10] In February 1777 the engineer calculated that there were eighty-two King's Negroes in all, whose maintenance cost about £672 per year or about half the entire fortification allowance, but only forty-eight were needed, and the others were "mostly old and runaways."[11] There were also the incidental costs of managing a community of enslaved Africans, particularly when most were obtained by forfeiture from civilian jails when owners failed to claim runaways caught and detained there. The commissioners spent 18s 9d in 1769, for instance, on discovering, taking up, and detaining an enslaved man named Morris who had been absent from Fort Augusta for nearly two years, only to have to hand him over to his legal owner, William Halstead, who had presented an application to them three years before.[12] Maintaining a permanent workforce to keep the forts in good repair was therefore difficult; purchasing stockpiles of materials for the use of the fortifications in peacetime was just as problematic. Consequently, two major problems that stymied any attempt to keep fortifications in order were the high prices of (1) labor and (2) materials that engineers faced in wartime whenever they were ordered to do so by the assembly of the island.

Most or all of essential materials such as bricks, stone, timber, slates, tiles, and lime had to be imported from North America or elsewhere, along with provisions, and warfare after 1776 cut off exports and pushed up the costs of providing the necessary commodities. Hard and durable timbers such as mahogany were best for constructing floors, roofs, stairs, and other parts of the forts and barracks, but these cost about 5d per yard even in 1772, compared to about 3d per yard for the lighter timbers and pitch pines.[13] As a result the contractors for constructing the new barracks and hospital in Spanish Town got permission from the commissioners in November 1776 to use pitch pines for the beams, for instance, due to "the great difficulty getting hard timber."[14] Lime was required in great quantities for cement and mortar, and cost about 5s per ton in November

Mid-Eighteenth-Century Jamaica

1772, but had risen to 7s 6d by January 1782, and in June the commissioners were forced to allow contractors 10s per ton, the price it carried in Kingston, in order to secure enough for the fortifications at Port Royal.[15] Contracts were advertised for stone in January 1782 at 7s 6d per ton, but within a fortnight the commission agreed to increase the price to 8s 1½d per ton for persons willing to supply stone "with all expedition."[16] The governor nevertheless noted in June that "notwithstanding the liberal offers . . . there had not been more stone supplied than was sufficient to keep about twelve masons employed," and the commissioners therefore agreed to raise the price to 10s.[17] The contractor, David Allan, complained that the lack of materials had caused delays and left his tradesman idle, "at times unemployed for whole days and sometimes many days together, notwithstanding they were still continued there in expectation of such material being supplied, and during such time did neither work nor serve whatsoever."[18] He therefore offered to supply stone himself "for the greater expedition in doing work for the future," at 11s 6d per ton, an offer the board turned down.

The same problems faced the engineers in securing labor for their projects. In peacetime the commissioners had relied on the island engineer and the contractors to provide their own tradesmen and workers or hired them from other contractors at the best rates they could, but from November 1778 the parishes were ordered to levy contingents of enslaved workers from local planters and send them to work on specified forts at the rate of 1s 10½d per day plus 1s 10½d per week.[19] In September 1779 the growing manpower shortages encouraged the board to permit the engineer to place advertisements in local newspapers increasing the rate to 2s 6d per day and allowing masters to send their enslaved Africans directly, while also offering a "liberal hire" of double that for all black tradesmen, both enslaved and free, and 10s per day "to hire fit and proper white people to oversee the Negroes employed in the public works."[20] As the situation became more desperate the board was forced to offer even higher terms for labor. In July 1780 the governor reported that the French and Spanish fleets had left for Jamaica and urged "the necessity of immediately putting Fort Charles into a strong posture of defense . . . and desired that the Board would employ the powers vested therein by law to procure Negroes for carrying on the works on the said fort."[21] The board accordingly ordered parishes to levy one enslaved person out of every hundred from local planters for work on the forts and fortifications, with hoes, bills, and baskets. Two years later, as the allied fleets once again threatened Jamaica, the assembly ordered the board to raise the rates to 3s 9d per day, and, "for the further encouragement of the proprietors of able labourer Negroes to hire the same to the public to work on the fortifications now carrying on," to allow 2s 6d for female laborers and "inferior Negro men," and their subsistence.[22]

The island engineer was therefore forced to rely in peacetime on a small cadre of King's Negroes and contractors' enslaved workers to maintain the forts, and to hire or levy a larger number of enslaved Africans in wartime to provide the necessary manpower, at far higher prices. The relative importance of hired labor in providing a "surge" capacity is shown by the shift in the profile of labor after 1778. Invoices presented to the commissioners for payment show that the island engineer hired laborers and tradesmen who worked about 39,000 days during this period, nearly 15 percent of 270,000 days of work expended on fortification construction between 1778 and 1783.[23] Contractors also continued to provide their own workforce, such as the head mason at Stoney Hill, John Kelly, and his family, whose laborers worked for 3,231 days, or the partnerships of Gordon and Grant at Castile Fort and Nicoll and Johnston at Port Royal, whose laborers and tradesmen worked over 7,000 days. Several overseers also submitted claims for workforces, presumably the jobbing gangs they had redeployed from work on the plantation. For example, Thomas Simcocks was made superintendent of the works at Stoney Hill and brought with him both laborers and tradesmen who worked for nearly 16,000 days. However, labor provided by these contractors only accounted for about 72,000 days in total, and for the remaining 160,000 days of work the island hired enslaved workers from nearly 180 separate individuals. Some received payment for only a few days of work from their enslaved men and women, but six people account for the bulk of the days worked, around 140,000 days in total, suggesting that the board was relying on a few major subcontractors to provide the bulk of their enslaved labor with many smaller owners then making up the numbers as required.

Finance

The problem that faced the Commissioners of Forts and Fortifications in maintaining Jamaica's fortifications, at least between 1768 and 1783, was therefore not so much the lack of other materials or labor but the high price of both when they came to purchase them for work on the forts. For example, in 1772, a bill of 23s 9d per perch for masonry work and materials was closely scrutinized by the board because it far exceeded the usual rates, but a decade later in December 1782 the board was prepared to accept a higher rate of 28s for work and materials at Castile Fort.[24] This led to financial strains on the commissioners, who threw out their existing estimates and budgets. They reported an overspenditure of £7,244 7s 7½d in December 1783, for instance, "entirely owing to the price of Negro labour, and of all the materials and articles employed in carrying on the Fortifications having increased immoderately, after the estimates of the expenses thereof had been formed, agreeably to the rates and prices of former times."[25] Part of the problem therefore was that the money voted by the assembly invariably bought less than it did at other times, because spiraling prices made prewar estimates obsolete. Engineers were therefore forced to scale back their ambitions, to accept inferior workmanship or materials, or to continue spending.

This required a series of financial expediencies intended to bridge the gap between the urgent and pressing demands of the contractors, for funds to cover their own costs, and the slow collection of revenue from taxation and other sources. It was usual practice for the island engineer to advance money out of his own pocket, as he explained to the commissioners in February 1776: "in carrying on the works ordered at the several fortifications he would be obliged to advance large sums of money for the hire and allowance of Negroes and for the purchase of materials for the said work," and the receiver-general or island treasurer was duly ordered to pay £1,000 to him on credit.[26] But this merely threw the burden of credit onto the receiver-general, and by November 1782 his own credit was exhausted. The governor reported that it was "impracticable, upon the present mode of purchasing and paying for materials for the public works, to procure a sufficient quantity for carrying on the same, with the necessary dispatch."[27] The board set aside £10,000 for buying materials and ordered a committee to print 125 "orders" or paper certificates, in £50 and £100, for the payment of contractors, carrying interest at 10 percent.[28] These formed an expensive public debt that the assembly then had to retire after the war.

Politics

The continually unsatisfactory state of the fortifications in Jamaica was therefore ultimately a reflection of a financial policy that starved the island engineer of funds required for maintenance and construction when prices of labor and materials were low, and only released money in wartime, when the rising costs of both outstripped the sums allocated for forts and fortifications. This had its roots in particular political and constitutional arrangements of Jamaica and the other islands of the British West Indies, notably the creation of a colonial legislature with the exclusive power of taxing its inhabitants. A legal ruling of *Campbell v. Hall* in 1773 confirmed that even islands conquered from or ceded to the British Crown, such as Grenada, Dominica, Tobago, and St. Vincent in 1763, could not be taxed by the imperial government once they had been granted their own assembly. Along with British political institutions, British political culture and ideologies had also arrived, including the rhetoric of taxation, representation, liberty, autonomy, and self-government that would be used so loudly and tendentiously by American colonists after 1763. The possibility that the imperial government was trespassing on the liberties and properties of colonists was a constant concern even for favored colonies in the British West Indies, and taxation and funding was therefore used as a weapon by colonists to curb government power. Revenues were kept small and strictly hypothecated or allocated to specific uses, and although governors repeatedly argued that it was more efficient to keep up funding for fortifications in peacetime rather than throwing money at them in wartime, Jamaican planters refused to accept this because they feared the funds would be misused.

This process can be seen particularly clearly in the complaints of Edward Long, a Jamaican planter and former judge and legislator who wrote a comprehensive and ideologically inflected history of Jamaica in 1774. This pointed out how previous governors had abused the fortification fund of £1,250 in their efforts to corrupt the legislature and undermine the liberties of the colonists. The fund was under the control of the island's executive council, who had applied to the assembly in 1763 to be repaid for several advances that had been made against the credit of the fund since 1756. A closer examination by the assembly showed that some £6,000 had been spent not on fortifications but on boosting the miserly fixed salaries or sinecures of various imperial officials in the island, rendering them independent of colonial influence. "They had drawn the money out of that fund which by law is strictly required to be kept sacred and applied solely to repairing the forts," Long said, "and dissipated it in expenses which the law does not warrant."[29] The governor had asked the house to raise total imperial revenues from £8,000 to £10,000 per year, ostensibly to meet the growing costs of maintaining the forts, but this had been refused, much to Long's approval. "The assembly had too much regard for their constituents to clap another pannier on their shoulders," he wrote, "and thought that the assembly . . . showed itself worthy [of] the confidence of the people by refusing to comply with a requisition so unreasonable," which had forced the council to back down.[30] Close control of expenditure was therefore necessary in order to keep the governors in check, even if this meant holding back the funds needed to maintain fortresses.

The insistence on strict allocation and hypothecation, for political reasons, also meant that even when funds were available, they could not be borrowed and applied to other purposes. For instance, in June 1772 the commissioners received a report of the emergency repairs that would be necessary for the governor's house in Spanish Town. The island engineer was ordered to lay before them at the next meeting the costs of repairs, where they would consider "whether the appropriations will, over and above payment of the contract and debts already payable thereout, afford sufficient for defraying that additional charge."[31] A committee of the Commissioners of Forts audited the accounts in November 1772 and found that they had nearly £13,000 in unspent cash at their disposal, but that it was split up among fifteen distinct "funds," some of them dating back to 1761.[32] In wartime, when demands changed rapidly as prices altered and new threats emerged, the system held back construction by dividing up funds into categories that swiftly became irrelevant, and as the pressures of war mounted, the commissioners therefore embarked on increasingly desperate searches for any spare funds that might justifiably be charged for work carried out but not properly and legally approved. In March 1780, for instance, they received invoices from artisans and slaveowners working on the fortifications for nearly £5,000. They ordered the receiver general to pay them, "together with interest upon the said several accounts until the time of payment, and [to] charge [them] to any public funds or monies in his hands."[33]

Two years later, the situation was more desperate, and the assembly was persuaded to pass an act consolidating the remaining funds unpaid and allowing them to be laid out on any expenditures already approved by the house. On November 2, 1781, the commissioners had instructed their secretary to abolish the existing allocations entirely, and "to transfer the balances now remaining of any old Funds to the credit of such of the latest funds as shall be established for similar purposes, to the end that the Board may perceive at one view the extent of the monies they are empowered to dispose of."[34] Once this was presented to the house on November 22, the benefits of suspending the process of appropriation and allowing the £15,313 8s 0d remaining to be used for current expenditure were recognized, provided that political control could be upheld. The house therefore passed a strongly worded resolution stating that while sufficient funds remained available for spending, any spending that had not been approved was illegal, and that as a result the commissioners "ought to allow [i.e., pay] such of those accounts only which arose for work heretofore approved by this House."[35]

The context for this decision was a bitter political struggle between the planters and the former governor, John Dalling, who had recently resigned, over the limits of his political authority, in particular his proposals to strip the island bare of troops in order to support the war against France, Spain, and the rebels in North America.[36] Underlying their decision was perhaps the calculation that greater investment in the fortifications would not only provide the governor with the patronage necessary to corrupt contractors and politicians but also enable him to withdraw troops by claiming that the fortifications would provide an adequate protection. Only by keeping the governor to strict limits and ensuring that funds were only spent on repairs or improvements that had been approved by the assembly down to the last detail could this be prevented. Even in the middle of a war, planters clearly continued to see the issue of fortification in political terms.

Conclusions

There were undoubtedly common challenges that faced British, French, and Spanish engineers in the eighteenth century when it became necessary to construct and maintain the fortifications erected on all islands. Skilled and unskilled labor, and materials such as timber, shingles, stone, brick, lime, and fittings, were always at a premium as sugar plantations required the same materials and could pay higher prices for them. The key difference was the political context. Neither French nor Spanish imperial governance was free from conflict, such as between governors, intendants, and the councils in French islands such as Saint-Domingue, and this necessarily had an impact on the pace and scale of fortification. Ultimately, these all came down to the key but contentious question of resources: who was to pay for the expensive work of fortification? In British islands such as Jamaica the problems were exacerbated as the imperial government was particularly unwilling to spend money subsidizing the defense of the rich sugar islands and could not raise it locally without the cooperation of the planters. The planters, in turn, were unwilling to put under the control of the imperial government large financial resources that might easily be diverted from their intended channel and used to corrupt colonial politics. When defense was not wholly under their control, they therefore voted funds for fortification and defense grudgingly and only under immediate necessity and attempted to regulate spending tightly. Consequently, island engineers usually only received funds in wartime, which then proved inadequate to meet the spiraling costs of materials and labor. The poor state of the fortifications of Jamaica in the mid-eighteenth century therefore reflected the context of the island and demonstrates the diverse nature of the challenges that faced imperial regimes.

4

Vernacular Architecture and the Defense of Antigua, 1670–1785

Christopher K. Waters

Antigua's fortification history starts ignobly. In 1666, a squadron of seven French West India Company vessels sailed from the recently captured St. Kitts into Five Island's harbor, dropped anchor, and started ferrying soldiers and militiamen to the shore. On landing, the French engaged "two batteries mounting eight and six guns, but owing to the absence of any parapet, gabion, or embrasure, they were quickly silenced."[1] Surprised by their easy victory, the French marched inland, engaging with the Antigua militia in battle, before forcing the capitulation of the island. Declaring victory, the French proceeded to plunder the island, removing 500 of the 800 enslaved Africans found there, as well as movable infrastructure like sugar coppers, cannons, and small arms. Before leaving, the French commander, M. de la Barre, ordered an additional indemnity of 200,000 pounds of sugar before embarking his troops and returning to the French islands. Antigua was returned to England the following year under the terms of the Treaty of Breda.[2]

For the next 120 years, the trauma felt by the Antigua plantation elite from the French invasion of 1666 translated into how the island's elites viewed defense and protected the island. Rather than rely on a distant metropolitan government, the Antiguan legislature established a series of forts and coastal batteries around the island, built using enslaved labor conscripted from nearby plantations, paid for out of specially raised taxes levied on the local population, and garrisoned with military contractors willing to play the role of gunner or matross. The result is a highly localized phenomenon, cloaked in an explicitly military aesthetic, but lacking in any engineering theory or military training. Instead, Antigua's fortifications served as political extensions of the planation elites who traded on the military cachet that the fortifications afforded them, while providing only a veneer of defensibility. This resulted in defensive features that look like forts but lack the strategic and tactical planning or necessary engineering to be of any defensive use.[3]

This chapter expands on the design limitations of Antigua's fortifications and places these weaknesses into the longer-term context of being a local government public works project between 1670 and 1783. I start with a brief strategic and tactical overview of how Antigua's legislature created defense policy and identify their priorities in fortification placement and construction. Next, I highlight several examples of what constituted a fort in the eyes of the Antiguan government and how their placement and construction followed political expediency, rather than any kind of military planning. To emphasize the expedient nature of the decision-making policies, I introduce the case study of the defenses around St. John's Harbour. I conclude with a discussion of the Antiguan fortification vernacular and call for a greater consideration of the impact that local elites had in controlling military and colonial sites.[4]

At only 281 square kilometers (108 square miles), Antigua is a small island. The farthest point inland from the coast is just 6 kilometers (3.75 miles) (figure 4.1). With the tallest peak measuring only 402 meters, the island is also relatively flat, with the northwestern two-thirds of the island dominated by rolling hills. For defense, Antigua's geography is important. First, unlike in the Greater Antilles, there was no hinterland to retreat to in an invasion. The inability to hide and conduct guerilla operations was further exacerbated by the rapid and complete deforestation of the island for sugar cultivation. By 1750, every acre was given over to sugarcane fields, further reducing the ability for groups of people to hide effectively.[5] Second, as an island, external threats were waterborne: defenses had to be organized to counter sailing vessels and soldiers. The long, heavily indented coastline further complicated defense, with the many deep bays and inlets offering protected anchorages and sheltered beaches ideal for landing troops.[6] Finally, Antigua sat on a nexus of currents and prevailing winds. From Antigua, vessels were able to sail in any direction: northeast to Europe, south to the Windward Islands, north to North America, and west to Jamaica and the Greater Antilles. Traveling even only a short distance west of Antigua made eastward movement all but impossible because of the prevailing winds. Recognizing this strategic position, Governor William Mathew, writing to London in 1749, declared the island, "the key of the British Navigation to all the Sugar Islands, and even to Jamaica itself."[7] These three pressures underlie how Antigua's fortification history evolved.

To protect the island, more than fifty-eight forts, coastal batteries, and guardhouses were built by the Antiguan legislature between 1670 and 1783.[8] The legislature was a bicameral body consisting of an elected Assembly and an appointed Council. A royally appointed governor functioned as the executive. While the governor was the direct representative of the British Crown, his charge included three other major islands—St. Kitts, Nevis, and Montserrat—and several additional dependencies such as Anguilla and some of the Virgin Islands, forcing him to divide his time. If he was off island, which some governors were for years at a time, power devolved to the president of the Council who also served as the lieutenant governor: always a local planter of high social standing. Additionally, while the governor held, in theory, near absolute power, the elected Antigua Assembly controlled the treasury and the ability to raise local taxes, forcing the governor to rely on compromise and debate. Additionally, for much of the seventeenth and eighteenth centuries, the governor was a local planter himself, already embroiled in the local social and political structure of the island. This devolved power structure ensured that local politics took precedence over metropolitan objectives—a status quo that was maintained until the end of the American War of Independence.[9]

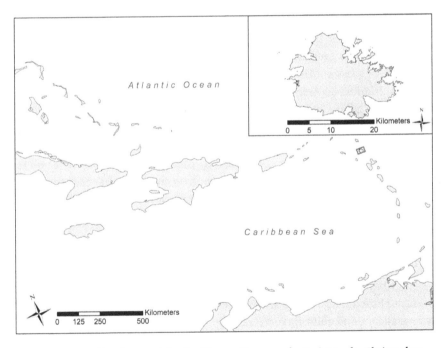

Figure 4.1. Map of Antigua and the Caribbean. (Base map by Esri. Map by Christopher K. Waters.)

Local autonomy extended to defense policy. While part of the British world, costs associated with defense were borne locally. Britain's military infrastructure on the island, the forts, barracks for soldiers, even the structures at the Naval Dockyard at English Harbour, were planned by and paid for by the Antiguan government. Even the Crown forces occupying these positions were subsidized out of the Antigua treasury, and local elites held military commissions, enabling the island's elite to manipulate royal forces to do their own bidding.[10] This worked to the advantage of the British treasury, which could avoid large expenditures protecting Antigua and other Caribbean islands. However, this also meant that other instruments of imperial power—notably the Royal Engineers and Royal Artillery—were not made regularly available until 1779.[11] The results of this vaguely defined relationship manifested in how, and by whom, the island was fortified.

The origins of this independence stem from the ignoble defeat at the hand of the French in 1666. At the time, Antigua was under the proprietary government of William, Lord Willoughby, administered through his headquarters on Barbados. The government in Barbados, a much larger and more lucrative plantation island than Antigua at the time, was accused of siphoning off military supplies—cannons, firearms, gunpowder, and soldiers—sent to defend Antigua and the other Leeward Islands, thereby rendering them helpless in the face of French aggression. Using this delay in support, Antigua and the other three Leeward Islands successfully petitioned for their own government in 1670, concomitant with their desires to dictate their own daily affairs, including defense.

Antigua's fortification policy between 1670 and 1783 was characterized by long periods of neglect punctuated by frenetic activity when threats suddenly arose. Decisions about where to build new fortifications, which defensive points were kept or abandoned, and how many gunners and matrosses each fortification needed, were debated during legislative sessions. Once a decision to build was made, contracts were let out for local overseers and masons, built on plans dreamed up by the legislators. Labor was provided by conscripted enslaved men from nearby plantations. Once a fortification was completed, it was handed over to a joint committee of both houses, with subcommittees assigned direct responsibility over several of the fortified sites. The members of the committee were supposed to visit these sites regularly, ensure that the proper equipment was available, and audit financial records. The defensive results from this process were badly constructed fortifications with few working cannon, poorly trained gunners and matrosses, and locations in areas that benefited the plantation elites to the detriment of the defensibility of the island as a whole.

Design by committee caused some major design flaws, compounded by the general lack of relevant experience by the committee members. Military service in regular British units among Antigua's elites was relatively rare before 1700 and almost nonexistent after 1710. Antigua's fortification system was originally designed by three governors with considerable military experience, Christopher Codrington II (1690–1699), Christopher Codrington III (1699- 1704), and Daniel Parke (1706–1710), yet they were the exception. Codrington II led local offenses against nearby islands in the Caribbean, while Codrington III and Parke both fought in the Low Countries and were familiar with siege warfare. Most of the planters, especially after the second generation, were focused on agricultural, economic, and political pursuits, with the goal of amassing enough wealth to retire to Britain and join the landed gentry.[12] This meant that the closest many of these local elites came to a military engineering background was seeing fortified sites from the outside as they traveled around the Atlantic world. Without access to properly trained engineers, Antigua's fortification committees were reduced to replicating what they had seen from afar and suspected to be inside.

Without the expertise of engineers or artillery officers, the resulting defensive structures illustrate a complete lack of military theory. First, holistic defensive planning where firing angles were carefully considered so that there were no blind spots was largely ignored. Of the sixteen renderings of Antigua's fortifications in Kane William Horneck's (1752) collection, only four had defensible and complete circuit walls. Three more sites were completely enclosed; however, the rear walls were not defensible, being no thicker than 40 to 50 centimeters, and stood only at chest height—hardly defensive and certainly unable to withstand cannon fire. The remaining nine sites are depicted as having significant gaps in the circuit, or only existed as half-moon batteries, leaving them completely vulnerable on the landward side.[13] Rather than a holistic conception of defense promulgated by European engineers, and what could be assumed to be possible if directly designed by a strong colonial government, Antigua's elites only considered threats coming from the sea, and only rarely considered the implications of an enemy successfully landing.[14]

The tactical shortsightedness of defending only against waterborne attack was compounded by the lack of military knowledge. For instance, in a dispute with the Royal Navy over the arrival of new heavy ordnance, the compromise eventually struck was predicated on a poor understanding of ordnance. The guns were originally intended to be spread around the island, however, the navy wanted to better defend the newly enlarged Dockyard at English Harbour. A compromise was struck to arm Monk's Hill, "where some good Cannon are very much wanted has so much the Command of English Harbour, that no Enemy can safely attempt the Same by Land but must be intirely exposed from thence." This was defensively necessary as the navy in the Dockyard "will never be able to defend itself from an Attack by Land, all the Forts & Batteries Erected there being Calculated to oppose an Attack from the Sea only."[15] While parts of the Dockyard are indeed visible from Monk's Hill, the distance from the closest defensive battery on Monk's Hill to the isthmus separating at English Harbour is 2,200 meters, the center of the Dockyard facility is 2,700 meters away, and to the entrance of the harbor 3,250 meters, well outside any effective range, and therefore an absurd defensive proposition (figure 4.2). This defect was only recognized by Antigua's legislature in a debate in 1782 in which Governor Thomas Shirley observed that even if the batteries were in impeccable condition, if obliged to retreat into that fortification, they could only "be spectators to the destruction of the Dock Yard, and the magazines and stores there upon which the existence of our navy in these seas must depend without being able to prevent the mischief."[16] This stark confession finally galvanized the Antiguan government into agreeing to pay for a new fortified camp on the ridge above the Dockyard (Shirley Heights). Although much of the financing and labor came from the island, the site was controlled by the military, designed by the Royal Engineers, and garrisoned by the British Army: the first time in Antigua's history when metropolitan military forces had direct control over a part of Antigua's defenses.

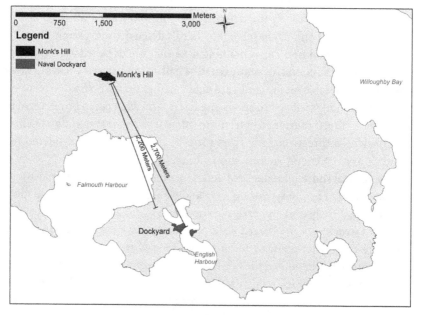

Figure 4.2. Map demonstrating the linear distances between the batteries at Monk's Hill and the dockyard at English Harbour. (Base map by Esri. Map by Christopher K. Waters.)

The lack of military engineering knowledge and experience among the island's elites is evident in other fortification features too. Uniform to all of the island's legislature-constructed fortifications are thin walls. Constructed out of local masonry, the walls are generally clad with poorly shaped stone, faced on only the visible side. The center of the walls are layers of rubble held together with mortar, creating a dense filling. Where measured, the walls range in thickness between 65 and 130 centimeters (figure 4.3). None of the fortifications have a terreplein to absorb shot concussions, or any other kinds of defensive features designed to keep walls intact and the enemy at a distance. In contrast, the two military-built fortifications, the navy battery at Fort Berkeley (1745), and Fort Charlotte (1790), have considerably thicker walls. The second battery, built by Commodore Knowles of the Royal Navy, has walls that are 450 centimeters thick, and deep, protective embrasures.[17] Fort Charlotte, on the opposite side of the harbor entrance, had walls that were 336 centimeters thick at the parapet and tapered into a proper scarp.

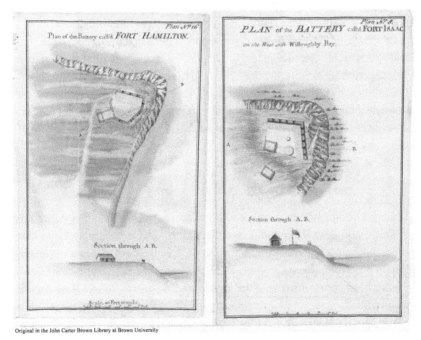

Figure 4.3. Northeast section of a map of Antigua. Fort Hamilton (*left*) and Fort Isaac (*right*) as depicted by Kane William Horneck in 1752. Note the small sizes of these fortifications, and the military design but lack of military engineering. In particular, note the thinness of the parapets.

Historically, there were several indictments of Antigua's fortifications by engineers and experienced military officers traveling through Antigua. Daniel Parke, in an attempt to sway the Antiguan elites to abandon their efforts to fortify the entire island and instead adapt his plans to entrench St. John's Town, brought his friend, the Ordnance Officer Colonel Lilly from his posting in Barbados in 1709. They utterly condemned Antigua's fortifications, writing, "there is not such thing in the whole Country as deserves the name of a Fort for that which is built on Munks hill is not so Since an Enemy may upon his first Landing (without having occasion bringing Canon against it) easily made himselfe master of it with Sword in hand."[18] Parke continued, describing the island's defenses as loose piles of stone, reminiscent of the newly constructed garden follie by the Duke of Bedford at his Badminton Estate in England.[19] Nor was this an isolated incident. Governor William Mathew, writing in 1734, took particular issue with Fort Hamilton, commenting that, "If Fort Hamilton had been better placed, as well as laid out as the worst fort in Europe," then it may have had some utility.[20] As it was built by the Antiguan government in the 1730s, it did not serve any use in Mathew's estimation. In a final indictment, Captain Thomas F. Lancey of the Royal Engineers wrote in 1831 that, "Forts, which last, where the Property of the Colony, are for the most part in a neglected and dilapidated state, several small Batteries too, with insufficient parapets, old Guns and unserviceable, colonial-made Carriages,"[21] showing despite their names, the fortifications themselves lacked even the basic defensive features and regular maintenance. In short, while called forts, these sites lacked the basic military features necessary to make them even remotely effective, a conclusion contrary to the military knowledge a colonial possession is meant to have at its disposal.

Fort Hamilton, Fort James, the Cripplegate, and the Protection of St. John's Harbour

The coastline around the St. John's Roads, encompassing the Cripplegate Battery, Fort James, and Fort Hamilton, exemplifies how local elites created a military aesthetic without any fortification theory. St. John's Town, the island's capital and main port, is on the western, leeward side of the island. The prevailing easterly winds blow across the island, through town, and over St. John's Harbour, and out the entrance and into the Caribbean Sea. The contrary winds made sailing into St. John's Harbour difficult for small vessels and impossible for large square-rigged ships that could not sail directly upwind. Additionally, as John Luffmann wrote in a letter to a friend in 1786, "its best security is the Bar, a shoal so called, extending almost across it . . . the depth of water on this shelve is from eight to fourteen feet," preventing most large vessels from entering.[22] Large shipping was confined to anchoring outside of the harbor, in relatively shallow and calm water, while produce and people were ferried in local boats from the quays in town.

The fortifications built to protect St. John's fulfilled two missions. First, they had to protect the entrance to St. John's Harbour and the wealth accumulated in the eponymous town from external attack. Second, and perhaps the larger daily threat, these forts had to provide the necessary cover for merchant vessels anchored in the St. John's Roads by providing enough of a deterrent that privateers could not seize these vulnerable vessels. Since Antigua and St. John's were never attacked in force after 1666, the first mission ostensibly succeeded.[23] Protecting shipping, however, proved to be more difficult.

Sugar was immensely profitable. Its cultivation generated new industries across the Atlantic world to support the burgeoning industry. Provisions and timber products flowed from North America and Ireland, while manufactured goods arrived from Europe. Newly enslaved Africans were forced onto vessels and brought in as labor. The Caribbean, and Antigua in particular, formed the nexus where these vessels converged. To understand the scale of this trade, between October 4, 1707, and September 22, 1708, 127 vessels cleared customs in St. John's Antigua in wartime conditions. Between 1784 and 1787, 1,505 vessels arrived in St. John's, connecting Antigua to the rest of the world.[24] These vessels were the commercial lifeblood of the colony, bringing raw materials and enslaved labor in, and shipping sugar, molasses, and rum back out.

Construction started at Fort James, the second largest fortification in Antigua after the citadel at Monk's Hill, in 1683. Built at the southernmost tip of a long, sandy peninsula, the fort protected the entrance to St. John's Harbour. Initially earthen embankments, in 1704 the inner fort was formalized in stone. The final expansion to its current state happened during the War of Jenkins' Ear between 1739 and 1740 specifically to counter threats from Spanish privateers.[25] This final expansion included a longer sea battery and an additional hornwork bringing additional cannons to bear on the anchorages.

Fort Hamilton was built in 1727. Located 1,300 meters north of Fort James, this battery was designed as a ravelin: a detached outer work for a larger fortification, only without a larger fortification near enough to protect it. Built on a small headland, the fort added additional ordnance defenses for the anchorages off St. John's as well as creating a hardened defensive point commanding Runaway Beach, a long stretch of sand and calm water identified as one of the most likely landing places on Antigua. Additionally, Fort Hamilton provided the secondary role of protecting the landward approaches to Fort James. To emphasize this fort's importance, a 1729 return of forts on Antigua shows that Fort Hamilton was issued the largest caliber cannons, all in good condition, barring only Fort James and Monk's Hill.[26] The fort, however, was too small, and the embrasures cut into the parapet were not well sighted, leaving the entire beach out of the cannon firing arcs. By 1728, the fort was considered useless,[27] and by 1740, the Antiguan legislature considered it a major threat to Fort James itself. Worried that Fort Hamilton could not withstand an attack, the government ordered all large caliber cannons out of the fort so that the large guns would not be captured and turned on Fort James.[28]

By reducing Fort Hamilton, the legislature committed several tactical errors. First, they left one of the most vulnerable beaches even less defended and the shipping riding at anchor less protected. Rather than correct the construction errors or expand the fortifications, the first instinct was to reduce the site's capabilities. Second, the mutually supportive relationship between Fort Hamilton and Fort James was forgotten. In the expansion of the latter, the former was still required to provide the necessary landward protection. In the final iteration of Fort James, landward defenses were ignored, leaving much of the terrestrial approaches without adequate ability to effect counterfire (figure 4.4). New embrasures were not cut into the parapet, and no effort was made to correct this weakness; all additional expansion plans were abandoned after the legislature pronounced its satisfaction with how the fort looked. Indeed, Fort James looked like a properly engineered fort from the outside, however vulnerable the fort actually was.

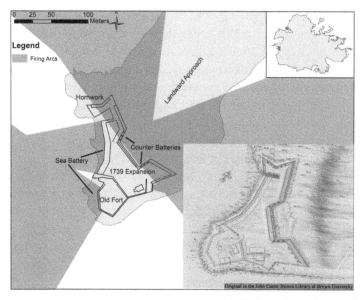

Figure 4.4. Fort James, Antigua, and the estimated cannon firing arcs based on the locations of the embrasures taken from an archaeological survey by Christopher K. Waters. (Base map by Esri. Map by Christopher K. Waters. Inset from figure 4.3.)

While landward defenses were poor, the forts protecting the anchorage were likewise out of place, and effective defense was hampered by a lack of military knowledge. Vessels riding on the St. John's Roads had to anchor in water deep enough that they would not run aground. For small vessels, this was not much of an issue, with water depths between 10 and 15 feet (3–5 meters) fairly close to Fort James and Fort Hamilton. Deeper water, however, only happens more than 1,000 meters from Fort James. At this distance, effective cannon fire becomes more difficult, affecting the ability of the gunners to defend the shipping in front of them. Privateers seized on this shortcoming, cutting vessels out from under the guns. Initially, a small battery was built on a spit of land directly west of Fort James at the Cripplegate, around 1707.[29] Although only an earthen embankment, the fortification was set at 30 meters elevation with an excellent view over the St. John's Roads, with deep water running practically underneath the fortification. However, its primary mission was soon forgotten, and the battery was abandoned while Fort James was expanding in the 1730s. This likely exacerbated the conditions allowing privateers to cut out merchant vessels from under Fort James's guns. This situation was only readdressed in 1778, explicitly to "be an Everlasting protection to allow Shipping which may lay over the Barr at the Mouth of the Harbour of Saint John, which from their distance from Fort James are under little or no Protection & are very liable to be Cut out by the Enemy."[30] The inability to construct a proper fort or to tactically think about their defensive situation resulted in poorly built fortifications of no defensive value whatsoever in Antigua (figure 4.5). Rather, the island elites chose to focus on the architectural aesthetics instead of seeing to a moderately effective defense.

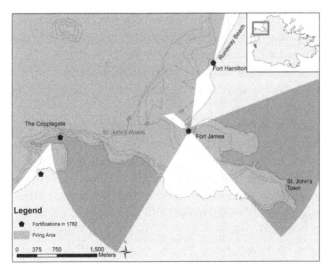

Figure 4.5. Defense of St John's Roads in 1782. Bathymetric depths are in feet. (Base map by Esri. Map by Christopher K. Waters.)

Fortification as Vernacular Architecture

While the defensive engineering of Antigua's fortifications is questionable, at best, the designs adhere to a military aesthetic. In fact, they look exactly like what a fortification should look like if one had seen a fortification from the outside and at a distance, especially when viewed from the water.[31] Without engineers or other experienced military personnel, the men in the Antiguan government, and the contractors they hired, had to work from a popular template of what a fortification should look like: stone walls, punctuated by embrasures, or at least a low parapet, a guardhouse, and a flagpole. Even the basic shapes of the fortifications were copied, either as half-moon batteries recalling seawall fortifications present in the major ports and cities in Europe, or more angular, resembling bastions or ravelins in terrestrial settings. This resulted in defensive features that were much more an homage to fortification design aesthetics but fell vastly short of the functional engineering necessary to make these sites effective.

The American folklorist and architectural historian Henry Glassie defines architectural vernacular as those buildings that "embody values alien to those cherished by the academy."[32] He goes on, stating that, "Vernacular technology depends on direct connections: direct access to materials and direct connections among suppliers, producers, and consumers who simultaneously shape landscapes, social orders, and economic arrangements."[33] In short, the Antiguan elites controlling Antigua's defense policy inadvertently created a fortification vernacular: a series of structures they believed looked like a military-engineered defensive feature. With their limited experience, poor construction habits, and limited tactical thinking, they chose locations, expanded defense, and abandoned sites based on political and social calculations rather than military thinking. Indeed, defensive sites in Antigua are best explained by social convention rather than tactical consideration. Entrances of harbors got fortified because that was where fortifications existed in other places; in Antigua's case, however, they tended to be placed at the outermost points, far away from spaces they were supposed to protect.

Antigua's fortifications between 1670 and 1783 provide an important counterpoint to the teleological colonial narratives where the military and the metropole are intimately intertwined, replicating plans developed in Europe and transplanted directly into a colonial context. As I show, the local elites in Antigua held exclusive power over the military decisions surrounding the island, to the point of usurping imperial symbols to maintain their political autonomy. This resulted in a defensive system protecting the island that relied on military aesthetics rather than military engineering. Thinking about fortification in the

Caribbean, and in the wider Atlantic world, then, requires decentering military and imperial perspectives and reevaluating how communities in colonial contexts bent the symbols of metropolitan power to best suit their local needs. This leads ultimately to the interesting question, if the colonial government's interest and knowledge were not being exploited to protect their possessions in the seventeenth and eighteenth centuries, how much direct control can we attribute to the daily lives and historical trajectories of these territories? By examining the fortifications as a vernacular in Antigua, we see a much more politically complex and multidirectional relationship between metropole and colony and destabilize dominant colonial narratives in the Atlantic world by restoring local agency.

5

The English Settlement of Guantánamo, Cuba

Urban and Defensive Features

Pedro Luengo

Many Caribbean cities were created during the second half of the eighteenth century. Usually designed under Enlightenment parameters, they generally included the most recent innovations in fortifications alongside European architectural rhetoric, which appeared more profoundly than previously. The Mopox Commission in Cuba (1796–1802) and French projects in modern-day Haiti offer good examples of these resettlement initiatives.[1] Far less attention has been paid to earlier eighteenth-century encampment attempts, especially those managed by the British Crown, such as in modern-day Belize or the ephemeral Guantánamo effort. Because they were considered new and somewhat utopian projects, they now offer good examples through which we can examine different urban aspects, including their defensive traits, social organization, and the imperial image they sought to relate. More specifically, this chapter addresses Cumberland, a 1741 British encampment near Guantánamo (Cuba) and compares it with similar projects in other parts of the Caribbean.

This chapter defines the military contribution of British encampment foundations during the first half of the eighteenth-century Caribbean, starting with the Cumberland case, connecting the solutions carried out by the English in their settlements, demonstrated by Graham (chapter 3) and Waters (chapter 4), with the Spanish ones, reconstructed, for instance, in the works of Manuel Gámez Casado (chapter 11), José Miguel Morales Folguera (chapter 14), and Nuria Hinarejos Martín (chapter 13). This comparison is especially relevant despite the limited interest it has received from academics. Only Jeremy Black, commenting on the encampment plan, and Asunción Baeza, analyzing the later attack on Santiago, have focused on the Guantánamo site.[2] The site's importance lies in being the best-known English expansionist settlement project in the Caribbean created in the period between the end of the piracy era and the beginning of successful attacks on French and Spanish ports. From here, this chapter examines how the first settlers chose the place and planned the city in terms of social organization. Secondly, this chapter also analyzes the defensive plan to demonstrate how the British maintained a clear method of fortifying these enclaves based on a common theoretical foundation. Finally, the essay identifies which architectural elements the colonists used to maintain Britishness in comparison to other European or native architectural traits. From all these perspectives, this chapter does not try only to reconstruct a short history of the small settlement, but instead defines the strategy the British employed at this time and contrasts it with those the French and Spanish employed in terms of campaign defense systems, urban planning, and residential design in the Caribbean.[3] All this can now be addressed thanks to graphical research on historical sources preserved in British, Spanish, American, and French archives, such as the Windsor Castle Archive, the British Library, the Archivo General de Indias, the Biblioteca Nacional de España, the Library of Congress, and the Bibliothèque Nationale de France. This information now permits us to compare with what was previously known about other Caribbean settlements under the British, Spanish, and French.

The British based their presence in the Caribbean during the first decades of the eighteenth century with Barbados as the key point of the Antilles alongside Jamaica in the center of the sea.[4] On one hand, the capital of Barbados, Bridgetown, does not follow a clear urban plan, although military structures played an important role beginning in the seventeenth century. The English located minor forts and batteries around the city and the island and built military edifices and some noteworthy estates such as Washington House around a large camp, and these facilities were likely used for military activities. On the other hand, Jamaica was captured from the Spanish in 1655 and from this moment, Kingston received some attention from British military engineers, who once again increased fortifications with small structures near the city. Both ports supported triangular trade with the North American colonies through their commercial role, which was based on agricultural production. At this same time, Anglo-Spanish international tensions led to conflicts in the Caribbean, including in Panama and in Cartagena de Indias. Although the British were unsuccessful in many of these conflicts, the conflagrations demonstrated the need to have geostrategic nodes in the region to support future campaigns and to hinder Spanish activities. This new military stratagem combined with the growing use of piracy and the proliferation of new log-cutting settlements established along the coast between the Bay of Campeche (Mexico) and modern-day Nicaragua, as

70   Pedro Luengo

well as on large coastal islands. For example, in 1713 the British fortified a chain
of posts extending from Cozumel Island (in modern-day Mexico) southward.[5]
Continuous struggles with Spain forced its limited population to coalesce into
an unofficial settlement near the Belize River from at least 1717 onward, and for
political reasons it received scant financial or military support from the British
Crown. As such, very little information has been located on its urban characteristics. In fact, something similar can be said about the fortified settlement of
Roatan Island, or the one known as Black River, which was active since 1742.[6]
Some years later, between 1743 and 1744, Spanish intelligence documented the
British foundation of the settlement of Rio Tinto that apparently had been active earlier.[7] From these small undistinguished positions the British organized
an attack against Truxillo (Honduras), exemplifying the new English strategy
of the period, that is, supporting campaigns from nearby camps or settlements.

   These military camps, at least partially, served as bases for attacks, and this
was characteristic of the time. In earlier times superior British naval power often permitted the easy conquest of enemy ports, but the English rarely settled
or developed the conquered port. In fact, before the Seven Years' War, intelligence, especially about geographical landmarks, was the crucial information
necessary for later amphibious approaches, as was clear in Guadalupe, Marti-
nica, and Havana, among others.[8] During the middle decades of the eighteenth
century the British developed an intermediary option, using naval forces to
land army forces kilometers away from their target, and from there starting
a land-based terrestrial flank. This tactic complemented their offensive operations after 1762 because they prepared only land approaches in the traditional
manner, obviating the advantages of a combined naval-army assault exploiting
geography, as they ultimately did some decades later.

Cartagena, Colombia

As part of this military project, the English established an encampment in Cartagena at the beginning of the assault in 1741, which represented a clear anteced-
ent of Cumberland. Located in Tierra Bomba, the British designed it after they
destroyed the Spanish forts of San Luis and San José at the mouth of the bay.[9]
The British laid out the camp along the coast with a small number of plots organized in two rows. Here, some of the rudiments that defined the basic elements
of British encampment can be found. To protect it, they repaired two small
forts, called Saint Iago and Saint Philip, and a battery. At the harbor's entrance,
two Spanish buildings remained, the star-shaped Fort San Luis de Bocachica
and Fort San José, located on a small island, which has recently been enlarged.[10]
The English map (figure 5.1) clearly shows that the urban development of the

camp was very limited, without data about government edifices, fountains, hospitals, or public spaces. Even the fortification was adapted from Spanish remains, without creating a distinct urban space. Despite the large number of British troops, the encampment only had room for a few regiments in a tiny space, especially when compared with Cumberland later.

Cumberland represents one clear geostrategic settlement connected with these conflicts. Nothing is preserved today of the camp, which must have been located near modern-day Cayamo (Caimanera, Guantánamo Province, Cuba; 20°01'24.5"N 75°13'17.4"W). Traditionally, it has been reported that Admiral Edward Vernon and General Thomas Wentworth created the camp along the south coast of Cuba in 1741. Some sources prove that this place was previously used, and an eighteenth-century French map of the area shows that it had been used by Vernon in 1738.[11] This date is incredibly significant and unknown until now. At this time, no war was declared between England and Spain; it was a year before the British attempt against Havana (between September and November 1739) and the successful attack against Portobelo in December 1739. Vernon, along with Wentworth, were known to have arrived in the Caribbean in 1739 after previously visiting Jamaica. Founding a camp in Cuba is difficult to explain in the context of the English presence in the Caribbean. Either Jamaica or Barbados seemed to be better candidates, even if the goal were to launch an attack on Portobelo. As Castillero and Morales contend, Spanish forces knew of the English war plans against Portobelo (1739) ahead of time, which explains the fortifications that Philip V brought about.[12] It is possible that the Spanish knew of the arrival of the British fleet in the Caribbean as early as 1738, although the foundation of Cumberland remained unknown until 1741.

Cumberland, Cuba

The name of Cumberland was chosen in honor of the Duke of Cumberland (Prince William, 1721–1765, the son of George II). Vernon and Wentworth had unsuccessfully attacked Portobelo and Cartagena between March and May 1741,[13] while Lawrence Washington, brother of future U.S. President George Washington, resided with Vernon in Bridgetown. Washington probably returned to Barbados via Jamaica, while Vernon and Wentworth decided to attempt a similar attack in Santiago de Cuba, carried out between July and December 1741. This port's sixteenth-century fortifications and its geographical features made a naval attack precarious, necessitating instead a territorial approach. To do so, ships entered Guantánamo Bay, which Vernon probably knew well, moved up the Catalina River and conquered the town of Catalina, ultimately establishing a camp from which to formulate an attack against Santiago. The British troops landed about 100 kilometers from Santiago and quickly encountered tropical diseases and local resistance. The Spanish avoided a terrestrial confrontation, relying instead on constant hit-and-run attacks against the camp, while the heat and disease sapped British health and morale during the four months spent preparing for the approach. Despite continual skirmishing, the British constructed various types of fieldworks, both documenting the geographical space and building trenches.[14] Ultimately, the troops returned to Jamaica in December 1741, ending their activity in Cumberland.

This British encampment has received little attention from scholars, despite representing an exceptional urban project in the eighteenth-century Caribbean (figure 5.2 and figure 5.3). Logically, the most detailed sources on the settlement can be found in English-language institutions, especially those in Great Britain[15] and the United States.[16] A general view, found in archives in both countries, was published, but only briefly analyzed, by Black.[17] But it was not only the English that sent information on the camp. The French also had plans for the camp, though their plans were very general and unattributed. Spanish authorities also attempted to get timely information on the settlement, and there are at least six depictions made between 1741 and 1745 (figure 5.4, figure 5.5, and figure 5.6).[18] All these maps are anonymous except for the one preserved in Washington, which is signed with a monogram (figure 5.7). While difficult to confirm, it is possible that this was a later copy by Balthasar Ricaud de Tirgale, who arrived in Havana in 1761 after working at the Academy in Barcelona. He maintained the original date of 1751, although the map must have been made a decade before. Apart from these sources, there is a group of very similar representations of Guantánamo. They follow the characteristics of the Escuela de Navegación de Cádiz, already studied by Morales.[19] For this reason, it seems probable that they correspond to training copies and were not used for military campaigns, based on the previous examples.[20]

According to one Spanish source, the camp had 535 houses, along with around 200 located at the islets of Guantánamo Bay and the east beach (figure 5.8 and figure 5.9).[21] For comparison, Kingston (Jamaica) must have 1,194 inhabited lots in 1745 according to contemporary maps. The troops sent from Cartagena, probably more than 25,000, were clearly reduced in number here, not reaching five thousand, including one thousand Jamaicans. Thus, at least a few of these houses in Cumberland may have been reserved for the Black population. Some other sources identify 500 mercenaries from the American colonies that joined the campaign in hopes of obtaining lands in a port likely to become the operational center of British expansion in the Caribbean.[22] The English had to design a settlement organized by military rank, including the most recent innovations for a racially complex community.

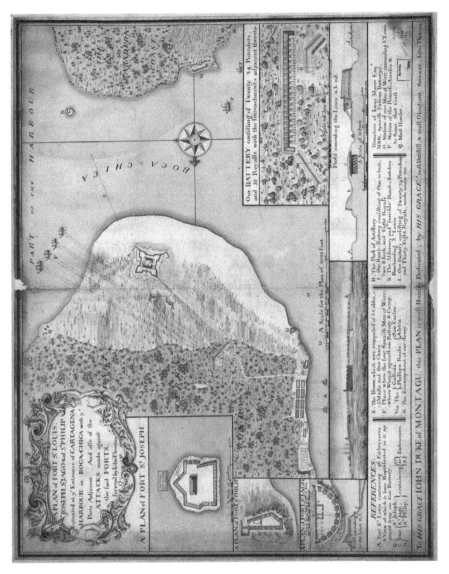

Figure 5.1. John Thomas, *A plan of Fort St. Louis, St. Joseph, St. Jago & of St. Philip scituated at ye entrance of Cartagena Harbour or Boca-Chica with ye parts adjacent and also of the attacks made against the said forts.* (Library of Congress, G5294.C3S5 1741.T5.)

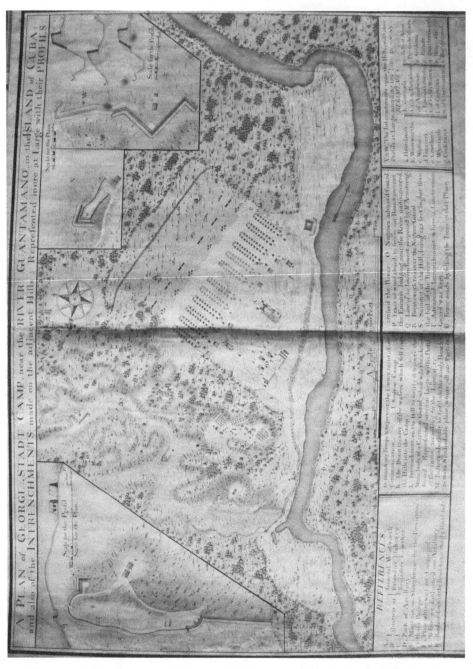

Figure 5.2. *A Plan of George Stadt Camp near the River Guantamano in the island of Cuba and also of the intrenchments made on the adjacent hills, represented more at larg with their profils.* (Courtesy of Royal Collection Trust / © Her Majesty Queen Elizabeth II 2019.)

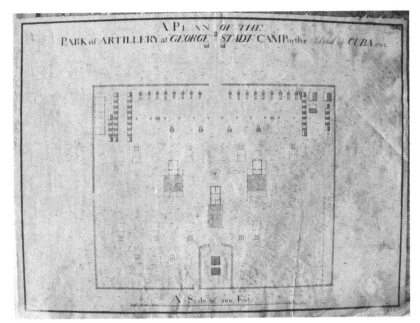

Figure 5.3. *A Plan of the Park of Artillery at George Stadt Camp in the Island of Cuba*, 1741. (Courtesy of Royal Collection Trust / © Her Majesty Queen Elizabeth II, 2019.)

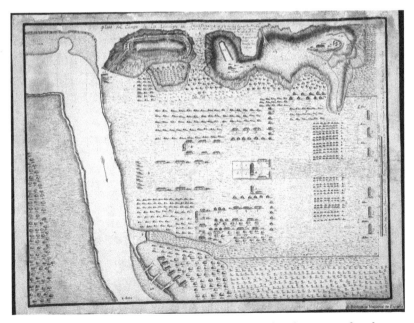

Figure 5.4. *Plano del Campo de los enemigos en Juantánamo, al pie de Las Lomas de Melcor, en el año de 1741, desde el principio de expans hasta el fin de dicho año.* (Image from the collections of the Biblioteca Nacional de España, MR/42/483. CC BY-4.0.)

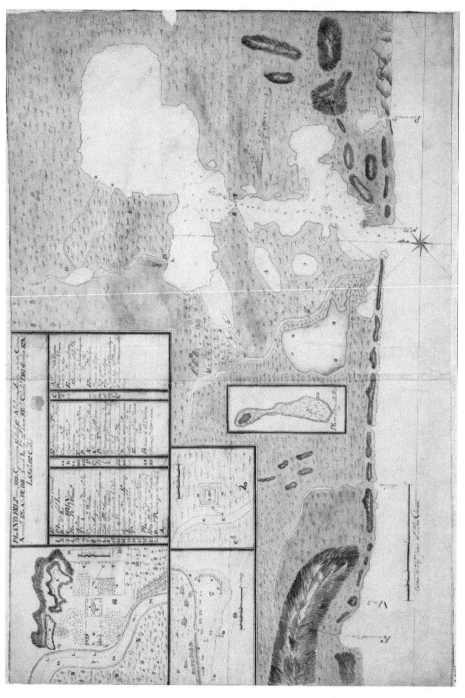

Figure 5.5. *Plano del Puerto de Guantánamo en donde el xpansión Vernon estuvo con su armada el año de 1741.* (Image from the collections of the Biblioteca Nacional de España, MR/43/226. CC BY-4.0.)

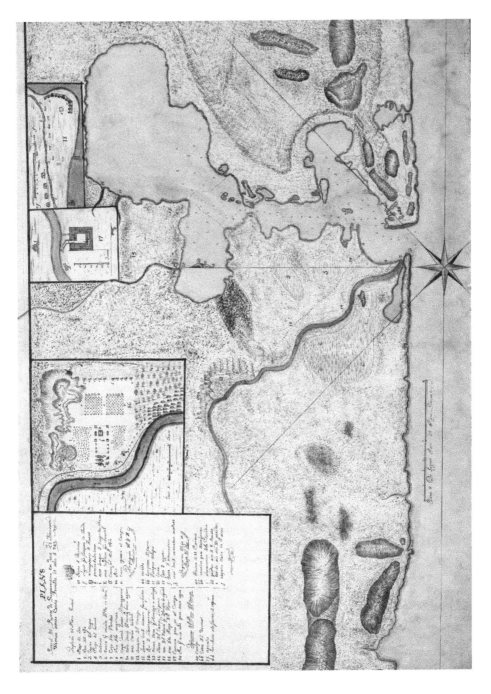

Figure 5.6. *Plano General del Puerto de Guantánamo en donde el Almirante Wernon estuvo con su armada el año de 1741.* (Image from the collections of the Biblioteca Nacional de España, MR/43/223. CC BY-4.0.)

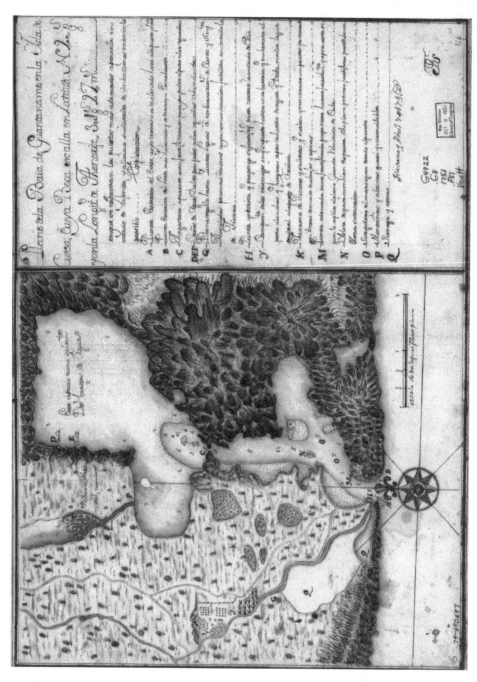

Figure 5.7. *Plano de la Bahía de Guantánamo, en la isla de Cuba, cuya boca se haya en Expansió N. 20 grados, y en la Expansión de Tenerife 301 grados. 27 minutos,* 1751. (Library of Congress, G4922. G8 1751 .P5.)

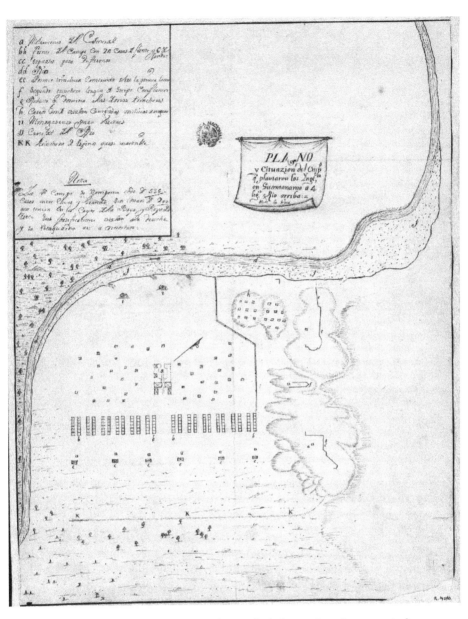

Figure 5.8. *Plano de situación del campo que plantaron los ingleses en Guantánamo a cuatro leguas río arriba desde la boca.* (Image from the collections of the Biblioteca Nacional de España, MR/43/218. CC BY-4.0.)

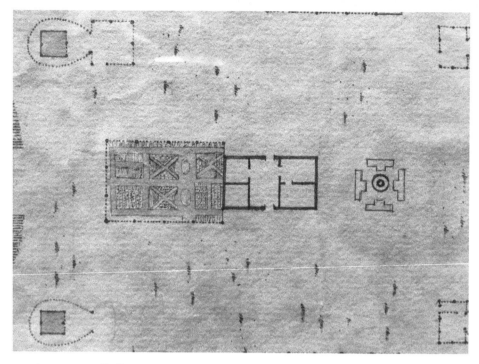

Figure 5.9. Detail of houses in park or artillery of Cumberland. A Plan of the Park of Artillery at George Stadt Camp in the Island of Cuba, 1741. (Courtesy of Royal Collection Trust / © Her Majesty Queen Elizabeth II 2019.)

Fortifying a Camp

The English provided detailed information that could be far from the final reality. For this reason, it is necessary to compare this data with that given by enemies' intelligence. The Spanish government started spying on the settlement soon after the British arrival. Just after the information on the English arrival of seventeen ships between July 29 and 30, 1741, the military engineer Antonio de Arredondo was sent to the south because of his knowledge on the area.[23] Francisco Langle, most likely a French engineer in the Spanish service, was sent to Guantánamo to inform on the English presence the same year.[24] Slightly later, in 1742, two other engineers, Carlos Desnaux and the Spaniard Juan Bautista MacEvan, were asked again about the actions to be carried out as a result of the English camp.[25] The sources are clear to stress that it was not in use after 1741, although attention remained focused on it. According to some studies on espionage and counterintelligence in the contemporary Caribbean, it can be said that the information received by the Spanish on the English settlement was far more detailed than from any other American port. A few campaigns were developed in Jamaica,[26] while the British information on other Spanish and French ports was not always as detailed.[27] All this information supports the assertion that Cumberland represents a noteworthy example of England's new fortification and military strategy of the time, in addition to being better documented. It relied on particularities found in other English examples in the Caribbean, managed in most cases by military officers. Despite London's minimal governmental control, a common strategy can nonetheless be identified.

Like the Dutch, the English did not rely much on permanent fortifications in the Caribbean, in contrast to the French, the Spanish, or even the Danish. Despite the variety of ports the English governed, most of them had a weak system for defense. As has been studied in recent years, while Barbados had a sequence of small forts around the island starting in the seventeenth century, its capital, Bridgetown, barely had any forts to protect it.[28] The situation was worse in Jamaica, where the coast lacked any such structures apart from a small one in Port Antonio, and those in Kingston Bay. Although other English Caribbean islands also had defensive structures, a similar pattern followed. Distant small buildings were located at geostrategic places to contain attacks temporally. The real defense was entrusted to the Royal Navy and, to a lesser extent, to open-field confrontation.

The fortification of Cumberland was very interesting compared with other cases in the Caribbean at the time, which could be considered another distinctive feature of these British encampments. While the French and Spanish relied on geometry and the most avant-garde theory, the English preferred pragmatism. The southern flank was considered secure because of the river's course. Thus, the storehouse and powder keg were located there, with their characteristic rectangular plan with a little pit surrounding it. The northern flank still preserved local flora, presenting a complex geographical orography. Taking advantage of the terrain, one of the characteristics of the second half of the eighteenth-century English warfare in the Caribbean, the British designed only three small forts. In the western section, a wall was carved on the hill, with a passageway behind it to the northwest side. More complex was a very narrow bastion at the center of the northern flank, controlling what must be a crossroads. Finally, a larger triangular ravelin was built on the eastern side (see figure 5.2). These structures can be found on the English maps as well as on the Spanish ones, which implies that they were ultimately built. On the contrary, the English maps also inform us of a fortification proposed by Armstrong that was never started. Across the river, the defense system was designed with trenches, including a wall with two bulwarks and a half-bulwark. At one of the extremes, closer to the storehouse, an interesting building was designed, a pentagonal bastioned fort in the antiquated Italian style.

These were the structures surrounding the camp, but the English maintained other buildings in the bay. For example, there was a squared-trench fort at the mouth of a river. It was probably developed to provide protection to the English fleet in case of conflict. In addition, a long battery was installed in Playa del Este to protect the landing in the docks with twelve cannons.

In addition to comparing these fortifications with other English contemporary examples, they can be viewed from the theoretical perspective. The best-known theorist of this time in England is John Müller (1699–1784), whose work was quickly translated into many languages during the second half of the eighteenth century. Likely, his treatises were merely the result of his teachings, and alterations developed in London after his arrival. He moved to London in 1736, before he was appointed deputy head of the recently created Royal Military Academy in Woolwich in 1741. Both from a profound knowledge of Vauban, usually cited in his writings, and his contemporary experiences, he tried to offer practical and homogenous solutions to the expanding English world. As Cumberland shows, and other European engineers copied, Müller succeeded. His texts gave much attention to new geometrical patterns in fortifications, in line with other contemporary European treatises, but also included information on how to design specific buildings such as hospitals and artillery fields, probably as a result of his experience in gunnery or lines of contravallation. Hospitals were considered a very important part of Müller's approach, as he recognized that one out of every twenty-five soldiers would become ill.[29] He fails to recommend a specific plan for them, but cited a French design, to build rectangular rooms of 42 × 21 feet (ca. 13 × 6 meters), which would allow for a layout of two rows of beds, five beds each row.[30] Although it is difficult to confirm the measurements of such small buildings in the Cumberland depiction, it may be possible that these corresponded to Müller's model, allowing the hospital to host around ten sick men from each regiment in twelve buildings, or 120 sick soldiers in total. He highly recommended locating them far from rivers or water, something especially important in the Caribbean due to the threat posed by mosquitos. As can be seen in the plan, in Cumberland they are located at the farthest line away from the river.

The artillery park forms a square section distant from the rest of the camp (see figure 5.3). Its features are very similar to the description given later by John Müller in his treatise.[31] The curious thing is that this park has not been found in any of the Spanish sources, so it seems probable that it was not ultimately built, although it was designed strictly according to the theory of the time. Importantly, this organization has not been found among fortification plans of other European powers, either Spanish or French, it being an element of the English fortification tradition. Also, in this treatise, the trenches forming a wall with triangular bastions are described and drawn as a line of counterval-lation.[32] A small structure of this type can be found at one of the extremes of the defense system. Finally, the profiles of the saps are clearly similar to those in Müller.[33] The technique used here, with the inner structure of the trench made in wood, required skilled workers and was not common in other countries, relying once again on the English manner of fortification. Such a close relationship between Müller's treatise and the works performed in Cumberland allows us to consider that the barracks might follow the same characteristics. The profiles and the descriptions are fully developed in the treatise and probably were known among English officials.[34] Recurrent references to Müller's proposal in Cumberland and general homogeneity in eighteenth-century English Caribbean fortification allow us to consider that his work in London was well known in military circles, influencing military engineers' later tasks in the colonies and providing a unifying feature to English fortifications overseas.

In addition to the fortifications, Cumberland's urban plan was also designed based on the rhetoric of the English naval empire, providing new public spaces and a clear ethnic organization, elements that support a common framework for British structures in the region. All this can be compared with the other English settlements in the Antilles, including Bridgetown, Kingston, and Belize. However, its location in Cuba allows a transnational example of how British urban planners dealt with a different geography in comparison to eighteenth-century foundations laid out by Spaniards. More particularly, houses of the highest-ranking military officers will be analyzed. In so doing, this chapter addresses how the traditions in gardening or house building were used to enforce a rhetoric of an innovative British empire. From this point, it would be easier to explain how local elites adopted these European patterns in large contemporary mansions in the Caribbean, such as plantation houses found in Cuba or Santo Domingo, or even new government palaces such as Sans Souci in Haiti. How models were created, developed, or rejected in such nearby settlements, although under different imperial regimes, is a relevant point to understand cultural groupings.

Commonly, an encampment is organized according to regiments, which appears in the map without much detail (see figure 5.2). Cumberland is organized according to four regiments[35] and four battalions of Americans in columns, while every row corresponded with the rank: colonels, officers (one or two houses each regiment), captains (two), lieutenants (four), "bells of arms," and privates (twelve). Behind these, there was an open space to organize the parade. Every regiment, finally, had its own quartermaster, two hospital buildings, and two boghouses. The organization of the troops was in line with their leaders: General Wentworth, Brigadier Blackney, and Brigadier Lowthes. Both

84   Pedro Luengo

brigadiers were provided with similar buildings of rectangular plan with gardens at the rear. The general had a more developed structure with an h-shape design. At the entrance of this building two small pavilions were located while proportionally larger gardens were laid out at the rear. A similar pattern was followed in the neighboring artillery park where private gardens of these three officials were even larger and more elaborate (see figures 5.3 and 5.9). As was shown for the fortification, this organization can be also found in Müller's later treatise, describing the governor's houses and their gardens.[36] Finally, Maroons were located in a different space, outside this reticular plan. Despite this, the Black soldiers' tents were also grouped in squares of 5 × 5, 5 × 4, or 6 × 2, while at least another twenty-nine seem to be scattered with a recognizable organization. This ethnic differentiation was also visible in other English settlements such as Kingston (Jamaica).

Unfortunately, little information is provided for these houses. Except from Müller's recommendations, the three large ones can be analyzed from the contemporary development of a gentleman's house.[37] The general's domicile can be considered a reinterpretation of the h-shape houses that were built in England from the beginning of the century, such as the Burlington House in London. Apart from this primary example, the other buildings were compact rectangles with a single bay, although one example had three. Probably they were one-and-a-half storied with a hipped roof and a relatively unornamented front, such as in other Atlantic examples.[38] Not many examples of this kind have survived in the English Caribbean except for Washington House in Bridgetown (Barbados), visited by the Washington brothers, Lawrence and George, in 1751. From the late seventeenth century onward, this typology included rear gardens in the French manner. Parterres and hedges were used to create geometrical decoration in squared sections, as was done in Hampton Court at the beginning of the century, although here with limited possibilities. These examples served as the basis for the Georgian houses that later spread throughout North America after the American War of Independence.

Despite the brief history of this settlement, the English taste was highlighted in some elements. For example, at the center of the artillery park, in between the three houses, it seems that a fountain was installed (see figure 5.9), in line with Müller's recommendation.[39] Furthermore, the camp had hydraulic works to control water descending from the surrounding hills. These two examples, together with the urban plan and the gardens, connect with the efforts carried out by the English in the Caribbean to maintain a homogenous imperial image. In this vein, Kingston was decorated with classical architectural structures, as in the crossroad of Lower Kings Street and Harbour Street.[40] These houses and urban services had no military purpose in an ephemeral camp.

Their aim was to maintain English "civilization" and "taste" overseas. The navy and their buildings must serve as a mirror of the metropolis, which at that time preferred French gardening culture over English traditions.

These examples demonstrate that the English changed the strategy in the Caribbean during the first half of the eighteenth century, in an innovative way compared with other European powers. They refused to address piratical assaults on American ports or to design long-term attacks preceded by the organization of camps. This happened at least in Cartagena (1741), Santiago de Cuba (1741), Roatan Island (1742), and Black Waters (1743), although it was not identified yet either in Havana (1739) or Portobelo (1739). Connected with this new plan are the visual initiatives Morales presents (chapter 8). Most of them were only known by enemies' descriptions, being very poorly developed for several reasons. An exception to this is Cumberland, which the British developed for the unsuccessful attack on Santiago de Cuba (1741), or maybe before that on Havana in 1739. The fortifications are also English. Although Müller's treatise postdates this foundation, the solutions are similar, highlighting common campaign fortification techniques, which were not usual in other European schools. Regarding fortification, the pattern followed is the same found in other English settlements of the time, supporting the contention that this was a general strategy by the government and not merely the consequence of the fortification interest of local communities. In addition to fortification features, the urban plan of Cumberland was designed from the perspective of a military hierarchy as in no other example, but in keeping with the English image as in other Caribbean capitals such as Kingston or Bridgetown. These differences with other settlements, even with those designed before by the same crew, can be explained by its long history, if we accept that it started in 1738. Regarding other contemporary urban attempts, differences with Huet's proposals, presented by Pedro Cruz Freire (chapter 7), are clear. The Spanish preferred to stress representative buildings, while no racial distinction was clearly shown. As a consequence, military, religious, and administrative personnel must be included in future studies as significant elements of European powers to shape imperial rhetoric.

6

Fortification Systems Designed to Counter Charles Knowles's Attacks in Cuba and Saint-Domingue in 1748

Ignacio J. López-Hernández

The triangle formed by the islands of Cuba, Jamaica, and Hispaniola was arguably one of the most important geopolitical spaces in the Americas. The eighteenth-century Caribbean was the place where the main European conflicts between the Spanish-French bloc and Great Britain unfolded. For that reason, these islands became instrumental in the War of Jenkins' Ear (1739–48) and the Seven Years' War (1756–63). British, French, and Spanish historiography has extensively examined the diplomatic, commercial, territorial, and military relationship among the three competing empires. The literature has also explored Spanish, British, and French military architecture in the Caribbean.[1] However, these works have not examined comparatively the imperial defensive system built in these three islands. Our previous evaluation has suggested that a comparative analysis of eighteenth-century military architecture in the Caribbean developed by the British, Spanish, and French empires was required for an assessment of the fortification model created in the region.[2] Recent scholarship on the Anglo-Spanish Atlantic has shown the necessity for further imperial comparisons.[3] In accord with this academic trend, a comparative examination of fortifications designed and envisioned by these competing empires in the Caribbean will contribute to our understanding of the knowledge transfers that resulted in the striking development of military architecture in this region. Specifically, this chapter aims to compare the fortification systems implemented by Spain and by France to repel the attacks on Santiago de Cuba and Saint-Louis-du-Sud carried out by the British by Rear Admiral Charles Knowles in 1748.

British Ambitions in the Caribbean: The Control of the Windward Passage

Despite the name, the War of Jenkins' Ear, and the propaganda used during the conflict, the casus belli was far from a simple royal insult. The real causes of the 1739 British declaration of war were exclusively economic and commercial.[4] That year, the *asiento* contract ratified by the Treaty of Utrecht, which provided the British Empire with the right to supply enslaved Africans to the Spanish territories in the Americas, was near its end (1743). For that reason, British commercial lobbies pushed Sir Robert Walpole's government not only to renew the concession but also to reinforce British presence in the Caribbean. Even though Walpole opposed the idea at first, the prime minister was obliged to declare war against Spain on October 23, 1739.[5] Success in this war rested with the capture of one of the Spanish ports along the route of the Spanish treasure fleet. The capture of Havana was the most ambitious desire, as shown by the contemporary printing *The Seat of War in the West Indies*: "Havana is the only Place the possession of which can possibly secure our Trade to the West Indies, and prevent the Spanish depredations."[6]

The primary consequence of this ambition was Vernon's campaign in the Caribbean. However, after Vernon's well-known successful attacks on Portobelo and San Lorenzo de Chagres, the operations ended in a disaster after the attempt to capture Cartagena de Indias and Santiago de Cuba in 1741. Fortunately for Great Britain, the war was subsumed by the War of the Austrian Succession, and the Spanish victory in the Caribbean was marginalized in importance. This second stage in the conflict introduced France as a new participant in the Caribbean warfare. From this point forward, Commodore Charles Knowles was in charge of British naval operations in the Caribbean. First, under orders from Chaloner Ogle, Knowles attacked La Guaira and Puerto Cabello in 1743, but he was beaten back by Spanish forces twice, on March 22 and April 24, 1743.[7] Once Knowles became a rear admiral on July 15, 1747, and commander in chief of the Jamaica Station, he was presented with the opportunity of planning a new attack on both Spanish and French territories.

As a direct witness of Vernon's campaign, Knowles knew that he could not afford another clamorous defeat. Thus, his objectives were less risky than the capture of one of the ports of the Spanish treasure fleet through a lengthy siege. However, Knowles's aims were no less ambitious than Vernon's. Like the vice admiral's last objective, Knowles intended to control the transit through the Windward Passage, which provided a direct connection between the Caribbean Sea and both the Old Bahama Channel and the Atlantic Ocean. Furthermore, a naval station to the north, such as at Guantánamo Bay, would be advantageous for any maritime encounter, as this location provided a squadron with the windward advantage.[8] This ambition could explain the British presence in Guantánamo since 1738, according to what Luengo revealed in chapter 5 of this volume. The southern coast of Hispaniola was also a strategic refuge for anchoring and resupply, with a direct connection to Jamaica. For that purpose, Knowles planned to attack western Cuba and the French colony of Saint-Domingue, but in a different manner than Vernon. Knowles's offensive had to be quick so that his forces would not have to combat the climatic conditions, which were the foremost cause of Vernon's defeats in 1741.

On February 17, 1748, only ten days after his arrival in Port Royal, Knowles left Jamaica on his eighty-gun, six-hundred-man flagship *Cornwall* accompanied by nine warships with more than three thousand men aboard.[9] Knowles set sail for Santiago de Cuba intending to attack it directly, but the winds were unfavorable. As such, he postponed his first objective and steered for Saint-Domingue.

Knowles's Attack on Saint-Louis-du-Sud and Saint-Domingue's Fortification

At the time of Knowles's arrival, Saint-Domingue was a prosperous French colony, as it had been since 1697. That year, Spain recognized French sovereignty over the western part of Hispaniola and the Isle of Tortuga by the Treaty of Ryswick. Since then, and for almost half a century, France had implemented a plan for the foundation of new cities to control vast territories of the island commercially and militarily that were left unprotected and unoccupied by Spain. Beginning with the creation of Petit-Goâve as the first French commune in 1665, all the buildings in Saint-Domingue relied on fortifications planned and designed by engineers sent from France. One of the most prestigious of these engineers was François Blondel, who considered the Antillean cities in this period far from fortified according to European theoretical thinking.[10]

Nevertheless, by as late as 1749, no city on Saint-Domingue was protected by walls, and they all depended on coastal batteries and a few small fortresses. As an example of the use of both typologies, Port-de-Paix was fortified in 1676 as the new capital of Saint-Domingue.[11] There, the governor's house was built on the top of a hill and fortified with towers and surrounded by batteries while the city was completely unprotected.[12] As a result of this defensive weakness, other settlements such as Fort-Dauphin and Cap-Français started gaining importance thanks to their strategic and more defensible locations. For this reason, Cap-Français was declared the new capital of the colony in 1711. It was situated at the end of an open bay. However, the numerous reefs required ships to sail through a narrow channel close to the coast where batteries were built. After

Fortification Systems in Cuba and Saint-Domingue

1736, Fort Picolet was the main fortification that guarded the access to the city's waterfront. It was designed by the engineer Louis-Joseph La Lance as a two-level battery that was adapted to the irregular slope of a steep hill.[13] In a similar manner, the engineer Coudreau proposed a new battery to lock a second channel formed between the coast and the Grande Mouton sandbank in Cape Foison (figure 6.1).[14] Once war against Great Britain broke out in 1744, the same engineer built two wooden fascine batteries on the city's waterfront.[15]

The third main city in the northern coast of the colony was Fort-Dauphin, located within the deep bay of Bayaha, close to the French-Spanish border. The first fortification project for this bay was designed by the engineer Marc Payen,[16] but it was Louis-Joseph La Lance who developed the ultimate solution in 1727, undertaken during the following years with some variations.[17] The entrance to the harbor was a long, narrow channel protected by three batteries. The main defensive point at this place was Fort la Bouque, an oddly shaped fortress designed by La Lance as a curved battery and a quadrangular redoubt surrounded by a ditch.[18] The entrance was reinforced by the guns of Saint Charles battery and Saint Frederic battery, placed along the channel.[19] Inside the bay, the city was protected by Fort Dauphin, a polygonal bastioned fortress that was adapted by La Lance to the shape of a peninsula that covered the city.[20]

The control of the enormous coastline of the Gulf of Gonâve required the founding of numerous cities, obviously a challenge to this multicentered context. Among them, the existence of little batteries in Leogane, Saint Marc and Gonaïves, and some interesting projects for Petit-Goâve are documented.[21] Petit Goâve was founded in 1663 on the northern coast of the Tiburon Peninsula as the first French settlement on the island.[22] Here, a small battery was successively modified until becoming a bastioned square redoubt. However, its open bay was difficult to defend. First, other batteries were proposed and finally it was decided to build a bastioned pentagon. It was placed in front of the other fort to provide crossfire and protect navigation in the bay's waters. This fortress was designed by the engineer Coudreau and built with logs and earth. It was completed with a ravelin and a water-filled ditch (figure 6.2).[23] These main fortifications were complemented with six more fascine batteries at the time the war started.[24]

Finally, due to the military and commercial interests of the southern coast of Tiburon Peninsula, the settlements of Jacmel, Les Cayes, and Saint-Louis-du-Sud were founded as headquarters for the Compagnie de Saint-Domingue.[25] Among them, Saint-Louis-du-Sud was located at the end of a deep bay used in 1654 by the English fleet that attacked and captured Jamaica in 1655. Its defensibility depended on an islet, placed in front of the town that formed a defendable channel. For that, the islet was completely fortified with a bastion fort in the same way that Spain did in San Juan de Ulúa (Veracruz) in the late

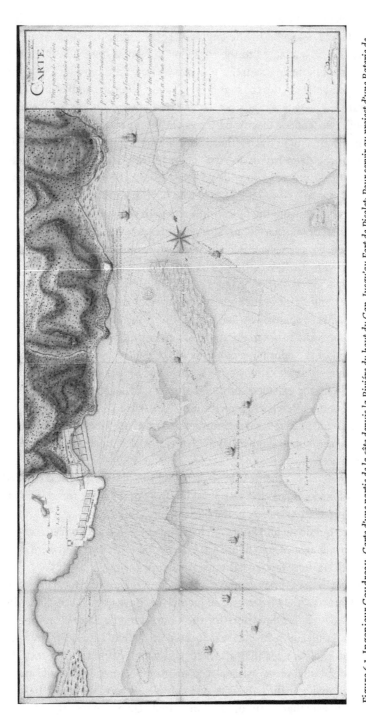

Figure 6.1. Ingenieur Coudreau, *Carte d'une partie de la côte depuis la Rivière du hout du Cap, Jusqu'au Fort de Picolet; Pour servir au project d'une Baterie de vingt pièces de canon proposée a faire su la pointe a Foison* (Map of part of the coast from the Rivière du hout du Cap, to Fort de Picolet; To be used for the project of a twenty-piece gun battery proposed to make known the Pointe a Foison), 1743. (Archives Nationales d'Outre Mer, 15DFC339terA.)

Fortification Systems in Cuba and Saint-Domingue 91

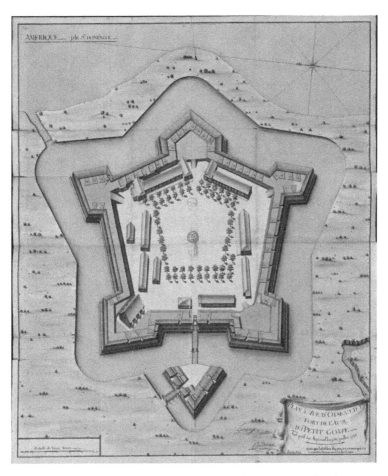

Figure 6.2. Ingenieur Coudreau, *Plan du fort de l'Acul du Petit Goave tel qu'il est aujourd'hui 31 juillet 1745* (Plan of Fort de l'Acul du Petit Goave a s it is today July 31, 1745), 1745. (Archives Nationales d'Outre Mer, 15DFC730A.)

sixteenth century.[26] According to Moreau de Saint Mery, the engineer Renau was responsible for designing Fort Saint Louis. His plan was supervised and corrected from the metropolis by Vauban himself and built under the direction of the engineers De la Broue and Philippe Cauvet.[27] The fortress was finished in 1705 and repaired two years later after a partial collapse. The final design was an irregular polygon with two bastions in front of the town and three demibastions defending the exterior bay (figure 6.3).[28] However, although the strength of the fortress entirely built of stone was apparent, there was no support battery to provide crossfire. This made Fort Saint Louis vulnerable, as subsequent events showed.

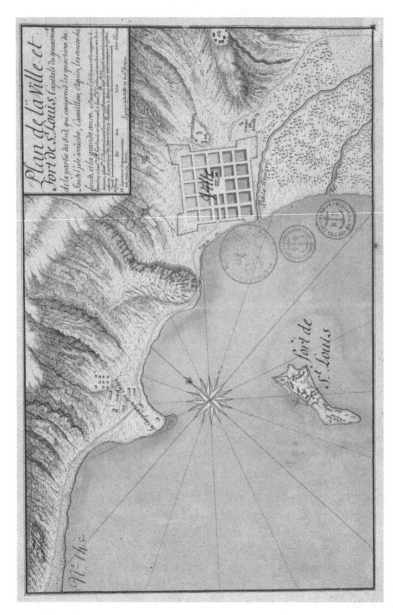

Figure 6.3. *Plan de la ville et fort de Saint-Louis, capitale du gouvernement du Sud* (Map of the city and fort of Saint-Louis, capital of the government of the South), 1742. (Archives Nationales d'Outre Mer, 15DFC14C.)

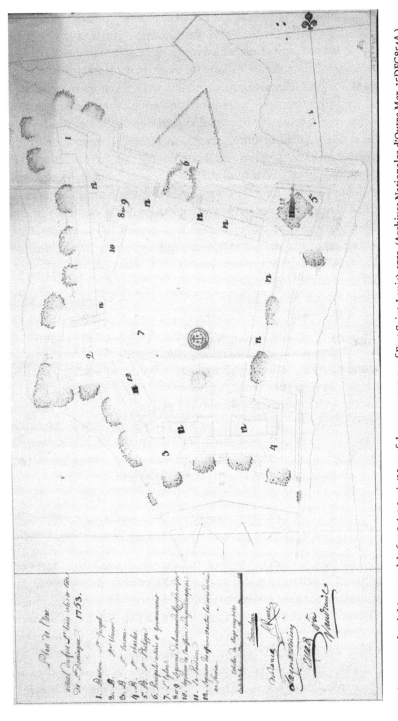

Figure 6.4. *Plan de l'état actuel du fort Saint-Louis* (Map of the current state of Fort Saint-Louis), 1753. (Archives Nationales d'Outre Mer, 15DFC854A.)

After finding it impossible to sail windward in his first attempt to reach Santiago de Cuba, Saint-Louis-du-Sud was Knowles's target of choice as the best harbor in his proximity from which to attack Saint-Domingue. The offensive was organized from the Ile à Vache for more than a week until the attack began on March 22.[29] However, the defenders were taken by surprise when Knowles's squadron formed in a line appeared sailing into the harbor. With the intention of not repeating the repelled attack on La Guaira, Knowles ordered the captains to not fire until every ship was placed in its position.[30] A few minutes before midday, the ships sailed into the bay and surrounded the islet. Fort Saint Louis opened fire at five minutes past twelve, but, as was ordered, the ships did not answer until they were anchored within a pistol shot of the walls. After a continuous cannonade that took three hours, Governor Étienne Cochard de Chastenoye capitulated under the agreement to surrender the garrison as prisoners of war and not to take up arms against the British king for a year and a day.[31] Fort Saint Louis was plundered and blown up, leaving the town completely undefended (figure 6.4).[32]

This easy victory persuaded Knowles to continue the campaign in Saint-Domingue with other attacks on Cap-François, Leogane, and Petit-Goâve,[33] as their fortifications were also easily overcome, like Fort Saint Louis. However, an enormous contingent was required to hold the territory: "We both [Governor Trelawny and Knowles] heartily wish we had more force to follow up the blow we have struck against the French, and a regiment be spared from England and one in the winter from Cape Breton, as I proposed to his Grace the Duke of Newcastle some time ago."[34] Consequently, Knowles decided to refocus his attention on his first objective: Santiago de Cuba. This decision demonstrates how challenging it was to attack the French multicentered approach, especially when contrasted with doing the same against the Spanish.

Knowles's Attack on Santiago de Cuba and the Defense of Western Cuba

There were two ways to capture Santiago de Cuba, which was located at the end of a large bay. If the enemy decided to attack the city from the bay, it was first necessary to attack the narrow entrance protected since the seventeenth century by the castle of San Pedro de la Roca, the fort of La Estrella, and other minor batteries. The other way to attack the city was by land. Santiago was never protected by walls and only relied on the castle of San Francisco, a bastion fort that, as Fernández Martín (chapter 9) has shown, was placed exactly in the city center, completely surrounded by other buildings. The Spanish and the British were familiar with this fort's uselessness. Once the troops arrived near the city, there was no possibility of defending it. However, the enemy had first to disembark on one of the few available beaches around the rugged coastline of Santiago. For these reasons, the priority for the governors of Santiago was to strengthen the fortifications of the bay entrance, fortify the coastline within a 15-kilometer radius and build trenches along the routes to the city.[35] Most of this work was undertaken by the French engineer Francisco de Langle under the supervision of Governor Francisco Cajigal de la Vega in 1741.[36] Once Langle and Cajigal left Santiago, the fortifications were completed by second lieutenant Isidro Limonta under the supervision of Governor Alonso Arcos Moreno by 1748.[37]

As the main defense of the fortification system of Santiago, the castle of San Pedro de la Roca (also known as El Morro) was substantially reinforced to increase its batteries and to protect the landward approach. The origin of this fortress dates back to 1637, when the engineer Juan Bautista Antonelli built an irregular bastioned castle on top of the hill that guarded the entrance to the bay.[38] Between 1664 and 1668, Juan de Císcara added a low battery on the bottom of the hill and another intermediate one called Santísimo Sacramento. In 1741, the capacity of this fort was insufficient to resist the attack of a large squadron, so Francisco de Langle increased the size of the Santísimo Sacramento battery

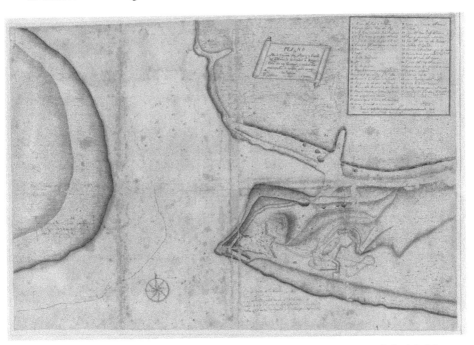

Figure 6.5. Francisco de Langle, *Plano de la entrada del Puerto y Castillo del Morro de la ciudad de Santiago de Cuba* (Plan of the entrance of the Port and Castillo del Morro in the city of Santiago de Cuba), 1741. (Archivo General Militar de Madrid, Cartoteca, CUB-56/08. CC BY-4.0.)

by carving into the mountainside and opening caves for ammunition depots. Outside the fort, he protected the landward approach by building different batteries to create a line of defense; this strategy could be considered an interesting precedent of the ones studied by Hinarejos in Puerto Rico.[39] Langle also renovated the fort of La Estrella by dismantling the old batteries and building another one in a place that provided a direct firing line to the bay's entrance. These alterations allowed the defenders to combine fire and to crossfire in the event the attackers might be able to force their entrance (figure 6.5). At the moment Knowles was preparing his attack on Santiago, Governor Arcos Moreno ordered the repair of the seventeenth-century battery of Santa Catalina, situated inside the channel close to La Estrella. The governor also ordered a fascine battery to be mounted at a coastal point known as La Redonda, from which the British could reach El Morro with their bombardments. Finally, Arcos Moreno blocked the entrance with two fire ships.[40]

As mentioned, fortifying any potential landing beaches that surrounded Santiago was required to prevent a land attack. To this end, Governor Cajigal put the engineer Francisco de Langle in charge of designing this coastal fortification system. When Langle received the commission, the war had already broken out. For this reason, every one of these batteries and forts had to be built as field fortifications with fascines and gabions. The diligence of Langle and Cajigal was crucial for the success of the defense of Santiago considering that the engineer finished the first field survey by September 28, 1740, and all the batteries and forts were built by the arrival of Vernon's squadron in July 1741.[41]

One of the most dangerous places was the beach of Aguadores, on the eastern coast of Santiago. From there, Christopher Myngs's troops captured Santiago in 1662 by sailing through the Aguadores River.[42] To prevent a similar occurrence, two batteries were built on top of the cliff at the mouth of the river.[43] Similarly, a fascine hornwork was raised between the two rivers that flowed in the beach of Juraguá Chico, 18 kilometers away from the Santiago Bay to the east. This battery was reinforced with a small fort that provided crossfire and a total control of the beach.[44] It was built in 1748 by Second Lieutenant Isidro Limonta as a triple battery with a small barrack.[45] Closing the eastern flank of this fortified line, another fort was built in Juraguá Grande. As this location presented a double exposure from the sea and the land, the fort was designed as an irregular bastioned tetragon. It was formed by a ditch, two demibastions defending the beach and two complete bastions protecting the land front.[46] Finally, the western coast of Santiago was significantly more defensible due to the lack of landing beaches and especially the difficult path to Santiago from there. The Bay of Cabañas would have been a good option to land, but its one-kilometer entrance channel was narrow and well defended by a high battery

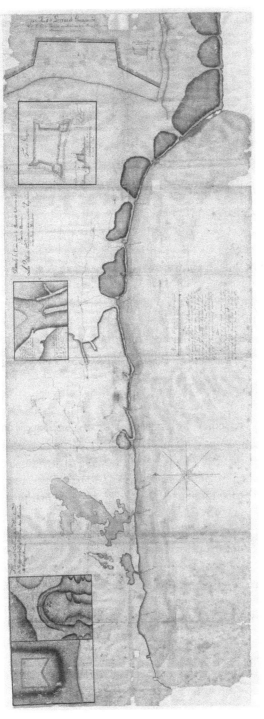

Figure 6.6. Francisco de Langle, *Plano de la Costa desde la Punta de Cabrera a la Punta de Berracos. Los Puestos Fortificados se mas bien Explicados en los Planos Particulares* (Plan of the Coast from Punta de Cabrera to Punta de Berracos. The Fortified Posts are explained in the Particular Plans). 1741. (Archivo General Militar de Madrid, Cartoteca, CUB-126/19. CC BY-4.0.)

placed in one of the two hills that guarded the access. The last landing beach was Bueycabón Nuevo (modern Mar Verde), where a two-sided battery was raised as the first point of an entrenched path that ended in a narrow passageway where the defenders could easily ambush the enemy (figure 6.6).[47]

Most of these defenses were surveyed by Vernon in 1741, so by the time Knowles arrived, he was aware of almost the entire fortification system, as a 1743 British map (kept among his documents) proves.[48] The British squadron arrived at the coast of Santiago on April 8. By this time, Governor Arcos Moreno was warned by French emissaries, so he closed the entrance with the fire ships, which were linked by a hawser. The next day, once the wind was favorable, Knowles ordered Captain Dent to lead the attack. Dent relied on the knowledge of a former prisoner and a Spanish pilot to go through the entrance by avoiding the fire ships. He noted to Knowles that the entrance to the bay would not be difficult.[49] However, the morning of April 9, it seemed to the British that a Spanish ship was brought down in the channel.[50] For this reason, Dent reconsidered his position, but Knowles ordered him to shoot his pilot "or throw him overboard" if he raised any objections.[51] The operation began when Dent's *Plymouth* followed by the *Cornwall* set sail to the entrance while Knowles's *Canterbury* bombarded the castle of San Pedro de la Roca with a mortar. A few minutes later, Dent was informed by an officer and the Spanish pilot that, in addition to the cable, there was a chain (and probably more) protecting the entrance. As the *Plymouth* had no chance of breaking the chain and considering it suspicious that Spanish batteries had not opened fire yet, Dent decided to abort the attack.[52] At that very moment, the *Plymouth* and the *Cornwell* were fired on by the new batteries of the castle of San Pedro and the battery of La Estrella. Both ships were finally able to retreat with severe damage.[53] Ironically, we can prove that there was neither the sunken ship[54] nor a chain, because Governor Arcos Moreno later admitted when he asked the secretary of state for funding to make a chain: "[the enemy] tried to force the harbor supposing there was one [a chain] but it was just a cable of the frigate that was placed [there] to be sunk."[55] Knowles never believed that the entrance was insurmountable, and he blamed Captain Dent for the defeat: "I am far from thinking it impracticable especially if an officer of solid resolution and judgment leads."[56] Dent was judged by a court-martial, before which some witnesses declared that they did not see any further obstruction. However, the court-martial absolved Dent based on the fact that if Knowles really thought the entrance was practicable, then he should have tried again. Certainly, the rear admiral never resumed the attack on the entrance of the bay, positing some reasons that the court did not consider strong enough.[57] On April 10, the squadron left Santiago and set sail to the Bay of Cabañas. There, the ships arrived with the intention of disembarking with barges, but they were repelled by the new defenses. That same evening, Knowles retreated to Jamaica.[58]

Conclusions

Knowles's campaigns in western Cuba and Saint-Domingue allow us to compare separately the fortification systems implemented by Spain and by France for the defense of their islands. On the one hand, it has been shown how Santiago's government implemented a strong plan for the fortification of the city and its coastline, similar to the strategy employed in Havana during the same conflict.[59] On the other hand, despite the efforts made by France to defend most of its cities and settlements in Saint-Domingue, French fortification in the island was never designed to confront a large professional army. However, this preliminary analysis does not necessarily mean that while the Spanish strategy was successful, the French strategy was not. Considering that when the war ended, both French and Spanish sovereignty over Saint-Domingue and Cuba remained intact, it is possible to conclude that the defensive strategies of both islands were effective.

The differences between French and Spanish fortification plans could be explained by the respective territorial administrations of their colonies. With regard to the Spanish territories in America, they always had a similar administrative status to other European regions, which were integrated into the Crown's possessions. Because of that, Spain developed in America a huge administrative structure that depended on the capitals of their viceroyalties, Captaincies General, and Royal Audiencias. Cities such as Mexico City, Havana, San Juan, and Cartagena brought together the entirety of Spanish power in their respective territories. Consequently, the domination of a vast part of the Spanish possessions in the continent rested on the control of these capitals. This problem determined the defensive strategies and fortification plans undertaken by the Spanish military engineers in America and particularly in Cuba. As the capture of Havana or Santiago de Cuba would mean the de facto control of a half part of the island, the fortification plan undertaken by military engineer Francisco de Langle was focused on Santiago and its closest coastline, while other strategic places such as the Bays of Guantánamo and Nipe were not fortified.

Furthermore, the depopulation of the region implied an additional danger. This threat already led to the loss of the Spanish territories of Hispaniola and their subsequent French occupation during the seventeenth century. This weakness was one of the reasons on which Vernon's strategy relied for his planned attack on Santiago and the creation of a naval station in Guantánamo.[60] However, Knowles had personally experienced Vernon's and Wentworth's mistakes, so he did not contemplate a long and wide-ranging amphibious operation like those undertaken in Santiago and in Cartagena in 1741.[61]

Both scenarios were studied by Langle when he designed his defensive plan, but he knew fortification in Cuba required a specific adaptation to the characteristics of the war in the Caribbean. As he had written to Governor Caji-gal, fortifications in Cuba did not require the strength and configuration of the contemporary models used in Europe.[62] For that reason, the main part of the defensive plan rested on field fortifications, which were intelligently distributed across the coastline by Langle very rapidly. This method of planning fortification in the Caribbean can be linked with other experiences such as that one presented by Waters's chapter in Antigua. However, while in the British islands many of these works were undertaken by civilians, in Santiago the defensive plan was adopted and inspected by men in uniform.

Yet no city was defended with a deployment similar the one seen in Saint-Domingue. As mentioned, even when the defenses of cities such as Cap-Français and Petit-Goâve were reinforced with field fortifications, they never were prepared to confront an amphibious attack, because no Saint-Dominican city fortified its land approaches. French officials were plenty conscious about this, as numerous contemporary projects for the construction of bastioned walls in Cap-Français, Fort-Dauphin, and Petit-Goâve show.[63] These attempts intended to transplant Vauban's fortification models to the Caribbean colony, but they were never erected since they required an enormous investment. So, the colony remained protected against corsairs, pirates, and small fleets but never to confront large squadrons like the one commanded by Knowles. This vulnerability was revealed in Saint-Louis on March 22, 1748, but the fact this was the only attack on the colony demonstrates that its control was as difficult as the plan for western Cuba. A huge operation to control several Saint-Dominican cities was required, as Knowles himself declared.

Thus, the defensive strength of Saint-Domingue hinged on a sort of administrative "polycentrism'" that provided the colony with several strategic points. The French colony never had the territorial administration Spain developed in its American territories, which determined that its control did not depend on a capital such as Havana, Santiago, or Cartagena. Even though Cap-Français was the capital during this period, the capture of the city would not have meant the control of the whole colony. However, this conclusion does not mean that this strategy was thought about, but it was the result of the lack of investments and its specific colonial organization. The effectiveness of the French defensive strategy was proven once again during the Seven Years' War. Therein, the British captured Martinique and Dominica by only controlling Fort-de-France and Basseterre, but there was no substantial attack on Saint-Domingue.[64] However, the strategy implemented by Spain during the War of Jenkins' Ear was no longer suitable, and a new fortification system was required to reduce the weakness underlined by Morales during the capture of Havana in 1762.[65]

7

The Versatility of the Military Engineer Luis Huet

Engineer, Urban Planner, and Spy

Pedro Cruz Freire

Once the Spanish succession disputes were concluded during the first decade of the eighteenth century, a series of reforms were carried out to modernize a country decimated by wars and regencies. The new Bourbon monarchy catalyzed numerous political modifications, yet among these was the continuing need to organize a duly qualified elite military organization. To this end, the French Corps Royal du Génie and the Belgian Royal Military Academy in Brussels were used as examples, because both organizations had functioned successfully in the second half of the previous century.

The newly organized military engineers initially prioritized updating the empire's defenses, but as the century wore on, their tasks increased. A good example of this increasing complexity in their expectations is shown in the case of one of the most outstanding engineers working in the Caribbean, the Italian Luis Huet. Huet's career is reconstructed in this chapter, which highlights his versatility.

In 1709, the Marquis of Bedmar, at that time secretary of war to Philip V, proposed to the king the creation of a corps of military engineers in collaboration with Field Marshal Jorge Próspero de Verboom, as Muñóz Corbalán notes in chapter 1. After an exhaustive analysis of the number of existing engineers in Spain and the Crown's need for additional professionals of this sort, the first General Plan of the Engineers was created, issued by the monarch in Zaragoza on April 7, 1711. Once the corps of engineers was created, the services that its members should perform were debated for several years. This resulted in an ordinance enacted in 1718 that laid out their main functions. The outfit's statutes specified that its members must possess a noteworthy level of specialization in numerous fields of knowledge. Thus, in architectural matters, military engineers had to perform tasks of both a civilian and a military nature, whether these came from public or private entities. However, they should be experts in management, articulation, and territorial control. For this, it was necessary to master the execution of plans and geographical maps, planning of terrestrial communications and hydraulic infrastructures, and so forth. Likewise, they must be fully trained in the art of war, that is, to master the use of artillery, strategy, siege warfare, defense tactics, militia distribution, and the use of natural resources to benefit the established purposes. There is no doubt that, as confirmed by Capel and other researchers, that this institution "was entrusted with functions that went far beyond those that specifically belonged to it."[1]

Although these were the primary assignments required by engineers throughout the eighteenth and nineteenth centuries, there were exceptional cases, especially at the political level. Such are the cases of Carlos Briones Hoyo y Abarca, lieutenant governor of the Hacha province in the middle of the eighteenth century, Ignacio Sala and his work as governor and general commander in Cartagena de Indias during the middle of that century, and Miguel del Corral and Luis Diez Navarro as acting governors of Veracruz and Costa Rica, respectively, during the last quarter of the same century.[2]

Luis Huet, an Italian Military Engineer

Within this group of engineers who served the Spanish Crown's purposes during the eighteenth century, this study highlights the wide-ranging work carried out by the Italian engineer Luis Huet. He was born in Liorna in 1722. At the age of thirteen, he began his military career as a cadet in the regiments of Burgundy and Brabant, rising to second lieutenant in 1740 and lieutenant four years later. During this initial period of his life, he participated in campaigns on the northern Italian peninsula, where he had his first assignments. He oversaw the construction of barricades and temporary bridges in the Piedmont region. He also participated in the siege of Conia, the retreat of Nice, and the expedition to the valley of Onella, where he took part in Gazelli's and Chuzanico's defenses. His participation in the conflict concluded at Tortona, where he was commissioned to defend the town and its castle. Once the war ended, he continued working in different locations in eastern Spain. He oversaw defensive works in Alicante, Valencia, Cartagena, Murcia, and Denia. In addition, he has been located in Andalusia contributing to the improvement of the port of Málaga and in northern Africa, where he collaborated in the defensive posts of Ceuta, Melilla, and Perejil Island. Those works allowed him to be promoted from captain and *ingeniero ordinario* in 1756 to colonel and *ingeniero director*, a rank that he achieved on November 4, 1770.[3]

Owing to his work on the peninsula, Huet earned the confidence of the Spanish authorities to go to Havana, one of the places most in need of military engineers in the last quarter of the eighteenth century. In 1772, he was granted a license to "travel with his family, in the usual way, in the *urca Santa Ana*, which is ready to carry marine equipment to that port."[4] In Havana, Huet carried out a list of activities that would confirm him as one of the great professionals in this organization's history. First, he was in charge of modifying Silvestre Abarca's designs for the Castillo del Príncipe, overseeing its construction between 1776 and 1782. Likewise, he carried out the construction of the provisional fort of San Diego, a small bastion that completed the project he inherited from his predecessor in the defensive remodeling of the city.[5] However, his duties on the island were not limited merely to finishing the defensive program proposed beginning in 1763. As *ingeniero director* of Cuban fortifications starting in 1779, he made a series of maps of the island's main ports, including Havana itself, which he represented on many occasions, as well as Mariel, Baracoa, Guantánamo, and Matanzas, to name the most relevant.

After Huet's extensive work in the Cuban capital he was assigned to Cádiz, where he assumed the oversight of the defensive works carried out in Andalusia.[6] During the final years of his career, he focused on finishing the always challenging Vendaval wall in Cádiz, constantly hit by high tides and inclement weather.[7]

This study aims to present two little known aspects, but at the same time of great interest, in which Huet stood out during his stay in the Americas. First, his role as urban planner will be addressed in two projects developed for the cities of San Julián de los Güines and San Juan de Jaruco, two population centers that emerged in the final decades of the eighteenth century. Second, the primary services he executed as an informant of the Spanish army will also be examined. His espionage work, including information collection, preparation of plans of enemy-controlled areas, and interrogations, were crucial for some of the operations of the Spanish army to succeed in the complicated military and diplomatic framework of the century's end.

The Urban Plan as a Military Problem

Urban works were not an unexplored field for the members of the Royal Corps of Spanish Engineers, which relied on these technicians' versatility, but not all of them participated as territorial planners. Nonetheless, there are some outstanding examples of their work from this century, both in Spain and in the Americas. In this regard, Vicente Ignacio Imperial Digueri y Trejo's work for the Spanish Navy's new settlement on the Isla de León stand out.[8] There are also noteworthy examples from the Western Hemisphere contemporaneous in time. For example, there are the cases of José Tantete's labor in Santiago de las Vegas or Guillermo Duncan's in San Antonio de los Baños.[9]

As a result of the conquest and later return of Havana in 1763, a policy of new settlements was carried out, very similar to the one practiced in the southeast of the United States after independence.[10] These settlements pursued two main objectives. First, they sought to consolidate some places of proven importance to prevent new attacks, either by the British or by the French. Second, they aimed to promote the commercial development and the exploitation of agricultural production, which would be translated into economic improvement in areas severely devastated by the Seven Years' War.[11] As Luengo (chapter 5) indicated, one of the main assignments that military engineers developed in Cuba was demographic and industrial development, where sugar and tobacco plantations were essential for the island's economic growth.[12]

As a general rule, the new settlements were designed according to the Ordinances of Philip II (1573), with a grid design distributed around a main square intended to be occupied by the main ecclesiastical and civil buildings. The first of Huet's interventions in urban matters occurred in the city of San Juan de Jaruco. Located a few kilometers east of Havana, there is evidence of the initial attempts for its foundation dated to 1766, started by Don Gabriel Beltrán de Santa Cruz. In 1769, the first works in the city began in earnest.[13] However, there must have been discrepancies with the distribution of the land and the size of the population. In 1773, Huet modified the first project with his *Plano de la Nueva Ciudad de San Juan de Jaruco, reducido a las dimensiones que se deven observar en su edificación, en Plazas, manzanas o quadras de casas y calles* . . . (Plan of the New City of San Juan de Jaruco, reduced to the dimensions that must be observed in its building, in squares, blocks or blocks of houses and streets . . .)[14] (figure 7.1). Huet proposed a reticular plan around a main square of 150 *varas* on each side. This plaza held different buildings. To the east, he placed the church, the cemetery, and the priest's domestic offices. The governor's palace was positioned to the west. To the south, the capitulars' house and jail were placed. Finally, two blocks with twenty-four houses each were placed to the north. In addition, the engineer placed other blocks in the corners of the square, also intended for housing. A second set of blocks, indicated with the letter L on the map, suggested the possibility of widening the city, if necessary, in the future. As Huet indicated to Marqués de la Torre, governor of Havana, his main contribution was to vary the measurements of the city's square and streets, each 10 *varas* wide. Eventually, the settlement grew considerably at the end of the century, as the historian Ignacio José de Urrutia y Montoya describes: "At eight leagues to the east is the city of S. Juan de Jaruco, a new settlement and estate of the

Counts of this title with one-hundred-and-fifty scattered houses, a church with its priest and sacristan, two-hundred plots and farms, as well as eight-hundred souls in its territory."[15]

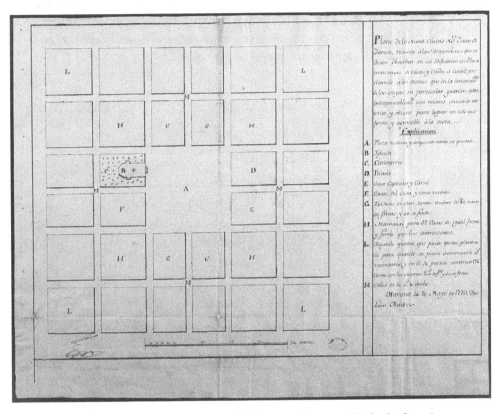

Figure 7.1. Luis Huet, *Plano de la Nueva Ciudad de San Juan de Jaruco, reducido a las dimensiones que se deven observar en su edificación, en Plazas, manzanas o quadras de casas y calles* (Plan of the New City of San Juan de Jaruco, reduced to the dimensions that must be observed in its construction, in squares, blocks or blocks of houses and streets), 1776. (Archivo General de Indias MP-Santo Domingo, 380.)

The urban planning of San Julián de los Güines represented a different scenario. Its foundation arises from the distribution of lands belonging to the Ayala family, in which Miguel Ayala, his son, and grandson took part. The territory that would belong to San Julián de los Güines was a vast plain with fertile land mainly used for the cultivation of tobacco, in which a modest church had been built in 1735 for the few workers hired on the tobacco plantation.[16] In 1784, Huet proposed carrying out a plan that indicated the project for the new settlement, which he left in charge of the military engineer José del Pozo Sucre. Up to three plans were made for this purpose, two related to the village's planimetry and another specific to the church, although the one analyzed here is the *Plano de San Julián de los Guynes y el proyecto de la nueva villa, echo de orden de S. M. por el brigadier e ingeniero director don Luis Huet* (figure 7.2).[17] This is yet further evidence of the enormous list of competencies assumed by military engineers, also well prepared to construct religious edifices.

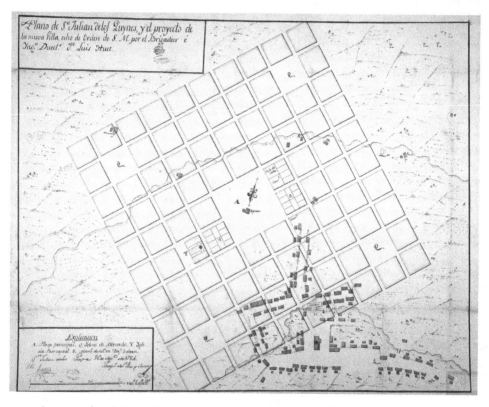

Figure 7.2. *Plano de San Julián de los Guynes y el proyecto de la nueva villa, echo de orden de S. M. por el brigadier e ingeniero director don Luis Huet* (Plan of San Julián de los Guynes and the project of the new town, made by order of H. M. by Brigadier and Director Engineer Don Luis Huet), 1784. (Archivo General de Indias, MP, Santo Domingo, 503.)

Del Pozo Sucre maintained the principles adopted in the Ordinances of Philip II. The city was composed by a reticular design, the axis of which was the central square, from which the different blocks emerged. The church, the governor's house, and the jail, all designed by Del Pozo in 1784, were located in this space.[18] This organization created a spatial order that did not exist in the current settlement, as reflected in the lower margin of the map, where it is shown that the primitive nucleus population was organized without any kind of order around the original church.

Both cases exemplify the capability of Huet in urban planning and spatial conception. He not only carries out the necessary modifications in the case of San Juan de Jaruco, correcting the original project, but also is later responsible for evaluating and approving the plan of San Julián de los Güines.

Engineers and Intelligence Missions

Given the training of these professionals in terms of defensive tactics and siege systems, military engineers played a decisive role in many of the conflicts that developed between nations throughout the eighteenth century. In this sense, their military role was not merely limited to devising defensive buildings that granted advantages over the invader, but they were also in charge of formalizing attacks and collecting information about siege targets.

During Huet's time in Havana, the Spanish Crown indirectly participated in the American War for Independence. This involvement was presented as an ideal opportunity to recover Florida, handed over to Great Britain after the Seven Years' War in 1763. For this reason, it is understandable that Spain supplied the rebellious British colonies with military equipment, taking advantage of the Mississippi River traffic, and simultaneously besieging the diminished British defenses at their weakest points.

For the success of this operation, the knowledge that the besieger possessed over the enemy was usually a decisive element. The information available was usually biased and outdated, so the speed of data collection by informants or spies was a tactic as valuable as it was difficult to obtain. These tasks were sometimes carried out by the military engineers, although as Muñoz Corbalán indicates in chapter 1, it was necessary to work quickly to guarantee a subsequent victory.[19]

In 1781, a magnificent opportunity arose to discern Great Britain's number of troops, the state of its fortifications, the quantity of its war supplies, and its warlike intentions. That year, two Spanish marines, Hipólito Salmon and Carlos Gurtel, had managed to escape after more than a month of captivity in Kingston, Jamaica. After their escape and arrival in Cuba, Huet demanded they come to Havana for an interrogation.[20]

The first part of the questioning reveals the main concern of Huet—to discern the status and disposition of British military power in the Americas. These intelligence efforts increasingly exemplified a new feature in these technicians' versatility. He inquired about the status of Jamaican fortifications, the number of troops that were on the island, ships currently in the bay, and the knowledge of Jamaican authorities about the future Spanish attack on Panzacola (modern-day Pensacola, Florida). In Huet's mind, because the war against the thirteen British colonies was greatly limiting the number of troops available in Florida, the most effective assistance, both in terms of time and numbers, would come from Kingston. These questions were answered with information of tremendous utility for Spanish interests. In the first place, Salmon and Gurtel indicated that they were not able to find out the status of Jamaica's defenses because "to not make ourselves suspicious, we neither wanted to see or to ask."[21] Nevertheless, they were able to provide an approximation of the number of troops who resided on the island, which revolved around the five thousand men, divided between five and six regiments, as well as the number of ships docked in its port, between eleven and twelve, although five of them remained stricken due to a hurricane, so Huet did not consider that these ships "could enter combat as they were."[22] Finally, he indicated that Jamaica's authorities were aware of the imminent Spanish attack on San Miguel de Panzacola. The second part of the interrogation was aimed at clarifying what the English concerns were in Europe, especially Gibraltar and in the Low Countries. Obviously, Great Britain did not intend to neglect Gibraltar under any circumstances. To this end, Huet asked about the number of fleets that had arrived in Jamaica from Europe, to which Gurtel replied that only one ship had arrived while he was imprisoned. Regarding Gibraltar, Gurtel said that he did not hear any words from the officers. Quite the opposite, he stated, the skirmishes with Flanders meant that a fleet was preparing to split between helping New York and attacking neighboring Curaçao.[23] The information obtained from these accidental informants turned out to be very useful in continuing with the plans established against San Miguel de Panzacola and the subsequent Spanish success in this matter.

Among other military functions developed by Huet in this context are his works as barracks master. This appointment entailed a series of responsibilities such as demarcating in the camps where to settle troops during an assault, reconnoitering territories, illustrating attacks, and drafting battle orders. Huet's work in relation to this employment is visible in two maps with two completely different purposes. First, his *Plano que demuestra el desembarco que deve hacerse junto a la población y castillo de Panzacola* (figure 7.3).[24] The drawing, made by Huet in 1779, shows the fighting disposition of the frigates, boats, and packets against the city and the fort, and once that was successfully carried out, entering the bay. Once stationed facing the city, Huet indicates the manner to besiege it. The frigates had to focus their fire on the castle, while the boats and packets had to be placed in the first line at the vicinity of Arroyo de San Miguel and Segunda Boquilla to continue the crossfire and to disembark. However, the plan presented was rejected because of the severe damage that this assault would bring about in the town.[25]

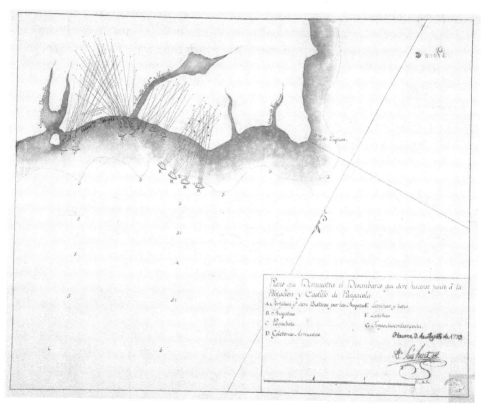

Figure 7.3. *Plano que demuestra el desembarco que deve hacerse junto a la población y castillo de Panzacola* (Plan that shows the disembarkation to be made next to the town and castle of Panzacola), 1779. (Archivo General de Indias, MP, Florida Louisiana, 86.)

The case is different for the map "Ysla de Providencia"[26] (figure 7.4), also developed by Huet in 1784. The drawing shows the city of Providencia, modern-day Nassau in the Bahamas, along with its fortifications, batteries, governor's house, and ships in attack formation along the coast. This does not represent an unapproved attack plan, but reflects the assault carried out by Bernardo de Gálvez on the island in 1781. The barracks master was in charge of illustrating what occurred during the conflict, in light of its utility in a future attack on the location.

The military engineers were in charge of numerous activities at the service of the Spanish Crown. Huet's example is one of the most noteworthy, given the number of duties he performed and the quality of the services he provided. Although this chapter only addresses his work as an urban planner and military officer, there are many more incidences in which Huet played a key role and that deserve to be studied. His work designing new cities is clearly in line with the Spanish tradition, which differs with that of the English, for example, as Luengo shows for the Caribbean encampments of the period (see chapter 5). Therefore, it is expected that this work will serve as a launching point for new and necessary research on this important professional engineer for Spanish interests in America in the final decades of the eighteenth century.

Figure 7.4. Luis Huet, *Mapa de la Isla de Providencia* (Providencia Island Map), 1784. (Archivo General de Indias MP, Santo Domingo, 470.)

8

Text and Image

The 1762 Capture of Havana

Alfredo J. Morales

During the eighteenth century, the Caribbean was the main theater for the armed conflicts between the Spanish and British Crowns. The rivalry between both powers, which had already played out on the same stage during the sixteenth century, reached its climax two hundred years later. The British eagerness to weaken Spanish power was aligned with Britain's interest in ending Spain's control over American territories and in choking the communications systems that linked it with the metropole. This network, constructed by the Spanish Crown in the second half of the sixteenth century, had been maintained, unaltered, over the centuries and had its main nodes in different Caribbean ports.[1] As a result, it is not unexpected that the British Crown focused its attacks on such places. During the sixteenth and seventeenth centuries, these

attacks were overseen by pirates and corsairs who were supported, incited, and even celebrated by the English monarch after their misdeeds against Spanish settlements. The examples of Sir Francis Drake and Sir Henry Morgan are, without a doubt, the most well known, their attacks being considered the most destructive and bloody.

While these early efforts were characterized by transitory attacks, during the eighteenth century, battles incorporated a more developed attack plan complemented by a strategy targeted at molding public opinion, in which visual discourse was crucial. More specifically, this chapter shows how the British created the image of victory on Havana in 1762 through paintings and drawings, which later were used by the incipient press.

British Interest in the Spanish Caribbean

By the eighteenth century, the British army itself became responsible for the attacks against Spanish cities in the Caribbean. In this regard, the attacks against Portobelo, Santiago de Cuba, and Cartagena de Indias led by Edward Vernon, who was named commander in chief of all the British naval forces in the western oceans, are well known. The two against Santiago de Cuba and Cartagena de Indias, both occurring in 1741, failed. In the first, the British troops were defeated by the small Spanish force commanded by Governor Francisco Cajigal de la Vega. Even more resounding was the failure at the city of Cartagena de Indias, where Blas de Lezo and a few troops held out in the Fort of San Felipe de Barajas by repelling the large and obstinate British attack. Vernon's confidence in his triumph meant that medals for a nonexistent victory were struck, as the confrontation signified a humiliating defeat for the English.[2] Logically,

Figure 8.1. Dominique Serres, *The Capture of Havana, 1762: The Morro Castle and the Boom Defence before the Attack.* (National Maritime Museum, Greenwich, BH0408.)

Figure 8.2. Richard Paton, *Bombardment of the Morro Castle, Havana, 1 July 1762*. (National Maritime Museum, Greenwich, BHO407.)

these failures were kept quiet in the British media. Moreover, Vernon himself, to avoid taking responsibility, attributed the defeat in Cartagena to General Thomas Wentworth, commander of the British ground forces. The failure against this city made the plan organized with George Anson, by which Anson would attack Panama from the Pacific, unfeasible because it was vital to have already taken Cartagena. This plan anticipated isolating the Spanish viceroyalties, New Spain in the north of the American continent and New Grenada and Peru in the south, from each other as a departure point to occupy and to exploit other territories in Spanish America.

Although this project was cut short, the British zeal to control the Spanish ports in the Caribbean and its Asian possessions did not disappear. Evidence of this fervor was the capture of Havana and Manila in 1762, during the Seven Years' War (figure 8.1). The occupation of both cities by British armies is telling proof of the global conflicts that were carried out between the two great European powers, Spain and Britain, during the eighteenth century. The capture of the Philippine capital relies on various studies and analysis, among which stands out the one produced by Díaz-Trechuelo in her monograph about architecture in the Philippines, a work of seminal reference despite the passage of time since its publication, as well as the more recent studies of Fish, Tracy, Luengo, and Cruz Freire.[3]

Likewise, Havana's occupation has aroused the interest of researchers.[4] Proof of it is the ample bibliography to which it has given rise, among the most recent contributions being the pages that Cruz Freire dedicates to it in his study on Silvestre Abarca and Schneider's monograph.[5] The importance that such an event had by itself increased as it was widely disseminated in the British world. Different images and types of texts contributed to its propaganda, as well as a wide range of depictions in prints and paintings on canvas (figure 8.2). It was not the first time in the eighteenth century that the British appealed to the visual media to disseminate a victory of its armies over a Spanish enclave in the Caribbean. In this regard, one should recall the prints that emerged from Samuel Scott's drawing when Vernon captured Portobelo.[6] The same artist created some paintings portraying the attack on and the capture of the city, which took place on November 21, 1739.[7] Additionally, one must cite the medal that was struck for that reason and that was widely disseminated, as well as the production of various items, including ceramics and fans, depicting the British victory and extolling the figure of Vernon.[8] These pieces and representations form part of a well-constructed plan of propaganda in which the images had a special agency. The portrait of Edward Vernon himself, painted by Sir Joshua Reynolds, serves as an example.

Victory as Visual Rhetoric of the British Empire: Hawk's View of Havana

The propagandistic phenomenon was repeated on the occasion of the taking of Havana. Similarly, for this reason, some excellent portraits of its main protagonists were painted. For example, there are those that depict Sir George Pocock, painted by Thomas Hudson, and the one devoted to General William Keppel, also belonging to Reynolds, in which the protagonist appears at the forefront pointing at Havana's Morro Castle as it is stormed by British troops. Moreover, a series of prints were published and paintings were created examining different moments in the attack. Among the prints, those preserved in Windsor Castle, known by the title *Britannia's Triumph*, stand out. The series is composed of twelve engravings that used the drawings and paintings carried out by Dominic Serres from the notes developed by Lieutenant Philip Orsbridge, who participated in the military action aboard the ship *Orford*.[9] This circumstance is evident in the texts that accompany each of the images, because it says they were produced live and that the engravings were carried out in accordance with law.[10] To counteract their high cost, it was necessary to resort to a popular subscription. Its authors were Pierre Charles Canot and James Mason, specialists in the middle of the eighteenth century in portraying maritime scenes and landscapes. They offered different moments in the British expedition and assault on Havana, and the images were finished with legends and coats of arms, in one instance that of the British royal family and in others the blazons of the admirals, generals, and officers of the English armies, who are referenced in the texts. The number of cannons that each ship carried is indicated along the borders of some of these engravings. The scenes depicted begin with the departure of the enormous fleet that was collected in Barbados to travel through the Old Canal of the Bahamas toward the Cuban capital, and end with the final bombardment of Havana. Between those endpoints are scenes of supplying the ships with arms and ammunition; the capture of La Chorrera, Cojimar, and the port of Bacuranao; the attacks on and the occupation of the Morro Castle; and the trapping of the Spanish fleet.[11] To these images, one must add the works of Dominic Serres, a French artist specializing in maritime and naval paintings (see figure 8.1). They were carried out for the Keppel family, three members of which played a leading role in the planning and development of the attack on the Cuban capital. One of them was General William Keppel, another his brother Augustus, and the third was George, Earl of Albemarle, who oversaw the assault on and the occupation of Havana alongside General George Pocock (figure 8.3, figure 8.4, and figure 8.5).[12]

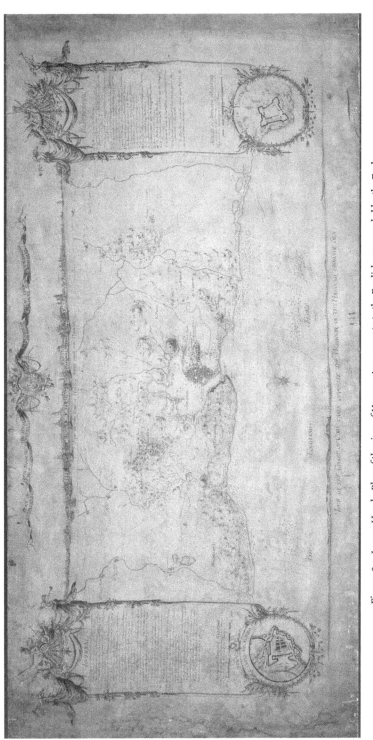

Figure 8.3. James Hawk, Plan of the siege of Havana Aug. 12, 1762 to the English commanded by the Earl of Albemarle General and Sir George Pocoke K. B. Admiral. (Library of Congress, G4924. H35L.)

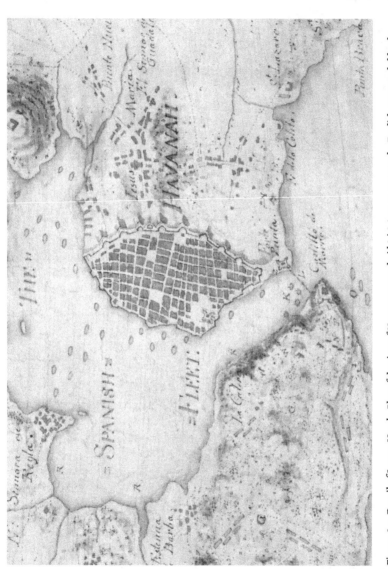

Figure 8.4. Detail of James Hawk, *Plan of the siege of Havana surrender'd [sic] Aug. 12, 1762 to the English commanded by the Earl of Albemarle General and Sir George Pococke K. B. Admiral*. (Library of Congress, G4924. H351.)

Figure 8.5. Detail of James Hawk, Plan of the siege of Havana surrenderid [sic] Aug. 12, 1762 to the English commanded by the Earl of Albemarle General and Sir George Pococke K. B. Admiral. (Library of Congress, G4924. H351.)

Within this body of work is the drawing that will be analyzed here, preserved in the Library of Congress in Washington, DC. This also contains ample explanatory text (see figures 8.3 to 8.5).[13] It contributes to the knowledge of this episode and the image of the city of Havana and its surroundings at the time of the British attack. The drawing stands out for its size, for its meticulous depiction of the territory, for offering one of the oldest images of Havana, and for the artist's interest in endowing it with artistic value, although clear deficiencies in the figurative motifs are evident. The cartographer James Hawk signed it in the lower right corner.

A large, inscribed band that emerges from a royal coat of arms provides the legend that identifies the depiction: *Plan of the siege of Havana surrender in* [sic] *Aug. 12, 1762 to the English commanded by the Earl of Albermarle General and Sir George Pococke K. B. Admiral*. This coat of arms belongs to King George III of Great Britain and Ireland. Among garlands, vegetable stems, and flowers appears possible depictions of the English rose, the Scottish thistle, and the Irish shamrock. A small angel holds the coat of arms in the lower part and another two playing trumpets are on the flanks. The coat of arms had an oval shape and the arms of the three aforementioned kingdoms are depicted in its quarters. Surrounding it is the garter of the Order of Garter along with its motto: *Honi soit qui mal y pense*. It lacks the tenants, the crowned lion, and the chained unicorn, which represent England and Scotland, as well as the motto *Dieu et mon droit*. The crowned lion that generally sits atop the Crown of St. Edward is also not portrayed.

Underneath the shield and the motto, an image of Havana is provided, viewed from the port, at least according to what the text says, although, in reality, it has been taken from the shore of La Cabaña. This placement allows for a more extensive panorama of the city. To the left appears the interior bay, with a small hill that could be Soto Hill, where later the Castle of Santo Domingo de Atarés would be built, with a church identifiable as San Francisco de Paula occupying the urban limit.[14] Buildings of different heights belonging to warehouses and domiciles follow, until arriving at the convent of San Francisco, clearly recognizable by its tower. The church has been represented laterally, seen from the immediate square, and not taken from the correct position, by which it would display its chancel. Other residential buildings follow, then a tower that might be San Felipe Neri, and other buildings of greater volume that might belong to the Castle of Real Fuerza. The city's profile continues with buildings of different heights and a set of towers difficult to identify, although one could belong to the church of the Ángel Custodio. On the extreme right of the city the Castle of San Salvador de la Punta and the mouth of the bay with the Morro Castle on the opposite shoreline have been depicted. In this opening, the rigging of the three Spanish ships, the *Asia*, the *Europa*, and the *Neptuno*, which were sunk to impede the British entrance, are seen. Around them, another vessel that could allude to the British ship *Bouat*, which gained access to the bay, has been drawn. Other ships depicted before the port and the city must belong to the Spanish fleet that remained in the interior of the bay during the British assault, as is indicated in the map located below the urban vista.

This map illustrates the city of Havana and its surrounding territory. The space extends between the Bacuranao River and the Marianao (or Mayanabo) River, portraying the extreme points of the British assault. It represents a vast geographical extension exceptional in the period's cartography. In fact, it was commonplace to depict the bay and its defenses from the access point, the city with his walled perimeter, and the most immediate surroundings. Even when the engineer Silvestre Abarca developed his project of fortifications for the Cuban capital in December 1763, once he returned to the place, the corresponding plan reiterates this model, although he widens it slightly toward the east to situate Aróstegui Hill and the Castillo del Príncipe.[15] It will be necessary to wait until the 1776 plan signed by the engineer Luis Huet to have another map that brought together the state of the city's defenses and that had such a broad depiction of the territory surrounding the city of Havana.[16] By that time, almost fifteen years had passed since the date of the plan that Hawk signed, which is here examined. It could be considered a coincidence. However, another nineteenth-century plan exists, signed by Colonel Carlos Benítez that, despite being oriented toward the north, coincides in geographical extension with the one found in the Library of Congress.[17] In the inscription that appears above the linear scale, on an unrolled paper, reads: *Carta Geográfica que comprende 5 leguas en contorno de la Ciudad de la Habana formada cuando la invasión de los Yngleses en el año de 1762* (Geographic Map that consists of 5 leagues in contour of the City of Havana created when the English invaded in 1762). The coincidences of the territory depicted, and this information, make me suspect the existence of a plan of that date that would be the one copied by Benítez, which has not been preserved or has not been located.

Another quality of Hawk's map is its thoroughness and the high level of detail achieved in the representation of territory surrounding Havana. Different geographic elements such as rivers, streams, and ponds are indicated, using watercolor to point out hills and other uneven terrain. The coastal forts of Bacuranao, Cojimar, San Lázaro, La Chorrera, and Marianao are situated. The communication routes are represented, and the neighborhoods outside the capital's walls, for example, Jesús y María, along with other towns in the area, for example, Regla, are situated. So are the factories and the mills, providing the name of each one of these. Such degree of information seems to demonstrate an intricate knowledge of the territory. This could have been acquired after the city's occupation, and for this end the maps and plans of the Spanish engineers that were stored in the Cuban capital may have been employed. However, I believe that it could have been prior to the assault and a consequence of a program of espionage on the part of the British. As has been pointed out, there were different occasions in which the English could have known of Havana's geographic environment and even the city's resources and defensive deficiencies with a certain amount of thoroughness. For instance, in 1756 the Cuban governor, Francisco Cajigal de la Vega, invited the governor of Jamaica, Admiral Charles Knowles, to visit the Cuban capital. During Knowles's stay, he was able to verify the strategic value of La Cabaña, information that would turn out to be of great importance for the 1762 assault, because at this location batteries that continually bombarded the city and that compelled its surrender were placed.[18] The situation was repeated in 1781, when in the midst of war, the British general, John Campbell, and some of his officers visited the city and looked over its fortifications, accompanied by Lieutenant Colonel Francisco de Miranda, assistant to *capitán general* (captain general) Juan Manuel Cagigal. This situation led engineer Luis Huet to complain and resulted in a denunciation to be sent to Minister of the Indies José de Gálvez. As a consequence, Miranda's imprisonment was ordered. Two years later, the English fleet under the command of Admiral Samuel Hood, which included Prince William, the Duke of Lancaster and younger son of King George III, visited Havana, and the governor, Luis de Unzaga, facilitated the visit to the fortifications for them. At these moments, the Castle of San Carlos de la Cabaña was already built and the city's defensive system was already updated, allowing the British to gather information in anticipation of a possible new assault on Havana, although one never occurred.[19]

Below the map of the capital and its surroundings, above the fragment of the sea wherein the location of the British fleet is indicated, a compass rose pointing out north has been drawn. Below this, a view of the Cuban coast between the Bacuranao and Marianao Rivers has been depicted, as it would have been seen from a ship that was approaching the entrance to Havana's bay and port. An inscription clarifies what is depicted: *View of the Coast of Cuba taken opposite the Harbour of the Havanah from the Sea*. In the drawing, the different levels of terrain, the hill and tower of Mariano, the Fort of La Chorrera, Aróstegui Hill, the city's profile, the Castle of La Punta, the entrance to the bay with a series of ships, Morro Castle, and the wooded lands of La Cabaña are made out. This depiction has an appearance of a quick sketch taken from real life. It is a very different image to the one carried at a later date and with clear cartographic rigor in the Real Academia de Guardiamarinas (Royal Academy of Midshipmen) in Cádiz, which is also preserved in the Library of Congress, along with maps of the Cuban coasts.[20]

Flanking the triple depiction, two vertical cartouches have been arranged. They are wrapped up in flags of a certain oriental resemblance and framed by garlands, curtains, and military trophies. The left one portrays at the end a seated soldier, wearing a uniform archaic for the time period. He wears a crossed band on his chest, feathered helmet, and a cape that swirls around. He wields a sword with his right hand, while the left holds up a shield with the image of the sun. On the sides, some children move between the flags, cannons, drums, and elements characteristic of military trophies. Other figures of small angels appear to hold up the flag, located over the curtains that emerge from it, and that give rise to the frame of the little angels with splendid ribbons playing trumpets. The curtains have flowered borders and are extended to serve as a frame for the cartouche, finished with ribbons, from which military trophies hang. The cartouche's base is placed among stems, flowers, garlands, and trophies. In the upper part, among some dry branches, a child carries a compass in his left hand, while the right one holds up a linear scale expressed in miles and British feet. The measurement corresponds to the existing distance between the Castle of San Salvador de la Punta and of Morro Castle, which protects the entrance to Havana's bay. An accurate plat of Morro Castle occupies the tondo. It is a very faithful representation, the presence of Los Doce Apóstoles battery in its final configuration being noteworthy. This demonstrates the knowledge the British had of the Cuban capital's defenses, definitely due to the espionage work.

All these elements serve as a framework for the campaign diary. It is an extensive text akin to a chronicle of war relating what happened on each day, from June 6, the date of the fleet's departure, to August 12, the day in which the surrender was signed. It tells us that the fleet was composed of thirty-seven warships and 150 transport vessels, carrying on board nine thousand men.[21] It points out that Guanabacoa was taken on July 8 and General Eliott posted two thousand soldiers there. It notes on July 14, Colonel William Howe landed with 1,200 men to the west of Havana and that on July 28 and August 2 reinforcements arrived from the North American colonies. On the first of these dates, 1,500 men arrived and an additional 2,000 landed on the second date. It also reported on the number of participants in the offensives carried out by the Spanish defenders on June 29 and July 22 and of the casualties that they suffered in this final offensive. The campaign diary describes the occupation of La Cabaña by Lord Albemarle on June 9, the cutting down of the forest in preparation for the attack on Morro Castle, the construction of batteries, and the start of the bombardment on the fort on July 1, until it surrendered on July 30. It also pointed out how the bombardment of the city from La Cabaña began on the following day, the attack intensifying from August 9 with fire from the west from the Castle of la Punta, until achieving the surrender and capitulation, which was signed on August 12. After the British seized the city and the fleet, along with its goods and riches, the Spanish troops were sent back to Spain. The cartouche found on the right side of the depiction offers slight variants to the traits already described. The protagonist resides in the position of the solider that crowns it, because he carries a palm in his left hand and he rests on an armillary sphere on which maps and documents are unfurled. The military trophies that surround him depict some drums, in addition to flags, cannons, and pikes. In the tondo, located in the lower area of the cartouche, the plat of the Castile of San Salvador de la Punta is depicted along with a child lying on it carrying a stick in the right hand and supporting a linear scale with the left. This is expressed in feet and Spanish leagues, pointing out the distance between the Castle de la Punta and Morro Castle. As in the tondo at left opposite, the faithfulness in the drawing of the castle's plat stands out, with its irregular forms and angular bulwarks.

In the cartouche (see figure 8.3), the letters written on the map of the city and its surroundings relative to the various episodes of the assault are identified. With these, the position of the boats that landed troops near Bacuranao (A), that of the forces led by Keppels and Pocock (B, C, and U), the placement of the ships that fired on the Castles of Cojimar, La Chorrera, and Bacuranao (D), the location of the boats that transported troops toward La Chorrera (M), the vessels sunk by the Spanish at the entrance to the port and the passage between them of the British ship *Bouat* (K and L) are indicated. Moreover, it serves to locate the British troops' encampments (I and Q), the march toward Guanabacoa, the Spaniards' place of refuge (E and F), as well as to identify the batteries and ships that fired on Morro Castle, the point in it wherein a breach was opened, and the location of the Spanish floating batteries in the bay's interior (N, O, P, and R). It also serves to situate the batteries that fired on the city (W), the stronghold built by the Spanish after the Morro's capture (X), the location of the British headquarters (T), the stronghold that the English built to attack the city from the west, and the line opened behind the Castle de la Punta that forced the city to surrender (Y and Z). With all the depictions finished, the movement of the British troops is indicated in red while the movement of the Spanish troops is indicated in yellow.

The drawing presented here is a unique work, not only its dimension and its type of pictorial support but also its theme and the importance of the graphical and textual information. Its specific purpose is unknown, although it is evident that it fits into the propagandistic policy developed by the British to highlight their great military victories. Clearly, the episode narrated raised the competition between England and Spain to a new level, and it had important consequences not only for the Spanish monarchy and its American territories but also for the world order itself. The loss of Havana and of Manila in the same year was a catastrophe for Spain, while it signified an enormous triumph for England. From then on, the Spanish monarchy, under the increasingly powerful threat from the English enemy, had to reconsider its military policy. Despite this uniqueness, this piece demonstrates how the British were interested in the possibilities of these visual tools, including also the urban proposals presented by Luengo (chapter 5), or the administration noted by Waters (chapter 4) and Graham (chapter 3). Conversely, the Spanish were not worried about providing a visual interpretation of conflicts, while their image was clearly maintained in urban and architectural practice, as many chapters of this book show.

Part III

The Spanish Plan

Fortifying the Caribbean Sea

9

The Interior Defense of Santiago de Cuba

The Fort of San Francisco

María Mercedes Fernández Martín

Previous chapters have shown how military architecture was understood in Europe at the end of the seventeenth century. Various Western powers attempted to support their expansionist policies in the Caribbean on an academic basis, but the result differed greatly from their intentions. Even around 1700, works in the most important Caribbean ports, such as Santiago de Cuba, were overseen by amateur architects without any academic training. Only during the eighteenth century, with the creation of the Corp of Engineers, examined by Muñoz Corbalán, did trained military engineers arrive in the Caribbean. To understand the previous situation more thoroughly this chapter focuses on Santiago de Cuba's Fort of San Francisco, a typical seventeenth-century work in the Americas. This chapter reconstructs its building process, emphasizing the projects' features from this time period.

The Geostrategic Significance of Santiago de Cuba in the Caribbean

Among the most significant precursors of the eighteenth-century defenses in the Caribbean Sea is the fortification of the island of Cuba. Given the island's strategic characteristics, Havana was the most protected city on the island for a long period, lasting from 1512 to 1898, because it was the final stop on the return voyage of the West Indies Fleet. Nevertheless, fortifications were spread out across the island over the years and increased in those areas of greatest strategic value or those most vulnerable to piratical attacks, for example, the ports of Matanzas or Santiago de Cuba. The latter was founded in 1515 by Diego

Velázquez de Cuéllar at the rear of a wide and protected bay but, unlike Havana, it was only moderately protected until 1639, when the construction of the defensive system was begun, this first stage lasting until 1669. A century after its founding, the city relied only on a few small forts, trenches, and observation points as its defense, along with the so-called Adelantado pillbox, a poor building of the medieval tradition, possibly of wood and earth, that was built in 1616 over the original construction of 1545.[1]

Santiago's defensive system took on new momentum because of the Dutch threat in the second quarter of the seventeenth century, and it was converted into an important enclave after the English assumed control of Jamaica.[2] In this period, Juan Bautista Antonelli, nicknamed el Mozo, arrived in the city, entrusted with the construction of the Castle of San Pedro de la Roca del Morro as the only protection for the port and the city of Santiago. Located on a hill that controlled the entire bay, its construction represented the most important defensive element and the organizing element of the remainder of the defenses that were later constructed.[3] Its construction was begun in 1639 and it must have been in use four years later, although it underwent major renovations both in 1691 and between 1771 and 1777, the latter period under the oversight of the architect Francisco Pérez, forming a complex of bastions, batteries, storehouses, and every type of military space.[4]

The English raid on Santiago in 1662 encouraged the Crown to strengthen the city's defenses. Orders were given for the reconstruction of the destroyed Morro and for the rebuilding of the city that had sustained major onslaughts. Per an express recommendation of the Crown, Santiago's defensive system was going to be developed further inland with the construction of various minor defenses such as the batteries La Estrella and Santa Catalina and the Fuerte Real or Fuerte de San Francisco in the city's interior.

In 1663, a year after the attack, Governor Rodrígo Flores de Aldana wrote to the king and described the city as disproportionate, with the houses dispersed, making its fortification difficult.[5] Flores's successor, Governor Pedro Bayona Villanueva, in his second term as Santiago's governor (1664–70), proposed the city's removal, an idea that the people clearly opposed, as it was decided in 1668 instead to reinforce its port and protect the city, planning for its defense, given the defenseless state in which the people lived.[6] The person put in charge of the project was Juan Síscara, or Císcara, who redefined the urban core as reflected in the plans developed between 1668 and 1669. With limited economic resources, he had to establish priorities, deciding in 1664 to build the Fort of La Estrella and the Fort of Santa Catalina, postponing work on the Fort of San Francisco and other lesser defenses.[7]

The Fortification Proposal of Juan de Císcara

Juan de Císcara was born in Madrid and joined the army of Catalonia, where he contributed to different coastal fortifications as an assistant. In 1663, he was promoted to the position of engineer, which was created for the reconstruction of Santiago de Cuba, traveling to his assignment along with the recently named governor, Pedro Bayona Villanueva. Considered as the greatest military engineer of seventeenth-century Cuba, his initial works in Santiago were the Castle of La Estrella and the platform of Santa Catalina, located on the mouth of the bay, as well as the transformation of the convent of San Francisco in a fortified enclosure within the city. His stay in Santiago lasted ten years, after which he was called by Governor Andrés de Magaña to Havana in 1673 to oversee the works on the city's rampart. He also planned two levels of the future Castle of San Severino in the port of Matanzas. He remained in Havana until his 1691 death, except for a short stay in Florida, where he was asked to oversee and to assess the military buildings that were being constructed there.[8]

The need to protect the population in anticipation of a new enemy attack overtaking the bay's defenses was a serious issue. Juan de Císcara, credited with the plan where the wide and deep Bay of Santiago de Cuba is depicted, devised a defensive plan where the havoc created by the English attack did not disrupt the city or its urban core.[9] In the lower-left corner, the explanatory cartouche, decorated with volutes and flanked by anthropomorphic figures arranged in profile, contains the title, *Planta del Morro y ciudad de Santiago de Cuba* (*Map of the Morro and the city of Santiago de Cuba*), and the numerical key of the places that are portrayed. This represents a model of a cartouche that will be repeated in different drawings signed by the engineer. At the bay's mouth, an irregular fortification is depicted, marked with the number 1 and identified as "the castle blown up by the English," preceded by a defensive platform. Halfway to the embouchure arises San Pedro de la Roca, defended with eight artillery pieces and reinforced by two platforms with five and four artillery pieces, respectively. The set is completed with the infantry barracks, the supply storehouses, and a little higher up, the Santa Catalina platform is equipped with another four pieces. At the back of the bay are salt mines with a few houses and the city of Santiago, portrayed with a reduced number of dwellings, with the primary buildings around the Plaza de Armas (main square), with the cathedral, the church of San Francisco, the governor's houses, and the Hospital Real (Royal Hospital), a location for which no type of defense is yet evident.

The city's vulnerability raised the possibility of its fortification or its removal to near the Castle of San Pedro de la Roca, a choice the population rejected.

Nonetheless, the first option of walling it off must have been considered. This is reflected in the plan signed by Juan Síscara, who designed a plat that, although frequently used in Europe, was very unique in the American context.[10] He proposed a regular construction of a hexagonal plat, with six bulwarks with their respective curtains, with those that faced the bay being of greater length and surrounded on its entire perimeter without a moat.[11] In general terms, this solution might be considered as an ambitious one for the second half of the seventeenth century in the region, there not existing similarly constructed examples. In the same plan, three gateways are opened that link respectively with the bay, the Morro, and the Matadero. The fortification surrounds the Plaza de Armas, today Parque Céspedes, the original core from which the city developed, along with the convent of San Francisco, the cathedral, and the governor's house with its guardhouse, including in that space the ruined Santa Catalina church.[12] Outside the fortified perimeter was part of the small village composed of houses made of straw and, toward the bay, a rough, difficult-to-access terrain formed by rocks that separated the city from the beach where a parapet of pickets and earth protected the starting points of the roads that traveled toward the city.

The reasons for the rejection of Císcara's project are unknown, although it might relate to the differences with contemporary proposals for the Americas. Instead of Císcara's project, the construction of an irregular fort within the urban space was chosen.[13] Presumably, this choice was due to the terrain determining the fortification by altering the supposedly perfect measurements of a regular plat, with an irregular plan that is better adapted to the orography being chosen instead.

The Fort of San Francisco, of which only a few archaeological traces remain, was the only important bastioned work built in Santiago, if we disregard el Morro. As the documentation makes clear, at first the construction was limited to a simple wooden fortification in the urban center around the convent of San Francisco, the designs of which were later entrusted to the engineer Juan de Císcara, who designed a structure outside the range of seventeenth-century siege cannons. He came up with a square structure with five bulwarks, four of which were in the corners and one joined to the entryway, considering two of them to be half bulwarks, thus forming an irregular contour. The works were carried out with the people's participation, contributing labor or materials under penalty of fine.

The works were constructed quickly because of the fear of new attacks by pirates. Nonetheless, they were not exempt from numerous critiques, mainly because of the hasty choice of land, dominated by a hill, and because of the little consistency in the materials used, which supported the limited defensive value that it had.[14] For these reasons and others of an economic nature (on various occasions its demolition was considered) some renovations were carried out in 1684 and 1773 until, after the 1766 earthquake, the fort risked falling into ruin, so it was decided to rebuild it, which was brought to fruition by the engineer Francisco Suárez Calderín.[15] There were some difficulties, the same ones inherited from previous stages, for example, the choice of land, earthquakes, and lack of funds to carry out its renovation, which led to its disappearance at the end of the eighteenth century.

The Proposals, from a Collection of Preserved Plans

Among the immense map collection preserved in the Archivo General de Indias (General Archive of the Indies) are different copies of the project. There are in total four designs, two of them unpublished, wherein the fortification is reproduced with slight variations between them. The first and most complete of these designs is dated, and is titled *Planta de la fuerça de San francisco hecha por el maestro de Campo Don Pedro Baiona Villanueva, gobernador de la plaza de Santiago de Cuba por su Magestad, en el año de 1668* (Map of the Fort of San Francisco made by the Maestro de Campo Don Pedro Baiona Villanueva, governor of the place of Santiago de Cuba by his Majesty, in the year 1668).[16] The design is very careful and correct, highlighting the decorative figureheads of the cartouche, marked with soft glazes, and a careful writing in which some orthographic variants stand out with respect to the standards currently in use. The plan is framed in a box, with the legend at the top with the explanation and the alphabetical references of the different bulwarks. This design, an irregular bastioned square, could be considered as one of the most common solutions in seventeenth-century American ports, such as San Pedro, Santa Lucía, Santa Catalina, San Juan Degollado, and San Antonio de Padua. Underneath this, the design of the defense works is reproduced, with their five reinforced bulwarks and respective sentry boxes, except for the San Juan Degollado bulwark. In the center is placed the church of San Francisco, surrounded by a line that indicates the space that the convent and its cells occupied. Likewise, it shows the defense that each bulwark had with its *líneas radiantes* or *redientes* (radiant lines) by means of dotted lines.[17] In the lower part, the scale is reproduced in geometric feet and a scale with the legend of "Five measurements of this make a geometric foot," and in the lower right corner the engineer's signature is inscribed on a rock.

With a similar heading and few variants in the cartouche's information is a second design in which the name of Císcara is included.[18] The only significant changes in the fortification's design are the layout of the church of San Francisco, which appears oriented toward the opposite direction relative to the previous design, indicating on the right margin *north* and on the left margin *south*. Moreover, in addition to the main gateway, another gateway, of smaller proportions, marked with the letter *B*, is reproduced on the front side.

A third design, where the title and the design vary slightly, presents identical characteristics.[19] On this occasion, the cartouche and the project appear independently in separate boxes. In the left one is the plan of the fortification with the convent of San Francisco in the center, but, in contrast to the previous ones, it reproduces neither the bulwarks' sentry boxes nor the stonework on its external reinforcement. In the right box, the cartouche is repeated, crowned on this occasion by a cross and flanked by anthropomorphic heads, where the title *San Francisco fortificado por el Maestro de campo Don Pedro Baiona Villanueba Gobernador de la ciudad de Cuba por su Magestad* (*San Francisco fortified by the Maestro de Campo Don Pedro Baiona Villanueba, Governor of the Cuban City by His Majesty*) is located, and underneath is the plan's explanation, identifying each one of the bulwarks by name. At the foot appears the signature Ingeniero Juan de Síscara (Engineer Juan de Síscara).

The drawing, with scale in geometric feet, is of high quality, using perspective and lines to give volume to the motifs depicted. A similar drawing located presents the same characteristics, although this time it does not appear to be signed, and the legend, similar to the previous one, is included in a simple registry without decoration.[20]

Finally, the fourth design of the bay of Santiago de Cuba with the placement of fortifications that, in contrast to the first one noted here, includes the fortified square of San Francisco, is preserved.[21] It shows the rugged orography with the defenses and the reinforcement of several platforms surrounding the Morro of San Pedro de la Roca and the mouth of the Aguadores River, near the bay's entrance, indicating the routes by which the English attacked the city. The lower part contains the explanation of the map, and an arrow designates north.

The different copies of the projects are dated 1668, the year in which the works were started, as is clear from the letter sent by the governor in the middle of that same year in which he dealt with building the fort.[22] The estimated time to completion was five months with a budget of 30,000 pesos. The works developed at a good pace because, a month after starting them, Bayona himself noted that the San Juan bulwark was already completed and the works on the San Antonio and San Pedro bulwarks were coming along quickly. However, Bayona did not see the entire work finished, and in 1670 his successor, Andrés de Magaña, criticized the fort's location and the limited defensive value. He also stated that the embankments were still unconstructed at that time.

A few years later, after the 1678 earthquake, the fort's demolition was considered, which again the townsfolk rejected. Its reconstruction was catalyzed around 1681 by Governor Juan Villalobos, who formed a commission, composed of the sergeant major, the presidio's captains, and the master builders, tasked with evaluating the works. Among the questions that were mulled over for the fortification truly fulfilling its defensive role was the demolition of the San Pedro bulwark, located to the right side of the entryway to raise it again aligned with the San Juan Degollado bulwark. In this manner, it would be a regular construction with a square footprint and four bulwarks. Likewise, it was proposed to tear down the church's vault and what remained of the convent of San Francisco, create embankments, and open a moat with a raised bridge. Despite the interest in the fortification and the reports sent to Spain, the Crown postponed the reconstruction during the final quarter of the century. As a result, during the administration of Palacios Saldurtum (1698–1700) knocking it down and building one a little higher, at the peak of Santa Ana, the hill that dominated the town, were considered.[23] It would not be until 1767 when Suárez Calderín proposed a new military use for the Castle of San Francisco.[24]

As has been stated, the Fort of San Francisco was built in a short space of time, although it was not free from debates and critiques about the suitability of its construction, which required that maps of the location of the city's fortifications and different copies of the fort's project be made.[25] It is not exceptional that different copies were made because, sometimes, they were sent to Spain for their recognition or approval, in addition to informing the Crown what had to be defended or controlled so that, in part, the copies can be considered as instruments of control on the part of the power. In their entirety, the projects and maps planned by Juan Císcara for the Fort of San Francisco reflected the military strategies of the governors, but beyond this, they form a tool of great importance to understand the complex process of engineering and stand out by their simplicity and functionality, following models from the first half of the seventeenth century.

Císcara's training is largely unknown, but his relationship with Italian engineering, specifically with the Milan school, is clear. In fact, Císcara requested the rank of military engineer supported by the Neapolitan friar Genaro María Aflitto, reader in theology, professor of mathematics, and professor in the Academia de Matemáticas y Arquitectura Militar (Academy of Mathematics and Military Architecture) founded by Philip II, which functioned intermittently in Madrid between 1583 and 1697.[26] Likewise, he is the author of *Compendio de modernas fortificaciones* (Compendium of Modern Fortifications), translated into Spanish in 1657 by Baltasar Císcara. This is a very brief treatise, divided into thirteen chapters, which, although it does not present revolutionary contributions, instead repeating previous ideas, and is of little importance for the development of technical knowledge, codifies the models, with examples of irregular fortifications such as the example that concerns us.

This example of Santiago de Cuba, and especially the case of Císcara, shows that the training of military engineers in the Caribbean at the end of the seventeenth century was autodidactic, or at best supported by some local scholars. This contrasts with the academic training developed in Europe during this century and the organization of studies by the Corp of Engineers during the eighteenth century. As a consequence of the work of Verboom in Spain, work in the Caribbean ports was requested by academic military engineers. The French would follow a similar pattern, sending engineers from Europe, although little is known about their previous training. Other European powers, such as the English, preferred to rely on military experience, which they viewed as better than theoretical training.

10

Engineering and the Articulation of Territory

Juan de Herrera y Sotomayor and the Canal del Dique Improvement Project in Cartagena de Indias, 1725–1728

Francisco Javier Herrera García

◆

The works by military engineers in the Caribbean were closely linked to fluvial knowledge. In addition to its importance for the correct design of fortifications, it was used to improve interior communications on rivers or canals. This new engineering branch must be incorporated to those previously addressed: as intelligence agents, architects, politicians, and urban planners, among others. A good example to show this phenomenon in the Caribbean is the work of Juan de Herrera y Sotomayor in the Canal del Dique (Cartagena). This facet of expertise in hydraulics and aquatic geography, in rivers, canals, shallow channels, and lagoons, was vital for the interests of the colonial power, defensively, logistically, and economically. These skills would also manifest themselves in North American territories, as the works of José Miguel Morales Folguera (chapter 14) or Gene Allen Smith (chapter 15) demonstrate.

With regard to Cartagena de India's Canal del Dique, the *Diccionario de gobierno y legislación de Indias* notes the need for the improvements in the middle of the 1720s: "The King is informed of the little care that has been taken in cleaning the so-called Canal (Dique), that departs from the Port of Cartagena through the pass of Pasa-Cavallos straight towards the Barranca del Rey on the border of the great Magdalena River, such that in the case of sightlessness, it was easy to lose one's navigation, and that is so useful for the saving of expenses, which previously required the transport of fruits overland; he ordered the governor to arrange for the cleaning at the expense of the lessees, who in 1726 had taken charge of it to make it navigable, and in case of not executing it, for having completed their lease, the Cabildo of that City do it, for whose expense they were demanded for each canoe and sampan the same rights that the aforementioned lessees earned."[1]

These improvements were ordered by the governor[2] and the *cabildo* (colonial town council) of Cartagena, which this chapter focuses on. More specifically, this chapter highlights how this infrastructure constituted one of the most important of the city's public goods, the leasing and exploitation of which in the hands of private individuals were the norm since it began operating in 1650. Fixed and modernized, it currently continues to fulfill the mission for which it was conceived, placing the port of Cartagena de Indias in contact with the Magdalena River, the main fluvial artery of modern-day Colombia, formerly Nueva Granada.[3]

As part of this approach from the military engineers, the management of the canal's construction is analyzed, examining especially how private interests— at times composed of various groups and institutions such as both local and transatlantic merchants, the *cabildo*, landowners, interior farmers, the Tierra Firme fleet that linked Spain and South America across the Atlantic Ocean, smugglers, military officials, the royal treasury, and the port city's inhabitants— generally interacted with each other.

A Link with the Magdalena River: Logistics and Supplies

Throughout the sixteenth century, the extreme difficulties and dangers involved in entering the Magdalena channel from the river mouth, where banks of sediment were numerous, along with the powerful flow of the river itself as it entered the sea, had become evident (figure 10.1). Moreover, the maritime journey from Cartagena to Bocas de Ceniza was inadvisable. Canoes were not suitable to be used on this stretch as they were not able to handle the frequent storms and were easy prey for the corsairs. For this reason, several land routes that directly connected the bay to the river, several kilometers from its mouth, were attempted. However, it was an uncomfortable way to travel through a flooded area, composed of an intricate network of swamps, shallow channels, mangroves, and jungle lands. Nonetheless, during the sixteenth and a good part of the seventeenth century, it was the only route to enter the capital and the interior cities of the New Kingdom of Granada. In the best-case scenario, one could more easily travel through part of this section in a canoe across a few swamps that connected with the Caribbean Sea, although it was necessary to move in caravans and make nightly stopovers in haciendas (manor houses), because the route required three or four days.[4] Beginning in the end of the sixteenth century, the canal project took shape, using natural rafts, shallow channels, and streams that supplied water, in addition to newly excavated stretches that would connect the Barranca (the river pier) de Mateo Rodríguez on the left shore of the river to the Matunilla estuary, then to head to the bay via the Strait of Pasacaballos.[5] Governor Pedro de Zapata inaugurated the project on August 20, 1650, after the intervention of the military engineer Juan de Somovilla y Tejada. The total distance was 29 leagues, about 122 kilometers, resulting in a series of small villages distributed along the course (Pasacaballos, Rocha, Bambote, Mahates, San Estanislao, and Barranca), as well as haciendas, all of which served as stopover points.[6]

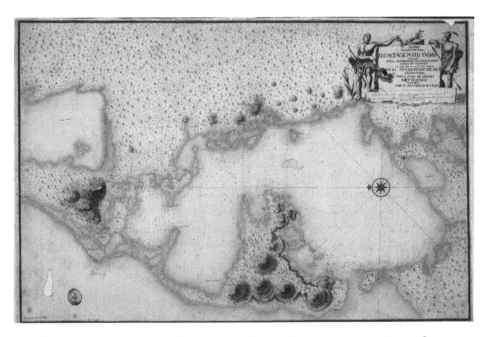

Figure 10.1. Cartagena de India's bay map, 1735, by Juan Herrera y Sotomayor. (Image from the collections of the Biblioteca Nacional de España, MR/43/113.)

The marshes and shallow channels experienced strong drainage flows that dried out the canal, and the river's floods were likewise an inconvenience, because they flooded a large part of the territory, affecting cattle as they spread, leaving the waterway unused as the sediments and plant residues were deposited. From its foundation, it depended on the city and the galleons being able to find supplies for the return trip, including a varied range of foods at reasonable prices, much lower than when they were transported by land.[7] The benefits were thus of the first order, and there was no hesitation in the need to invest in the Dique's maintenance. The shortage of funds, the refusal of the lessees to pay for the needed repairs, and the technical difficulties themselves led instead to the waterway being unavailable for most of the year, a circumstance that was almost perpetual between 1679 and 1726. The old roads and the navigable stretch between Matunilla and Mahates, the "middle Dique," were resorted to. Protests from the fleet captains were commonplace, stressing the high cost of mule transport.[8] It is estimated that the price of some products could increase by upward of 300 percent when the transport by this waterway was impossible.[9]

This being the case, after several years of irregular or nonexistent operation, in 1725 a work that would ensure comfortable navigability without prolonged interruptions of its channel was again decided on. Different lessees had assumed its management, always refusing to carry out the necessary works, thus it is not so strange that the system of lessees was counterproductive and was the cause of so many years of underutilization.[10] The general context that encouraged the route's opening, maintenance, and proper functioning has to do with the agency that the Caribbean and its port cities acquired from the middle of the sixteenth century onward. Cartagena became vital for the redistribution of goods coming from Europe, basically consisting of high-value manufactured goods, through the Caribbean, the New Kingdom, Peru, and other points in South America through the Panamanian isthmus. At the same time, it acted as a receiving city for precious metals (gold and silver), pearls, emeralds from New Granada's mines, and Caribbean fish. We should also remember the unfortunate traffic in enslaved humans coming from Africa, for which Cartagena acted as both a receiving and a distribution point.[11] If we add to these milestones the growing population eager for consumption, the sterility of the countryside, which could only produce some corn, rice, bananas, cassava, and small-scale livestock products,[12] it is difficult to estimate how vital the Magdalena waterway was for the transport of people, metals, foodstuffs, and European imports bound for the cities of Santa Fe, Tunja, Pamplona, Vélez, Villa de Leiva, Mariquita, and so on. As we have indicated, the Canal del Dique offered comfort, speed, and lower costs to this traffic. An aim not always achieved was the good supply of the port city, at prices affordable to the entire community, a difficulty that could be avoided thanks to contraband.[13] The Canal del Dique also, if it functioned adequately, played an important role at the time of dissuading the illegal "introductions" of goods (figure 10.2).

Figure 10.2. Map of the provinces of Santa Marta and Cartagena, with the Canal del Dique and Magdalena River mouth by Antonio de. Arébalo, 1766. (© Ministerio de Cultura y Deporte, Archivo General de Indias, MP-Panama, 174.)

The record preserved in the Archivo General de Indias in Seville, Spain, notes all the procedures for the canal's leasing, operation, and improvement. Dated from 1724 to 1725, the record's main protagonists are the city's *cabildo*, Cartagena's governor Luis de Aponte, the galleon commander Francisco Cornejo, the owner of one of the fleet's supply boats in the port, the competition's bidders (Francisco San Martín and Francisco Herranz), and especially the engineer Juan de Herrera y Sotomayor, who provides the precise technical solutions, demonstrating simultaneously his extensive knowledge of the actual needs of Cartagena and its surroundings in economic, logistical, and defensive matters.[14]

The quick-but-complex contractual process, marked by multiple reports advising the lease, doubts about the same, rivalries and pressures between parties, consultations to the Real Audiencia, and such, began with the bid that San Martín and Herranz tendered to Cartagena's *cabildo* requesting they serve as lessees and rehabilitators of the now-unused channel. The city's merchants advised leasing the channel and making it suitable. They were represented by *comandante* (commander) Francisco Cornejo, fervent promoter of the project, simultaneously supported by the military governor himself, Luis de Aponte. This group relied on another skilled supporter of the Dique's operability, the engineer Herrera y Sotomayor, who provides technical solutions to ensure navigation and preservation based equally on the ideas of progress and public benefit. Nonetheless, after a few months there was reticence on the part of the *cabildo*, fearful of the risk involved in the operation, its low profitability, the financing of specific works, and the collateral damage that may result from the canal's opening. All these concerns apparently mirrored another reality, the interests of a certain group represented there, the *hacendados* (manor house owners),[15] whose lands were situated in the regions around the canal and roads, as well as the persistent problem of illegal trade in which the entire social strata of Cartagena were involved to a greater or lesser extent.

Before both bidders made their economic proposals and conditions with the *cabildo*, it would be Don Francisco Cornejo,[16] commander of the galleons anchored in the bay, who would raise his arguments to the president of Santa Fe's Real Audiencia, the main colonial government agency in the New Kingdom of Granada, seeking its approval and support. This petition was dated March 13, 1724, and it clearly reviews the interests, benefits, and problems that came with the Dique's navigability project. The sailor and transporter express the urgent need of opening the water route with the aim of benefiting food producers and all types of New Grenadian highlands goods, especially flour, which is produced abundantly and at good prices in the region, in addition to gold, silver, emeralds, hides, leather, goatskins, salted meats, sugar, honey, corn, cassava, beans, hams, cocoa, fish, tobacco, sweets, chickens, garlic, onions, cheeses, horses, mules, and Brazil wood. With all of this, the city should be well supplied at any time of the year, especially at peak times when the galleons of the fleet are there. He goes on to estimate Cartagena's environs are only capable of providing some 10 percent of the convoy's needs. The low prices of provisions and other products thus provided by water transport could then compete with those distributed from the northern Caribbean and North America by the English *asiento* firm for the Africans (the British South Seas Company), as well as those transported difficultly by sea from the Gulf of Sinú or Tolú. The intelligent mariner thinks about the benefit derived for the entire kingdom, because as such the agricultural economy of the interior will be boosted. It is clear that with the Dique in operation, the merchants would achieve a greater fluidity in relations with the capital and other cities and their rich lands, not only in being able to export European products easily but also encouraging the arrival of larger remittances of gold and silver with which to acquire them as well as establishing new possibilities for financing commercial operations and other enterprises. Although not cited precisely in Cornejo's writing, the increasing arrival of these valuable metals, as well as emeralds, is among the main aspirations of Cartagena's merchants and transporters, along with flour and other edible products.[17]

Daily Contraband and the Channel as Remedy

Another chapter important for the fleet, also reflected in the letter to the president, is the constant need of good wood for repairing boats' defects. In this sense, Francisco Cornejo again mentions the difficulties of wood's transport by the water route from the Bay of Sinú, where vessels are exposed to winds and sea breezes, when it would be easier and cheaper to move them to the interior via the channel.

If we were to look for a constant in Cartagena's history, we would find it in contraband, illegal commerce, "illicit introductions," or "hospitalities," a mechanism through which the city could survive and acquire luxury products or necessities at reasonable prices, without paying royal taxes. The problem increased in the eighteenth century, during which almost all of the citizens, officials, military officials, aristocrats, common people, ecclesiastics, and friars were involved. The sloops arrived from the Dutch, English, and French Caribbean islands with shipments that they deposited in protected places on the coast, such as Sinú, Tolú, the Island of Barú, or Ríohacha, for their subsequent transfer, generally at night, to the stronghold. Nonetheless, the primary means through which contraband was delivered was the English *asiento* galleon, established in 1713 after the Treaty of Utrecht signed between United Kingdom and Spain to deal with the sale and distribution of enslaved Africans, whose bodega was stocked with much more than was legally allowed.[18] In one of those reports about this uncontrolled economic and social phenomenon, dated September 8, 1724, Capt. Don José García de Luna defends himself against the accusations made against him that the previous governor, Don Carlos Sucre (1719–20), declaring that when the *oidor* (judge) Antonio de la Pedrosa y Guerrero,[19] willing to fight and to stop the illegal traffic, arrived, the residents feared being caught wholly "by public royal thieves." As a result of that momentary restrictive policy, the prices of products such as wine, fabrics, and such, rose immensely, for example, a *vara*[20] of so-called Dutch-weave and ribbon fabrics went from 4 *reales* to 12 *pesos*. The captain cites one of the classic examples of high-level contraband, such was the case of Viceroy Jorge de Villalonga (1720–24), among whose executive mandates was the combating of contraband, who participated in illegal commerce at his leisure during his stay in Cartagena and returned to Santa Fe with a notable shipment of "illegal clothing." Capitan García de Luna continues on to state that both in Cartagena and Portobelo, all the ministers of state "are introducers," their large houses being merchandise storehouses.[21]

Returning to the ideas extrapolated by Capitan Francisco Cornejo, the recurring theme of smuggling is again seen, pointing out how the food products that transit through the channel from the interior plateaus might compete with those provided by the smugglers, stopping this illegal trade. Flour would be cheaper, as would be meats and other edible products. The channel would therefore become an effective weapon to end contraband, which would no longer be as profitable.

It is equally possible to understand the aversion of the *hacendados* from around Cartagena, unable to produce foodstuffs in different quantities, maintaining abusive prices, as well as controlling terrestrial roadways and providing an expensive and slow means of transport to the commercial trade between Cartagena and the river. They are the owners of these "hazenduelas," and as such they have a greater interest in the channel's interruption because they exploit the costly and lucrative means of animal transport.[22] The trees and plant debris that clog the ravine and several points of the route, notes Cornejo, have been intentionally left by the owners of such lands who moreover argue that the Dique might lead to the inundation of their lands: "Part of the aforementioned subjects are also opposed because they have mules that they rent from here to the *barranca* with which they will increase the prices and thus make the traffic in clothing that goes up as well as the few fruits that go down the channels difficult. For these reasons they give for being opposed that when it has been the dique running they have experienced with the River's increases much damage in their *haciendas*."[23]

With respect to fiscal benefits, there is no doubt that it would have repercussions on the royal coffers, by having a customs office that will control the shipments and will set moderate tariffs and, of course, the city as proprietor of the public good, will receive an income, needing to recover itself financially from the previous decades when the city brought in 14,000 pesos annually when the canal was navigable. Cornejo estimates that this route would even contribute to the best and most effective defense of the port city, because if it was well supplied, it would result in a prolonged resistance, being able to be besieged for a long time, in contrast to what occurred in 1697 with the attack and plundering of the French privateer and soldier, Baron de Pointis, also known as Bernard des Jean (1645–1707). The optimal provision of the Tierra Firme fleets was even discussed, which in the case of danger in the Caribbean or Havana itself, could return to Spain directly from Cartagena.[24]

The reasons put forward by the galleon commander represent a compromise between economic, commercial, fiscal interests and the general interest of the population, including the Cartagena *cabildo*. The decline of the New Kingdom in light of the inability to compete with the illicit Caribbean trade and the need to adopt measures that reactivate all sectors is already foreshadowed in his words. In short, the good articulation of communications between the inland of the New Kingdom and Cartagena, through the operation of the channel, will reap benefits for international trade as well as domestic and economic activity generally. Above all, his interest in transatlantic trade, in which Cornejo participates, understood as an economic engine, is noted. It is not surprising that these ideas were supported by Cartagena's larger merchants, involved in the importation and sale of manufactured products, in exchange for gold and silver.

Lessees, *Cabildo* Members, Discrepancies, and the Contract's Signing

The bidders Francisco de San Martín y La Madrid[25] and Francisco Herranz de Meñaca[26] are linked to the importation trade and the exchange of precious metals, as intermediaries, as it seems was characteristic of the Cartagena population.[27] It is possible that the other merchants and Captain Cornejo himself previously agreed to the business that was to be arranged with the city's *cabildo*, having taken into account the forecasted benefits to commercial traffic. Immediately, the applicants proposed some conditions that raised doubts, reluctance, and until the public refusal, arguments over legal questions on the part of the *cabildo*. In each parties' proposal, their mercantile interest and costly operation of the canal is evident. They proposed to open a new *barranca* on the river, with its corresponding channel with a first section already excavated that will pass through the natural shallow channels of Machado and Soledad, continuing toward the Colador marsh, which receives the water from the Magdalena River, thus being shorter and more direct from the river, whose water would penetrate directly into the channel, relieving the low water levels. The lease would be established for ten years, eight required and two optional, at a price of 1,000 pesos annually, half the cost of the previous lease. They protected themselves in that they will have to tackle the opening of the current *barranca* and the works of the new route, part of which they estimate will be borne by the income of *cabildo* members. They allow for traffic control by the captain general to the *barranca* and urge the signing of the contract, because in so doing they could advance the needed works to have the route open and available on October 11, 1725, the date on which the current license comes into force. An interesting detail was to require any resulting litigation not to go to the ordinary courts but instead go only to the captain general and the governor,[28] in this case Luis de Aponte, unequivocal evidence of the support of the city's highest authority for the merchants and their protection.[29]

The initial refusal of the *cabildo* largely reflects the interests of some of its representatives. Since the seventeenth century, the group was composed of the urban elites, property owners, and public officials such as the accountants, treasurers, customs administrators, and high-ranking military men,[30] all to a greater or lesser extent owners of rural properties and mule trains employed as a means of transport.

Thus, the reason for their opposition to the modernization of transit over the Magdalena River is unnecessary to explain. After the appropriate announcement, the signing was delayed, the *cabildo* members did not view the previous agreement as successful, and the bidders stressed the argument of putting the route into use as soon as possible, because the rainy season would prevent any progress in the works.

On the part of the *cabildo* members, their distrust can be summarized in the low expected income, their consideration that the new ravine and the journey to the swamps would be unnecessary, their doubting its effectiveness, in addition to their auguring the even greater possibility of flooding of the haciendas and the losses that it would entail. They also disagreed with the legal ability to grant leases by themselves for such an extended period, ten years, and they even come to assert that the channel would be an easy access route "for the enemy pirates with their launches, pirogues, and canoes can be introduced to the interior lands, and create much damage while the news is coming to the remedy."[31] While they recognize the benefits generated, they come to question the projects and ideas of the engineer Juan de Herrera y Sotomayor. The *cabildo* was also urged by the representatives of the *armada*'s galleon captain, who stated the need to have cheap food for a journey of four months, that is, from the departure and stay in Portobelo, then to Havana and the return trip across the Atlantic.[32]

The *cabildo* members raise new doubts that will have to be confirmed in the Audiencia of Santa Fe, as the representative of royal authority. Gaining time and avoiding a quick solution to the problem is the *cabildo* members' tactics, so now they worry if it is legal to open a new mouth on the Magdalena River, thus extracting its water, without royal permission, as any navigable river is the king's property. Treating the fluvial channel as a royal prerogative, any extraction of water must be authorized through royal decree. With this, the two bidders agree, and it is postulated that the matter should be raised, to save time, to the Audiencia of the New Kingdom where the king is not found but in fact "His Imperial Image, very true to life, is venerated, which provisionally supplies in such cases the same Royal personage," that is, the portrait of Philip V at Santa Fe would be sufficient "in his name" to issue a concurring royal endorsement. Months later, on August 8, the *cabildo* read and agreed to put into practice the royal provision that arrived from Santa Fe, which proposed the lease of the channel in the terms previously agreed on, the previous proclamation of the contract, and especially to follow the technical prescriptions of the royal engineer Juan de Herrera "for being of his profession and being his science and noteworthy experience," so that his project is again exhibited,[33] to which we will later refer. Not without reluctance and certain disagreements among the lessees and the *cabildo*, the signing of the leasing contract finally took place on August 27, committing the lessees to opening the new channel and its mouth, according to as Herrera arranged, and to the maintenance such that it could be navigable the greater part of the year; the terms of the lease as was foreseen, remained fixed at ten years, eight obligatory and two optional, at the rate of one thousand pesos per year; the bidders will be responsible for collecting the tariffs from the following October 11, when it should be ready for the movement of canoes and sampans; the precise workforce will be provided by the *cabildo*, however, the lessees will pay their salaries; finally, any litigation resulting from the contract will be heard in the *cabildo*.[34] On September 14, the lessees requested that the governor, Don Luis de Aponte, order all the captains of the jurisdiction to provide a workforce for the opening of the shallow channel and the mouth.[35]

Juan de Herrera and His Projects

A key figure, conscious of the province's political, economic, and military obstacles, was the engineer Juan de Herrera y Sotomayor, to whom the necessary technical proposals are attributed. As in other cases, Herrera assumed his role as infrastructure planner to tend to the economic, spatial, logistical, and political problems of the time, in such a way that the engineering projects that we will analyze progress over the following issues: commerce, the speed and economy of transport, the benefit to the population and the public coffers, the defense against occasional enemies and contraband, space management, and so on. Various authors have highlighted his importance and transcendent activity as an engineer, which would bring him after his training in Europe to various places in the Americas, such as Valparaíso, Valdivia, and Buenos Aires, where he found himself between 1681 and 1690 largely under the supervision of his father, José de Herrera, governor of Buenos Aires. After returning to Spain, he was sent to Havana and to Cartagena de Indias in 1699, where he remained until his 1732 death, developing an intense and varied curriculum vitae as an engineer. He is considered the first active scientific engineer in Tierra Firme,[36] as shown in his various activities both in the field of poliorcetics and in infrastructure building and cartography, for which he traversed and explored the Caribbean coast. His frequent mobility is one of the facets that distinguishes him,[37] along with the founding of the "Academia Militar de Matemáticas Cartaginesa" (Cartagena Military Academy of Mathematics) on April 9, 1731, where he taught the theory and practice of mathematics as applied to military and defensive ends, as well as cartography.[38]

There has been talk of an American fortification school and a system unique to Herrera that, however, seems inconsistent when the typologies and solutions practiced by the engineer are compared with those laid out by European avant-garde treatises, especially those from France.[39] His post in Cartagena focused on the need to replace the defenses that were largely destroyed in 1697 during Baron de Pointis's assault (figure 10.3).[40] The domain of geography, knowledge of space, geological and plant nature, and such, are inherent to the engineering discipline and will continue to be commonplace, after Herrera, in later engineers who work in and around Cartagena, such as Antonio Arévalo and Manuel de Anguiano, as Manuel Gámez Casado explains in chapter 11. The need to understand and plan the surrounding space, quite a distance from the metropolis, is an astonishing feature of all of them.

We have mentioned the importance of the waterway for Cartagena's communication with the interior. It is not by chance that over the course of the eighteenth century its maintenance and improvement received increasing attention. Keep in mind that the ideas surrounding its preservation can be framed within the massive advances that are produced in Europe and America in terms of canal and hydraulic engineering.

During this century, the great navigation canals were consolidated in the Old World, and this type of solution arrived as well to the Americas, especially to North America. In this vein, the sophisticated canal reform proposed by Antonio de Arévalo in the final decade of the century must be understood,[41] without forgetting the critical moment of the Bourbon reformist policy, intensified in terms of modernization of communications and trade, after the 1778 "free trade treaty."[42]

Figure 10.3. Plans, aerial views, and sections of several fortifications of the Cartagena de India's bay, by Juan de Herrera y Sotomayor, c. 1730. (© Instituto de Historia y Cultura Militar, Archivo General Militar de Madrid, JT.7-C.1-34. CC BY-4.0.)

The improvement proposals for the Dique formulated by Juan de Herrera, at the behest of the governor and the galleon commander, date from the beginning of 1725, after the engineer embarked on a risky and dangerous visit in November of the previous year to the canal's channel, then unrecognizable as a result of the great inundations, which were a result of the overflow of the river and of heavy rains that affected the region. On March 17, 1725, he described his project requiring the opening of a new river mouth, 3 leagues above the one then existing, forming a new *barranca*. It would be characterized by its orientation to the river's current, so that it would better capture its waters as a funnel that would gradually narrow. It would follow a new channel, wider and deeper than the prior one, of some 3 leagues. It connected the river with marshes that would act as a deposit basin for the waters resulting from the floods of the Magdalena River, and it would pour its reserves into the canal during the low-water periods. He insisted on the need to excavate the bed of the channel and widen it, so it could act as a collector during the rainy season and not flood the neighboring haciendas, as had happened in recent years. The Barranca del Rey would also shorten the road to Honda by about 3 leagues, thus benefiting the transport of people, merchandise, and mail, and permit goods to be stored in warehouses to assist the bodegas where travelers would "mansion" and their goods could be safeguarded. He did not see any problem regarding the possible use of the channel as a route for pirates or enemies to penetrate the interior, because it would be very easy to ambush them in the channel itself and nothing more would be heard from their presence, suggesting that the channel and especially its entrance from Cartagena Bay would be permanently guarded, a circumstance that might explain the project developed by Herrera in 1730, of a redoubt for cannons and gunfire that would be located at the exit to the sea from the Pasacaballos Strait and would have the purpose of securing the routes to the Magdalena River, through the Dique, and by sea to Tolú, Bahía del Sinú, and other coastal locations (figure 10.4).[43] The elements of greater peculiarity that the engineer director tried to incorporate in the channel to improve the connection with the "large river" and to facilitate the transit of canoes and sampans were the floodgates and locks that would have to be located in the *barranca*, in the new mouth, a system that will also prevent the entry of sediments such as mud and sand in the navigable waterway. This tested the technical knowledge of Herrera, an experienced hydraulic engineer. He pointed out in this regard, as the entrance of an eventual and devastating flood of the Magdalena River "is impeded through two locks that should be made next to its mouth with the art and talent that it is practiced in Flanders and Holland so that in such a case only that water necessary for navigation enters the channel and that it be maintained always cleanly."[44]

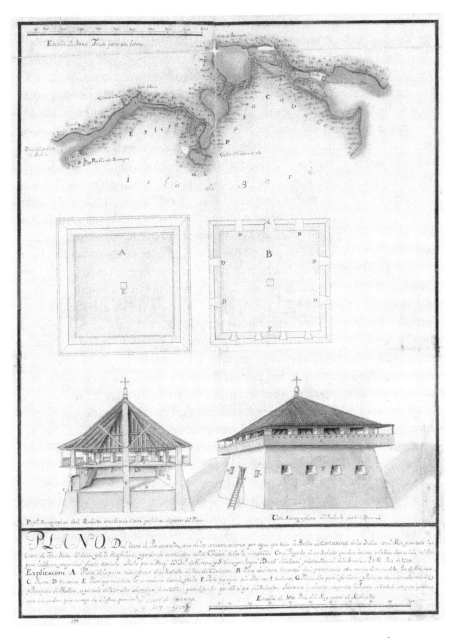

Figure 10.4. Plat of the strait of Pasacaballos and project of redoubt in its sea mouth, Cartagena de Indias, 1730s, by Juan de Herrera y Sotomayor. (© Intsituto de Historia y Cultura Militar, Archivo General Militar de Madrid, JT.7-C.1-36[b]. CC BY-4.0.)

With the licensing process issued by the Real Audiencia resolved, prior to the signing of the contract by the lessees and the *cabildo*, the *cabildo* members demanded a report from the engineer, focused especially on an explanation of the lock system, its viability, and the cost that its construction may incur. In the detailed exposition dated August 21,[45] Herrera declares, "locks are termed in Flanders, Holland, and France those receptacles that are formed, or already are in, the rivers and the seashores for the ships and other boats to be able to navigate the channels, which without this precaution would be impossible," while recognizing their usefulness for "flooding and drying out countries, for fortifying places, and many uses,"[46] a good test of the engineer's knowledge of and experience in the material acquired in northern Europe. Herrera plans two holding containers, locks, covered with square-section wood pylons, conjoined through a type of groove. Well-pressed together and tied to each other, the locks would impede the loss of water and the introduction of sands and debris from the surrounding lands. Each one would be 100 *varas* long (84 meters), and the first would be arranged at 25 *varas* (21 meters) from the river's mouth. The gates are arranged on square pillars of two *varas* sideways (1.68 meters), with deep foundations, in which some logs fitted with grooved guides and joined at the top by a bridge fit together, forming a kind of door. The gates would move through the guides rising or descending. Laterally, a channel with a small gate would be provided, to decrease or to increase the lock's water. The idea is that they would enter into operation when the river crests, so as to make it impossible to flood the nearby lands, while simultaneously facilitating navigation. However, they would hinder the penetration of sediments, preventing the channel's clogging.[47] It was a simplified solution of the lock systems that he would have seen, and analyzed, in Flanders and Holland.[48]

In fact, despite the opening of the new mouth and the indicated section of channel, the locks never were built. We do not know whether it was due to a shortage of building materials or doubts about their effectiveness. In 1728, at the request of the lessees San Martín and Herranz, Herrera once again informed us about the canal's state. The new mouth and the *barranca* were in operation shortly after the contract's signing, as was the channel, owing to the continual maintenance work. It was possible to navigate for most of the year, during about ten months, and the savannah's haciendas had not suffered flooding. A result of the engineer's observations is the determination of the difference between the levels of the river's floods and its low-water levels, which he estimated at eight *varas* (6.72 meters), as well as the effectiveness of the marshes to absorb excess water injected by the fluvial course to provide liquid to the channel in drought conditions. The main problem that was discovered at the time of deepening the channel is the appearance of outcrops of hard stone, which were difficult to eliminate, specifically because of the lack of labor capable of doing so. Herrera also determined the importance of the streams that discharged into the swamps, vital to prevent the canal's drying out.[49] The engineer's geographical and environmental knowledge is thus demonstrated.

Hydraulic Engineering at the Service of Progress: Knowledge and Treatises

Although not largely carried out, Herrera's project reveals his training in hydraulic systems.[50] Although the familiarity with certain treatises by the first scientific engineers who arrived in the Americas, such as the followers of engineers Cristóbal de Rojas, Vauban, or Fernández Medrano, has been proposed,[51] it seems clear that Herrera's theoretical knowledge went beyond these classical authors, and Herrera was familiar with the works of architecture, mathematics, astronomy, artillery, and such. Multidisciplinary training in different scientific subjects is foundational to all seventeenth- and eighteenth-century military engineers, as Muñoz Corbalán has demonstrated at the beginning of this volume. If we take into account Herrera's seven-year stay in Flanders, as an infantry soldier in a company of the *tercio*[52] of Don Juan de Toledo y Portugal, between 1667 and 1680,[53] it is easy to deduce Herrera's experience in channels, locks, floodgates, techniques for water diversion, and so on, without overlooking the use of these constructions and contraptions with defensive purposes, for the protection of cities and citadels. He was also likely trained in the pressure cooker of the famous Spanish Military Academy in Brussels run by Sebastián Fernández de Medrano (1646–1705), founded in 1675, although he does not appear among the names of this academy's known graduates.[54]

The use of hydraulic engineering in the service of the articulation of territory, logistics, economy, transport, and public purposes is linked to the Enlightenment mentality, not in vain. In the eighteenth century, there were many large navigable canal projects in Spain built in the second half of the seventeenth century, for example, the Canal de Castilla and the Canal Imperial de Aragón, inspired by the French canals of Midi or Languedoc.[55] The well-known ordinances of the Spanish corps of engineers of 1718 show the importance of this facet of the engineer's training. They state "that the rivers that could be made navigable, and places that could be put to use to open canals and ditches, be identified, discovering subterranean waters as well, which will not only ensure the increase in commerce and the greater benefit to the people by the ease of use and the very little expense with which they would transport fruits, materials, and goods from one province to another."[56]

It is likely that Herrera was familiar with the most recent works of hydrology, developed in Holland, especially for the systems for draining lands through ditches and windmills, navigable canals regulated via locks, moats to protect cities, and so forth, in large part a technology designed for and thought to serve military strategy, which required experience in the so-called maneuvers of water, consistent in adequately addressing water flows to fill or to drain trenches, redirect water through fluvial channels toward canals that flood lands to make them impassable.[57]

Among the Flemish and Dutch engineers whose theoretical work Herrera might have been familiar we have one of the greatest figures on the subject of hydraulic engineers, an expert in canals, locks, and windmills, the mathematician and engineer Simon Stevin (Bruges, 1548–1620).[58] In his abundant theoretical production, the first-known treatise about locks, *Nieuwe maniere van sterctebov door spilsluysen*, which appeared in Rotterdam in 1617, stands out.[59] The engineer Fernández de Medrano referred to it in complimentary terms: "It was this highly celebrated author from the principality of Orange, Mauricio of Nassau, who knew his usefulness and that there [Brussels] was without work, used it, taking advantage of his great science and ability, so much so that he was called par excellence, Doctor Stevin. This essay, a folio volume, deals with fortification, moats, and locks, to detain and level the waters."[60]

Regarding the defensive use of locks and the floodgates that close them, Stevin recognizes a triple utility in such gadgets: (1) to fill or to empty moats, canals, or rivers with the purpose of isolating places or bulwarks, (2) to avoid clogging the water channel, and (3) to permit the navigation of boats, adapting them even to the masts' heights.[61] We can see how the floodgates Herrera proposed followed the most elementary model illustrated in the Dutch treatise: they were composed of a vertical closing plank, they were operated by a wheel around which a rope was wound, all inserted into a type of wooden frame (figure 10.5).

In the case of the Dique, traversed by mast-less canoes and sampans, it was sufficient. This type of floodgate, according to the Flemish treatise writer, was advisable for the conduits to flood moats or for canals through which small-sized or low boats moved.[62] Following Stevin's ideas, Herrera likewise recognizes the defensive use of locks and their suitability to avoid accumulations of sandy materials at the bottom of canals and rivers, flooding of lands, and so forth. The other technical detail that the engineer cited to isolate the tub or lock and contain the surrounding terrain, is a type of pylons "in the form of squared stakes of such type joined and nailed into the earth that they do differ from a support," also seems to be learned from Stevin.[63] This waterproof and resistant closure system, composed of quadrangular woods, assembled by a means of a slot in which the tongue of the adjacent one fits, also relies on the solution provided by the Flemish mathematician to isolate the locks, forming a type of circle of sheet piling joining together (figure 10.6). He is considered the inventor of this engineering solution.[64]

Figure 10.5. Floodgate model for locks. Simon Stevin, *Nouvelle maniere de fortification par escluses*. Rotterdam, 1618. (From the collection of Francisco Javier Herrera García.)

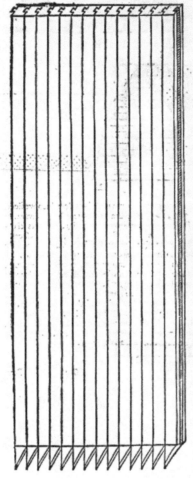

Figure 10. 6. Simon Stevin, *Nouvelle maniere de fortification par escluses* (Model of squared stakes for enclosure locks), Rotterdam, 1618. (From the collection of Francisco Javier Herrera García.)

In Italy in the previous century, similar solutions to dam and to regulate the waters, such as floodgates of a straight or angular enclosure that moved in a vertical or rotary movement around an axis, had been devised to allow for river navigation. This is demonstrated by the Milanese engineer Giovanni Francesco Sitoni (1532–1608) in his *Trattato delle virtù e proprietà delle acque* (1599)[65] and even better yet by the Paduan Vittorio Zonca (1568–1603) in his *Nuovo Theatro di machine* (1607), where he illustrates and explains the system adapted to an elliptical plant lock.[66] Later, in accordance with Stevin, the Dutch engineer Menno Van Coehoorn (Britsum, 1641–1704), relies on the locks as a suitable element to defend places and to regulate the moats' water levels.[67]

Greater technical quality is seen in the locks and floodgates created by eighteenth- century engineers, although we are not going to examine them because they were not chronologically within the period of Juan de Herrera, such as the well-known Bernard Forest de Bélidor (1698–1761) and the Spaniard Sánchez Taramas (1733–1789), translator of the treaties of the German John Müller (1699–1784),[68] but who may have been consulted by the following engineers who worked on Cartagena's Dique including Juan Jiménez Donoso (1776) and especially Antonio de Arévalo (1794–1798), who again proposed locks secured with pylons and their corresponding floodgates.[69]

There is no doubt about Juan de Herrera's mastery of the theoretical approaches about engineering in the Spanish Low Countries, Holland, and Italy from the sixteenth century. Now we can better understand the vast technological knowledge of military engineers and particularly Herrera. A good example of how he submitted to the solutions proposed by the engineer-mathematicians of northern Europe we have in his proposal to rebuild Cartagena's seawall open to the Caribbean, exposed continually to storms and waves. This walled exposure had been destroyed by strong winds in 1714. The project put forth by the engineer included a breakwater on the first line, semidetached from stone boxes by pylons connected with guaco vines, all this entering into the sea, then a walkable embankment, and the steep wall of ashlar and masonry adjoining the city limit.[70] The first defensive line, with a rocky breakwater, would not hinder the enemy's penetration for long, but it would serve to hold back the waves, as advocated by another great Dutch engineer, Samuel Marolois (1572–1627), in whose fortification treatise this resource is applied, *"fortifier une place situèe a bord de la mer, &y acommoder un havre"*[71] with his corresponding illustration, replicated by Herrera in his well-known project preserved in the AGI (figure 10.7 and figure 10.8).[72]

To conclude, we must recognize Juan de Herrera's scientific expertise and willingness to serve, which characterized military engineers in the eighteenth and nineteenth centuries. His efforts to improve the Canal del Dique highlight his experience in hydraulic engineering at the service of economic, political, and strategic interests and demonstrate his training in canalization and locks and his capacity for mobility, as well as interest in and the precise observation of the geography.

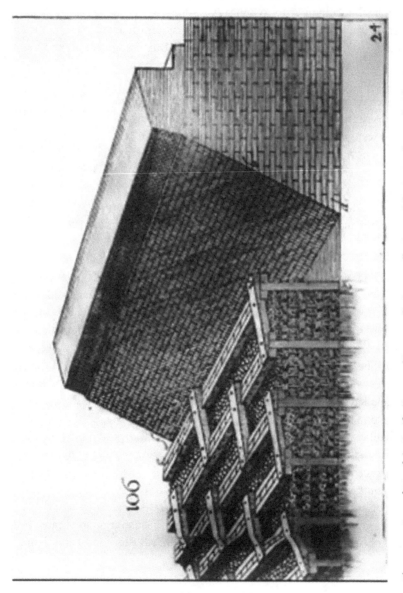

Figure 10.7. Samuel Marolois, *Fortification ou architecture militaire tant offensive que defensive*. Border sea fortification, Amsterdam, 1627. (From the collection of Francisco Javier Herrera García.)

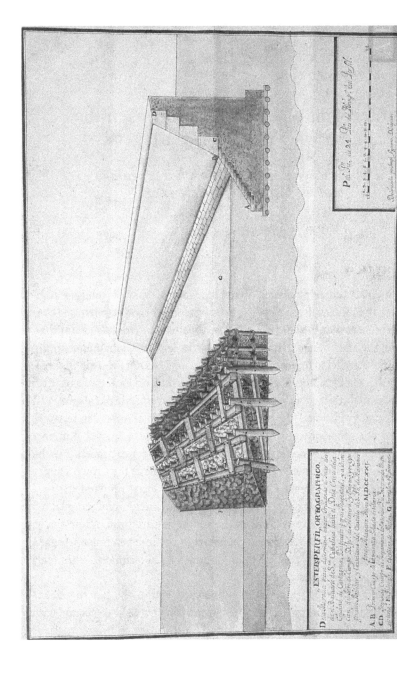

Figure 10.8. Border wall of Cartagena de Indias, 1721, by Herrera y Sotomayor and José Figueroa. (© Ministerio de Cultura y Deporte, Archivo General de Indias, MP-Panama, 124.)

11

Projects and Defensive Reforms at the End of the Viceregal Cartagena

The Military Engineer Manuel de Anguiano and the Martyrs of Independence

Manuel Gámez Casado

The principal studies published about the work of Spanish military engineers in the Viceroyalty of New Granada have sought to document the constructive processes that they developed in various places. This has meant that, on occasion, the enormous task undertaken by these professionals concerning other activities parallel to their constructive functions has not been highlighted. Along with this concern, the engineers clearly also took on local customs after being in continual contact with natives, completing an episode of cultural reciprocity that puts traditional ideals of the hispanicization of American territory in doubt. In this sense, it turns out to be telling that it was Spanish engineer Manuel de Anguiano who was at the forefront of independence processes in the Colombian city of Cartagena de Indias, forsaking his role as the Crown's envoy and demonstrating an intense involvement with the social needs of the people (figure 11.1).[1] Thus, this chapter documents Anguiano's engineering labors related to Spanish defensive systems in the southern Caribbean. Additionally, this chapter shows how this engineer took part in the independence struggle. Therefore, there remains a contradiction in how a royal technician ultimately could support popular uprisings.

In this chapter, a different facet is analyzed within the heterogeneous production of military engineers, who have been continuously associated with the design and construction of fortifications. In this case, a different lens is provided through which it can be seen how the engineers were integrated into the society of Cartagena de Indias, being participants in their concerns and in

Figure 11.1. Bust of the military engineer Manuel de Anguiano, ca. 1850, by Luis Felipe Jaspe Franco, Paseo de los mártires, Cartagena de Indias. (Photograph by Manuel Gámez Casado.)

the political debate that arose at the end of the eighteenth century. This chapter offers another vision of these military officers, addressing other historical problems distinct from those treated in the previous chapters in an attempt to expand our knowledge of American geopolitics.

The integration of Spanish military engineers in American society is a fundamental requirement to understanding the development of territorial policies. The Spanish Crown needed military engineers to paralyze the different subversions generated in different parts of the Caribbean, carrying out diplomacy and political control work together with other representatives of the viceregal authority. As a consequence, the engineers gained some experience in matters related to governance and geopolitical protection not only through the construction of fortifications but also through expeditions that enabled contacts with other powers such as France and England. Setting off from these contentions, the main function of the military engineers who passed through Cartagena during the colonial period was to outline an effective defensive structure that would protect the city from enemy attacks.[2] This caused continual and varied alterations in its fortifications since the city's founding, a succession of heterogeneous approaches being undertaken that sought to tackle an improvement, greater than the opponent's offensive plans. This was identified with the European powers who were trying to secure possessions in the southern half of the Caribbean, for example, the French and the English. The latter became the principal enemies of the Spanish Crown after the signing of the Third Pacte de Famille peace accord with France.[3] A test of this enmity was the English Vice Admiral Edward Vernon's attack on Cartagena de Indias in 1741, which led to the destruction of the city's main fortifications.[4] This bloody event also served as a catalyst for the development of a definitive project for the defense of Cartagena Bay, which would ensure the security of what was the most important commercial port in the region. In this manner, the most fertile period for Cartagena's military engineering began, supported by the arrival of many professionals with extensive training, vast experience, and a broad knowledge of military arts.

Antonio de Arévalo's death coincided with the end of the eighteenth century, a century during which different projects have been well documented and studied. However, the situation changes for the years spanning 1800 and November 1811, the date on which Cartagena de Indias was liberated from the Spanish Crown, as there are no important historiographical contributions in that instance. Of course, new information about the diplomatic and strategic processes developed in the first decade of the nineteenth century has been provided. These include, for example, unpublished papers that demonstrate how the engineer Manuel de Anguiano, Arévalo's successor, continued with his ideal of perfecting the defensive enclosure of the place to prevent possible attacks. Additionally, his engineering labors were related with the new ideas developed by the pro-independence institutions, a result of the union created from the coexistence between two cultures within the period's unique global contexts. Anguiano's understanding and acceptance of local proposals led him to occupy a momentous role in the independence struggle. Precisely this circumstance leads to his execution on the order of the Spanish Consejo de Guerra (War Council) in 1816, passing into history as one of the nine martyrs of Cartagena de Indias.[5]

A Late Eighteenth-Century Military Engineer in Cartagena de Indias

Anguiano occupied the post of *ingeniero director* of Cartagena's fortifications after the death of his teacher Antonio de Arévalo. Anguiano was born in Oran, a city in which one of the main academies for the training of Spanish military engineers had existed since 1732.[6] There, his father, Sebastián de Anguiano, spent his career in the artillery corps until ultimately being promoted to captain, being moved along with his son and his wife, Francisca Ruiz y Díaz, to Málaga, a city in which the young Manuel spent part of his life.[7] Moreover, the locating of his transit license to the Indies allows us to know that his move was approved by José de Gálvez, secretary of the Despacho Universal de Indias, in Aranjuez on May 7, 1787, as an *ingeniero extraordinario*, a rank he occupied for nine years. This voyage to America started in Cádiz on August 11, 1787, as he boarded the frigate *Vizcaína* along with his forty-four-year-old servant Salvador Flores, a native of Santiago de Compostela.[8] He started a trip that altered his personal and professional development, because on the western side of the Atlantic he fulfilled the ideological and constructive concerns that he had demonstrated in his early writings.

Immediately, the engineer joined in on the work of renovating Cartagena's ramparts and fortifications, which allowed him to advance quickly through the professional ladder of the Spanish engineer corps. Thus, on April 3, 1797, he was promoted to the rank of *ingeniero en segundo*, which he held until Arévalo's death three years later—a moment in which the definitive administration of the defensive works passed to him owing to his merits. To complete a defensive system suitable for the effective security of the port and the bay, he wrote a status report of the different edifices that composed Cartagena's urban space. Thus, in the plan now published, he included all the city's buildings, differentiating them by grouping, for example, military and naval, including convents and hospitals, and thereby being able to acknowledge the city's infrastructural needs (figure 11.2).[9] This document, of course, makes it possible for historians to understand the location of buildings that have been subsequently destroyed or renovated. However, the primary value of this plan rests in the defensive role that Anguiano proposed for certain civil buildings, advising that convents, hospitals, or warehouses be converted into barracks, arsenals, or bulwarks. Thus, his intention was to prepare the city's defense beyond the construction of buildings assigned to this end, demonstrating a broad knowledge in matters relating to the adaptation of urban space and of public architecture to the defensive needs of a place.

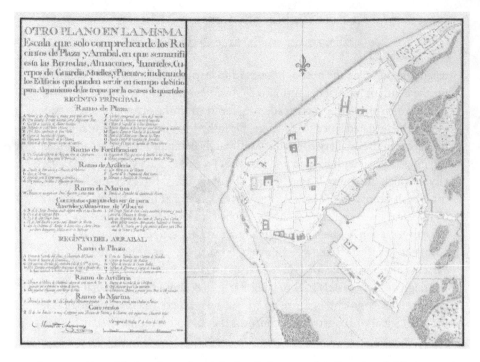

Figure 11.2. Manuel de Anguiano, *Plano de la plaza de Cartagena de Indias y el arrabal de Getsemaní* (Plan of the place of Cartagena de Indias and the outskirts of Getsemaní), January 1, 1805). (Servicio Geográfico del Ejército, Ministerio de Defensa, JT.7-C.3-158. CC BY-4.0.)

With the same aim, the engineer suggested the need to improve the defensive system of the territory between that place and Darien, the main center of contact between natives and the English as well as the traditional native battlefield against the Spanish Crown, in various audiences held throughout the summer of 1805 with Anastasio Cejudo, governor and commanding general of Cartagena.[10] The only bastions that protected the Spaniards who transported supplies between these settlements were composed of the squadron of mounted dragoons from El Corozal and the two small batteries located to the leeward side in Tolú, at the midpoint of the coastline.[11] Those locations needed to be reinforced to ensure their capture, and the consequent lack of provisions in Cartagena was exceedingly difficult. Therefore, among the first measures Anguiano undertook was the protection of a few provisional batteries both on the beach of Chamba and on La Popa Mountain, thus reinforcing the fortified grid of the province and the access to the location. From his proposal, it is deduced that Anguiano's initial plan did not include constructing large defensive buildings because those built years before were considered sufficient. The engineer suggested projects of palisades and areas of reinforcement that would cooperate with the city's large fortifications in the tasks of protection, because he wanted a degree of security that such an important port required. To achieve these objectives, it is clear that the engineer carried out a series of expeditions through the area, expeditions in which he made contact with the local tribes, became concerned with their issues, and assumed certain responsibilities on their behalf.

The initial suggestions presented by Anguiano were sent to the then viceroy of New Granada, Antonio José Amar y Borbón, who studied them as did the officers of the artillery commands, who eagerly expressed their needs. The viceroy was conscious that after the signing of the Peace of Amiens in 1802, an accord that had been reached between the United Kingdom and France, the need for developing defensive works and in covering for the lack of supplies had been greatly reduced, now that there were some years of certain peace between the principal European powers in the Caribbean theater. Nevertheless, Amar y Borbón approved provisions for the royal treasury to make the necessary funds available to fulfill the military engineer's proposals, even though the extraordinary Junta de Guerra (War Board) had not yet definitely accepted or approved the recommended changes. Ultimately, this body decided to approve the engineer's request to increase the number of fixed-regiment infantry troops in the Tolú, Cispatá, and Barranquilla batteries protecting the ports that surrounded Cartagena and permitted the passage of ships that would cover these routes. But with this measure, the board did not approve requests for increasing the number of troops at El Corozal, for seeking an improvement in the defenses of the Caribbean coastline or for coordinating the region's commercial network. As such, the board permitted the free transit of ships through Caribbean waters, which introduced a new measure in the fight against contraband, one that would increase the circulation of new ideas springing up about the relationships established between the Crown and the colonial populace.[12]

However, Anguiano took part in the junta to explain his building proposals for the provisional batteries on La Popa and on the beach at Chamba. In his speech, he described the fortification model that he would use for these enclaves, seeking nonpermanent reinforcements for the large stone forts and ruling out new stone buildings in favor of those already in existence, maintaining some remains of the batteries on the mountain of La Popa that had been built during the final years of the eighteenth century (figure 11.3).[13]

Nonetheless, Manuel de Anguiano's main contribution to Cartagena's defensive architecture comes from the meeting held on September 17, 1805.[14] At this meeting, the engineer presented his plan for the general defense, based in

Figure 11.3. Remnants of the batteries on La Popa Mountain, Cartagena de Indias. (Photograph by Manuel Gámez Casado.)

part on the modifications that Brigadier Agustín Crame had recommended on Antonio de Arévalo's project in the previous decades.[15] Based on this approach and in relation to the square, Anguiano suggested raising the northern rampart from the Santa Cruz bulwark to the Santa Clara bulwark, given that it was not at the ideal height. This section had been rebuilt by Arévalo after being almost entirely destroyed following a storm. He advised further incorporating a breakwater that would limit the impact of the sea against the curtains.[16] Apparently, this project had not allowed the walls to rise to an effective level, something that Anguiano proposed. Likewise, from the Santa Cruz bulwark, the engineer hoped to build a wall to the immediate crossbow platform, because until then there was a small, weak, and hardly resistant wall. However, both proposals were rejected by the junta owing to the excessive time and cost that such modifications entailed. Instead, it was ordered that the area would be defended through a temporary fascine parapet and the cutting of the beach of Santa Catalina through the installation of a piloting and stockade breakwater in the manner of a pincer that would run toward the Santo Domingo bulwark. This created a new obstacle to repel a possible attack near the marina rampart. Although certainly the nature of the work carried out would be short-lived, it did address a problem already detected by Crame and now solved by Anguiano (figure 11.4).

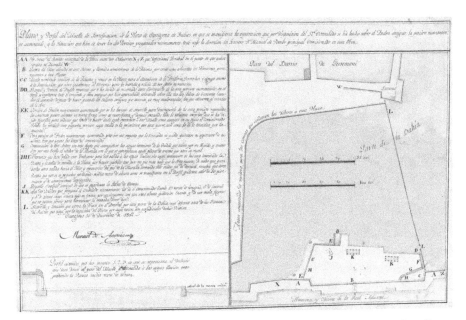

Figure 11.4. Manuel de Anguiano, Plano y perfil del muelle de la plaza de Cartagena de Indias (Plan and profile of the dock of the place of Cartagena de Indias), December 16, 1802. (Servicio Geográfico del Ejército, Ministerio de Defensa, JT.7-C.2_85. CC BY-4.0.)

Another proposal involved the building of a large gunpowder store and three other medium-sized ones that would supplement the already finished vaults of Santa Clara. This building housed both the militia and military supplies, greatly increasing the danger should it be destroyed. This possibility prompted Anguiano to propose building some new storehouses that would improve the stockpiling of military supplies. This project, which had already been outlined by Crame and approved by a royal decree of February 12, 1786, now authorized construction of one of these with a capacity of two thousand *quintales*. The Junta de Guerra approved it. Likewise, Anguiano planned for two shacks for the gatehouse in Bocagrande and another in Palo Alto's hornwork, which would complete the military renovations of the place. Nevertheless, the fragility of the materials used for such constructions did not make their preservation possible, and the neglect suffered by these buildings over decades led to their destruction.

Beyond the modifications proposed by Anguiano, the most ambitious project of those he presented was the renovation of the legendary castle of San Felipe de Barajas (figure 11.5). The engineer tackled the remodeling of the most important fort of those protecting the city and the outskirts of Getsemaní, and owing to his efficient articulation, British Vice Admiral Edward Vernon could

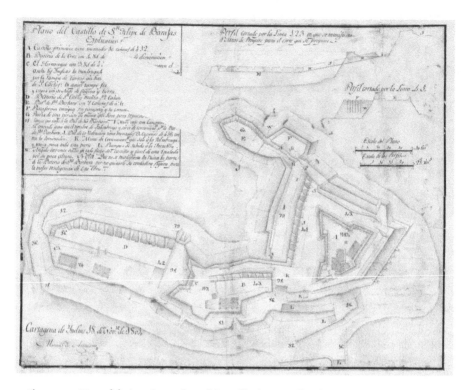

Figure 11.5. Manuel de Anguiano, Plano del castillo de San Felipe de Barajas de Cartagena de Indias con la batería de Santa Bárbara descubierta (Plan of the castle of San Felipe de Barajas of Cartagena de Indias with the Santa Bárbara battery uncovered), November 18, 1801. (Servicio Geográfico del Ejército, Ministerio de Defensa, JT.7-C.2_84. CC BY-4.0.)

not conquer or destroy the place. The San Lázaro fort, which resulted from a series of modifications and additions to the original early seventeenth-century construction, produced a building enormously irregular in its planimetric disposition; after English troops destroyed it in 1741, Antonio de Arévalo had it restructured, and its renovation reflected the ideas of many engineers who passed through Cartagena at the time. The result resembles a palimpsest, the apparent disorder of which derived from the superposition of batteries and hornworks. Regardless, it was not in line with the disciplined engineering approaches carried out by academically trained soldiers. This accumulation of spaces displeased Manuel de Anguiano, as he offered in a November 1803 letter describing the building.[17] In it, the engineer stated that on examining the structure, he only found a series of batteries adapted to the mountain, without any type of coherent system that would make the defense of the region possible. Moreover, he alluded to a general plan Agustín Crame developed to support his own theory; in article 32 he warned of the lack of efficiency of an edifice that is disorganized and without a coherent structural arrangement. But among all the elements added in San Felipe de Barajas, Anguiano acknowledged Santa Bárbara battery to be the least useful, because of its disposition to the east and distance from the plaza, which made it useless for protecting both Cartagena's port and its main enclaves. The improper site of the battery was not its only weakness. It had also been poorly constructed with reused materials from the old edifice the English had destroyed. In this sense, although the defensive plan for the castle was based on firing from different overlapping bodies, according to the plan of Arévalo himself, the Santa Bárbara battery wound up being the smallest in size and the least important. Arévalo based his negative assessment on its location, because having been built on the building's main front, to the northeast, it needed the presence and size of guns appropriate for a battery located on the front line of battle. The absence of such characteristics in this stretch of the fortification, along with a lack of strength in this area of the mountain, were sufficient arguments for Manuel de Anguiano to argue that the Santa Bárbara battery be destroyed.

The engineer presented a project to demolish this section of the castle of San Felipe de Barajas before the Junta de Fortificación y Defensa de Indias (Board of Fortification and Defense of the Indies), accompanied by a plan for the whole town drawn up in November 1801 and that now is published for the first time (see figure 11.5).[18] In it, he outlined the general plat of the fortification, differentiating each of the batteries, ramps, and communication elements that composed it. In this manner, starting from the original castle as the central axis of the mountain, he set out to the west and firstly the de la Cruz battery, then the hornwork, wherein the English intended to enter in April 1741, and in the westernmost, the San Carlos battery. This collective formed the space of greatest defensive importance because from here the security of the historic city must have been dealt with. This had already been demonstrated during Vernon's attack, so Anguiano insisted on reinforcing this region before any other. Therefore, his intention was to change the front of attack from the one that had historically been used to the one that faced the outskirts of Getsemaní and the square. While it is true that the previous additions had been arranged along this outline, Anguiano proposed to focus the constructive efforts on embellishing these batteries and freeing the opposite side from visual and building obstacles. Similarly, in the plan, he pointed out the underground communications passages, the Redención battery, and the faussebraye that joins this latter with the reviled Santa Bárbara battery. This space, despite the Spanish engineer's intentions, is found in a perfect state to make the best understanding of the fort as a whole possible. Thus, starting with this idea, Anguiano incorporated an addition in the plan that would allow for the covering of the region to destroy, enabling him to depict a general view of the fort of San Felipe de Barajas after the cutting off of the Santa Bárbara battery (figure 11.6). All of this served to make the Junta accept the engineer's proposal. However, the court prevented the demolition of this part of the castle, although they could not halt the abandonment of the battery given Anguiano's disinterest, according to his opinion, about that section of the fortification.

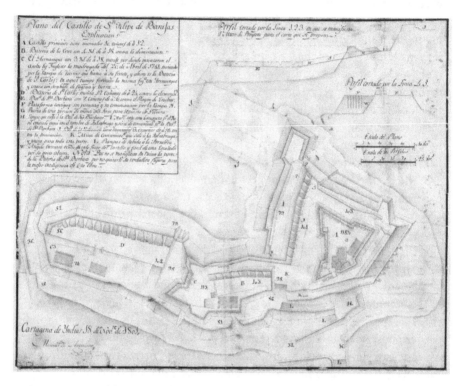

Figure 11.6. Manuel de Anguiano, *Plano del castillo de San Felipe de Barajas de Cartagena de Indias con la batería de Santa Bárbara cubierta* (Plan of the castle of San Felipe de Barajas of Cartagena de Indias with the Santa Bárbara battery covered), November 18, 1801. (Servicio Geográfico del Ejército, Ministerio de Defensa, JT.7-C.2_84. CC BY-4.0.)

In addition to Anguiano's interest in knocking down the Santa Bárbara battery, he is eloquent in the criticism of the whole of San Felipe in his *Relación sobre la situación y utilidad de la Plaza de Cartagena de Indias* (*Relation about the situation and the utility of the Place of Cartagena de Indias*), a manuscript dated in 1805 in which the engineer analyzed the defensive possibilities of Cartagena's fortifications. In addition to what has already been discussed, the engineer warned of the precarious state in which the esplanades that connect the batteries were found, basic elements for the castle's functioning to be used for the movement of artillery to different points on the mountain. With the proposal for the aforementioned battery's demolition rejected, for Anguiano all that needed to be done was to renovate the connecting esplanades with earthenware brought from Spain, which, according to the aforementioned engineer, would best resist the erosion created by the iron gun carriage wheels. The engineer merely had to resign himself to the fact that the court would not accept his main proposal, which would have altered not only the castle's profile that we see today, but also the defensive strategy of Cartagena's outskirts (figure 11.7).

Figure 11.7. Santa Bárbara battery of the castle of San Felipe de Barajas, ca. 1760, Cartagena de Indias. (Photograph by Manuel Gámez Casado.)

Anguiano and the Independence Movement

After analyzing the engineer's building proposals, it becomes apparent that one of the principal chapters of his life story centers on the role played in the complex political, social, and cultural processes taking place in Cartagena de Indias during the early years of the nineteenth century. First, the Crown paid little attention to the engineer's plans, because the majority of his projects were not accomplished or even approved by that institution. From the personal point of view, such a circumstance would create a certain unease in Anguiano, who was aware of the excellent attention that the court had provided to colleagues like Arévalo. Even so, the value that the boards and the governors placed on his proposals was different, because these officers always showed absolute support for the engineer's ideas, understanding that these ideas sought to perfect the security of the city, its economy, and its daily life. By this, we do not mean to establish an affinity with local institutions, but to demonstrate how the court could not take on the necessary expenses for such purposes, since the important crisis produced on the peninsula by the independence war had created other budgetary priorities distinct from those presented here. Moreover, the first independence movements under the auspices of the founding of the *toledista* and the *piñerista* parties were beginning to be monitored. The latter initiated a movement that brought about a declaration on behalf of the Junta Suprema de Gobierno de la Independencia de Cartagena de Indias (Supreme Governing Board of the Independence of Cartagena de Indias), arguing for the absolute neglect on the part of the king and based on a revolutionary ideology that protected the people's liberty.[19] It is well known how the response on behalf of Ferdinand VII consisted of sending troops to the cities declared in rebellion, a battalion commanded by the naval officer Pablo Morillo landing on Cartagena's coasts, which required 106 days of siege by sea and land to carry out the city's recapture. His taking of the city was absolute, even though the townspeople entrenched themselves in the fortifications constructed by the Spaniards. In this context, the engineer Manuel de Anguiano declared himself a partisan of Cartagena's independence and resigned from his post when the creole governing assembly was constituted, as he had managed to ingratiate himself among its inhabitants by developing the most recent defensive projects analyzed herein. This circumstance meant that he was included in the list requested by the viceroyalty's *asesor general* and *auditor de guerra* (general assessor and military auditor), Anselmo Bierna y Mazo, in which the names of those guilty of supporting the revolutionaries had been collected, made up of the most noteworthy local leaders and those worthy of being executed in the Plaza de la Merced.[20]

Thus, Anguiano and the other eight men responsible for the pro-independence uprising, after undergoing interrogations in which the authorities aimed to obtain information about the goals of the revolutionary group, were shot by Spanish troops in 1816, an event known in the region around Cartagena as the execution of the nine martyrs.[21] Of all of them, Manuel de Anguiano was accused of having supported Cartagena's independence in clear disloyalty to the king, of having instructed the local cadets to carry out revolutionary actions, and of having published various instructions and slogans in support of the cause against the orders promulgated by his superiors.[22] Of little use were the arguments he presented in his defense, in which he alleged that his activity had occurred by mandate of the Cartagena government, which he considered he had to obey, because he was convicted for having praised the province's revolutionaries against the king. He was shot in the back in February 1816.

The last of the many engineers who had made Cartagena the unconquered city described in stories, engravings, and novels was executed by his own countrymen. Doubtlessly, this was the first step in achieving the goal desired by those liberators, the surrender of the Spanish government led by Governor Gabriel de Torres, who in October 1821 relinquished authority to the Colombian army.[23] With this, the close connection achieved by the military engineers with American society is demonstrated, serving as a paradigm for rejecting the interpretations that excluded them from the native populations. This example must be brought together with those already collected in the historiography that emphasizes the need for integration of the militia troops with the indigenous populations through the processes of hispanicization. Contact was created owing to the various diplomatic missions carried out by engineers within their varied duties in the American viceroyalties, expressing themselves as not only being occupied in converting those territories into the most fortified of those that Spain ruled but also in establishing some social and cultural foundations that still remain today.

12

The Fort of San Carlos de Perote

The Historical Context of Its Construction

Mónica Cejudo Collera and Germán Segura García

The conquest and defense of America were, during the initial centuries of the Spanish presence in those territories, a labor more of improvisation and private imitation than of an example of a perfectly structured plan. The Spanish monarchy had neither the ability nor the opportunity of sustaining such exorbitant efforts, even if a medal was struck in the time of Philip II with the engraving that read *Non sufficit orbis* (the world is not enough). Time and space, on a global scale, were conditions that weighed heavily on any undertaking. Only the "indomitable perseverance" and "the patient virtue of the Spanish," in the words of Sir Walter Raleigh, allowed Spain to settle most of the Americas and defend them against enemy incursions.[1] Spain's advantage consisted in being able to direct its incursions at any point in the vast American expanse; the disadvantage lay in being exposed to tropical diseases and lacking sufficient naval anchorages, without which a fleet did not have many opportunities to stay long on the continent's coasts. The attacks against the Spanish possessions, a result also of uncoordinated efforts, could be comfortably repelled by the illustrious garrisons that defended the fortifications of the original defensive system erected during the times of Philip II. But throughout the seventeenth century, the rival powers were becoming bolder at the same time that Spain lost its grip, finding itself engulfed in endless European conflicts. As early as 1697, Cartagena de Indias witnessed an assault from the French squadron under the command of Baron de Pointis, demonstrating the fragility of the Spanish defensive framework and the limitations of a sparse and scattered naval power.

At the beginning of the eighteenth century, Spain found itself immersed in a long war of succession in which the various powers supported a claimant to the Spanish throne with an eye on, among other things, the attainment of commercial privileges in the Americas. By then, even the traditional West Indies Fleet or Spanish treasure fleet, which had been held in the Caribbean for more than two years, had to be escorted to the Iberian Peninsula by a French squadron in 1702. It would not be until after the conflict's conclusion that the Spanish navy could be rebuilt by the new monarch, Philip V of the House of Bourbon, who also left his mark on American politics.

Mexican territory played an important role in the configuration of the Spanish empire's defenses. Initially, ports such as Veracruz, Campeche, and Acapulco, and later inland structures such as Bacalar or Perote, created one of the most significant military networks in eighteenth-century America. To define how this project was developed, this chapter will reconstruct the building process of the fort of San Carlos de Perote, from the first geostrategic challenges at the beginning of the century to the final works of the second half. To show how these structures were crucial for later Mexican history, a reconstruction of its role during the nineteenth and twentieth centuries is narrated, including its other uses and recent restorations.

The Eighteenth-Century American Context

The new dynasty put its effort into the preservation of acquired territory and into the reform of an outdated and corrupt administration. Thus, the domains were subdivided into four viceroyalties—New Spain, Peru, New Grenada, and Río de la Plata—and four captaincies general—Santo Domingo, Guatemala, Venezuela, and Chile—introducing intendancies to oversee local administration and strengthening the *visitas* (inspections) and the *juicios de residencia* (trials of residence) of the officials designated by the monarch. On defensive matters, the fixed battalions of Havana, Cartagena, Puerto Rico, and Panama were created between 1719 and 1739. Later these were complemented by those of Veracruz, Callao, Valdivia, and Yucatán.

But the British, regularly complaining about Spain's noncompliance with the agreements reached at Utrecht (1713) by which the United Kingdom had obtained the thirty-year *asiento* monopoly of Africans and an annual permit ship, did not restrain the drums of war from sounding. The War of Jenkins' Ear (1739–48) was the first war in which the two European powers engaged for strictly American motives. Once again, the enemy squadrons turned toward the American coast to attack the Spanish posts in La Guaira, Chagres, Portobelo, and, thrice, Cartagena de Indias.[2] The failure of the final British expedition against this last place, defended by Viceroy Sebastián de Eslava and a tenacious Blas de Lezo, might have fed unwarranted faith in the favorability of the Spanish defensive system, though this was just a mirage, as would soon be evident. Nevertheless, for the moment, the conflict finished at the negotiating table: Spain agreed not to inspect British ships on the high seas and the United Kingdom renounced the *asiento* of Africans and the permit ship (1750). British contraband was already carried out on such a scale that there was no need to retain such perks.

Spanish-British animosity came back to the fore as part of the Seven Years' War (1756–63), when Spain took the side of France and co-signed with it a third Family Compact or *Pacte de Famille* (1761) to counteract the British abuses in its indiscriminate commercial raiding. The reaction of the government in London was energetic, launching its squadrons against Havana and Manila, which could not hold out against the superiority of the expeditionary forces (1762). The most memorable of these episodes was the loyalty demonstrated by the Cuban and Filipino people, who mobilized their militias to oppose the invaders and impede their progress beyond the places they conquered. But, as Ricardo Wall, Spanish secretary of state, confessed to the president of the Neapolitan regency council, "in a miserable war, it is impossible to create an advantageous peace."[3] The peace terms, in a conflict in which Spain entered late and poorly prepared, led to the loss of Florida, which was compensated by France with the cession of part of Louisiana, while the British returned Havana and Manila.

Facing the failure experienced in the defense of its main enclaves in the Caribbean and in Asia, Charles III's government seriously had to rethink its overseas defensive policy. The starting premises were not very favorable. First, there was an almost-chronic shortage of funds to support troops, and it was increasingly difficult to find the necessary replacements to fill out the units' personnel. The pay was low, and arrived late, to which it might be added that overseas service often entailed a final farewell to one's native land. Indeed, troops sometimes considered a posting in the Americas a death sentence. As such, defense had to rely on the native population, which had given a good account of itself in recent events. On the other hand, Spanish ministers had taken into account that the main threat to confront came from a foreign enemy and that, accordingly, it was necessary to control the coasts (to avoid new amphibious assaults) and the land border (for the special case of the Apachería). No internal threat worthy of review was contemplated, such was the Spaniards' faith in the loyalty of the Americans. Finally, the defensive system was conceived to preserve the monarchy's domains on the continent, not to embark on new conquests. Given that great battles could not be expected, all of the effort was focused on garrisoning the fortified locations appropriately and resisting the enemy's assaults until a drawn-out defense or a relief army, aided by the weather, secured victory.

Ultimately, the system was articulated around three foundations, the triad formed by the navy, a truly American army, and fortifications.[4] With regard to the first foundation, after the War of the Spanish Succession, Secretary of State José Patiño already had begun to provide Spain with a powerful fleet and to create the bases necessary for its maintenance. Despite setbacks and having to compete with the army's budget, the Spanish navy was favored in the middle of the century by the dedication of the Marquis of Ensenada. Even in the 1770s, Spain invested more than 20 percent (almost 30 percent in 1785) of the monarchy's total expenses in the navy, making it the second most powerful, after that of the United Kingdom, in the number of ships of the line.[5]

In relation to the creation of a permanent army in the Americas, it was decided to send regular troops from the Iberian Peninsula to form companies with a force of around one hundred men on staff. Much later, as the number of infantry companies grew, these were conformed into battalions and ultimately fixed regiments. As the personnel was increased, the units were composed more and more by American staff, especially *criollos* (creoles), and even led to the creation of *mestizo* (mixed-race), *pardo* (Maroon), and *moreno* (dark-skinned) companies that came to complete the personnel of some armies. Rarely did the regiments serve in full, as the forces were scattered in detachments, presidios, and posts far and wide throughout the territory. In addition to these endowed troops, America kept relying on, at specific times, expeditionary forces and on the always considerable aid of the regulated and local militias. In the territory of New Spain, Juan de Villalba Angulo Ponce de León was the one responsible for reorganizing the viceroyalty's forces starting in 1764,[6] slightly before the arrival of José de Gálvez as royal *visitador* (inspector) to these lands.

Finally, regarding the third foundation, defense and improvement plans for the American fortifications were developed, especially the II Plan de Defensa del Caribe (Second Plan for the Defense of the Caribbean) (1765), inspired by Alejandro O'Reilly, and the Plan Continental de Defensa (Continental Plan of Defense) (1779), created by the engineer Agustín Crame.[7] But also innumerable defensive projects of a local scale were brought about, as was the case for the plan of defense of Veracruz (1775),[8] signed by Juan Fernando de Palacio, Manuel de Santistevan, Agustín Crame, Nicolás Devis, and Segismundo Font. Based on the defensive plan of Havana (1771),[9] the Veracruz plan likewise starts from a hypothesis of an amphibious invasion, organizing the defense of the plaza and of the Castle of San Juan de Ulúa with the idea in mind of winning time until the weather conditions and illnesses that would doubtlessly devastate the enemy camp and hinder the attackers' efforts while Spanish forces awaited arrival of forces to relieve the place.[10] The strategy was prudent and perhaps the only one viable, given the immensity of space to defend and the Spanish monarchy's true capabilities. As the best minds were aware: "All states have their natural limits; and by this very true principle not having been recognized in Spain; the excessive desire to expand them blinded the imaginations; in order not to notice that it was such an extension that was the true cause of incessant weakening."[11]

The most famous route in the Viceroyalty of New Spain was the Camino Real (Royal Road) that connected the port of Veracruz with Mexico City. Across it, important commercial transactions between the coast of the Mexican heartland and the high plateau and even over the entire Atlantic-Pacific axis were carried out. Noteworthy was the Manila galleon, which unloaded Asian merchandise in Acapulco to be transported thereafter overland to Veracruz and afterward to the Iberian Peninsula. The transit between Veracruz and Mexico City could be undertaken over the so-called Veracruz Road, which left the high plateau north of Cofre de Perote, and the so-called New Road, which ran south of Pico de Orizaba. Both routes favored, from the economic point of view, different urban nuclei: the first, the group from Xalapa (aided in the eighteenth century by the viceregal government and Veracruz merchants), and the second, the group from Orizaba-Córdoba (favored by the merchants from Mexico City).[12] The conflict of local and viceregal elites to obtain hegemony over the transit route of merchandise was skewed significantly toward the Xalapa group when the decision was made to build the Fort of San Carlos de Perote on the first of these routes.

The Project of San Carlos de Perote

The imminent outbreak of war against the British in 1761 had sown fear in the Spanish government at a possible landing in Veracruz. The Marquis of Cruillas, by then viceroy of New Spain, ordered the adaptation of Veracruz's plaza and of the Castle of San Juan de Ulúa to face the possible threats on the Atlantic front, in addition to providing for the installation of provision storehouses in Perote, Xalapa, and Orizaba. With the conflict ended in 1765, various councils of war held in Mexico City decided on, among other projects, the construction of a fort in the interior as support for the important port of Veracruz. The only condition specified from the Spanish court in Madrid was that the place chosen had to be at least three regular troop transits from Veracruz (about 150 km) and on the plain where the Camino Real passed en route to the capital. It was the Marquis de Croix, Cruillas's replacement, who first pointed out San Miguel de Perote as a possible location in October 1766, highlighting the favorability of the climate for building storehouses for provisions and gunpowder.[13]

As he later noted, "I have always felt Pueblo de Perote to be the most appropriate place by being the most supplied for giving all the aid in provisions, arms, troops, and tools, dry and cold weather, very convenient for the preservation of the edibles of maize, flour, and other vegetables, and by its surroundings being a country of abundance, and finally the central point to go from there opportunely to all the paths and isolated crossroads that come from Veracruz and the coast."[14]

In August 1768, authorization was obtained from the Count of Aranda, president of the Council of Castile, and the designs were entrusted to the engineer Manuel de Santistevan, who presented a first plan at the beginning of 1769. It was a square-shaped fort of 120 *varas* (about 100 m) on the exterior side, with four bulwarks, a moat, and a covered road. But Aranda thought that the fort was very small, that its arrangement did not ensure the overlap of fire of the more than twenty guns that could be mounted on its bulwarks, and that it did not have sufficient storage capacity, although he left it to Viceroy Croix to decide on the most appropriate solutions.[15] In April 1770, Santistevan presented a second plan with a bastioned fortification, of four sides with bulwarks on the angles and with a front of 280 *varas* (about 235 m). Two months later, under Santistevan's supervision, the building works of the Fort of Perote began, which were effectively finished in 1775 and ultimately finished in 1777, by which point Antonio María Bucareli was viceroy. Meanwhile, the third floor proposed for the buildings allocated for troop lodging was eliminated, and it was decided to vault all the curtains to increase storage capacity. The fort was christened as San Carlos, in honor of the then-reigning monarch in Spain, Charles III from the House of Bourbon.

Years later, in 1780, Viceroy Martín Mayorga submitted a report to José de Gálvez, minister of the Indies, complaining of the poor quality and the unfortunate location of the Fort of San Carlos de Perote. Particularly, the foundations were considered rather defective, leaks in the buildings and infiltrations of water quickly being detected, which began also to damage the bulwarks and curtains. However, by being located on low ground, the fort was dominated by several *padrastros* (elevated sections of earth around fortifications that could be employed by enemies) on the town side, although this did not prevent him from considering it a convenient work for assigning it for general storage, with supplies of food, weapons, and gunpowder and personnel consisting of two infantry companies for its safekeeping. Still, at the end of the eighteenth century, successive viceroys thought that the fortification had so many technical defects that its defensive purpose was minimal, so it continued to be used as a storehouse and as a barracks for troops until the end of the colonial period.

San Carlos de Perote in the Nineteenth and Twentieth Centuries

Considered more of a storehouse than a fortification, properly speaking, the Fort of San Carlos de Perote had a number of roles over the course of its history. A royalist bastion during Mexican independence, within its walls were some noteworthy Mexican patriots until, after undergoing an eight-month siege, it fell into the hands of the Army of the Three Guarantees at the end of 1821. After the ephemeral Mexican Empire of Agustín de Iturbide, the provisional government set up an early officers' military academy (the Heroico Colegio Militar) there, where it remained from 1823 until 1828 (figure 12.1, figure 12.2, and figure 12.3). Afterward, it once again functioned as a prison, wherein the Texas rebels who sought the independence of that territory from the Mexican government were imprisoned. Guadalupe Victoria, the first president of the Estados Unidos Mexicanos, died there in 1843, years after he left power. General Antonio López de Santa Anna was imprisoned there before going off to exile for the first time in 1845. Two years later, San Carlos was occupied by US troops during the Mexican-American War (1846–48).

Figure 12.1. View of San Carlos de Perote with the municipality of Perote in the background, taken from a drone, 2017. (Photograph by Alejandro Marambio.)

Figure 12.2. Orthomosaic of San Carlos de Perote made with a drone, 2017. (Photograph by Alejandro Marambio.)

Figure 12.3. Main gate of San Carlos de Perote, 2017. (Photograph by Mónica Cejudo.)

In the 1850s, San Carlos de Perote was the scene of the bloody fight between liberals and conservatives until power rested definitively in the hands of the former in 1861, during the government of Benito Juárez. It would be snatched again from the Mexicans following the French intervention to impose Maximilian of Habsburg as emperor of the Second Mexican Empire (1863–67). The fort's governor received the order to blow up the fort so it did not fall into foreign hands, but the powerful explosion only altered one of the bulwarks and cut up some wall curtains (see figure 12.1 and figure 12.2). After the conflict, even as its installations held some noteworthy imperial collaborators, the troops assigned to San Carlos mutinied in light of the reelection of Benito Juárez, and federal forces had to intervene to put down the rebels, whose leader was shot to death in the fort.

Figure 12.4. Parade ground and main building of San Carlos de Perote, 2017. (Photograph by Mónica Cejudo.)

At the start of the twentieth century, the long-standing president Porfirio Díaz converted Perote into a military prison, a use that continued until the outbreak of the Mexican Revolution in 1910. Afterward, it was converted into a military instruction camp for the Mexican forces and was somewhat in disuse until it was renovated in 1939 to take in some 400 republican refugees (although some were settled in the town of Perote) who had to flee Spain as a result of the Spanish Civil War. During World War II, in which Mexico joined with the Allied powers, San Carlos carried out the functions of an internment camp, nearly five hundred German, Italian, and Japanese prisoners of war being confined in the fort, the majority of whom were crewmen on enemy ships, but also civilians imprisoned on suspicion of supporting the Axis forces. After the war's end, in 1949 the government established a Central State Prison, later called the Centro Estatal de Readaptación Social del Estado de Veracruz (State Center of Social Re-adaptation of Veracruz State) in San Carlos, essentially a prison for common criminals sentenced to prison terms. It continued in this role until its closure as a penitentiary and its transfer to the Perote *ayunamiento* (municipal government) on June 20, 2007 (figure 12.4 and figure 12.5).

Figure 12.5. View of a curtain with casemates, San Carlos de Perote, 2017. (Photograph by Mónica Cejudo.)

Since then, a series of rehabilitation, recovery, and improvement works have been carried out in the fortress, although as of yet the edifice's new fate has not been defined other than a few adaptations to accommodate cultural visits to the historic site.

13

The Three Defensive Lines Built on the East Front of Puerta de Tierra, San Juan, Puerto Rico

Nuria Hinarejos Martín

After the Europeans arrived on the American continent and the Treaty of Tordesillas (1494) was agreed to, the Spanish Crown became the first hegemon to receive, on a global scale, the privileges of exportation and conquest of all territories within the Americas. This papal-brokered agreement substantially transformed the relations among the major European powers and significantly modified international policy because the Spanish Crown forbade foreign participation in maritime trade to create a monopolized system protecting Spanish agriculture, manufactures, and wealth coming from the West Indies, as well as the ports and the main overseas possessions' navigation routes.[1] This Spanish expansion, its maritime trade, and Europeans' positive reception of products from the West Indies sparked the interest and greed of Europe's major powers, which saw these territories as an important source of income. These were circumstances that turned the Americas into a zone of constant conflict and a center for military operations during the modern era.

England turned into a maritime power of the first order that tried to take control of several Spanish overseas possessions. The international policy set forth by the Count-Duke of Olivares provoked the rupture of the Valtellina Agreement, also known as the Twelve Years' Truce, resulting in the founding of the Dutch West India Company in 1621, the purpose of which was to dominate Atlantic maritime trade.[2] These rivalries continued during the eighteenth century, forcing the Spanish Crown to sign the Pacte de Famille and the Treaty of San Ildefonso with France on August 18, 1796, aimed at developing a joint policy against England and helping each other militarily as needed.[3] As a result, the Spanish monarchy saw the need to build a complicated defensive system in the American continent's main ports to protect the trade routes and neutralize potential attacks.

In this historical context, Puerto Rico was a strategic point to be protected. The capital of the island, San Juan, was fortified from a very early date, but latter updates to gunnery required a regular renewal of its defenses. This chapter demonstrates how Spanish military engineers designed three defensive lines in East Front of Puerta de Tierra in the second half of the eighteenth century, with the intention of addressing the new international threats. To understand better how these structures are now preserved, the most recent history of the edifices is summarized.

Puerto Rico's Defensive System

Fortifications on the island of Puerto Rico, the focus of this study, began in 1509 when Juan Ponce de León built a strong-house in the village of Caparra, situated on the south side of San Juan Bay, to protect the Spanish troops from potential threats and store all weapons and war munitions. However, fortifications in the city of San Juan, the island's capital, did not begin for another decade. The capital's defense was reinforced through the construction of numerous fortifications: Casa Blanca, the fortress of Santa Catalina, the San Felipe del Morro Castle, the Boquerón Fort, and the battery platforms in Escambrón and Santa Elena. They were all built according to the military architectural model of the Italian Renaissance, which was founded in the edification of harmonic constructions with balanced, functional, monumental, geometric, and regular layouts, similar to fortifications erected in other Spanish possessions in the Caribbean and more, as mentioned in chapters 3, 6, and 11, among others.

During the eighteenth century, new fortifications were constructed, and the existing ones were modified and renovated because of the poor state in which they existed after the attacks carried out on the island by the British pirate Sir Francis Drake in 1595, George Clifford in 1598, and the 1625 fire started by the Dutch troops under Balduino Enrico. These clashes made clear the deficiencies of the structures built up to then, forcing the Spanish Crown to invest significant financial sums to reinforce the defense of San Juan's square through the construction of new battery platforms and small forts like San Jerónimo del Boquerón, Cañuelo, the battery platforms of La Perla, the city's walled enclosure, and San Cristóbal Castle. However, the city's defensive system was not finished until the late nineteenth century, when the United States took possession of the island after the Spanish-American War.

New fortifications were built during the eighteenth century along with the renovation of other existing ones due to the evolution of artillery, the effects of the War of the Spanish Succession (1701–14), and the establishment of the Bourbon dynasty. The War of the Spanish Succession became an international conflict during the reign of Philip V and ended with the signing of the Peace of Utrecht. This resulted in a series of negative consequences for all Spanish possessions overseas as England, France, and Holland viewed the New World as an important source of economic resources. As a result of these circumstances, the British attacked Portobelo (Panama) in 1739, besieged Cartagena de Indias in March 1741, and captured Havana in 1762. These events forced Charles III to propose the reinforcement and modernization of the defensive systems in all Spanish territories.

The monarch sent the Irish engineer Thomas O'Daly to Puerto Rico on May 19, 1761, so he could get to know the state of the island's defensive system.[4] After studying it thoroughly, O'Daly created a very detailed description wherein he referenced the landing made by Admiral Cristopher Columbus in November, 1493, the foundation of Caparra between 1595 and 1598, and the 1625 Dutch siege. The document analyzes in a very detailed manner all the defenses built in the capital up until that moment, the ruined state in which most of them were found, the limited amount of artillery they had, and the repairs made after the siege of Havana in light of the possibility of a new British attack.[5] This report was sent to Alejandro O'Reilly on September 27, 1764,[6] as he received a royal order just days before that forced him to move to the island to inform the monarch of the state in which the defense system was found and to organize the troops according to the model used in Havana.[7] Following his arrival in Puerto Rico, O'Reilly made a study of the island for several days along with governor Ambrosio Benavides; the volunteer engineer Pablo Castelló; the second engineer and head of the royal fortification works, Lt. Col. Thomas O'Daly; and Lt. Col. Pedro Carrasco, subaltern corporal and sergeant major of the city. In May 1765, O'Reilly issued his report about the island's economic, political, and social systems in which he stated the need to reinforce the capital's defensive system. O'Reilly's tactical-strategic study became the basis for all defensive projects and improvement works made by the military engineers who worked on the island in the Crown's service over the course of this century because the report's main objective was to turn San Juan into an impregnable city. This defensive project was sent to the Advisory Board of Fortification and Defense of the Indies along with several manuscript blueprints made by Thomas O'Daly, dated May 17, 1765, and a nautical chart drawn up by Lt. Manuel Miguel de León of the Spanish Navy.[8] It was approved on September 19, 1765, at the Royal Palace of La Granja de San Ildefonso (Segovia) at a meeting in which the following officials attended: Pedro Padilla, Manuel de Navacerrada, Joseph Hermosilla, the captain and ordinary engineer Juan Francisco Mestre, and the general commander of the Royal Corps of Engineers and the kingdom's general inspector of the plazas and fortifications Maximiliano de la Croix. Several documents located in

Mexico's General Archive of the Nation and the General Archive of the Indies allow us to confirm that in December of that same year the monarch arranged the shipment of seven hundred convicted smugglers hailing from Colombia, Spain, and Venezuela to work on the construction of San Juan's new defensive system. At the same time, the king reinforced the island's garrison with the León Regiment and several troops from Ceuta and Oran, as well as allocated 100,000 pesos annually from the Royal Treasury of New Mexico to Puerto Rico.

The building of the first defenses mapped out by O'Reilly started on January 1, 1766, and was overseen by the island's governor and captain general, José Dufresne, under the direction of the chief engineer of the Royal Fortification Works, Thomas O'Daly.

The Three Defensive Lines in the Puerta de Tierra Region

In addition to O'Daly, it is worth mentioning the presence of Juan Francisco Mestre,[9] who worked in the construction of the island's defensive system and succeeded O'Daly after O'Daly's death on January 19, 1781. A year after taking over, Mestre informed the king of the need to simplify San Juan's port following O'Reilly's recommendation made in 1765, as well as O'Daly's in 1772, even though it was rejected by the monarch because the king's priority was to reinforce San Juan's complex defense system. During the eleven years that Mestre remained on the island, he made several improvements to the Santa Catalina fortress, the San Felipe del Morro Castle, the Cañuelo and San Jerónimo del Boquerón forts, several barracks of the city, and the Royal Hospital, the edifice of which was transformed into a barracks by the mid-eighteenth century. That being said, there is no doubt that the largest contribution by this second engineer and head of the Royal Fortification Works was the defensive project he elaborated to reinforce the eastern front of San Juan's islet, also known as the Puerta de Tierra, dated September 13, 1783, which served the purpose of delaying any potential attack to the capital.[10]

He mapped out the construction of twelve gates on a solid ground of muddy clay located between the San Jorge Canal and the San Antonio Bridge to avoid possible landings in the vicinity of the Condado lagoon, the San Antonio Canal, the San Jerónimo del Boquerón fort, and the Escambrón battery platform.[11] They were built with earthen parapets and bomb-proof fascines designed as temporary works, even though later on they became permanent fortifications given that the constant rain on the island forced Spanish engineers to make several repairs and to reinforce the escarpment and counterscarp with a coating of mud, lime, and stone to avoid the humidity ruining its facade. Once the construction was finished, Mestre projected the edification of several external defenses within the vicinity of the San Cristóbal Castle, which he named: the Abanico Fort, the Princess's battery platform, and Santa Teresa battery platform. These were designed to neutralize any possible landing from the city's north side. Despite the number of reefs, mangroves, and the ground's irregularity, in the area Mestre, unlike O'Reilly, did not discount this possibility as the site of an English invasion.

The defense of the twelve gates was strengthened with the construction of the three defensive lines formed by trenches, equipped with curtains made of masonry, and ashlar protected by pits. They were known as the first, second, and third lines of defense, the nomenclature of which was related to their proximity to the San Antonio Bridge. These defenses have not been analyzed much until now because they have gone unnoticed by most of the experts on this subject. The exact date of their construction is still unknown because a document dated May 30, 1887, places their construction in 1797,[12] while Adolfo de Hostos states they were erected between 1780 and 1798. Moreover, according to Torres Ramírez, the third defensive line was constructed in 1794. Meanwhile, Pedro Tomás de Córdoba notes they were built after the 1797 British attack. The work *Lealtad y Heroísmo* dates these fortifications in 1798. Finally, Andrés Mignucci suggests the first defensive line was built between 1796 and 1802, the second one between 1850 and 1861, and the third was finished by the late eighteenth century.[13]

However, the first graphic source in which they are represented is a blueprint drawn by Mestre on September 13, 1783, and can be seen in numerous nautical charts made by the Captain Cosme Churruca in 1794 (figure 13.1).[14] These graphic sources allow us to confirm the presence of Mestre's twelve gates, which were part of the first line of cover, a second entrenched one, made from north to south located between the Salemas Canal and San Juan's plaza, and the Tajamar battery platform erected on one end of the third line. Therefore, it is possible to consider that all dates mentioned by these authors are actually incorrect.

The fist defensive line was a continuous entrenchment made from the tip of the Escambrón on the north up to the mangroves and the San Antonio Canal to the south (figure 13.2). It was projected to be defended by four hundred soldiers, artillerymen, and several battalion guns. In the immediate area of this line of coverage, all trees were cut and burned to prevent the enemy from building batteries and parapets reinforced with thick branches.[15]

On June 20, 1896, it was proposed to reinforce the defense of this fortification with a galvanized iron dome twenty meters thick made of hardened cast iron to place two bronze cannons of 12 centimeters, the cost of which were estimated to be 83,000 pesos.

Figure 13.1. *Plano de la plaza de Puerto Rico y sus inmediaciones* (Map of the Plaza de Puerto Rico and its surroundings.) (Archivo General Militar de Madrid, Cartoteca, sig. PRI-15/9. CC BY-4.0.)

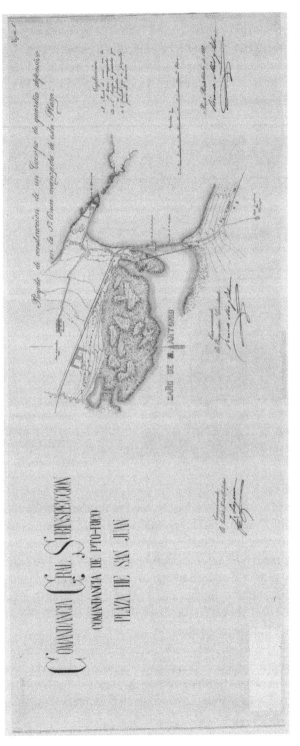

Figure 13.2. *Proyecto de construcción de un Cuerpo de guardia defensivo en la 1º línea avanzada de esta Plaza* (Construction project of a defensive guard corps in the 1st advanced line of this plaza). (Archivo General Militar de Madrid, Cartoteca, sig. PRI-51/4. CC-BY-4.0.)

The Escambrón battery platform and the San Antonio Bridge were linked by a parapet of musketry protected by a pit, the defense of which was reinforced by the San Ramón battery platform[16] located near the San Jerónimo del Boquerón Fort, which was defended by five artillery pieces, two of which were placed out in the open (figure 13.3).[17]

Figure 13.3. San Ramón battery platform's bartizan, 2017. (Photograph by Nuria Hinarejos Martín.)

Even though the high cost of this work meant that it was never carried out, the engineer José Laguna argued for the need to reinforce the artillery placed on the battery with four 12-centimeter bronze cannons, building several spare munitions depots, and four 2-meter-thick vaults equipped with two rows of overlapping cots capable of accommodating eighty soldiers. We have not been able to locate any graphical or documental source that allow us to confirm if this work was ultimately built or not, but a document found in the General Military Archive of Madrid does show that on March 12, 1897, it was reinforced with the eight 9-centimeter bronze cannons.[18]

The second line consisted of another entrenched system 400 meters long, located 460 meters from the San Cristóbal Castle, and 800 meters from the first line.[19] It extended between the mangroves to the north to the San Antonio Canal to the south, and its objective was to neutralize a possible landing in this region (figure 13.4).

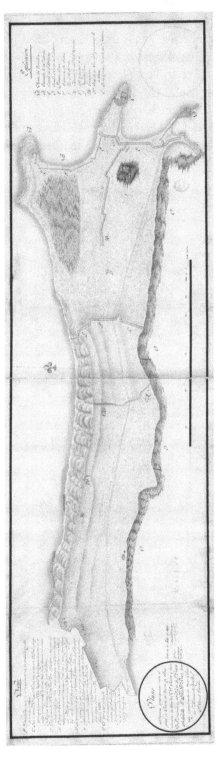

Figure 13.4. Manuel Sicardo, Plano del terreno comprehendido entre el glacis de Puerta de Tierra y obras esteriores, la costa del N. Puente y Caño de San Antonio en la Plaza de S. Juan Bautista de Puerto Rico, levantado geométricamente por el Guarda de Almacen de Fortificacn. Dn. Manuel Sicardo (Plan of the land comprised between the glacis of Puerta de Tierra and the exterior works, the coast of the N. Puente and Caño de San Antonio in the Plaza de S. Juan Bautista in Puerto Rico, geometrically raised by the Fortification's guardhouse store). The first and second line of defense, a large entrenchment that crossed the islet from north to south, and Tajamar battery erected in the third line of defense are shown. (Archivo General Militar de Madrid, Cartoteca, sig. PRI-21/10. CC BY-4.0.)

It was reinforced by banquettes, gunboats, masonry lined pits, and Isabel II's Battery, which was equipped with thirteen gunships, one of which was built out in the open and had five artillery pieces whose fire reached the outer ground (figure 13.5 and figure 13.6).[20] The defense of this battery was bolstered using a pit with embrasures and a ditch, which were finished in 1794.[21] Several documents located in the Military General Archive of Madrid and the National History Archive permit the analysis of the new improvement works made in this second line in the mid-nineteenth century.[22]

Figure 13.5. Isabel II battery platform, 2017. (Photograph by Nuria Hinarejos Martín.)

Figure 13.6. Isabel II battery platform, 2017. (Photograph by Nuria Hinarejos Martín.)

The third line, known as last withdrawal, was built parallel to the first one. It was a masonry wall parallel to the bay, approximately 274 meters long, which joined the Prince's Ravelin with the San Cristóbal Castle. Its purpose was to strengthen the defense of the castle's external works and reinforce the eastern side of the city. The Tajamar battery was built at the end of the wall closest to the sea, which Juan Manuel Zapatero described as a fortification made of ashlar, and the purpose of which was to strengthen the defense of the Princess's Battery, prevent possible landings, and avoid the presence of ships in the vicinity of San Cristóbal Castle and the Escambrón battery.[23] Today, one can still see some of the remains of the primitive battery even though the constant crash of waves has caused the collapse of most of its original construction (figure 13.7).

Figure 13.7. Tajamar's Battery, 2017. (Photograph by Nuria Hinarejos Martín.)

The need to strengthen San Juan's defense during the nineteenth century caused the emergence of the so-called controversial zones in the adjacent territories within the capital. These were spaces reserved for the Ministry of War and used as instructional fields for the troops, which forced the prohibition of any type of edification in these areas except those of a military nature. The first one corresponded to the neighborhood La Puntilla or the San Lázaro end, located in the southern side of the city, an area of vital importance for the maritime and terrestrial defense of the capital. The second area comprised the three lines of defense built in Puerta de Tierra, while the third one was determined by the Ballajá neighborhood located in the vicinity of the San Felipe del Morro Castle, where the Ballajá barracks were built in 1857 (figure 13.8).

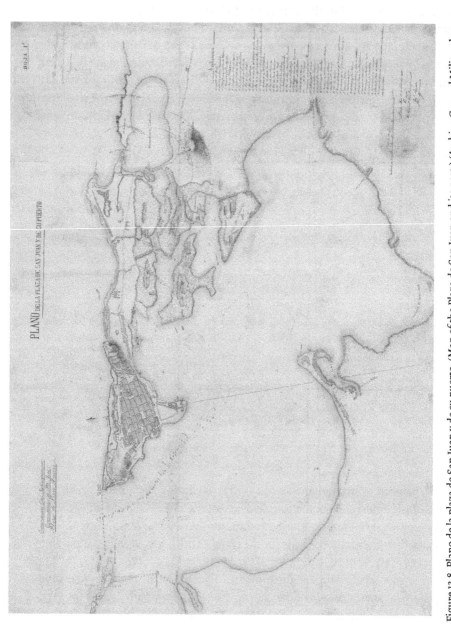

Figure 13.8. Plano de la plaza de San Juan y de su puerto. (Map of the Plaza de San Juan and its port.) (Archivo General Militar de Madrid, Carroteca, sig. PRI-17/6. CC BY-4.0.)

The three controversial zones remained under the Ministry of War's control until the population growth experienced during the nineteenth century—a result of the rural exodus to the city in search of employment and a better quality of life—forced the ministry to propose an expansion of the capital and several urbanization plans for the Puerta de Tierra area to avoid overcrowding. However, once the island was acquired by the United States in 1898, several modifications were made in this sector. On September 20, 1917, the construction of an urban park in honor of Luis Muñoz Rivera (1859–1916) was approved, located between the first and second line of defense. Bennett, Parsons & Frost, an architectural firm from Chicago, oversaw the work, in which they invested $400,000.[24] The project's design and execution were directed by the architect William Parsons, whose work lasted from November 1, 1926, until 1932, after which Francisco Valines Cofresí made some improvements. Andrés Mignucci states that Cofresí was replaced in 1935 with Victori M. Cott, who designed and directed the construction of several pergolas, sheds, and urban suites.[25] The park became the Museum of Natural History until it was transformed into a zoo in 1945. In the 1960s, new modifications were made. Finally, after Hurricane Hugo in 1989, Otto Reyes Casanova reported that restorations were needed.

14

The Defense of New Orleans as a Capital of the Government of Louisiana and Western Florida

José Miguel Morales Folguera

The collection of colonies that was Spanish America was forged for three centuries in a continuous improvement and conquest of its borderlands. In the second half of the eighteenth century, its northern border consisted of the extensive modern-day US states of California, Arizona, New Mexico, Texas, Louisiana, Mississippi, Alabama, and Florida, in which the Spanish Crown used the same methods of occupation, those it had been employing for centuries throughout its American possessions given the excellent results it had produced. If the Spanish presence in Louisiana had lasted only a few decades more, that region too would likely have achieved complete occupation and hispanicization.

The North American territories of the Spanish empire were considered a crucial geostrategic region during the second half of the eighteenth century. Therefore, many fortification projects were proposed and ultimately built, although an updated general perspective on all of them was still required. This chapter defines how the Spanish empire designed the defense of New Orleans as part of a broader territorial plan.

The Spanish dominion of Louisiana began in 1763, when France ceded this vast territory to Spain per the terms of the Pacte de la Famille between the Bourbons, signed after the Treaty of Paris. In 1800, the French emperor Napoleon took the territory back in the Treaty of San Ildefonso, although in practice Louisiana maintained the same administration. Three years later, it was sold to the United States. During these forty years of Spanish occupation, Spain attempted to impose a profound hispanicization of the territory, always looking to collaborate with the French creoles and the Indian tribes who resided in the territory. It was a political practice that had been developed with great success for three centuries in the colonization of Hispanic America.

The defense and fortification of the northern area of New Spain, which included the internal provinces, California, Texas, Arizona, Alabama, Mississippi, Louisiana, and the two Floridas, was one of the main concerns of the foreign policy of the Spanish Crown in the eighteenth century. The presence as visitors of senior administration officials, such as José de Gálvez, and the regulation of the presidios on the northern border, sought information about the situation of these extensive border territories and their defense in light of the Spanish tradition of construction of fortifications and presidios.[1]

The First Spanish Plan for New Orleans

The first Spanish fortification plan in Louisiana was carried out under the supervision of Governor Alejandro O'Reilly (1769–70), who arrived in New Orleans in 1769 at the head of an army composed of 2,056 men, including thirteen noncommissioned officers and the engineer captain Juan Cotilla. Louisiana was a dependency of the Captaincy General of Cuba, although legally it was subordinate to the Audiencia of Santo Domingo.[2] O'Reilly's project was based on the concentration of most Spanish troops in New Orleans, while allowing many of the military posts on the borderlands to disappear. He was also opposed to the creation of new fortifications, as he thought that *"la defensa de la provincia debía consistir únicamente en los defensores"* (the defense of the province must solely rely on defenders).[3]

The Second Spanish Plan for New Orleans

A second fortification plan was carried out by Colonel Francisco Bouligny, collected in his *Memoria de la Louisiana*, which was delivered to the Secretary of the Indies on August 15, 1776.[4] This important personage of Spanish Louisiana was born in Alicante in 1736. In 1769, after serving in Havana, he moved to New Orleans with O'Reilly. After traveling to Spain in 1775, Bouligny wrote his *Memoria de la Louisiana* for José de Gálvez. In the tenth chapter, he develops his plan of the province's fortifications. The first measure was the placement of a frigate with thirty or forty guns and with a *"costado tan fuerte que ninguna de las contrarias, que pudiese entrar en el río fuera capaz de ponerse a su lado"* (broadside so strong that no enemies, would they be able to enter the river, could get to its side) on the Mississippi River. This boat would always remain in the river as a floating battery to block the passage *"cuando convenga y a quien se quiera"* (when convenient and to whom it wanted).[5]

In the place called Torno de los Ingleses, a location four leagues downstream from New Orleans, a bend in the Mississippi forced ships to slow down;

he advised the reconstruction of the two batteries there, which the French had built originally. In the northern area of New Orleans, it was advisable to rebuild and increase the fort of the Bayú de San Juan, which was located on Lake Pontchartrain. This protected both places and indicated the convenience of building one or two batteries in the River Oyo or Bello Riviere. He also expressed the need to rebuild the fort of Manchak on the island of New Orleans, as well as the realization of another one on the opposite shore, to achieve an effective crossfire.

With these defenses, one hundred leagues of Spanish possessions on either side of the river, from the Gulf of Mexico to Manchak, would be protected from an attack by any potential enemy, as long as the works were carried out with good construction and with the pits and defenses, *"que pide el arte militar, aún en el caso de sitio"* (that calls for military artistry, even in the case of siege). With this proposal, Bouligny brought together static defense, traditional of the Spanish military engineering, with the dynamic defense, more adapted to English attacks, which were more likely to be marine in nature.

As for the city of New Orleans, Bouligny judged it convenient *"circundarla de muros siguiendo el mismo plan que actualmente está trazado allí con estacas pues tiene ya todas sus cortinas con sus correspondientes baterías de defensa, poniendo igualmente un fuerte baluarte a cada extremidad de la ciudad, mirando al río, y en el mismo puesto que el anterior Gobernador ha hecho hazer una batería"* (to surround it with walls following the same plan that is currently drawn there with stakes because it already has all its curtains with their corresponding defensive batteries, also placing a strong bastion at each end of the city, facing the river, and in the same position as the previous governor has made a battery).[6] All the forts had to have batteries to the river and to the land, to avoid being surprised in the rear. The works should have been brick and lime, and ideally not built in floodplains. The garrison must also be increased progressively and fortified to account for expected population growth.

The Third Spanish Plan for New Orleans

To the sixth governor of Louisiana, Francisco Luis Héctor, Baron de Carondelet (1791–1797), also known as the best Spanish governor of New Orleans for his efforts in the reconstruction of the city after the two terrible fires that destroyed the few remains of the French city, is credited with an ambitious policy of reconstruction and erection of forts. One of his first concerns was the defense of New Orleans, which by this time was surrounded by the construction of five forts, located on the four corners of the city walls, and the fifth in the center of the inner side of the rectangle, named San Luis, San Carlos, Borgoña, San Juan, and San Fernando.[7] On this work, Carondelet collaborated with the engineer Juan María Perchet, who arrived in New Orleans in 1794 to carry out the reconstruction of the city and its defenses after the 1794 fire, and the commander of engineers, Joaquín de la Torre.[8]

Shortly after having undertaken the construction of the fortifications around New Orleans, Carondelet ordered the execution of the new forts of San Felipe de Placaminas and Fuerte Borbón, located on both banks of the river at the entrance to New Orleans. He also proposed that a battery of guns be located in the territory between Lake Borgne and Lake Pontchartrain, on the pass known as Chef Menteur. In addition, he urged the construction of another battery in the Coquille to control the passage of ships between the two lakes. Another battery was to be built in Tierra Grande at the entrance to Barataria Bay to defend access to the city. All these recommendations would complete the defenses of Fort San Juan, which would be moved to a more advantageous position.[9]

Carondelet also ordered that a complete list be made of the amount that was considered necessary for the preservation and repairs of the province's fortifications, barracks, hospitals, warehouses, and other military buildings of each plaza, accompanying the plan and expression of the cost of the maintenance of the necessary residents in them. In addition, the plan for New Orleans, which was carried out in all its terms, also dealt with such important cities as Panzacola, Movila, Natchez, Nogales, Villa Gayoso, Nuevo Madrid, Baton Rouge, Gálveztown, San Luis, and the forts of San Marcos de Apalaches, San Juan del Bayú, Tombecté, Manchak, San Felipe de Placaminas, Arkanzas, Punta Cortada, Ouachita, Natchitoches, and Santa Genoveva de Ylinoa.

The Fourth Spanish Plan for New Orleans

The last of the great Spanish plans of fortification of Louisiana came from the architect and military engineer Francisco Sabatini, who wrote a report signed on August 15, 1794, in which he expressed the need to fortify Louisiana to defend it from the enemies of Spain:[10] "*teniendo la provincia de la Luisiana una gran posición de costa en el seno mejicano, hallándose rodeada por tierras de varias naciones de indios, que median entre ellos y los Estados Unidos de América, el reino de Méjico y la Florida, y atravesándola el gran río Mississippi, puede considerarse su ataque por tres diversos parages, ya sea por mar, haciendo un desembarco en la mencionada costa; ya se haga por tierra o bien se execute aprovechándose de la navegación del Mississippi, que parece proporciona por su curso y caudal la facilidad de esta empresa*" (The province of Louisiana having a great coastal position in the Mexican bosom, being surrounded by lands of several nations of Indians, which mediate between them and the

United States of America, the kingdom of Mexico and Florida, and crossing the great river Mississippi, its attack by three diverse places must be considered, either by sea, making a landing on the aforementioned coast; whether it is done by land or it is executed taking advantage of the navigation of the Mississippi, which seems to provide ease to this enterprise due to its course and flow).

Sabatini knew that at that time the United States did not have the capacity to carry out important operations at such a great distance from its territories yet, but that it was indispensable to take the necessary precautions now, making a defensive plan that would safeguard Louisiana and carrying out plans for the forts named Mazas and Nueva Movila. He also thought it necessary to know the distances from the forts of New Orleans, the Movila, and Panzacola to the borders of the United States. A complete description of the Mississippi River and adjacent rivers must also be submitted. Doing so was seen as necessary to attract the natives and avoid the settlement of foreigners. Important pieces in this defense were the reconstruction of Panzacola's forts and a contingent of four thousand veteran soldiers in New Orleans, which should be supported by a militia of eight thousand men.

Defending the Spanish City of New Orleans

The most important works of military architecture of the province were carried out in the capital, where the governor and most of the army resided. The works carried out during the French period were of little importance. They were made of wood and disappeared during the first years of Spanish rule. One of the first actions of the new Spanish administration was the completion of an inventory of the buildings belonging to his Magestad Christianisima in the city of New Orleans. This inventory, executed in the first years of the government of Alejandro O'Reilly, listed the public buildings inherited from the French administration. A second inventory carried out in 1799 already showed the works executed by the Spanish government over the previous thirty-six years.[11]

The inventory supported by O'Reilly indicated the following buildings belonging to the government:[12] a barracks for landed troops of fifty-six *toesas* along the river and 112 *toesas* deep; a general storehouse with provisions for Indians circumscribed the walls of the fortification, and a house was located at the rear. The land for these buildings, later to become an artillery park, had thirty-six *toesas* and four feet facing the river and forty-six *toesas* of depth. Another warehouse, which served the artillery branch, with a house behind it in its enclosure, had an area of twenty *toesas* and three feet by forty-six *toesas*. The guardhouse, the jails, and the city administration building disappeared in the 1788 fire, explaining why they were reconstructed already in the Spanish period. The house of the commissariat and the treasury, later used as the headquarters of the government, had a land of thirty-six *toesas* facing the river and fifty-six in depth. The doctor's house, where the botanical garden was located, was fifteen *toesas* by fifty- seven *toesas*. The storekeeper's house was fifteen *toesas* by thirty-five *toesas*. The gunpowder warehouse and the Marina Park, which also succumbed to fire, had an area of twelve *toesas* by nine-and-a-half *toesas*. The grounds of the four guardhouses for the city precinct were occupied by the fortification works started by Baron de Carondelet. Other buildings of less architectural interest were a warehouse for gunpowder with a room on the other side of the river, the warehouse at the pier of Bayú de San Juan, and the exit point of said bayou with the fort of the same name.

In a copy of this inventory, made in the year 1799 during the administration of Luis Unzaga, were also made certain architectural annotations, as well as appraisals of the edifices.[13] Because of this information, we can know that the soldiers' hospital was a brick masonry building, with galleries on the main fronts with a total of seventy-four columns. There was also an official hospital, made of masonry between poles, which was the characteristic structure of the Spanish buildings of New Orleans, with a gallery around it and six rooms inside.

Although the different governors contributed in unequal measure to the reconstructions or reconversions of the military buildings, none stood out as much as Carondelet. One could cite, however, the activity carried out previously by Bernardo de Gálvez, who built several towers at different distances from New Orleans to monitor possible attacks. Also during Gálvez's administration, barracks were completed for the troops, which stretched from the rear of the Ursuline convent to Barracas Street, facing the river, composing a large rectangle. These buildings were raised with brick, had two stories, and galleries on pillars in both front and back.[14]

Gilberto Guillemard was the military engineer commissioned by Carondelet to carry out an extensive program of work to provide New Orleans with enough defenses to make it safe from danger.[15] In the spring of 1792, he was overseeing the building of five land redoubts assisted by five armed drafts and a battery in the water. All were linked by a trench and a strong stockade, which covered the New Orleans circular road. Two of the forts were located at the corners of the walls and overlooked the river. The most important was the Fuerte de San Carlos. El Fuerte de San Luis was the only defense at the city's heights. The other three forts were located on the rear, covering the landward approaches. El Fuerte de Borgoña and el Fuerte de San Juan were in the two upper corners of the rectangle formed by the city, while the San Fernando fort was in the center. Each of them had guns on top and barracks for around one hundred soldiers.

The five forts were built in a regular shape, in a closed perimeter with a door to the interior of the city, equipped with sidewalks and a glacis.[16] We cannot truly know the plan of the forts, since the different historical plans draw them in different manners. On December 8, 1794, a fire destroyed the blocks of houses on the three streets parallel to the river located on the left side of the city, where most of the public buildings were located. To delimit the perimeter of the fire two plans are made, neither of which have the author's signature. The first[17] presents the city surrounded by a wall on three sides with the front open to the river. In the four corners and in the center of the opposite side of the river, there are four hexagonal forts, four batteries located between the forts, and two others located on the riverbed, that is, the earth wall that protected the city from floods of the river. The second plan[18] is more imprecise in terms of defining the plans of the forts, only describing them with a circular plan and with their respective names. Also, it indicates the presence of the four batteries on the walls, although one of the two existing ones on the levee disappears.

An English map dated in 1798 includes the five forts with a pentagonal-bastioned plan, the wall continues on three sides with four salient arrow-shaped batteries between the forts. This must have been the plan that the forts had, because, on an 1800 plan sent by Carlos Trudeau to Luis de Peñalver, bishop of Louisiana, representing the sector of New Orleans between Bienville and Gravier Streets in the suburb of Santa María, the forts of San Luis and Borgoña, which were located on the left side of the city, are perfectly drawn. Both forts have a basal pentagonal plan, and in the center of the wall between them stands a battery in the shape of a spearhead.[19]

The Final Spanish Plan for New Orleans' Defense

In 1801 Carlos Trudeau[20] drew what would be the last plan of New Orleans made during the Spanish period.[21] It is a plan of extraordinary quality, whose main objective was to locate public buildings and land belonging to the Spanish Crown during O'Reilly's administration. However, it also shows us the appearance of the wall with its forts, batteries, and the six existing doors with their corresponding guardhouses. The size of the batteries is striking, as is the battery located between the forts of San Juan and San Fernando in the shape of a triple bulwark. In one of the texts that accompany the plan, it is specified that *"esta Fortificación, con Palissadas de maderas de seis pulgadas quadradas, sobresalientes de nueve pies de altura. Con el terrapleno y fosso de la pallissada se mantuvo hasta el año 1779 y no queda en el presente que el fosso, alterado en la menor parte por la Nueva Fortificación"* (this fortification, with palisades of wood six inches square, overhanging nine feet high. With the embankment and moat of the palisade, it remained until the year 1779 and there no longer remains in the present such that the moat was altered in the lowest part by the new fortification).[22]

Between the forts and on the sides of the *leve o malecón* facing the river, six gates were opened, four of which bore the names of said forts: San Luis, San Juan, San Carlos, and San Fernando. These doors, formed of wooden palisades, were guarded by sentinels and closed at nine o'clock every night.[23] The fort of San Carlos was the most important military work. Carondelet considered it the final bulwark in the city's defense in light of a possible siege. The fort was protected with brick and endowed with a garrison of between eight hundred and one thousand men and defended by its double batteries, so it could *soportar un asedio de un mes* (endure a month-long siege).[24]

The description, made by the French general Victor Collot of New Orleans in 1796,[25] is quite explicit, since it is made by a soldier and possibly a spy in the service of France, another feature of this new group of military engineers, as shown by Cruz above:[26]

> The defense of this place consists of five small forts and a large battery, all distributed in the following way. On the side facing the river and at the ends of the city, there are two forts, which guard the route on the river. Its figure is that of a regular pentagon, having a parapet eighteen feet thick, covered with brick, with trench and covered path. The trench is eight feet deep by twenty feet wide. In each of these forts there is a guardhouse with one hundred and fifty men and a gunpowder store: twelve pieces of cannons of twelve and eighteen caliber make up their artillery. Between these two forts and in front of the city's main street, there is a large battery that is open to the river and that crosses its fires with the two forts. The first of these two forts, that is, the one on the right, which is the most important, is called Saint Carlos, and the other is Saint Luis. At the back and to cover the city on the land side, the other three forts (Nos. 4, 5, and 6) have been placed. They are less considerable than the first two. Two are located at the angles of the city square, and a third is located in the center in an advanced manner in the manner of an obtuse angle. These forts have not covered roads but only palisades. Each one has eight pieces of cannon (we ignore the caliber) and two accommodations for a hundred men. The five forts and the battery cross their fires with each other, and are joined by a trench forty feet wide and seven deep.

Collot thought that once the two forts located at the riverfront were overtaken, the conquest of the city was quite simple and could be accomplished with about five hundred men. Collot estimated that the distance between New

Orleans and the entrance to the Mississippi River was about ninety-nine miles. Its banks were inhabited only up to the area of the Torno or Curva de los Ingleses (English Turn), as these lands were highly susceptible to flooding and thus uninhabitable. The English had chosen this place to defend the entrance to the river with two forts, which were abandoned during the Spanish period, since a position located twenty miles upstream, called the Torno de Placcamin, was preferred. There they had established a very strong fort, called Fuerte de Placcamin. It was located on the left side of the river, at the mouth of a small stream or bay, called Mardigras. Its outline was so irregular and peculiar that one could not easily tell its shape. It was a bastion with two long arms in the center, which gave it the appearance of a horn. The parapets facing the river were eighteen feet thick and coated with brick. It was surrounded by a trench twenty feet wide by twelve feet deep. The two arms and the throat of the fort were only defended by a sand bank around them. Two barracks for three hundred men had been built inside as were the lodgings for the commander and the powder store. On the north side, a small levee had been built, which extended five hundred *toesas* along the river. It protected the fort from the river's flooding. Twenty-four pieces of cannon of all calibers formed the battery, with a captain and a hundred men, who formed the garrison and who were relieved every month. Collot estimated that the situation of the fort was excellent, making it very difficult to force entry to the river and access to the city of New Orleans.

Instead, the Torno de Placcamin was the true key to the defense of the capital of Louisiana. The curve of the river was actually a double meander, forcing the boats to make a double turn, and in the center, there was not only a fort, as Collot noted, but a bulwarked fort on the south bank, crossing his fires with another battery located opposite the bay of Mardigras, which had the name of Fuerte Borbón. The fort that Collot could only contemplate in 1796 was designed nine years earlier by the military engineer Joaquín de Peramás.[27]

In 1787, during the administration of Esteban Miró (1782–1791), construction of a fort was chosen for the Torno de Placcamin with the name of San Felipe, to cross its fires with the battery in front of the Fuerte Borbón, repeating in this way the strategy developed at the immediate approach to New Orleans.

The project of the new fort was made by the engineer Joaquín de Peramás, who executed three plans: one showing the site of the Placcamin meander with the placement of two forts,[28] a second with the plan of the fort,[29] and a third plan with the sections.[30]

The plan of the Torno de Placcamin is formed by the drawing of the meander of the river, the locations facing the fort of San Felipe and the battery or Fuerte de San Fernando, the Bayou Mardi Gras, which empties into the sea at a distance of two leagues, and two other bayous in front, also connected to the sea. These bayous were navigable by canoe, being entirely surrounded by thick forests of willows, bushes, and cane marshes.

The plan of Fuerte de San Felipe shows a strong bastion shape, like a spear point, facing the river. Access was achieved through a ramp, which led to the Plaza de Armas, from which a staircase that covered the trench ended at the fort gate with a drawbridge. Inside were the buildings. On the left, a building with an elongated rectangular floor plan intended for the officer's guardhouse, the troops' guardhouse, and four rooms for barracks were located. The remaining units located around the courtyard of the fort were: the gunpowder store, the equipment storehouse, the bakery, the commander's residence, the kitchen's officer, the troop kitchen, the mess officers, and a common space. Two ramps located at the angles of the frontal bastions served to drain the rainwater to the river. This was a very important aspect, because the abundant rains might lead to accumulated water, which might have ended up demolishing the walls.

The Fuerte de San Felipe was not built until 1792, when its construction was contracted to Gilberto Antonio de San Maxent. In that year, 14,419 pesos were spent on its structure. Shortly after these works a description of the fort noted it was "*Una fuerte batería dispuesta en la forma de baluarte dotada con 12 cañones del calibre 18, el resto está rodeado por un terraplén de arena cubierta de verde césped y el correspondiente parapeto de ocho pies de espesor, un camino cubierto rodea el fuerte con su correspondiente estacada y una alambrada en el pie del glacis*" (A strong battery arranged in the shape of a bulwark equipped with 12 18-caliber guns, the rest is surrounded by a sand embankment covered with green grass and the corresponding eight-foot-thick parapet, a covered path surrounds the fort with its corresponding stockade and a wire fence at the foot of the glacis).[31]

Several improvements were made in the following years, its maintenance being a constant concern due to the surrounding land's weakness. In his visit to the fort in 1796, Víctor Collot pointed out that the fort had lost more than three feet on the side of the bayou and another two on the eastern side.[32]

In front of the Fuerte de San Felipe, Joaquín de Peramás designed a battery known as Fuerte Borbón, with which it should cross its fire. It was a small redoubt of earth and wood containing five six-caliber cannons. Its excellent position meant that boats, when returning on the river's meander, did not see the fort until they were directly underneath its guns. In 1795, it was destroyed by a hurricane and Carondelet ordered it to be rebuilt, sending the following instructions to Colonel Favrot: "*elevar el parapeto del fuerte Borbón por el lado del río unos nueve pies, y el interior del fuerte . . . de manera que pudiera erigir una batería de tres piezas de artillería, con objeto de que dejara el resto del suelo libre para elevar el techo de la casa del guarda antes de llenar el resto de la plaza de armas hasta la misma altura de 3 pies y medio. Su batería circular, una vez finalizada con sus aspilleras abiertas, su interior y exterior cubiertos con vigas, formarán un dique alrededor del fuerte, siguiendo la línea que hemos señalado en el suelo para el parapeto del camino cubierto, de manera que las aguas no puedan cubrir el suelo del fuerte"* (raise the parapet of Fort Bourbon on the river side about nine feet, and the interior of the fort . . . so that it could erect a battery of three artillery pieces, to leave the rest of the ground free to raise the roof of the gatehouse before filling the rest of the parade ground to the same height of three-and-one-half feet. Its circular battery, once completed with its open loopholes, its interior and exterior covered with beams, will form a dike around the fort, following the line that we have indicated on the ground for the parapet of the covered path, so that the waters cannot cover the fort floor).[33]

15

"Without Any Fighting or Disturbance"

Conquering Spanish Baton Rouge and Mobile

Gene Allen Smith

Nineteenth-century Manifest Destiny meant expansion, ordained by Divine will, over an unspecified area that could include North America, or even the entire western hemisphere.[1] Thomas Jefferson, writing in 1786, had expressed that same hope: "Our continent must be viewed as the nest from which all America, North and South is to be peopled."[2] Just as the 1840s view of destiny believed the American peopling of the continent or hemisphere would happen in due time, as if God had sanctioned it, so did the Jeffersonians some three decades earlier. Shortly before the War of 1812, Jefferson informed John Jacob Astor that he "looked forward with gratification to the time when" the entirety of the Pacific coast would be populated "with free and independent Americans."[3] Earlier he had even offered a hemispherical view when he wrote "it is impossible not to look forward to distant times, when our rapid multiplication will expand itself... and cover the whole northern, if not the southern continent."[4] For Jefferson's Republicans, expanding throughout the continent and hemisphere provided for an "empire of liberty," which would preserve the young republic's cherished beliefs from European destruction.[5]

The Importance of Rivers in the Early United States

Expansion throughout the Western Hemisphere had to begin with the settlement and development of the trans-Appalachian west. Moreover, navigation of the Mississippi River, the lifeline of the West, would definitely need to remain open for successful expansion. The river had become the mainstay of transportation and communication for farmers and frontiersmen west of the Appalachian Mountains, and as long as that thoroughfare remained open, all were satisfied. Yet when there appeared a possibility of closing the Mississippi, American tempers flared. In 1785–86, during the Confederation period, American Secretary of Foreign Affairs John Jay negotiated a treaty with Spanish Foreign Minister Don Diego de Gardoqui proposing to close the Mississippi River for at least twenty-five years in return for favorable commercial concessions. Once Jay learned of the opposition to the agreement, his better judgment prevailed and he did not submit the Jay-Gardoqui Treaty to the American Confederation Congress; in fact, the river remained open.[6]

Spain's control of the Mississippi River and the Gulf Coast had blocked outlets for American commerce, threatened the security of the young nation, and infringed on the United States' "pursuit of happiness."[7] Despite these encroachments, possession of those lands in the Gulf South could not "be in better hands," Jefferson wrote in 1788. His only apprehension was that Spain was "too feeble to hold them till our population can be sufficiently advanced to gain it from them piece by piece."[8] After the purchase of Louisiana in 1803, Spanish forts and communities at Baton Rouge and Mobile represented two West Florida locations—or two pieces—that Presidents Jefferson and his successor James Madison believed should belong to the United States. In their official capacity, they conspired, cajoled, and encouraged like-minded Americans to overwhelm the locations so that populist movements could spring forward. That way the United States would not have to "declare" war on Spain or give the appearance of forcibly taking the region. Instead, piece by piece Americans would consume what they believed belonged to them by God given right. By 1810 enough Americans had moved into the Baton Rouge district to seize control themselves. Then once the War of 1812 began, the United States officially seized Mobile, but only to prevent British forces from using the Gulf Coast city during the conflict. In any case, less than ten years after the Louisiana Purchase the United States had acquired both West Florida forts—Baton Rouge and Mobile—in bloodless conquests.

As the Louisiana Purchase settled the prickly Mississippi question, Jefferson contended that "this removes from us the greatest source of danger to our peace."[9] But this prophetic statement was unfounded, for navigation of the country's other southern rivers would also become issues of contention. While the Louisiana Purchase settled the American claim to the Mississippi River, it did not provide the right to navigate or a right of deposit for the other river systems flowing into the Gulf of Mexico. The Pearl River, Pascagoula River, Perdido River, the Alabama River system, the Escambia River, and Apalachicola River were not included in the Louisiana Purchase and thus became sources of controversy between the United States and Spain during the first two decades of the nineteenth century.

These rivers flowing through Spanish West Florida remained issues of contention in Spanish-American relations until the James Monroe administration formally acquired Florida in 1821. While the Mississippi River system embodied the great watershed for lands between the Appalachian and Rocky Mountains, other rivers flowing into the Gulf were similarly important. The Alabama River system, including the Mobile and Tombigbee Rivers, and the Apalachicola system became essential transportation and communication routes for the southwestern territories of the United States. Those rivers became as important to the settlers of the Mississippi Territory and Tennessee as was the Mississippi to inhabitants of Ohio, Kentucky, and western Pennsylvania. Just as westerners had demanded that the Mississippi River remain open, American frontiersmen in the Gulf southwest insisted that these river systems, too, be opened to American trade.

James Madison, Jefferson's secretary of state, contended that navigation of the southwestern rivers was necessary for maximizing the use of the Gulf of Mexico.[10] Moreover, the congressional committee that recommended the appropriations for the Louisiana Purchase foresaw the importance of the Gulf Coast to continued American expansion and concurred with Madison: "If we look forward to the free use of the Mississippi, the Apalachicola, and the other rivers of the West by ourselves and our posterity.... The Floridas must become a part of the United States, either by purchase or by conquest."[11]

American Attempts to Acquire the Floridas

Just as Jefferson wanted access to the Mississippi River, he also wanted to bring within the American fold the Floridas, which controlled the rivers of the Gulf South.[12] In April 1791, Jefferson had informed President George Washington that Governor Juan Nepumaceno de Quesada y Barnuevo had invited Americans to settle in Spanish Florida. This offered a blessing in disguise, and Jefferson remarked that he wished 100,000 Americans would accept this invitation. Washington's secretary of state believed this would deliver to the United States "peaceably what may otherwise cost us a war."[13]

In 1803 Jefferson wished to acquire New Orleans and West Florida, and had instructed Livingston and Monroe to attempt to purchase land east, not west, of the Mississippi River in the hopes of settling the problems experienced by frontiersmen along the Gulf. To that end, the United States acquired New Orleans in the Louisiana Purchase, but the status of West Florida remained ambiguous. The eastern boundaries for the territory seemed unclear, leaving room for confusion. Monroe, who had helped negotiate the Purchase, was not confused by the provisions of the treaty at all. In fact, he insisted that the deal included Mobile as well as West Florida.[14] Livingston concurred with Monroe, arguing that the United States should take possession of West Florida as a part of the Louisiana Purchase.[15]

Even though the status of West Florida remained doubtful, Jefferson and Congress took steps to prove conclusively that it belonged to the United States as part of the Louisiana Purchase. At Jefferson's behest, Congress passed the Mobile Act in February 1804, which gave the United States legal control over part of the region. The act proclaimed the annexation of all navigable rivers and streams within the United States that flowed into the Gulf of Mexico. It also created a separate customs district at Fort Stoddert (north of the thirty-first parallel) to collect duties.[16]

The Marquis de Casa Yrujo, Spanish minister to the United States, protested the American claim under the Mobile Act. Jefferson's proclamation, May 20, 1804, asserting that the Mobile revenue district only included those waters within the boundaries of the United States, momentarily mollified Spain's protest. While Jefferson had been willing to risk war for the right to use the Mississippi, he was reluctant to take such action over West Florida. Most likely his belief that American settlers would eventually seize the West Florida lands that nature held for them, made him realize that war was unnecessary.[17]

Jeffersonian Republicans recognized the importance of both East and West Florida, but for more than reasons of navigation. True, the Floridas commanded the rivers of the Southwest, but the area was also important for security reasons. As long as a foreign nation possessed the Floridas that country threatened Jefferson's domain because the peninsula could be used as an operational base against the southern United States. Exactly, this had been done repeatedly during the colonial and revolutionary periods. The area could also be used as a refuge for hostile Indians and enslaved runaways. Confusion in the Floridas had been further exacerbated when the territory changed hands between Britain and Spain. Moreover, the region's multinational inhabitants reluctantly swore loyalty to a government that could not retain the peninsula or protect their interests. Problems such as these created a general atmosphere of lawlessness and insecurity along the frontier that threatened American existence.[18]

The disintegration of the Spanish empire created unforeseen problems for the United States. Jefferson had remarked that Spanish control over the Floridas did not threaten his country because Americans could wrest the lands from her in due time. Also Spain's weakness did not imperil American independence. But should France or Great Britain gain command of Florida, it could jeopardize independence or threaten American control over and access to the Mississippi River and Gulf Coast.[19] Jefferson had expressed this concern in 1793 when he remarked that Great Britain would seize Florida and "thus completely encircle us with her colonies and fleets."[20] In 1815 James Monroe reiterated the same sentiments when he declared that "East-Florida in itself is comparatively nothing but as a post in the hands of Great Britain it is of the highest importance." If Britain gained control over Florida, Monroe contended Britain would command the Gulf of Mexico and all its waters, including the Mississippi. Furthermore, the United States would lose "a vast proportion of the most fertile and productive parts of this Union, on which the navigation and commerce so essentially depend[ed]."[21]

The Spanish loss of Florida remained a constant threat during the first two decades of the nineteenth century. The uncertainties of the Napoleonic wars in Europe only fostered those fears. Florida resembled a pawn waiting to change European hands, and it appeared that the only way to prevent such a catastrophe was for the United States to use any method to seize the moment, just as Louisiana had been procured. Thus, during his administration Jefferson tried gentle persuasion, diplomacy, blustering, and even the threat of war to secure Florida, all to no avail.[22]

The American Acquisition of West Florida

Jefferson's hopes that his country would assume control over Gulf lands began to materialize in late September 1810. At four o'clock on Sunday morning, September 23, 1810, eighty armed Americans commanded by Philemon Thomas stormed the dilapidated Spanish fort in Baton Rouge, West Florida. As the invaders streamed through the undefended gate and gaps in the stockade and past the unloaded cannon, they demanded that Spanish troops surrender their weapons. Don Luis Antonio de Grand-Pré, commander of the bastion, bravely resisted as his few ill-equipped and invalid soldiers surrendered. Other than the brave young leader and one of his soldiers (Manuel Matamoros), who died defending their honor and the Spanish flag, there were no casualties. West Florida governor Carlos De Lassus, abruptly awakened by the screaming and gunshots, quickly dressed and hurried toward the fort. But before he had traveled the block from his house to the scene of activity, rebel horsemen overwhelmed and captured him. With the governor's apprehension, the conquest of Spanish Baton Rouge had ended in a matter of minutes.[23]

After the conquest, the Americans called a convention of delegates representing the region and, on September 26, issued a Declaration of Independence for West Florida, which resembled the US declaration. Soon thereafter the convention delivered a copy of the document to Governor David Holmes of the Mississippi Territory and Governor William C. C. Claiborne of the Orleans

Territory, insisting they forward it to the government in Washington. They also requested annexation into the United States and protection against Spanish retribution.[24]

Republican President James Madison faced a quandary. He wanted to annex Baton Rouge immediately, but he knew that he could not use military forces for such a venture without congressional approval, and that body would not meet until early December. Moreover, military occupation of Spanish territory would incur the wrath of not only Spain but perhaps even England and France. Madison feared that should the government not aid West Florida, there would "be danger of its passing into the hands of a third and dangerous party." Britain, the president had written to his friend Thomas Jefferson, had a "propensity to fish in troubled waters," and Madison realized that the moment would be lost should the United States not cast her line.[25]

Rumors of the impending arrival of Spanish troops from Cuba or Veracruz, combined with fabricated accounts of a British landing at Pensacola and stories of American adventurers seizing additional Spanish territory, forced Madison to take action before Congress convened. On October 27, 1810, Madison issued a proclamation instructing American officials to take possession of West Florida based on the Louisiana Purchase of 1803. The United States, the president declared, had not previously exercised its title to the territory, not because of any doubt of its legitimacy, but rather because of "events over which [the country] had no control." He announced that the time had arrived; "the tranquility and security of our adjoining territories are endangered," and the country's revenue and commercial laws as well as slave importation statutes were being violated. Although Madison made no reference to the Baton Rouge revolution in that message, he did admit that "a crisis has at length arrived subversive of the order of things under the Spanish authorities," and should the United States not act immediately it "may lead to events ultimately contravening the views of both parties."[26]

In conclusion, Madison instructed Governor Claiborne to take possession of the territory for the United States. The message also directed the inhabitants to obey the laws, to maintain order, and to cherish the harmony and protection of their life, property, and religion. The president had by executive order incorporated Spanish Baton Rouge into the American territory of Orleans; this claim included all of West Florida except the city of Mobile, which remained in Spanish hands.[27]

Tensions between Spanish forces and Americans in the region heightened considerably in the following months. Before the end of 1810 Lt. Daniel Dexter of the US Navy had accompanied a troop transport bound for Fort Stoddert on the Mobile River. Apparently, the West Florida revolutionaries involved with the Baton Rouge seizure had made overtures concerning the conquest of Mobile, and Fort Stoddert needed additional troops to prevent an unwanted uprising. But Spanish forces at Fort Charlotte in Mobile controlled the river's mouth, making the American fort inaccessible from the Gulf via water.[28]

In early January 1811, the American flotilla, laden with troops and supplies, anchored near Fort Charlotte. But Francisco Collell, commander of the Spanish bastion, refused to allow the Americans to pass or disembark. Almost a month passed before Collell allowed the troops to land and march overland to Fort Stoddert. Before the affair had been resolved, an unsubstantiated rumor circulated that four Spanish frigates had landed troops in nearby Pensacola with troops to regain the lands Spain had lost. Although the rumor proved to be exactly that, the two nations avoided a diplomatic crisis.[29]

In early June 1811 the navy sent a thirteen-ship expedition (eleven gunboats, the brig *Viper*, and a storeship) commanded by Lt. Joseph Bainbridge to ensure safe passage of military supplies to Fort Stoddert. US-Spanish relations along the Gulf Coast had worsened as Collell steadfastly refused to allow the passage of supplies north to the fort. Capt. John Shaw, commander of the New Orleans naval station, had responded by sending the squadron to deliver the supplies—by force if necessary.[30]

The gunboats arrived in Mobile Bay on July 2, 1811, and it appeared for a time that Collell would not acquiesce. As Bainbridge moved his vessels into position, he learned that the *Viper*'s draft prevented the flagship from crossing the sandbar that commanded the harbor. Bainbridge then transferred his pennant from the *Viper* to gunboat *No. 25* and informed Collell that he intended to execute his orders. Three days later Bainbridge ordered six of his gunboats to anchor about five hundred yards off Fort Charlotte with their guns ready for action. Meanwhile, gunboat *No. 25* proceeded upriver, followed by the sloop *Alligator* (gunboat *No. 166*), which towed the storeship. Collell did not order his Spanish troops to fire on the American convoy as it moved upriver toward Fort Stoddert. Episodes such as this characterized the tense state of affairs along the Gulf.[31]

On April 4, 1812, four days after the United States welcomed Louisiana's entrance into the Union, the US Congress incorporated Mobile and its surrounding area into the Mississippi Territory. David Holmes, the aggressive Republican frontier governor of the Mississippi Territory, was not officially informed of any change in Mobile's status, nor was he immediately given information concerning the area. In fact, he did not discover that the Mobile district had been added to his territory until three weeks later when he read a newspaper account that reported the congressional action. Once Holmes learned of the change, he began organizing the region as part of his domain. He appointed officials to control the territory, including a sheriff for Mobile County. He also divided the county into militia districts and established a city government for Mobile. And while he took these steps, Holmes did not try to enforce his decrees in the Spanish-occupied and controlled city.[32]

Spanish forces controlled Mobile when war erupted between the United States and Great Britain in June 1812. By the end of the summer, Governor Holmes's aggressive actions in the Mobile District had created a dangerous and unusual situation. The United States and Britain were at war, and Holmes's unsanctioned reorganizations threatened a war with Spain as well. Moreover, about 200 yards south of the city of Mobile stood Fort Charlotte, "a regular square of 120 yards front, built of brick, with four Bastions, Ditch, Coverway, and Pallisades [sic]." Although in a serious state of disrepair, the fort contained a garrison of about 130 men. And while this force certainly was not strong enough to expel Americans from the territory, it still provided a source of friction and potential trouble. Accordingly, the United States government made no official effort to seize the Spanish fort or city, nor did the Spanish interfere with American military forces in the area.[33]

This strange coexistence lasted until the following spring. On February 12, 1813, the US Congress, meeting in a secret session, finally provided President James Madison the authority to seize all of West Florida, including Mobile. Four days later Secretary of War John Armstrong sent a copy of the act to General James Wilkinson at New Orleans and instructed him to seize Fort Charlotte and the surrounding territory east to the Perdido River. When Wilkinson received his orders in mid-March, he immediately began preparations to bring Mobile under the Stars and Stripes.[34]

During the last two weeks of March 1813, Wilkinson hastily assembled about 800 men, including both infantry and artillery, and sent them via water to Pass Christian, some 75 miles west of Mobile. The general also requested that New Orleans naval station commander Captain Shaw provide gunboat escorts for his fourteen transports. Wilkinson's plan was to use the gunboats to occupy Mobile Bay and disrupt the city's communication with Spanish Pensacola. Finally, Wilkinson directed Colonel John Bowyer, stationed at Fort Stoddert, to move his four hundred troops into a position to assist with the attack.[35]

Wilkinson experienced a series of delays and did not depart New Orleans until March 29. He traveled by sea aboard the *Alligator*, but stormy waters tossed the vessel so badly that the general transferred to a barge. The barge proved even worse. As it neared Pass Christian it sank, taking down most of Wilkinson's personal baggage. The general and several of his associates avoided drowning by clinging to the barge's keel for some time before being rescued by Spanish fishermen. This helping hand, viewed from hindsight, is ironic because the fishermen towed the barge ashore and righted it, thereby allowing the general and his associates to proceed against the fishermen's countrymen.[36]

Although bad weather had delayed Wilkinson and Shaw's advance, it did not hinder the planned amphibious assault. In the early morning hours of April 12, Shaw's five gunboats (*Nos. 5, 22, 65, 156,* and *163*) provided cover and support as six hundred of Wilkinson's men went ashore three miles south of Fort Charlotte and marched in column toward their objective. Colonel Bowyer's men arrived by sunrise and moved their five artillery pieces into advantageous positions north of the Spanish fort. Meanwhile, a company of American volunteers from Mobile joined the US cause and helped cut off Spanish communications with Pensacola. Captain Cayetano Pérez recognized that he was under siege. Over the next three days, Pérez watched his situation deteriorate as Wilkinson made final preparations for a land assault. Meanwhile, Shaw's gunboats remained anchored in a line-ahead formation about two hundred yards off the fort, preventing escape or reinforcement via water.[37]

Pérez was in a helpless situation—his garrison now numbered about eighty hungry and dispirited men. Fort Charlotte could not withstand a sustained assault because Pérez had but few guns and limited powder and shot. The governor of West Florida, Mauricio Zúñiga, had not aided or supported Fort Charlotte. He had withdrawn men from Mobile the previous winter to bolster the defenses of the more important city of Pensacola to the east. Even so, the governor could still only muster sixty regulars and some 120 Black troops from Cuba for defense of Pensacola. Furthermore, the Spanish had only 280 soldiers in all of West Florida. Governor Zúñiga had anticipated five hundred additional Cuban troops and the support of the Creek Indians, but neither arrived in time to prevent the loss of Mobile.[38]

As Wilkinson prepared for his attack, he sent dispatches to the townspeople admonishing them to refrain from aiding the Spanish soldiers. He also informed Pérez that the Americans came not as enemies but rather "to relieve the brave garrison which you so worthily command, from the occupancy of a post within the legitimate limits of the United States." Wilkinson's "friendly" offer was an insult to the loyal Spanish commander, who issued a formal protest against the arrogant American claims. But the protest represented nothing more than bluster and an attempt to forestall the inevitable; Pérez knew he had no alternative other than to surrender. On April 13, 1813, Wilkinson and Pérez met and signed formal articles of surrender, turning Fort Charlotte and Mobile over to the United States. Two days later Shaw's gunboats evacuated Spanish forces to Pensacola with their personal weapons and equipment. All Spanish cannon and munitions remained within the fort. Captain Shaw later recalled that at five o'clock on the evening of April 15—amid formal salutes from the fort's cannon and American gunboats—"our Flag was display'd within their Works." Mobile had been incorporated into the United States "without any fighting or disturbance [and] everything has remained quiet since."[39]

The capture of Mobile stands as a model of cooperation between the US Army and Navy, despite the animosity that previously existed between Wilkinson and Shaw. It represented the United States' most successful joint military operation during the War of 1812. In fact, in no other engagement did the country gain so much with so little effort. Although Wilkinson and Shaw could boast of the "Invasion of the [city] & its tame surrender," they had not triumphed over the British but a weaker Spanish force not at war against the United States. Nevertheless, the action gave the United States unquestioned control over Florida, west of the Perdido River, and demonstrated the ease by which Spain could be expelled from the Gulf Coast, including perhaps even East Florida.[40]

Conclusion

Nineteenth-century historian Henry Adams proclaimed that the American capture and retention of Mobile was "the only permanent gain of territory made during the war." Moreover, it was "effected without bloodshed, [and had] attracted less attention than it deserved." The United States had purchased Louisiana in 1803 from Napoleon, who had pressured Spain to relinquish the territory; the legality of both of these transactions remained questionable, especially in British and Spanish eyes. In 1810 American settlers in Baton Rouge had revolted and seized the Spanish fort, proclaiming the area the West Florida Republic. During the months that followed, President James Madison avoided Spanish conflict by maintaining that the United States was occupying the Baton Rouge district as part of the Louisiana Purchase. This public announcement provided American justification because it subsumed the newly created Republic of West Florida and incorporated the area into the already established Louisiana Territory created by the 1803 Purchase. This gave the appearance that the United States was simply taking what they already claimed. During the War of 1812, US forces seized and retained Mobile while American settlers strengthened their hold on other West Florida lands. General Wilkinson claimed that the military occupation of Mobile was simply "to relieve the [Spanish] from the occupancy of a post within the legitimate limits of the United States."[41]

Did either of these acquisitions represent a military conquest? Given that the United States and Spain were not at war and that US military forces fired no shots in hostility, the seizure of Baton Rouge and occupation of Mobile fulfilled Jefferson's wish for conquering without war. And while the United States benefited greatly from Spanish weakness along the Gulf, questions remained about ownership of these areas of West Florida. Ultimately, the American victory at New Orleans during the War of 1812 erased all doubts about who possessed, who controlled, and who owned Louisiana and the Purchase. Likewise, the American incorporation of Baton Rouge and occupation of Mobile removed all misgivings about the US acquisition of that part of West Florida. In neither case did the Treaty of Ghent—which ended the War of 1812—and its status quo antebellum provisions apply to the lands Spain lost. While the United States had no acknowledged title to either Louisiana, Baton Rouge, or Mobile before the War of 1812, the American government was unwilling to return these possessions to Britain or her Spanish ally after the war.[42]

By 1815 Britain was ready to end the conflict and was ill-disposed to continue fighting a war with the United States over treaty violations or questions of Spanish territory. The Treaty of Ghent became an immediate way to end the fighting. Outstanding claims by both sides remained open for future negotiations for years, but the United States and Great Britain never addressed the issue of American Gulf Coast expansion. Former Spanish-owned lands remained under the Stars and Stripes after the war, despite repeated protests from Madrid. Status quo ante bellum, then, did not truly represent the peace arrangements because the state of affairs along the Gulf Coast appeared very different in 1815 than the situation in 1812. After the War of 1812, the American flag flew unquestionably over former Spanish possessions in Louisiana, Baton Rouge, Mobile, and throughout West Florida, west of the Perdido River. The ease by which Americans hoisted their flag in these regions revealed that Spain was too weak to maintain anything but de jure control over the Gulf Coast. Without Great Britain enforcing the Treaty of Ghent or supporting Spanish claims against the United States, it was only a matter of time before the Stars and Stripes would be comfortably "display'd" over the entire Florida peninsula.[43]

Epilogue

Pedro Luengo and Gene Allen Smith

Transimperial dialogue between the British and Spanish was crucial for the development of fortifications in the Caribbean. Both countries believed that they knew well the imperial plans of the other, sometimes even considering their opponents' plans as potential solutions to their particular problems. But in most cases, each country preferred to maintain their own metropolitan-centric original plans, which affected several fields: engineering, training, defense and finally intelligence activities. Initially, the Spanish relied on scientific training of military engineers in European academies, while other powers preferred to give them a deeper field experience, as shown by Muñoz Corbalán (chapter 1) and Ruíz Carrasco (chapter 2). Spaniards were taught about theoretical European fortification systems, from Müller to Fernández Medrano or Lucuz, and later adapted those theoretical principles to local geography. This common background resulted in a common solution of problems that was furthermore well controlled from the Royal Court. By the end of the seventeenth century regular fortifications inspired by Italian design principles became common in the Caribbean, as Fernández Martín (chapter 9) described. Meanwhile, the British were unable to develop a common or fluid London-based procedure for constructing defense works in the colonies, but instead encouraged local authorities and even private entities to build and take care of defenses, as Waters (chapter 4) described for Antigua.

This dialogue continued during conflicts when the British or Spanish worked as either defender or attacker, creating some differences between both models. As Graham contended in chapter 3, the English had little interest in fortifications, instead trusting more on terrestrial military or naval forces. This led to a reflection on Spanish engineers. For example, Alejandro Boligny opted for a dynamic defense rather than an unimaginative static one as Morales Folguera (chapter 14) revealed for New Orleans. On the contrary, most of examples show that Spain preferred traditional fortifications, regularly updated with considerations from the court. This approach affected not only the buildings but also administrative procedures that resulted by the early nineteenth century in the deterioration of fortifications because of Spanish overextension and underfunding of existing forts. For example, the American conquests of Baton Rouge (1810) and Mobile (1813), as described by Smith (chapter 15), happened because

Spain had not modernized or updated these defensive structures, which permitted rambunctious Americans to conquer them with little effort despite no formal declaration of war—these forts are described in military reports and personal accounts rather than with maps or building projects. Against what was common in Europe, the beginning of nineteenth century saw dynamic struggles that began to reshape Spain's American Empire, but those changes were not transferred to architectural drawings; while sometimes prints described the changes occurring these were often produced after the conflict had ended, and probably fostered more public interest than military analysis. On the contrary, Spanish officials frequently sent back to the court a rich collection of maps and plans of imperial fortifications, which offers a rich source for future projects.

Research into historic intelligence work clearly reveals two points that highlight an amorphous contested boundary. The development of espionage grew during the eighteenth century in the Caribbean as the British started it and the Spanish responded, as Cruz Freire revealed in chapter 7. Diplomatic visits to Havana or Kingston became opportunities to get updated information on fortifications and military equipment. Initially, short reports were created just before an attack, yet little by little they became a crucial prologue to any campaign. Only from these intelligence contributions, as López Hernández (chapter 6) and Luengo (chapter 5) prove, can innovative attacks be explained against Portobelo, Cartagena de Indias, Santiago de Cuba, and Havana, apart from many other French ports. Crucial intelligence work was not only useful for sieges, but even after the conquest. As Morales (chapter 8) contends, these materials were sent back to the metropolis, and they often became of interest more than any other map or plan explaining the campaign. They were used to create favorable public opinion to new military projects.

An intermediary point between the court and the local had to be found by military engineers regarding the need to update fortifications. War required a well-informed proposal to be efficient. Innovations were common, especially on attacks, requiring quick renovations of defenses. But this was not always easy or possible, given the local lack of skillful manpower, adequate materials, or even funds, frequently requiring a dialogue with local workers and unknown traditions. Adapting innovative solutions in terms of building techniques necessitated a deep dialogue between military engineers and local workers. Moreover, western innovations reached the Caribbean surprisingly quickly; as Hinarejos Martín (chapter 13) or Gámez Casado (chapter 11) showed for San Juan de Puerto Rico and Cartagena de Indias, the way of fortifying big ports was changing drastically from the original perspective common during the seventeenth century. Defensive lines and spread-out little structures were gaining in importance within the Spanish systems. From their experience at these ports, similar fortifications were designed for hinterlands, as Cejudo Collera and Segura García demonstrated for the monumental case of Perote (chapter 12). In parallel, engineers saw the defense of a port in terms of buildings rather than only forts. Hydraulic works, studied by Herrera García (chapter 10), or entire cities as Morales Folguera discussed (chapter 14), were significant when designing efficient protection.

This heritage is, little by little, becoming better known and is being used to write a new historical discourse focused on cultural dialogue rather than simply conquest or military action. This new discourse centers on preserving or culturally managing rather than conquering or destroying bastions. Demilitarization of heritage is providing societies with new spaces to reflect on their history as well as their place within the larger history of a borderland, a region, a country, or part of an empire.

Fortifications represented the crux of hegemonic imperialistic expansion in the Caribbean region during the eighteenth century. They were constructed to demonstrate imperial power over locales. Their construction represented the most advanced knowledge and theoretical understanding of defending territory and a location. The actual construction provided economic opportunities for locals and initiated a process of incorporating them into the power structure of the imperial power. While their place represented the lowest position with the imperial power structure, without their participation, the fortification would not have been completed. But as the fort evolved from protecting a frontier or borderland to being completely within the domain of the empire, it assumed a unique place in the local society and economy. The fort assumed less of a protective role, and instead became a symbol of power that had to be maintained or updated as time passed. Once the nineteenth century emerged, these anachronistic structures had little purpose. Their deterioration demonstrated the decline of the empire and could not serve as effective defenses any longer. Ultimately, forts survive today as memories of the past, yet we need to examine them as statements—of imperial power, of local adaptation, of cross-cultural dialogue, and of opportunities for cultural resource management. Forts are unquestioned architectural marvels as well as symbols of a time past.

Notes

INTRODUCTION

1. Elena Fasano Guarini, "Center and Periphery," *Journal of Modern History* 67 (1995): S74–S96; Pekka Hämäläinen and Samuel Truett, "On Borderlands," *Journal of American History* 98 (2011): 338–61; Jeremy Adelman and Stephen Aaron, "From Borderlands to Borders: Empires, Nation-States, and the Peoples in between in North American History," *American Historical Review* 104 (1999): 814–41; Richard White, *The Middle Ground: Indians, Empires, and Republics in the Great Lakes Region, 1650–1815* (Cambridge: Cambridge University Press, 1991); Andrew K. Frank and A. Glenn Crothers, *Borderland Narratives: Negotiation and Accommodation in North America´s Contested Spaces, 1500–1850* (Gainesville: University Press of Florida, 2017).

2. Stanley Stein and Barbara Stein, *Silver, Trade, and War: Spain and America in the Making of Early Modern Europe* (Baltimore: Johns Hopkins University Press, 2003); Alejandro de la Fuente, *Havana and the Atlantic during the Sixteenth Century* (Chapel Hill: University of North Carolina Press, 2008); Elena A. Schneider, *The Occupation of Havana: War, Trade, and Slavery in the Atlantic World* (Chapel Hill: University of North Carolina Press, 2018), 1–14; Jorge Cañizares-Esguerra, *Entangled Empires: The Anglo-Iberian Atlantic, 1500–1830* (Philadelphia: University of Pennsylvania Press), 201.

3. Richard Harding, *Amphibious Warfare in the Eighteenth Century: The British Expeditions to the West Indies, 1740–1742* (1991); Simms Nam, *Three Victories and a Defeat: The Rise and Fall of the First British Empire, 1714–1783* (London: Penguin Books, 2008); Satsuma Shinsuke, *Britain and Colonial Maritime War in the Early Eighteenth Century* (Martlesham, England: Boydell Press, 2013); Ignacio Rivas Ibañez, *Mobilizing Resources for War: The Intelligence Systems during the War of Jenkins "Ear"* (London: University College London, 2008); Kris E. Lane, *Pillaging the Empire: Piracy in the Americas, 1500–1750* (New York: Routledge, 1998); Robert Ritchie, *Captain Kidd and the War against the Pirates* (New York: Barnes and Noble, 1998); J. Leitch Wright, *Anglo-Spanish Rivalry in North America* (Athens: University of Georgia Press, 1971); C. R. Boxer, *The Dutch Seaborne Empire, 1600–1800* (New York: Penguin Books, 1989); Eliga Gould, *The Persistence of Empire: British Political Culture in the Age of the American Revolution* (Chapel Hill: University of North Carolina Press, 2000).

4. Tessa C. S. Machling, *The Fortifications of Nevis, West Indies, from the 17th Century to the Present Day: Protected Interests?* (British Archaeological Reports, 2012); Jeremy Black, *Fortifications and Siegecraft: Defense and Attack through the Ages* (Lanham, MD: Rowman and Littlefield, 2018).

5. Jorge Cañizares-Esguerra, *Puritan Conquistadors: Iberianizing the Atlantic, 1550–1700* (Stanford: Stanford University Press, 2006); J. H. Elliott, *Empires of the Atlantic World: Britain and Spain in America, 1492–1830* (New Haven, CT: Yale University Press, 2006); Eliga Gould, "Entangled Histories, Entangled Worlds: The English-Speaking Atlantic as a Spanish Periphery," *American Historical Review* 112, no. 3 (2007): 764–86.

6. Diego Angulo Íñiguez, *Planos de monumentos arquitectónicos de América y Filipinas existente en el Archivo de Indias* (Seville: Laboratorio de arte, 1933); José Antonio Calderón Quijano, *Visión general de las fortificaciones indianas en los distintos frentes coloniales* (Zaragoza: 1988); José Antonio Calderón Quijano, *Fortificaciones en Nueva España* (Seville: 1984); José Antonio Calderón Quijano, *Guía de los documentos, mapas y planos sobre historia de América y España Moderna en la Biblioteca Nacional de París, Museo Británico y Public Record Office de Londres* (Seville: 1962).

7. Horacio Capel Sáez, Joan-Eugeni Sánchez, and Omar Moncada, *De Palas a Minerva: La formación científica y la estructura institucional de los ingenieros militares en el siglo XVIII* (Barcelona: El Serbal and Consejo Superior de Investigaciones Científicas), and Horacio Capel Sáez et al., *Los ingenieros militares en España, siglo XVIII: Repertorio biográfico e inventario de su labor científica y espacial* (Barcelona: Universidad de Barcelona, 1983); José Omar Moncada Maya, "El ingeniero militar Miguel Constanzó en la Real Academia de Bellas Artes de San Carlos de la Nueva España," *Scripta Nova: Revista electrónica de Geografía y Ciencias Sociales* 7 (2003): 20–31. See also José Omar Moncada Maya, *El ingeniero Miguel Constanzó: Un militar ilustrado en la Nueva España del siglo XVIII* (Mexico City: UNAM, 1994); Antonio Ramos Zúñiga, *La ciudad de los castillos: Fortificaciones y arte defensivo en La Habana de los siglos XVI al XIX* (Bloomington: Asociación Cubana de Amigos de los Castillos, 2006). By the same author see also "La fortificación española en Cuba siglos XVI–XIX," *Atrio: Revista de Historia del Arte* 5 (1993): 49–64; and Juan Manuel Zapatero, *Historia de las fortificaciones de Cartagena de Indias* (Madrid: Ediciones de Cultura Hispánica, 1979); Ramón Gutiérrez, *Fortificaciones en Iberoamérica* (Madrid: Ediciones El Viso, 2005); Alicia Cámara and Fernando de los Cobos, "La experiencia de la monarquía española en la fortificación marítima del Mediterráneo y su proyección en el Caribe," in *Congreso Internacional Fortificación y Frontera Marítima* (Ibiza: 2005); Alicia Cámara Muñoz, *Los ingenieros militares de la monarquía hispánica en los siglos XVII y XVIII* (Madrid: Ministerio de Defensa and Centro de Estudios Europa Hispánica, 2005); *Fortificaciones del Caribe: Memorias de la Reunión de Expertos* (Cartagena de Indias: 1996); *Cartografía y relaciones históricas de Ultramar* (Madrid: Ministerio de Defensa, 1999); J. Mañas Martínez, *Puertos y fortificaciones en América y Filipinas: Catálogo de la exposición* (Madrid: CEHOPU, 1985); Ignacio González Tascón et al., *Obras hidráulicas en América colonial* (Madrid: CEHOPU, 1993); Ignacio González Tascón, *Ingeniería española en ultramar (siglos XVI–XIX)* (Madrid: CEHOPU, 1992).

8. Nuria Sanz, *Fortificaciones Americanas y la Convención del Patrimonio Mundial* (Paris: 2006); Tamara Blanes, *Fortificaciones del Caribe* (Havana: Editorial Letras Cubanas, 2001); Alfredo González Fernández, "Repercusiones espaciales en la fortificación colonial en La Habana," *ERIA* 35 (1994); Francisco Pérez Guzmán, "Modo de vida de esclavos y forzados en las fortificaciones de Cuba: Siglo XVIII," *Anuario de estudios americanos* 47 (1990).

9. Rodolfo Segovia, *El lago de piedra: La geopolítica de las fortificaciones españolas del*

Caribe (1586–1786) (Bogotá: El Áncora Editores, 2013); *Quiroga: Revista de Patrimonio Iberoamericano* 5 (2014).

10. Alicia Cámara and Bernardo Revuelta, *Ingeniería de la ilustración* (Madrid: Fundación Juanelo Turriano, 2015); Juan Miguel Muñoz Corbalán, *Jorge Próspero Verboom: Ingeniero flamenco de la monarquía hispánica* (Madrid: Fundación Juanelo Turriano, 2015).

11. Alicia Cámara, *El Dibujante ingeniero al servicio de la monarquía hispánica: Siglos XVI–XVIII* (Madrid: Fundación Juanelo Turriano, 2016).

12. Pedro Luengo and Gene A. Smith, *From Colonies to Countries in the North Caribbean: Military Engineers in the Development of Cities and Territories* (Cambridge: Cambridge Scholars Publishing, 2016); Pedro Cruz Freire and Ignacio López, *Ingeniería e ingenieros en la América Hispana: Siglos XVIII y XIX* (Seville: Universidad de Sevilla 2017); Pedro Cruz Freire, *Silvestre Abarca: Un ingeniero militar al servicio de la monarquía hispana* (Seville: Athenaica, 2018).

13. Ian Steele, *Betrayals: Fort William Henry and the "Massacre"* (New York: Oxford University Press, 1993).

14. Fred Anderson, *Crucible of War: The Seven Years' War and the Fate of Empire in British America, 1754–1766* (New York: Vintage Books, 2000); Fred Anderson, *The War That Made America* (New York: Viking, 2005).

15. Richard Ketcham, *Saratoga: Turning Point of America´s Revolutionary War* (New York: Macmillan, 1999); James Kirby Martin, *Benedict Arnold: Revolutionary Hero* (New York: New York University Press, 1997); Fred Anderson, *Crucible of War: The Seven Years' War and the Fate of Empie in British North America, 1754–1766* (New York: Vintage Books, 2000), 117–18, 185–90, 240–48, 340–43.

16. Albert Manucy, *The Building of Castello de San Marcos: National Park Service Interpretive Series, History No. 1* (Washington, DC: Department of the Interior, 1942); United States, National Park Service, Division of Publications, *Castillo de San Marcos: A Guide to the Castillo de San Marcos National Monument, Florida* (Washington, DC: Department of the Interior, 1993); John W. Griffin and Patricia C. Griffin, *Fifty Years of Southeastern Archaeology: Selected Works of John W. Griffin* (Gainesville: University Press of Florida, 1996); David Weber, *Spanish Frontier in North America* (New Haven, CT: Yale University Press, 2009).

Chapter 1

1. Juan Miguel Muñoz Corbalán, "*Universitas bellica:* Les Académies de Mathématiques de la couronne espagnole au XVIIIe siècle ou *Non nisi grandia canto*," in *Les savoirs de l'ingénieur militaire: Manuels, cours et cahiers d'exercices, 1751–1914. 5ème Journée d'étude organisée par Émilie d'Orgeix (INHA- Bordeaux 3), Isabelle Warmoes (Musée des Plans-Reliefs, Paris) et le Centre d'Histoire des Techniques et de l'Environnement. París, Institut National d'Histoire de l'Art,* 22 octubre 2010, ed. Isabelle Warmoes and Émilie D'Orgeix (Paris: INHA, 2013), 113–26.

2. Among them: *El Práctico Artillero, el Perfecto Bombardero, y el Arquitecto Perfecto en el Arte Militar* (Brussels: Francisco Foppens, 1680); *El Ingeniero, primera parte de la Moderna Arquitectura Militar* (Brussels: Lamberto Marchant, 1687); *L'ingenieur pratique ou l'Architecture militaire et moderne* (Brussels: Lamberto Marchant, 1696?); *Breve tratado del ataque, y defensa de una plaza real: Y todo en verso* (Brussels: Lamberto Marchant, 1698); and *El Architecto Perfecto en el Arte Militar* (Brussels: Lamberto Marchant, 1700).

3. Alicia Cámara Muñoz, ed., *Los ingenieros militares de la monarquía hispánica en los siglos XVII y XVIII* (Madrid: Ministerio de Defensa and Centro de Estudios Europa Hispánica, 2005); Horacio Capel Sáez et al., *De Palas a Minerva: La formación científica y la estructura institucional de los ingenieros militares en el siglo XVIII* (Barcelona: El Serbal and Consejo Superior de Investigaciones Científicas, 1988); Juan Miguel Muñoz Corbalán, ed., *La Academia de Matemáticas de Barcelona: El legado de los ingenieros militares* (Madrid: Ministerio de Defensa; Barcelona: Novatesa, 2004).

4. John Müller and Miguel Sánchez Taramas, *Tratado de fortificación, ó Arte de construir los edificios militares y civiles* (Barcelona: Thomas Piferrer, 1769).

5. Bernard Forest de Belidor, *La Science des Ingenieurs dans la conduite des travaux de Fortification et de Architecture civile, dediée au Roy* (The Hague: Pierre Gosse, 1754); Benito Bails, *Elementos de matemática*, 4 vols. (Madrid: Viuda de don Joaquín Ibarra, 1779–80).

6. Pedro Lucuze, *Principios de fortificacion, que contienen las definiciones de los terminos principales de las obras de plaza, y de campaña, con una idea de la conducta regularmente observada en el ataque y defensa de las fortalezas: Dispuestos para la instruccion de la juventud militar* (Barcelona: Thomas Piferrer, 1772).

7. Charles-François Mandar, *De l'architecture des forteresses, or de l'art de fortifier les places* (Paris: Magimel, 1801).

8. Guillaume Le Blond, "Fortification," in *Encyclopédie, ou Dictionnaire raisonné des sciences, des arts et des métiers*, ed. Denis Diderot and Jean Le Rond D'Alembert, vol. 7: (1751–72), 194.

9. Le Blond, "Fortification," 193.

10. Antonio Rodríguez Villa, *Noticia biográfica de Don Sebastián Fernández de Medrano* (Madrid: Manuel G. Hernández, 1882).

11. *Instruccion, y Ordenanza de 4 de Julio de 1718. Para los Ingenieros, y otras personas, dividida en dos partes. En la primera se trata de la formacion de Mapas, ò Cartas Geograficas de Provincias, con observaciones, y notas sobre los Rios que se pudieren hacer navegables, Azequias para Molinos, Batanes, y Riegos, y otras diversas diligencias, dirigidas al beneficio universal de los Pueblos; y assimismo el reconocimiento, y formacion de Planos, y relaciones de Plazas, Puertos de Mar, Bahias, y Costas; y de los reparos, y nuevas obras, que necessitaren, con el tanteo de su coste. En la segunda se expressan los reconocimientos, tanteos, y formalidades con que se han de executar las obras nuevas, y los reparos que fueren precisos en las Fortificaciones, Almacenes, Quarteles, Muelles, y otras Fabricas Reales, y sobre conservacion de las Plazas, y Puertos de Mar* (Madrid: Juan de Ariztia, 1718).

12. *Ordenanza, e Instrucción para al enseñanza de las Mathematicas en la Real, y Militar Academia que se ha establecido en Barcelona* (Barcelona: Francisco Suriá, 1739).

13. Juan Miguel Muñoz Corbalán, "Urgencias cartográficas militares en la España de la primera mitad del siglo XVIII: Ordenanza de ingenieros y Academia de Matemáticas," in *El dibujante ingeniero al servicio de la monarquía hispánica:.= Siglos XVI–XVIII*, ed. Alicia Cámara Muñoz (Madrid: Fundación Juanelo Turriano, 2016), 91–112.

14. Over the course of an eighteenth-century Spanish military engineer's career, he would be promoted through a series of ranks. These ranks were, in order from lowest to highest: *ingeniero delineador, ingeniero voluntario, ingeniero ordinario, ingeniero en segunda, ingeniero jefe*, and *ingeniero director*. In general, these ranks correlated with military ranks

like lieutenant, captain, and colonel, but this correlation was variable over the course of the century.

15. Juan Miguel Muñoz Corbalán, "La Real Junta de Fortificaciones de Barcelona," *Espacio, Tiempo y Forma: Revista de la Facultad de Geografía e Historia, serie VII "Historia del Arte"* 5 (1992): 351–73.

16. Archivo General de Simancas, Secretaría de Guerra, leg. 115.

17. Alicia Camara Muñoz, ed., *El dibujante ingeniero al servicio de la monarquía hispánica. Siglos XVI–XVIII* (Madrid: Fundación Juanelo Turriano, 2016).

18. Pedro Lucuze and Pedro Martín Zermeño, *Discurso de los Brigadieres Don Pedro Lucuze y Don Pedro Zermeño sobre conservar ô abandonar los tres Presidios menores: Melilla, Peñon y Alhuzemas*. Barcelona, March 4, 1765. Archivo General Militar, Madrid, Catálogo General de Documentos, 4-5-6-9.

19. Juan Miguel Muñoz Corbalán, "I plastici e la difesa del territorio spagnolo en el tempo di Carlo III: Fallimento e mancata assimilazione del modello francese," in *Castelli e Città Fortificate: Storia–Recupero–Valorizzazione*, ed. A. De Marco and G. Tubaro (Fagagna: Stampa Graphis and Università degli Studi di Udine, Istituto di Urbanistica e Pianificazione, 1991), 652–58; and Juan Miguel Muñoz Corbalán, "La 'Colección de Relieves de las Fortificaciones del Reino:' Essai d'organisation du Cabinet de Plans-Reliefs en Espagne pendant le règne de Charles III," in *Actes du Colloque International sur les Plans-Reliefs au passé et au present les 23, 24, 25 avril 1990 en l'Hôtel National des Invalides*, ed. André Corvisier (Paris: SEDES, 1993), 181–94.

20. José Ignacio de la Torre Echévarri, "Una maqueta para un rey: El estudio de fortificación de Felipe V," in *Tesoros del Museo del Ejército*, ed. María Jesús Rubio Visiers and Carmen García Campa (Madrid: Ministerio de Defensa, 2007), 99–124.

21. Archivo General Militar, Madrid, Atlas 194.

22. Archivo General Militar, Madrid, Atlas 161; "Juan José Ordovás," in *Atlas político y militar del Reyno de Murcia*, ed. José Antonio Martínez López and David Munuera Navarro (Murcia: Mimarq, 2005).

23. Juan Miguel Muñoz Corbalán, "La maqueta de Cádiz (1777–1779)," in *Milicia y Sociedad en la Baja Andalucía (Siglos XVIII y XIX). VIII Jornadas Nacionales de Historia Militar. Sevilla, 11–15 de mayo de 1998* (Seville: Universidad de Sevilla, Cátedra "General Castaños"—Región Militar Sur, 1999), 889–909.

24. Juan Miguel Muñoz Corbalán, "El dibujante ingeniero hacia la universalidad de la dualidad arte/técnica en la cartografía militar del siglo XVIII," *Quintana: Revista do Departamento de Historia da Arte* 14 (2015): 59–79; Isabelle Warmoes, Émilie D'Orgeix, and Charles Van den Heuvel, eds., *Atlas militaires manuscrits européens (XVIe–XVIIIe siècles): Forme, contenu, contexte de réalisation et vocations. Actes des 4es journées d'étude du Musée des Plans-Reliefs. Paris, Hôtel de Croisilles. 18–19 avril 2002* (Paris: Musée des Plans-Reliefs, 2003).

25. Fernando Rodríguez de la Flor, "Vauban lúdico (Un grabado de Pablo Minguet e Irol, juegos de la Fortificación, Madrid, 1752)," *Boletín del Museo e Instituto Camón Aznar*, 24 (1986): 115–32.

26. Juan Miguel Muñoz Corbalán, *Jorge Próspero Verboom: Ingeniero flamenco de la monarquía hispánica* (Madrid: Fundación Juanelo Turriano, 2015).

230 Notes

27. Fernando Rodríguez de la Flor, "El imaginario de la fortificación entre el Barroco y la Ilustración española," in *Los ingenieros militares de la monarquía hispánica en los siglos XVII y XVIII*, ed. Alicia Camara Muñoz (Madrid: Ministerio de Defensa and Centro de Estudios Europa Hispánica, 2015), 33–51.

28. Diego Saavedra Fajardo, *Idea de un Príncipe Político Christiano he representada en cien empresas* (Munich: Nicolao Enrico, 1640).

Chapter 2

1. About the Real Academia de Bellas Artes de San Fernando, see Claude Bédat, *La Real Academia de Bellas Artes de San Fernando, 1744–1808* (Madrid: Real Academia de Bellas Artes de San Fernando, 1989).

2. Real Academia de San Fernando, *Estatutos de la Real Academia de San Fernando* (Madrid: Real Academia de San Fernando, 1757).

3. José Enrique García Melero, "Orígenes del Control de los Proyectos de Obras Públicas por la Academia de San Fernando (1768–1777)," *Espacio, Tiempo y Forma, Serie VII, Historia del Arte* 11 (1998): 287–342.

4. "Junta particular del 10 de agosto de 1777," in Asociación de Amigos de la Real Academia de Bellas Artes San Fernando (hereafter ARABASF), *Libros de Actas de las Sesiones Particulares y de Gobierno*, 3–123, ff. 78v–86r.

5. The royal decree can be found in, Pedro Escolano de Arrieta, *Práctica del Consejo Real en el Despacho de los Negocios Consultivos, Instructivos y Contenciosos: Con Distinción de los que Pertenecen al Consejo Pleno, ó á Cada Sala Particular; Y las Fórmulas de las Cédulas, Provisiones y Certificaciones Respectivas* (Madrid, 1796), 2: 20–24.

6. ARABASF, Secretario general. *Reales Órdenes*, 5-151-1, s/f.

7. Juan José Martín González, "Problemática del Retablo Bajo Carlos III," *Fragmentos* 12–14 (1988): 32–43.

8. José Enrique García Melero, "Arquitectura y burocracia: El proceso del proyecto en la Comisión de Arquitectura de la Academia (1786–1808)," *Espacio, Tiempo y Forma, Serie VII, Historia del arte* 4 (1991): 283–348.

9. By a royal decree signed in the royal palace of El Pardo on the date mentioned, and accepted by the Academia's *junta ordinaria* on April 2, 1786. ARABASF, *Libros de Actas de las Sesiones Particulares, Ordinarias, Generales, Extraordinarias, Públicas y Solemnes*, 3–85, ff. 7r–11r.

10. Jesús María Ruiz Carrasco, "La Real Academia de San Fernando y la proyección de consistorios en los reinos andaluces (1777–1808)," *Ars Bilduma*, 8 (2018): 139–58.

11. See Horacio Capel, Joe Eugeni Sánchez, and Omar Moncada, *De Palas a Minerva: La Formación Científica y la Estructura Institucional de los Ingenieros Militares en el Siglo XVIII* (Madrid: CSIC, 1988).

12. Concerning the training of the majority of the academic architects active during the last two decades of the eighteenth century, it is worth highlighting the content found in Alicia Quintana Martínez, *La Arquitectura y los Arquitectos en la Real Academia de Bellas Artes de San Fernando, 1744–1774* (Madrid: Xarait, 1983).

13. See the Academia's *junta ordinaria* of March 7, 1773, when, with the intention to evaluate the treatise "Arquitectura Hidráulica en la Fábrica de Puentes" created by Fray

Antonio de San José Pontones, Hermosilla expressed his negative opinion on the matter against the standard of Ventura Rodríguez, Benito Bails, Jorge Juan, Pedro de Silva, and Miguel Fernández. This opinion was especially taken into account because the treatise was not published. ARABASF, *Libros de Actas de las Sesiones Particulares, Ordinarias, Generales, Extraordinarias, Públicas y Solemnes*, 3–83, ff. 190r–191v.

14. A royal decree, a copy of which was sent to the Real Academia de San Fernando by the Marquis de Grimaldi on September 21, 1774, to make known the statement that it makes in its text about the institution "preserving its privileges and powers." ARABASF, *Secretario general. Académicos. Privilegios y Exenciones*, 1–12–22, exp. 3, ff. 1r–4r.

15. With regard to the military engineers' civil works on the other side of the Atlantic, see Carlos Laorden Ramos, *Obra Civil en Ultramar del Real Cuerpo de Ingenieros*, 2 vols. (Madrid, 2008).

16. In this regard, see José Enrique García Melero: "Nexos y Mimesis Academicistas: América en la Academia de Bellas Artes de San Fernando," in *Influencias Artísticas entre España y América*, ed. José Enrique García Melero (Madrid: Editorial Mapfre, 1992): 261–359.

17. Which is reflected, alongside other irregularities, in an undated document, very probably drafted in 1789 or 1790, taking into account the matters that it concerns, and lacking a signature, drafted outside the Academia and titled "Informe sobre el Estado Actual y Goce de los Privilegios, Facultades y Prerrogativas de la Academia." ARABASF, *Secretario general. Académicos. Privilegios y exenciones*, 1-12-22, exp. 2, s/f.

18. To which only individuals approved by the Real Academia de San Fernando or by the Real Academia de San Carlos de Valencia could apply, the Valencian academic Rafael Jimeno being selected for the position. The opposition's announcement is contained in ARABASF, *Secretario general. Oposiciones y concursos*, 2-6-3, exp. 4, s/f. Conversely, this opposition's evaluation, by the Madrid Academia, is contained in ARABASF, *Secretario general. Relaciones con otras academias. Academia de San Carlos de México*, 2-36-3, exp. 2, s/f.

19. They did not find "merit in any of these works." ARABASF, *Secretario general. Relaciones con otras academias. Academia de San Carlos de México*, 2-36-3, exp. 4, s/f.

20. About this military engineer, see Pedro Cruz Freire, "Francisco Suárez Calderín y la renovación del Castillo de San Francisco de Santiago de Cuba," *Quiroga* 4 (2013): 88–93.

21. Ramón Gutierrez and Cristina Esteras, "La distancia entre Europa y América en la Colonia: A Propósito de la Catedral de Santiago de Cuba," *Cuadernos de Arte Colonial* 1 (1986): 47–63.

22. Archivo Histórico Nacional (hereafter AHN), Consejos, 21401, s/f.

23. Part of the information about Buceta's plan, along with the plans carried out by him, were revealed already in Diego Angulo Íñiguez, *Planos de Monumentos Arquitectónicos de América y Filipinas Existente en el Archivo de Indias* (Seville: Universidad de Sevilla, Laboratorio de Arte, 1933), 1: sheets 47–50.

24. Pedro Luengo Gutiérrez, "Movilidad de los Ingenieros Militares en Cuba a Finales del Siglo XVIII," *Quiroga* 6 (2014): 36–47.

25. Archivo General de Indias (hereafter AGI), MP-Santo Domingo, 446–48.

26. AGI, MP-Santo Domingo, 446. The one mentioned by Buceta is contained in Jo-

seph Francisco Ortiz y Sanz, *Los Diez Libros de Archîtectura de M. Vitrubio Polión, Traducidos del Latín y Comentados* (Madrid: Imprenta Real, 1787), 65.

27. In the plans, reference is made to the fact that the interior of the pillars of the future edifice would be made by wooden vertical columns, joined at their highest point to the two *soleras* (a board seated flat on a work, so that other vertical, diagonal, or horizontal ones rest on it) and the keys that must connect them and the pairs of roof trusses that would hold up the roof through bolts and curves. AGI, MP-Santo Domingo, 448. Concerning the union of woods and their conjunction with stones in buildings, see Miguel Benavente, *Elementos de Toda la Architectura Civil, con las Más Singulares Observaciones de los Modernos, Impresos en Latin por el P. Christiano Rieger* (Madrid: 1763), 59, 229, 237, and 243.

28. Enrique Camacho Cárdenas, "De Nuevo sobre las Catedrales de Santiago de Cuba," in *Temas americanistas: Historia y diversidad cultural*, ed. Sandra Olivero Guidobono and José Luis Caño Ortigosa (Seville: Editorial Universidad de Sevilla—Secretariado de Publicaciones, 2015), 595–606.

29. Likewise, the ornamentation that must have occupied the church's interior space, as well as the ashlar masonry, was simplified and the view of the ornamentation was improved. AGI, MP-Santo Domingo, 494–95.

30. AHN, Consejos, 21401, s/f.

31. AHN, Consejos, 21401, s/f.

32. Camacho Cárdenas, "De nuevo sobre las catedrales," 598.

33. ARABASF, Comisión de Arquitectura. Informes. Catedrales, 2-32-5, s/f.

34. José Enrique García Melero, "Arquitectura y Burocracia: El Proceso del Proyecto en la Comisión de Arquitectura de la Academia (1786–1808)," *Espacio, tiempo y forma. Serie VII, Historia del arte* 4 (1991): 283–348.

35. ARABASF, Secretario general. *Libro de Actas de la Comisión de Arquitectura*, 3–139, ff. 146r–146v.

36. ARABASF, Comisión de Arquitectura. Informes. Catedrales, 2-32-5, s/f.

37. For a compilation of the construction projects assigned outside the Iberian Peninsula and that were examined by the Real Academia de San Fernando, where the data, among other things that concern us, are located, see Silvia Arbaiza Blanca-Soler, "La Comisión de Arquitectura y los Expedientes de Ultramar en la Real Academia de Bellas Artes de San Fernando (I)," *Academia* 110–11 (2010): 89–146.

38. ARABASF, Comisión de Arquitectura. Informes. Catedrales, 2-32-5, s/f.

39. After its acceptance, it was ratified by the special meeting on September 4. See ARABASF, Secretario general. *Libro de Actas de Sesiones Particulares*, 3–124, ff. 173r, 174r–174v.

40. About this important academic architect, consult Carlos Sambricio, "Datos sobre los discípulos y seguidores de D. Ventura Rodríguez," in *Estudios sobre Ventura Rodriguez (1717–1785)*, ed. F. Checa Goitia (Madrid: Real Academia de Bellas Artes de San Fernando, 1985), 244–304; Carlos Sambricio, *La Arquitectura Española de la Ilustración* (Madrid: Consejo Superior de los Colegios de Arquitectos de España, 1986), 363–70; Inocencio Cadiñanos Bardeci, "El arquitecto Manuel Martín Rodríguez, discípulo de Ventura Rodríguez," *Academia* 71 (1990): 411–80; Juan Luis Blanco Mozo, "La Cultura de Ventura Rodríguez: La Biblioteca de Su Sobrino Manuel Martín Rodriguez," *Anuario del Departamento de Historia y Teoría del Arte* 7–8 (1995–96): 181–221.

Notes 233

41. ARABASF, Comisión de Arquitectura. Informes. Catedrales, 2-32-5, s/f.

42. ARABASF, Secretario general. *Libro de Actas de Generales y Públicas*, 3–86, ff. 72v–73r. Likewise, the notification of the foregoing to Cerdá, dated April 30, is contained in ARABASF, Comisión de Arquitectura. Informes. Catedrales, 2-32-5, s/f.

43. ARABASF, Secretario general. *Libro de Actas de la Comisión de Arquitectura*, 3–139, ff. 300r, 302v.

44. Gutierrez and Esteras, "La distancia entre Europa," 57.

45. See the correspondence between Antonio Porcel, Bernardo de Iriarte (the Academia's vice protector), and Martín Rodríguez on this issue, dated between June 6 and June 23, 1800. ARABASF, Comisión de Arquitectura. Informes. Catedrales, 2-32-5, s/f.

46. Camacho Cárdenas, "De nuevo sobre las catedrales," 602.

47. See, for instance, the designs carried out by Hermosilla himself for the execution of the altarpiece of the parish church of Omnium Sanctorum in Seville. Alberto Fernández González, "Trazas y Proyectos para el Desaparecido Retablo Mayor de Estuco de la Iglesia Parroquial de Omnium Sanctorum de Sevilla," *Laboratorio de Arte* 20 (2007): 203–28.

48. In this respect, emphasis is continually and correctly placed on Camacho Cárdenas, "De nuevo sobre las catedrales," 596, 597, 599.

49. See Martín Rodríguez's plan in Gutierrez and Esteras, "La distancia entre Europa," 54–55; Miguel Ángel Castillo Oreja and Mónica Riaza de los Mozos, "Entre el Barroco y el Neoclasicismo: La Academia de Bellas Artes de San Fernando y las Últimas Empresas Construct ivas de los Borbones en América," in *Actas del III Congreso Internacional del Barroco Americano: Territorio, Arte, Espacio y Sociedad* (Seville: 2001), 708–24.

50. Some information about the life and work of this military engineer, including the development of the plans of the city of New Veracruz in 1800 (AGI, MP-Mexico, 479), are contained in CAPEL, Horacio Capel et al., *Los Ingenieros Militares en España, Siglo XVIII: Repertorio Biográfico e Inventario de Su Labor Científica y Espacial* (Barcelona: Universitat de Barcelona, 1983), 317–18.

51. ARABASF, Comisión de Arquitectura. Informes, 2-29-6, exp. 12, s/f.

52. Specifically, the construction of the new Real Fábrica de Tabacos de México was decreed on April 20, 1776, by the Crown. Although the person in charge of the project was initially the military engineer Miguel Constanzó, in 1787 the works were brought to a standstill for unknown reasons and the viceroy, Juan Vicente de Güemes Pacheco, put Mascaró in charge of the work. Moreover, the two buildings would be located "facing the Alameda, between the Hospicio de Pobres and the Convento del Corpus Christi," where the work would cost less "than if it were carried out in the city's center." María Lourdes Díaz-Trechuelo Spinola, Concepción Pajaron Parody, and Adolfo Rubio Gil, "El Virrey Don Juan Vicente de Güemes Pacheco, Segundo Conde de Revillagigedo," in *Los Virreyes de Nueva España en el reinado de Carlos IV*, ed. Jose Antonio Calderón Quijano (Seville: Escuela de Estudios Hispano-Americanos de Sevilla, 1972), 1: 126.

53. The lower and upper levels, the elevation, and the sectional of the Casa de la Dirección de la Renta de Tabacos, as well as the upper and lower levels, the sectional, and the elevation of the Fábrica de Tabacos, are contained in, respectively AGI, MP-Mexico, 696–99. They were published also in Guillermo Céspedes del Castillo, *El Tabaco en Nueva España* (Madrid: Real Academia de la Historia, 1992).

234   Notes

54. AGI, MP-Mexico, 695.

55. AGI, MP-Mexico, 406. Moreover, the project, in addition to the mention of the other engineering and urban-planning works carried out by Mascaró, can be seen in Carlos Laorden Ramos, "Obras Civiles en América del Arma de Ingenieros," *Revista de Historia Militar*, special edition 1, (2012): 137–54.

56. ARABASF, Secretario general. *Libro de Actas de la Comisión de Arquitectura*, 3–139, f. 179r.

57. ARABASF, Secretario general. *Libro de Actas de la Comisión de Arquitectura*, 3–139, f. 179r.

58. About the naming of Velázquez and his work as director of architecture of the Real Academia de Bellas Artes de San Carlos de México, see ARABASF, Secretario general. Relaciones con Otras Academias: Academia de San Carlos de México, 2-36-3. Conversely, about the figure of this architect, see Glorinela González Franco, "José Antonio González Velázquez, Arquitecto del Neoclásico," *Boletín de Monumentos Históricos* 15 (1991), 30–39. On the other hand, about him and other well-known architects of the period in New Spain, see Elizabeth Fuentes Rojas, *La Academia de San Carlos y los Constructores del Neoclásico* (Mexico City: Universidad Nacional Autónoma de México, Escuela Nacional de Artes Plásticas, 2002).

59. ARABASF, Secretario general. *Libro de Actas de la Comisión de Arquitectura*, 3–139, ff. 179r–179v.

60. About this military engineer, a member of the Real Academia de Bellas Artes de San Carlos de México, see José Omar Moncada Maya, *El Ingeniero Miguel Constanzó: Un Militar Ilustrado en la Nueva España del Siglo XVIII* (Mexico City: Universidad Nacional Autónoma de México, Instituto de Geografía, 1994) and, José Omar Moncada Maya, *Miguel Constanzó y la Alta California: Crónica de sus viajes, 1768–1770* (Mexico City: Universidad Nacional Autónoma de México, Instituto de Geografía, 2012).

61. José Omar Moncada Maya, *El ingeniero Miguel Constanzó*, 235–36.

62. José Omar Moncada Maya, "El ingeniero Militar Miguel Constanzó en la Real Academia de Bellas Artes de San Carlos de la Nueva España," *Scripta Nova: Revista electrónica de Geografía y Ciencias Sociales* 7 (2003), s/f.

63. ARABASF, Secretario general. *Libro de Actas de la Comisión de Arquitectura*, 3–139, f. 232r.

64. ARABASF, Secretario general. *Libro de Actas de la Comisión de Arquitectura*, 3–139, ff. 232r–232v.

65. Presently called the "*la ciudadela*." See Sonia Lombardo de Ruiz, *La Ciudadela: Ideología y Arquitectura del Siglo XVIII* (Mexico City: Universidad Nacional Autónoma de México, 1980).

66. He took part in the towers and the sacristy of the Cathedral, in the church of the Third Order of Saint Francis, the one in Rosario, the one in San Francisco, and the convent of Santo Domingo in Bogotá; he restored the prison and the headquarters of the Real Audiencia of the city as well as drafted the first plan for the city of Bogotá. He designed the original Central Cemetery and completed both the Puente del Común and the old coliseum. Jaime Torres Sánchez and Luz Amanda Salazar Hurtado, *Introducción a la Historia de la Ingeniería y de la Educación en Colombia* (Bogotá: Universidad Nacional de Colombia, 2002), 109.

Notes   235

67. Robert Ojeda Pérez, Adriana Castellanos Alfonso, and Sebastián Torres, "Incendio del Palacio Virreinal de Santa Fé: Resonancia Histórica y Patrimonial," *Módulo Arquitectura CUC* 12 (2013): 163–81.

68. Enrique Marco Dorta, "El Palacio de los Virreyes de Bogotá: Un Proyecto Fracasado," *Anales del Instituto de Arte Americano e Investigaciones Estéticas* 2 (1949): 88–98.

69. ARABASF, Secretario general. *Libro de Actas de la Comisión de Arquitectura*, 3–139, ff. 263r–263v.

70. ARABASF, Comisión de Arquitectura. Informes, 2-29-6, exp. 15, s/f.

71. ARABASF, Comisión de Arquitectura. Informes, 2-29-6, exp. 15, s/f.

72. ARABASF, Secretario general. *Libro de Actas de Generales y Públicas*, 3–86, ff. 90v–91r. About Juan Pedro Arnal, see Carlos Sambricio, "Juan Pedro Arnal, Arquitecto del Siglo XVIII," *Archivo español de arte* 183 (1973), 299–328; Carlos Sambricio, "Juan Pedro Arnal y la Teoría Arquitectónica en la Academia de San Fernando de Madrid," *Goya* 147 (1978): 147–57; and Carlos Sambricio, *La Arquitectura española*, 93–108, 304–9.

73. ARABASF, Comisión de Arquitectura. Informes, 2-29-6, exp. 15, s/f. Moreover, once the letter signed by the secretary for the Council of the Indies (Silvestre Collar) was received, the Academia dealt with the matter in the *junta ordinaria* of December 6, 1801, in the minutes of which it is stated that Juan Pedro Arnal would carry out the project as as soon as possible. ARABASF, Secretario general. *Libro de Actas de Generales y Públicas*, 3–86, ff. 172v–173r.

Chapter 3

1. National Library of Jamaica, MS 40, "Report to the Board of Trade" (1754) ff. 12r–13v.

2. British Library (hereafter BL), King's MS 205 ff. 407r411r.

3. BL, MS 12411 ff. 13r–17v.

4. For the political, social, economic, and imperial contexts, see Richard Sheridan, *Sugar and Slavery: An Economic History of the British West Indies, 1623–1775* (London: Canoe, 1974); Andrew O'Shaughnessy, *An Empire Divided: The American Revolution and the British Caribbean* (Philadelphia: University of Pennsylvania Press, 2000); Frederick Spurdle, *Early West Indian Government, Showing the Progress of Government in Barbados, Jamaica, and the Leeward Islands, 1660–1783* (Palmerston North, NZ: The Author, 1962).

5. Aaron Graham, "The Colonial Sinews of Imperial Power: The Political Economy of Jamaican Taxation, 1768–1838," *Journal of Imperial and Commonwealth History* 45 (2017): 188–209.

6. This ambitious scheme is outlined in BL, King's MS 214, Archibald Campbell, "A Memoir Relative to the Island of Jamaica, 1782."

7. What follows is based on a close study of the minute books of the Commissioners of Forts and Fortifications in Jamaica between 1768 and 1783 (Jamaica Archives [hereafter JA], 1B/5/15/2 vols. 1–2). The second volume is unpaginated, so the page citations given are my own references. For the commissioners, see Spurdle, *Early West Indian Government*, 129–37.

8. Barry Higman, *Slave Population and Economy in Jamaica, 1807–1834* (Cambridge: Cambridge University Press, 1979), 14–17, 26– 35; Nicholas Radburn and Justin Roberts, "Gold versus Life: Jobbing Gangs and British Caribbean Slavery," *William and Mary Quarterly* 76 (2019): 223–56.

9. Higman, *Slave Population*, 37–40.

10. JA, 1B/5/15/2/1 ff. 2v, 17r–v.

11. JA, 1B/5/15/2/2 ff. 66b–6.

12. JA, 1B/5/15/2/1 ff. 21r–v.

13. JA, 1B/5/15/2/1 f. 73r.

14. JA, 1B/5/15/2/2 f. 53a.

15. JA, 1B/5/15/2/2 ff. 128a, 130b.

16. JA, 1B/5/15/2/2 ff. 128a, 129b–130a.

17. JA, 1B/5/15/2/2 f. 130a.

18. JA, 1B/5/15/2/2 ff. 131a–b.

19. JA, 1B/5/15/2/2 ff. 82b, 84b.

20. JA, 1B/5/15/2/2 ff. 87b–88a.

21. JA, 1B/5/15/2/2 f. 99b.

22. JA, 1B/5/15/2/2 f. 130b; *Journal of the House of Assembly of Jamaica*, vol. vii, 465, 473, 474.

23. This has been reconstructed from the claims for labor submitted to the Commissioners of Forts by the contractors. A day has been (arbitrarily) calculated at eight hours of work.

24. JA, 1B/5/15/2/1 f. 68v and JA, 1B/5/15/2/2 f. 141b.

25. JA, 1B/5/15/2/2 f. 157b.

26. JA, 1B/5/15/2/2 ff. 44b–45a.

27. JA, 1B/5/15/2/2 f. 139b.

28. JA, 1B/5/15/2/2 ff. 139b, 140a.

29. Edward Long, *A History of Jamaica* (London, 1774), 1: 63–64.

30. Long, *History of Jamaica*, 1: 64–68.

31. JA, 1B/5/15/2/1 ff. 70r–v.

32. JA, 1B/5/15/2/1 ff. 74v–78v.

33. JA, 1B/5/15/2/2 ff. 95a–97a.

34. JA, 1B/5/15/2/2 f. 120a.

35. JA, 1B/5/15/2/2 f. 120b.

36. George Metcalf, *Royal Government and Political Conflict in Jamaica, 1729–1783* (London: Longmans, 1965), 199– 208; O'Shaughnessy, *An Empire Divided*, 189, 193, 203.

Chapter 4

1. Vere Langford Oliver, *The History of the Island of Antigua, One of the Leeward Caribees in the West Indies, From the First Settlement in 1635 to the Present Time*, 3 vols. (London: Mitchell and Hughes, 1899), 1: xxxii. Original spelling and grammar from archival sources are retained throughout the text.

2. Brian Dyde, *A History of Antigua: The Unsuspected Isle* (London: Macmillan Education, 2000), 20–24. The National Archives, Kew, UK (hereafter TNA), Colonial Office (hereafter CO), 9/22: August 19, 1755.

3. Christopher K. Waters, "Putting Forts in Their Place: The Politics of Defense in Antigua, 1670–1785" (PhD diss., Syracuse University, 2018).

4. See Shannon Lee Dawdy, *Building the Devil's Empire: French Colonial New Orleans* (Chicago: University of Chicago Press, 2008).

Notes

5. Dyde, *History of Antigua: The Unsuspected Isle*, 52. Until 1730, several small bands of maroons—runaway enslaved persons—formed communities in the Sherkerley Mountains that were periodically targeted by the local government for eradication. The last band was hunted down in 1730 (TNA CO 9/7: October 12, 1730). Rates of convictions for running away, considered a capital crime, also declined from seventy individuals between 1740 and 1750, to fourteen between 1750 and 1760, and only five between 1760 and 1770. This suggests that long-term maroonage was not possible in Antigua by the mid-eighteenth century, reflecting the intense deforestation and sugar cultivation that had overtaken the island. For more, see David Barry Gaspar, "Runaways in Seventeenth-Century Antigua, West Indies," *Boletin de Estudtios Lantinamericanos del Caribe* 26 (1979), and David Barry Gaspar, *Bondmen and Rebels: A Study of Master-Slave Relations in Antigua* (Durham, NC: Duke University Press, 1985).

6. Mrs. Langahan, *Antigua and the Antiguans: A Full Account of the Colony and Its Inhabitants from the Time of the Caribs to the Present Day* (London: Saunders and Otley, 1844).

7. TNA CO 9/20: March 17, 1749.

8. Waters, "Putting Forts in Their Place"; Desmond V. Nicholson, *Forts of Antigua and Barbuda* (St. John's, Antigua: Museum of Antigua and Barbuda, 1994); Christopher K. Waters, "Indefensible Landscapes: Power Dynamics, Social Relations, and Antigua's Eighteenth-Century Fortifications," in *Power, Political Economy, and Historical Landscapes of the Modern World: Interdisciplinary Perspectives*, ed. C. R. Decorse (Albany: State University of New York Press, 2019).

9. The original autonomy thesis was proposed by Elsa Goveia, *Slave Society in the British Leeward Islands at the End of the Eighteenth Century* (New Haven, CT: Yale University Press, 1965). See also Douglas Hall, *Five of the Leewards, 1834–1870: The Major Problems of the Post-Emancipation Period in Antigua, Barbuda, Montserrat, Nevis, and St. Kitts* (St. Laurence, Barbados: Caribbean University Press, 1971); Dyde, *History of Antigua: The Unsuspected Isle*; Natalie A. Zacek, *Settler Society in the English Leeward Islands, 1670–1776* (Cambridge: Cambridge University Press, 2010), 12, 209, suggests that Antigua's legislature saw itself as an equal to Parliament in London and therefore outside of that jurisdiction. Instead, Antigua raised a 4.5 percent customs duty on all sugar exports for the Crown, and in return was largely left alone. This is largely due to a series of weak monarchs between Charles II and George II (1660–1760) who were focused on consolidating power at home and did not have the means or security to pursue imperial ambition (except for Queen Anne, 1702–1714). See Steven Saunders Webb, *The Governors-General: The English Army and the Definition of Empire, 1569–1681* (Chapel Hill: University of North Carolina Press, 1979) and Steven Saunders Webb, *Marlborough's America* (New Haven, CT: Yale University Press, 2013).

10. The Thirty-Eighth Regiment (South Staffordshire) was stationed on Antigua between 1707 and 1763. During their tenure, the Colonels of the Regiment rarely made it to Antigua, with command devolving to the next highest officer. Taking advantage of this situation, several Antiguan planters held de facto command, such as Daniel Parke (1706–10), Valentine Morris (1707–40), and George Lucas (1724–47). Webb, *Governors-General*; Webb, *Marlborough's America*; Oliver, *History of the Island of Antigua*; Roger Norman Buckley, *The British Army in the West Indies: Society and the Military in the Revolutionary Age* (Gainesville: University Press of Florida, 1998); Ivor Waters, *The Unfortunate Valentine*

238   Notes

Morris (Chepstow: Chepstow Society, 1964); Waters, "Putting Forts in Their Place"; Waters, "Indefensible Landscapes."

11. National Archives of Antigua and Barbuda, St. John's Antigua [hereafter NAAB], 330: August 26, 1779.

12. Richard B. Sheridan, "The Rise of a Colonial Gentry: A Case Study of Antigua, 1730–1775," *Economic History Review* 13, no. 3 (1961): 342–57. Christopher Chase Dunn, *Sugar and Slaves: The Rise of the Planter Class in the English West Indies, 1624–1713* (Chapel Hill: University of North Carolina Press, 1972); Webb, *Governors-General*; Webb, *Marlborough's America.*

13. Kane William Horneck, *A report of the state of the fortifications In the island of Antigua and particularly those of English Harbour In the said Island in the year 1752.* Manuscript, hand colored, nineteen plans. Originals held at the John Carter Brown Library. Of the sixteen sites, ten have been surveyed archaeologically by the author. While there are some design discrepancies between the Horneck images and the archaeological remains, the overall design, including the presence or absence of a circuit wall, did not change. Archival research indicates that only minor changes, such as the addition of a gunpowder magazine, happened after a site was initially constructed. Design flaws were only rarely addressed.

14. For military treatises, see John Müller, *A Treatise Containing the Elementary Part of Fortification, Regular and Irregular with Remarks on the Constructions of the most Celebrated Authors, particularly of Marshal de Vauban and Baron Coehorn, in which the Perfection and Imperfection of their several Works are considered: For Use of the Royal Academy of Artillery at Woolwich* (London: Lamb, 1756); John Müller, *The Attac and Defense of Fortified Places,* 2nd ed. (London: J. Millan, 1768); and Sebastien LePetrie de Vauban, *A Manual of Siegecraft and Fortification,* trans. G. A. Rothrock (Ann Arbor: University of Michigan Press, 1968).

15. NAAB 324: July 11, 1745.

16. TNA CO 9/41: August 22, 1782.

17. Fort Berkeley was expanded in 1745 to protect the expanding Naval Dockyard in English Harbour. Both projects were funded and planned by the Antiguan legislature, which sought to lure the Royal Navy into maintaining a permanent presence on Antigua. The original fort from 1704 was expanded to include a long firing platform for eleven cannons. The walls were only 195 centimeters thick. Commodore Knowles, the ranking naval officer, was concerned that the Antiguan legislature was not building adequate-enough defenses, so on his own initiative constructed a second battery using navy resources, NAAB 324: April 1, 1745. For his actions, Knowles was officially reprimanded by the navy, but was acquitted at his court-martial, NAAB 324: July 11, 1776; Julian Gywn, *An Admiral for America: Sir Peter Warren, Vice Admiral of the Red, 1703–1752* (Gainesville: University Press of Florida, 2004), 62–63. Fort Berkeley remained in the possession of the Antiguan government until 1783 when it was deemed too expensive to maintain and handed over to the navy, TNA CO 9/41: September 24, 1783.

18. TNA CO 9/1: April 23, 1709.

19. Calendar of State Papers, Colonial: North America and the West Indies, "America and West Indies: June 1709, 21–30," in *Calendar of State Papers Colonial, America, and West Indies: Volume 24, 1708–1709,* ed. Cecil Headlam (London, 1922), 370–408. *British History Online,* June 26, 1709.

Notes   239

20. CSPWI, "America and West Indies: September 1734, 11–15," in *Calendar of State Papers Colonial, America, and West Indies: Volume 41, 1734–1735* (London, 1953), 199–242. *British History Online*, September 14, 1734.

21. TNA, Map Room (hereafter MR), 1/1070.

22. John Luffman, *A Brief Account of the Island of Antigua, Together with the Customs and Manners of Its Inhabitants, White as well as Black . . . in Letters to a Friend* (London: Eighteenth Century Collections Online Print Editions, 2010), Letter VI, September 3, 1786.

23. Antigua was probably not attacked in force after 1666 because of its position slightly to the windward of the rest of the Lesser Antilles, making sailing large warships and troop transports upwind to the island that much more difficult and time consuming. Additionally, St. John's is on the west side of the island, protected by reef systems to the north and south that made a direct approach to the island for square-rigged vessels even more difficult and very slow. In contrast, St. Kitts, Nevis, and Montserrat, which are farther west of Antigua, were all seized by the French many times after 1666, while Antigua was left largely alone.

24. TNA CO 157/1 and TNA CO 10/1, respectively.

25. TNA CO 8/1: 47–49, NICHOLSON, Nicholson, *Forts of Antigua*, 10; David Buisseret and Barrie Clark, *A Report on the Chief Monuments of: Antigua, The British Virgin Islands, the Cayman Islands, Dominica, Grenada, Montserrat, Saint Lucia, Saint Vincent, and the Turks and Caicos Islands*. Submitted to Museum of Antigua, 1971, NAAB 324: February 1, 1739/40, NAAB 324: March 14, 1739/40.

26. TNA CO 152/18/T99.

27. TNA CO 9/6: October 11, 1728.

28. NAAB 324: April 10, 1740.

29. TNA CO 9/1: August 9, 1707

30. NAAB 329: September 24, 1778. Recognizing their inability to create a proper fortification, the Antigua legislature agreed to commission a military engineer to draw up plans for the new battery.

31. Matthew Johnson, *Behind the Castle Gate: From Medieval to Renaissance* (London: Routledge, 2002), 2–10, notes the same phenomenon with late medieval British castles. While they present impressive facades indicating a military function, closer examination reveals that most of these structures have little to no defensive utility whatsoever. Instead, Johnson argues that these sites were intentionally designed to telegraph the aesthetic of power and prestige, enhanced by artificial embankments and specially created vistas. There was nothing military about them. In Antigua's case, the fortifications were intended as military; however, they did not have the architectural engineering necessary to be effective.

32. Henry Glassie, *Vernacular Architecture* (Bloomington: Indiana University Press, 2000), 20.

33. Glassie, *Vernacular Architecture*, 31.

Chapter 5

1. María Dolores Higueras, ed., *Cuba ilustrada: Real Comisión de Guantánamo, 1796–1802* (Madrid: Lunwerg, 1991).

2. Although Cumberland is not the main focus of the study, some details were included in Ascensión Baeza Martín, "Las argucias de la guerra: El gobernador Cagigal y el asedio inglés desde Guantánamo en 1741," *Temas Americanistas* 19 (2007): 37–51, and slightly later in J. R. McNeill, *Mosquito Empires: Ecology and War in the Greater Caribbean, 1620–1914* (Cambridge: Cambridge University Press, 2010), 164–66. See also approaches in José Sánchez Guerra, "Guantánamo in the Eye of the Hurricane," in *Guantánamo and American Empire: The Humanities Respond*, ed. Don E. Walicek and Jessica Adams (Cham, Switzerland: Palgrave Macmillan, 2017), 183–214. Regarding Vernon's assault on Santiago, see Ignacio J. López Hernández, "La defensa de Santiago de Cuba al ataque de Vernon de 1741: Principios de fortificación para la guerra en el Caribe," *Anuario de Estudios Hispanoamericanos* 76, no. 1 (2019) 177–207.

3. John H. Elliott, *Empires of the Atlantic World: Britain and Spain in America, 1492–1830* (New Haven, CT: Yale University Press, 2007).

4. Richard Sheridan, "The Formation of Caribbean Plantation Society, 1689–1748," in *The Oxford History of the British Empire: The Eighteenth Century*, ed. P. J. Marshall (Oxford: Oxford University Press, 1998), 394–414. See also Jenny Shaw, *Everyday Life in the Early English Caribbean: Irish, Africans, and the Construction of Difference* (Athens: University of Georgia Press, 2013).

5. Manuel Gámez Casado, "Buscando al enemigo inglés: Expediciones de guardacostas españoles al golfo del Darién, 1767–1768," *Anuario de Estudios Americanos* 7, no. 1 (2018): 211–36.

6. It was identified by the Spanish engineer Luis Díez Navarro as part of his works in Guatemala in 1743. See Miguel Ángel Castillo Oreja, "Puertos y defensas del Mar del Norte en la Capitanía General de Guatemala," in *Mares Fortificados: Protección y defensa de las rutas de globalización en el siglo XVIII catálogo de la exposición celebrada en el Museo del Canal Interoceánico de Panamá 15 de mayo de 2018–15 de julio de 2018*, ed. Pedro Luengo (Seville: Universidad de Sevilla, 2018), 46.

7. Luis Díez Navarro, *Plano del poblado que habían fundado los ingleses en Río Tinto, en la Costa de mosquitos*. AGI, MP-Guatemala, 50. See also Luis Díez Navarro, *Plano a la vista que demuestra la situación del establecimiento de Río Tinto llamando comúnmente por los ingleses Black River en la costa de Honduras*. Biblioteca Nacional de España, MR/42/621.

8. Pedro Luengo, "Tres defensas para el corazón del Caribe: Jamaica, Cuba y Saint Domingue," in *Mares Fortificados: Protección y defensa de las rutas de globalización en el siglo XVIII catálogo de la exposición celebrada en el Museo del Canal Interoceánico de Panamá 15 de mayo de 2018–15 de julio de 2018*, ed. Pedro Luengo (Seville: Universidad de Sevilla, 2018), 73–88. See also Ignacio J. López Hernández and Pedro Luengo, "Fortificaciones francesas en el Caribe frente a los ataques de la Guerra de los Siete Años," *Aldaba* 43 (2018): 273–89.

9. Carlos del Cairo Hurtado, "Mentiras verdaderas o la topología de la guerra: Aproximación arqueológica a la cartografía colonial de Bocachica, Cartagena de Indias," *Apuntes* 26, no. 1 (2013): 186–203. Regarding the fortification of Cartagena de Indias at this time, see Juan Manuel Zapatero, *Historia de las Fortificaciones de Cartagena de Indias* (Madrid: Ediciones de Cultura Hispánica, 1979), or more recently, Alfonso Rafael Cabrera Cruz, "El patrimonio arquitectónico y fortificaciones en Cartagena de Indias: Identidad, significado cultural y prospectiva" (PhD diss., Universidad de Granada, 2018).

Notes   241

10. John Thomas, *A Plan of Fort St. Louis, St. Joseph, St. Jago & of St. Philip scituated at ye entrance of Cartagena Harbour or Boca-Chica with ye parts adjacent and also of the attacks made against the said forts*, Library of Congress, G5294.C3S5 1741 .T5.

11. *Plan du port de Couve et de Goauantanamo* (1738), Bibliothèque nationale de France, département Cartes et plans, GE SH 18 PF 144 DIV 11 P 1 D.

12. Alfredo Castillero Calvo, *Portobelo y el San Lorenzo del Chagres: Perspectivas imperiales, Siglos XVI–XIX* (Panama City: Editora Novo Art, 2016), 2: 425–26. See also Alfredo J. Morales, "El istmo de Panamá: La defensa de una ruta comercial global," in *Mares Fortificados: Protección y defensa de las rutas de globalización en el siglo XVIII catálogo de la exposición celebrada en el Museo del Canal Interoceánico de Panamá 15 de mayo de 2018–15 de julio de 2018*, ed. Pedro Luengo (Seville: Universidad de Sevilla, 2018), 17–34.

13. Rafael López Guzmán and Alfonso Cabrera, "La visión del virrey Sebastián de Eslava del asedio de Cartagena de Indias en 1741: El funcionamiento de las fortificaciones," in *Ingeniería e Ingenieros en la América Hispana, Siglos XVIII y XIX*, ed. Pedro Cruz Freire and Ignacio J. López Hernández (Seville: Editorial Universidad de Sevilla, 2017), 49–76.

14. Francisco Angle, *Plano de la costa de Cuba que comprende desde la Punta de Cabrera hasta el río de Yatera, en que se contiene el puerto de Guantánamo y el lugar donde estuvieron acampados los ingleses el año de 1741*. Archivo General de Indias (AGI), MP-Santo Domingo, 212.

15. *A Plan of George Stadt Camp near the River Guantamano in the island of Cuba and also of the intrenchments made on the adjacent hills, represented more at large with their profils*. Windsor Archive. *A Plan of the Park of Artillery at George Stadt Camp in the Island of Cuba, 1741*. Windsor archive. VIII/44.

16. *A Plan of George Stadt Camp near the River Guantamano in the island of Cuba and also of the intrenchments made on the adjacent hills, represented more at large with their profils*. Library of Congress, G4922.G83R4 1741.T5.

17. Jeremy Black, *Maps of War: Mapping Conflict through the Centuries* (London: Conway-Bloomsbury, 2016), 70–72.

18. *Bahía de Guantánamo*. Biblioteca Nacional de España, MR/43/211; *Plano del Puerto de Guantánamo en donde el almirante Vernon estuvo con su armada el año de 1741*. Biblioteca Nacional de España, MR/43/226; *Plano General del Puerto de Guantánamo en donde el Almirante Wernon estuvo con su armada el año de 1741*. Biblioteca Nacional de España, MR/43/223; *Plano de situación del campo que plantaron los ingleses en Guantánamo a cuatro leguas río arriba desde la boca*. Biblioteca Nacional de España, MR/43/218; *Plano del plantaron los ingleses en Guantánamo a cuatro leguas río arriba desde la boca*. Biblioteca Nacional de España, MR/43/218; *Plano del Campo de los enemigos en Juantánamo, al pie de Las Lomas de Melcor, en el año de 1741, desde el principio de agosto hasta el fin de dicho año*. Biblioteca Nacional de España, MR/42/483; *Plano de la Bahía de Guantánamo, en la isla de Cuba, cuya boca se haya en latitud N. 20 grados, y en la longitud de Tenerife 301 grados. 27 minutos*. Library of Congress, G4922.G8 1751 .P51; *Plano de la bahía de Guantánamo en la isla de Cuba, cuya boca se haya en latitud N. 20 grados y longitud de Tenerife 301 grados 27 minutos*. Library of Congress, G4922.G8 1751 .P5. *Campo de los enemigos en Juantánamo, al pie de Las Lomas de Melcor, en el año de 1741, desde el principio de agosto hasta el fin de dicho año*. Biblioteca Nacional de España,

MR/42/483; *Plano de la Bahía de Guantánamo, en la isla de Cuba, cuya boca se haya en latitud N. 20 grados, y en la longitud de Tenerife 301 grados. 27 minutos.* Library of Congress, G4922.G8 1751 .P51; *Plano de la bahía de Guantánamo en la isla de Cuba, cuya boca se haya en latitud N. 20 grados y longitud de Tenerife 301 grados 27 minutos.* Library of Congress, G4922.G8 1751 .P5.

19. Alfredo J. Morales, "Cartografía de la costa y puertos de Cuba," in *Historia y globalización: Ensayos en homenaje a Alfredo Castillero Calvo* (Panama City: Editora Novo Art, 2017), 81–115.

20. Most of the maps of the escuela are preserved in Washington. See, for example, Agustín Blondo y Zabala, *Puerto de Guantánamo.* Library of Congress, G4922.G8 17-- .B5; *Plano de la Bahía del Guantánamo en la costa . . .* Library of Congress, G4922.G8 17-- .P5; *Plano de la Bahía del Guantánamo en la costa . . .* Library of Congress, G4922.G8 17-- .P51; *Plano de la Bahía del Guantánamo en la costa . . .* Library of Congress, G4922.G8 17-- .P52; and *Plano de la Bahía de Guantánamo en la isla de Cuba . . .* Library of Congress, G4922.G8 1751 .P5.

21. *Plano de situación del campo que plantaron los ingleses en Guantánamo a cuatro leguas río arriba desde la boca.* Biblioteca Nacional de España, MR/43/218.

22. Sánchez Guerra, "Guantánamo in the Eye of the Hurricane," 184.

23. Jorge Cerdá Crespo, *Conflictos coloniales: La guerra de los nueve años, 1839–1748* (Alicante: Universidad de Alicante, 2010), 218.

24. Horacio Capel Sáez et al., *Los ingenieros militares en España, siglo XVIII: Repertorio biográfico e inventario de su labor científica y espacial* (Barcelona: Universidad de Barcelona, 1983), 37.

25. Capel Sáez et al., *Los ingenieros militares en España, siglo XVIII,* 146–47.

26. Alfredo J. Morales, "Cuba y Jamaica: Conflictos en el Caribe," in *Ingeniería e Ingenieros en la América Hispana, Siglos XVIII y XIX,* ed. Pedro Cruz Freire and Ignacio J. López Hernández (Seville: Editorial Universidad de Sevilla, 2017), 13–28.

27. Pedro Cruz Freire and Pedro Luengo, "El Caribe durante la Guerra de los Siete Años: El espionaje británico sobre las fortificaciones españolas y francesas," *Colonial Latin American Review* 28 (2019): 556–76.

28. Luengo, "Tres defensas para el corazón del Caribe."

29. John Müller, *A Treatise Containing the Practical Part of Fortification: In Four Parts* (London: A. Millar, 1755), ff. 225–26.

30. Müller, *A Treatise Containing the Practical Part of Fortification,* ff. 225.

31. "Whilst the line of circumvallation is making, the Commander of the Artillery is employed in making the Park, which ought to be placed in the Part most remote from the town, and the least exposed to be insulted; it is made in the form of a square redoubt, with a breastwork and a Ditch round it, and the entrance is covered with a redan, or small ravelin."

Besides this, which for distinction's sake is called the Great Park, and which contains all the Artillery, Ammunition and Stores of the whole Army; there is also a smaller one, at the rear of each attack, to hold the artillery and stores which are used daily in the trenches, and which are continually supplied from the Great Park. These latter need not to be so well secured as the great one; provided they are free from cannon- shot, it is sufficient." John Müller, *The Attac and Defence of Fortified Places: In Three parts* (London: J. Millan, 1747), ff. 20–21.

Notes 243

32. Müller, *The Attac and Defence*, ff. 18–19 and Figure II and III.

33. Müller, *The Attac and Defence*, ff. 48–50 and Figure IX.

34. Müller, *A Treatise Containing . . .*, ff. 222–24.

35. The names of their superiors were Harrison, Wentworth, Wolfe, Frazier, Lowther, Wyniard, Cockran, and Cotterels.

36. Müller, *A Treatise Containing . . .*, ff. 211–13.

37. Stephen G. Hague, "Historiography and the Origins of the Gentleman's House in the British Atlantic World," in *"The Mirror of Great Britain": National Identity in Seventeenth-Century British Architecture*, ed. Olivia Horsfall Turner (Reading: Spire Books, 2010), 233–59.

38. Hague, "Historiography and the Origins of the Gentleman's House in the British Atlantic World," 236.

39. Müller, *A Treatise Containing . . .*, f. 212.

40. Michael Hay, *Plan of Kingston*. Library of Congress, G4964.K5G46 1745 .H3.

Chapter 6

1. David Buisseret, *The Fortifications of Kingston, 1655–1914* (Kingston: Bolivar Press, 1971); Tamara Blanes Martín, *Fortificaciones del Caribe* (Havana: Editorial Letras Cubanas, 2001); Pedro Cruz Freire and Silvestre Abarca, *Un ingeniero militar al servicio de la monarquía hispana* (Seville: Athenaica, 2018); Pierre Pinon, "Saint-Domingue: L'Île à villes," in *Les villes françaises du Nouveau Monde*, ed. Laurent Vidal and Émile d'Orgeix (Paris: Somogy Editions d'Art, 1999): 108–19; Gauvin Alexander Bailey, *Architecture and Urbanism in the French Atlantic Empire: State, Church, and Society, 1604–1830* (Montreal: McGill Queen's University Press, 2018).

2. Pedro Luengo and Ignacio J. López-Hernández, "Fortificaciones francesas en el Caribe frente a los ataques de la Guerra de los Siete Años," *Aldaba* 43 (2018): 273–89; Ignacio J. López-Hernández, "La defensa de Santiago de Cuba al ataque de Vernon de 1741: Principios de fortificación para la Guerra en el Caribe," *Anuario de Estudios Americanos* 76, no. 1 (January–June 2019): 177–207.

3. Jorge Cañizares-Esguerra, ed., *Entangled Empires: The Anglo-Iberian Atlantic, 1500–1830* (Philadelphia: University of Pennsylvania Press, 2018); Pedro Luengo, "Military Engineering in Eighteenth-Century Havana and Manila: The Experience of the Seven Years War," *War in History* 24, no. 1 (January 2017): 4–27.

4. Harold Temperley, "The Cause of the War of Jenkins' Ear, 1739," *Transactions of the Royal Historical Society* 3 (1909): 197–236; Rafael Donoso Anes, "La Compañía del Asiento y la Guerra de la Oreja de Jenkins: Sus causas económicas y algunos aspectos contables relacionados," *RC-SAR* 11, no. 1 (2008); Jorge Cerdá Crespo, *Conflictos coloniales: La Guerra de los Nueve Años, 1739–1748* (Alicante: Universidad de Alicante, 2010).

5. Edward Pearce, *The Great Man: Sir Robert Walpole; Scoundrel, Genius, and Britain's First Prime Minister* (London: Pimlico, 2008), 402–3.

6. Emanuel Bowen, *The Seat of War in the West Indies, containing new & accurate plans of the Havana, la Vera Cruz, Cartagena and Puert Bello . . .* (London, 1740). British Library, Cartographic Items Maps, 85. m.1.(3).

7. David Marley, *Wars of the Americas: A Chronology of Armed Conflict in the New World,*

244 Notes

1492 to the Present (Santa Barbara, CA: ABC-CLIO, 1998) 263. See also J. C. M. Oglesby, "The British Attacks on the Caracas Coast, 1743," *Mariner's Mirror* 58 (1972): 27–40.

8. Juan Pérez de la Riva, "Inglaterra y Cuba en la primera mitad del siglo XVIII: Expedición de Vernon contra Santiago de Cuba en 1741," *Revista Bimestre Cubana* 36 (1935): 64; Richard Pares, *War and Trade in the West Indies, 1739–1763* (Oxford: Clarendon Press, 1936), 92.

9. The squadron consisted of the *Cornwall* (Captain Richard Chadwick, 80 guns, 600 men), the *Elizabeth* (Captain Polycarpus Taylor, 70 guns, 480 men), the *Plymouth* (Captain Digby Dent, 60 guns, 400 men), the *Strafford* (Captain James Rentone, 60 guns, 400 men), the *Warwick* (Captain Thomas Innes, 60 guns, 400 men), the *Worcester* (Captain Thomas Andrews, 60 guns, 400 men); the *Canterbury* (Captain David Brodie, 58 guns, 400 men), and the *Oxford* (Captain Edmund Toll, 50 guns, 300 men), plus the sloops *Weazel* (6 guns, 100 men) and *Merlin* (6 guns, 100 men). See Marley, *Wars of the Americas*, 408.

10. François Blondel, *Nouvelle maniere de fortifier les places* (The Hague: Chez Arnout Leers, 1684), 5–6.

11. M. L. E. Moreau de Saint Mery, *Description topographique, physique, civile, politique et historique de la partie francaise de l'isle* Saint-Domingue (Philadelphia: Chez l'auteur, 1798), 1: 698.

12. *Plan du Port-de-Paix*, Paul Corneau, 1686, BNF, Cartes et Plans, GE SH 18 PF 150 DIV 7 P 2 D.

13. *Plan, profil et elevation de la batterie sur la pointe Picolet*, Louis-Joseph La Lance, 1736, ANOM, 15DFC334C.

14. *Carte d"une partie de la côte depuis la Riviére du hout du Cap, Jusqu'au Fort de Picolet; Pour servir au project d'une Baterie de vingt piéces de canon proposée a faire su la pointe a Foison . . .*, Ingenieur Coudreau, 1743, ANOM, 15DFC339terA.

15. *Plan d'une partie de la batterie du Quay en face de la Rade . . .*, Ingenieur Coudreau, 1745, ANOM, 15DFC341A.

16. *Plan géométrique de l'entrée et port du Bayahs de la coste* Saint-Domingue *avec deus batteries proposées à y faire pour ampêcher les vaisseaux ennemis d"y entrer . . .*, Marc Payen, 1688, BNF, Division 5, portefeuille 149, 01.

17. Pinon, "Saint-Domingue," 110.

18. *Fort Dauphin de St Domingue: Plan profils et élévation de la batterie et redoute de Fayet à faire à la bouche ou entrée de la baye du Fort Dauphin*, Louis-Joseph La Lance, 1732, ANOM, 15DFC290B.

19. *Carte de la baie du Fort Dauphin, pour faire voir les ouvrages qui ont été faits sur le Canal pour en défendre l'entrée*, 1748, ANOM, 15DFC298C.

20. *Plan du fort de Bayaha pour servir au projet arrêté par Monsieur le Chevalier de la Rochalar et Monsieur l'intendant*, Louis-Joseph La Lance, 1728; ANOM,15DFC298C, *Carte de la baie du Fort Dauphin, pour faire voir les ouvrages qui ont été faits sur le Canal pour en défendre l'entrée*, 1748, ANOM, 15DFC276bisB.

21. *Plan de la ville de Leogane et fort de la Pointe, lieutenance de Roi du gouvernement de l'Ouest*, 1742, ANOM, 15DFC13C. *Plan de ville de St Marc dans l'isle de St Domingue*, 1750, BNF, GED-3754.

Notes

22. M. L. E. Moreau de Saint Mery, *Description topographique*..., vol. II, p. 537.

23. *Plan du fort de l'Acul du Petit Goave tel qu'il est aujourd'hui 31 juillet 1745*, Ingenieur Coudreau, 1745, ANOM, 15DFC730A.

24. *Plan d'une partie de la côte de l'Acul pour servir à faire voir les batteries-retranchements qui ont été faits pour s'opposer aux descentes*, 1748, ANOM, 15DFC427A.

25. Giovanni Venegoni, "De la Hermandad de la Costa a la Compañía Real de Saint Domingue: Compañías comerciales, filibusteros y administración colonial en Santo Domingo, 1684–1720," *Boletín AFEHC* 58 (2013).

26. *Carte de l'Isle à Vache et de ses environs depuis la pointe d'Aquin jusqu'à la pointe de la Bacoüe*. 1720, BNF, département Cartes et plans, GE SH 18 PF 152 DIV 4 P 17.

27. Moreau de Saint Mery, *Description topographique*, 2: 537; 2: 625.

28. *Plan de la ville et fort de Saint-Louis, capitale du gouvernement du Sud*, 1742, ANOM, 15DFC14C.

29. Marley, *Wars of the Americas*, 408.

30. Herbert William Richmond, *The Navy in the War of 1739–1748* (Cambridge: Cambridge University Press, 1920), 1: 123.

31. Richmond, *The Navy in the War of 1739–1748*, 1: 123.

32. *Plan de l'état actuel du fort Saint-Louis*, 1753, ANOM, 15DFC854A.

33. Nicholas Rogers, *Mayhem: Post-War Crime and Violence in Britain, 1748–53* (New Haven, CT: Yale University Press, 2012).

34. Quotation from Knowles's letter published in Richmond, *The Navy in the War of 1739–1748*, 1: 124.

35. Lopéz-Hernandez, "La defensa de Santiago de Cuba."

36. *Descripción de los reparos y obra hechas en las Fortalezas del Puerto de la Ciudad de Santiago de Cuba y Puertos de desembarco a varlovento y sotavento deel abaliadas y executadas por su Yngeniero Don Francisco del Angle en Virtud de Orden de su Gobernador el Señor Coronel de los Reales Ecercitos Don Francisco Caxigal de la Vega Cavallero del Orden de Santiago*, AGI, Santo Domingo, 2106; There is limited information about this engineer. The only reference to Langle regarding the defense of Santiago was published by Leví Marrero, *Cuba: Economía y sociedad*, vol. 3 (Madrid: Playor, 1975). Additionally, Capel recorded some information about his activity, albeit imprecisely. See Horacio Capel et al., *Los ingenieros militares en España, Siglo XVIII, Repertorio biográfico e inventario de su labor científica y espacial* (Barcelona: Ediciones de la Universidad de Barcelona, 1983), 37, 346–47. Further details about his projects in Santiago de Cuba can be found in Ignacio Lopéz-Hernandez, "La defensa de Santiago de Cuba."

37. *El Gobernador de Cuba da quenta a VM de lo sucedido con la escuadra Ynglesa del cargo del Almiral Noules el 9 de abril de 1748*, April 14, 1749..., AGI, Santo Domingo, 1202.

38. Francisco Castillo Meléndez, *La defensa de la isla de Cuba en la segunda mitad del siglo XVII* (Seville: Diputación Provincial, 1986), 364; Omar López Rodríguez, *El Castillo del Morro de Santiago de Cuba* (Havana: Editorial Pablo de la Torriente, 1997), 8; Tamara Blanes Martín, "Historia y singularidad de una fortaleza, el Morro de Santiago de Cuba," *Arquitectura en Cuba* 377 (1998): 32–36; Ramón Gutiérrez, *Fortificaciones en Iberoamérica* (Madrid: El Viso, 2005), 141; Tamara Blanes Martín, *Fortificaciones del Caribe* (Havana: Editorial Letras Cubanas, 2001), 65–75.

246 Notes

39. *Plano de la entrada del Puerto y Castillo del Morro de la ciudad de Santiago de Cuba,* Francisco de Langle, 1741, AGMM, Cartoteca, CUB-56/08.

40. Governor Alonso Arcos Moreno's letter to the Secretary of State, Zenón de Somodevilla, 1st Marquess of Ensenada, April 14, 1748. AGI, Santo Domingo, 2108.

41. Francisco de Langle's report about the fortification of Santiago de Cuba and its coastline, September 28, 1740, AGI, Santo Domingo, 2106; *Descripción de los reparos y obra hechas en las Fortalezas del Puerto de la Ciudad de Santiago de Cuba y Puertos de desembarco,* AGI, Santo Domingo, 2106.

42. Charles Harding Firth, "The Capture of Santiago, in Cuba, by Captain Myngs, 1662," *English Historical Review* 14 (1899): 536–41.

43. Francisco de Langle to Governor Francisco Cagigal, October 10, 1741, AGI, Santo Domingo, 2106, pp. 4–5 and 14.

44. *Fuerte de Guragua.* Francisco de Langle, h. 1741, AGMM, Cartoteca, CUB-126/19 (detail 1).

45. *Plano del Puesto de Juraguasito y su nuevo fuerte q dista 4 leguas al este del Puerto de Santiago de Cuba Año de 1748,* Isidro Limonta, 1748, AGI, MP Santo Domingo, 248.

46. *Fuerte de Guragua.* Francisco de Langle, h. 1741, AGMM, Cartoteca, CUB-126/19 (detail 2).

47. *Plano del Camino de la Trinchera de Guaycabón que tiene 100 tuesas de Largo,* Francisco de Langle, c. 1741, AGMM, Cartoteca, CUB-126/19 (detail 3).

48. *A Plan of the Entrance and Fortifications of the Harbour of St. Iago on the South-Side of Cuba,* Edward Lewis, 1743. This was published in Herbert William Richmond, *The Navy in the War of 1739–1748* (Cambridge: Cambridge University Press, 1920), 126.

49. *A Plan of the Entrance and Fortifications of the Harbour of St. Iago on the South-Side of Cuba,* Edward Lewis, 1743. This was published in Herbert William Richmond, *The Navy in the War of 1739–1748* (Cambridge: Cambridge University Press, 1920), 126.

50. The Spanish documents preserved in the Archivo General de Indias show no ship was ultimately sunk at the mouth of the harbor. See Governor Alonso Arcos Moreno's letter to the Secretary of State, Zenón de Somodevilla, 1st Marquess of Ensenada, August 10, 1748, AGI, Santo Domingo, 2108.

51. Richmond, *The Navy in the War of 1739–1748,* 126.

52. Richmond, *The Navy in the War of 1739–1748,* 126.

53. Jacobo de Pezuela, *Historia de la Isla de Cuba,* vol. 2 (Madrid: Carlos Bailly-Bailliere, 1868), 416–17.

54. Governor Alonso Arcos Moreno's letter to the Secretary of State, Zenón de Somodevilla, 1st Marquess of Ensenada, April 14, 1748. AGI, Santo Domingo, 2108.

55. *"En dia 9 de abril quando intentaron forzar el puerto suponiendo que la avia y no era sino un cable de la fragata que se debia echar a pique,"* Governor Alonso Arcos Moreno's letter to the Secretary of State, Zenón de Somodevilla, 1st Marquess of Ensenada, August 10, 1748, AGI, Santo Domingo, 2108.

56. Richmond, *The Navy in the War of 1739–1748,* 129.

57. Richmond, *The Navy in the War of 1739–1748,* 129.

58. Governor Alonso Arcos Moreno's letter to the Secretary of State, Zenón de Somodevilla, 1st Marquess of Ensenada, April 14, 1748. AGI, Santo Domingo, 2108.

59. Antonio Ramos Zúñiga, *La ciudad de los Castillos: Fortificaciones y arte defensivo en La Habana de los siglos XVI al XIX* (Victoria: Trafford-Asociación Cubana de Amigos de los Castillos, 2004), 122.

60. Pares, *War and Trade in the West Indies*, 92.

61. Rafael López Guzmán and Alfonso R. Cabrera Cruz, "La visión del Virrey Sebastián de Eslava del Asedio de Cartagena de Indias en 1741: El funcionamiento de las fortificaciones," in *Ingeniería e Ingenieros en la América Hispana, Siglos XVIII y XIX*, ed. Ignacio J. López-Hernández and Pedro Cruz Freire (Seville: Universidad de Sevilla, 2017), 49–76.

62. Engineer Francisco de Langle's report to Governor Francisco Cagigal, September 1, 1740, AGI, Santo Domingo, 2106.

63. *Plan de la ville du Cap, capitale du gouvernement du nord*, 1742, ANOM, 15DFC8C; *Plan de la ville et fort projeté au port de Bayaha, Joseph Louis La Lance*, 1727, ANOM, 15DFC275B; *Plan général pour un port fermé avec une ville de guerre défendue par une enceinte, une forteresse et deux batteries avancées proposée pour la baie de l'Acul du Petit Goave*, M. Meynier, 1740, ANOM, 15DFC719B.

64. López-Hernández and Luego, "Fortificaciones francesas."

65. Luengo, "Military Engineering in Eighteenth-Century."

Chapter 7

1. Horacio Capel et al., *De Palas a Minerva: La formación científica y la estructuración de los ingenieros militares en el siglo XVIII* (Barcelona: Serbal/CSIC, 1988), 37.

2. Horacio Capel et al., *Los Ingenieros militares en España, siglo XVIII: Repertorio biográfico e inventario de su labor científica y espacial* (Barcelona: Publicacions i edicions de la Universitat de Barcelona, 1983), 82, 122–24, 151–53, 421–22.

3. *Libretas de servicios correspondientes a los individuos del cuerpo de ingenieros destinados en la isla de Cuba, por fin de Diziembre de 1779*.

4. Archivo General de Indias [hereafter, AGI] Santo Domingo, 2134. S/F AGI. Contratación 5517, N.1R.39. S/F.

5. Pedro Cruz Freire, "El hornabeque de San Diego y la conclusión del Plan de Defensa de Silvestre Abarca para la ciudad de La Habana," in *De Sur a Sur: Intercambios artísticos y relaciones culturales*, ed. Rafael López Guzmán (Granada: Universidad de Granada, 2017), 165–72.

6. His service sheet can be found in: Archivo General de Simancas [hereafter, AGS] Secretaría de Guerra, Indiferente, Docket. 5837, file 1. 5–14.

7. For further information about Huet's work on the Vendaval wall of Cádiz, see *Memoria histórica sobre la fundación de las murallas de Cádiz en el frente del Vendaval, origen de los destrozos que se han experimentado, épocas de sus ruinas, insuficientes medios aplicados a repararlas y tiempo que han subsistido estos*. Archivo Histórico Provincial de Cádiz (hereafter, AHPC). Fondo José Pettenghi, Sig. 35.658/34, fols. 1–13.

8. Vicente Torrejón Chaves, "Vicente Ignacio Imperial Digueri y Trejo: Ingeniero militar, marino, urbanista y arquitecto del siglo XVIII," in *Espacio, Tiempo y Forma*, serie VII, Hª del arte, vol. .2. (1989), 305–6.

9. Juan Ramón Jiménez Verdejo et al., "Considerations Concerning French Urban

Influence on Spanish Colonial Cities on the Island of Cuba," *Journal of Asian Architecture and Building Engineering* 2, no. 8 (2009): 334–36.

10. For more information about the politics of new settlements in the modern-day United States, see José Miguel Morales Folguera, "Urbanismo hispanoamericano en el sudeste de los EE. UU. (Louisiana y Florida): La obra del malagueño Bernardo de Gálvez y Gallardo (1746–1786)," in *Actas IV Jornadas de Andalucía y América* (Seville: Escuela de Estudios Hispanoamericanos, 1984), 119–40.

11. Carlos Laorden Ramos, "El ejército y la fundación de ciudades en Cuba," *Revista de Historia Militar* 78 (1995): 43–44.

12. Pedro Luengo Gutiérrez, "Movilidad de los ingenieros militares en Cuba a finales del siglo XVIII," *Quiroga: Revista de Patrimonio Iberoamericano* 6 (July–December 2014): 42.

13. The file regarding the city foundation can be found in AGI, Santo Domingo, 380.

14. AGI, MP-Santo Domingo, 380.

15. Ignacio José de Urrutia y Montoya, *Primeros Historiadiores, Siglo XVIII*, vol. 2 (Havana: Imagen Contemporánea, 2012), 253.

16. Manuel Hernández González, *En el vendaval de la revolución: La trayectoria vital del ingeniero venezolano José del Pozo y Sucre* (Santa Cruz de Tenerife: Idea, 2010), 53.

17. AGI, MP-Santo Domingo, 503.

18. José del Pozo y Sucre, *Croquis que manifiesta la ydea del plano [para la iglesia] de San Julián de los Guines, con un perfil cortado por la línea AB, y vista de la puerta principal colaterales y laterales*. AGI, MP-Santo Domingo, 505. *Plano de la casa de villa y cárcel proyectada en San Julián de los Guines, con las portadas de ambos edificios*. AGI, MP-Santo Domingo, 506.

19. Juan Miguel Muñoz Corbalán, "Espionaje a contrarreloj sobre el terreno por el ingeniero del siglo XVIII," in *El ingeniero espía*, ed. Alicia Cámara Muñoz and Bernardo Revuelta Pol (Segovia: Fundación Juanelo Turriano, 2018), 91–132.

20. Biblioteca Nacional de España, *Papeles relativos a la expedición de Alejandro O'Reilly a Nueva Orleans, y otros documentos sobre América Central*. Docket. Mss/17616.

21. Biblioteca Nacional de España, *Papeles relativos a la expedición de Alejandro O'Reilly a Nueva Orleans, y otros documentos sobre América Central*. Docket. Mss/17616.

22. Biblioteca Nacional de España, *Papeles relativos a la expedición de Alejandro O'Reilly a Nueva Orleans, y otros documentos sobre América Central*. Docket. Mss/17616.

23. Biblioteca Nacional de España, *Papeles relativos a la expedición de Alejandro O'Reilly a Nueva Orleans, y otros documentos sobre América Central*. Docket. Mss/17616.

24. AGI, MP-Florida Luisiana, 86.

25. Luis Arnal Simon, *Arquitectura y urbanismo del septentrión novohispano: Fundaciones en la Florida y el Seno Mexicano, Siglos XVI al XVIII* (Mexico City: Universidad Nacional Autónoma de México, 2006), 298–300.

26. AGI, MP-Santo Domingo, 470.

Chapter 8

1. The communications system has been studied by Ramón María Serrera, *Tráfico terrestre y red vial en las Indias españolas* (Barcelona: Lunwerg, 1992).

2. The subject has an extensive bibliography. The most recent publication belongs to Rafael López Guzmán and Alfonso Rafael Cabrera Cruz, "La visión del virrey

Sebastián de Eslava del asedio de Cartagena de Indias en 1741: El funcionamiento de las fortificaciones," in *Ingeniería e ingenieros en la América hispana, Siglos XVIII y XIX*, ed. Pedro Cruz Freire and Ignacio J. López Hernández (Seville: Editorial Universidad de Sevilla, 2017), 49–75.

3. See María Lourdes Díaz-Trechuelo Spinola, *Arquitectura española en Filipinas (1565–1800)* (Seville: Escuela de Estudios Hispanoamericanos, 1959); Shirley Fish, *When Britain Ruled the Philippines, 1762–1764* (Bloomington: 1st Books Library, 2003); Nicholas Tracy, *Manila Ransomed: The British Assault on Manila in the Seven Years War* (Exeter: University of Exeter Press, 1995); Pedro Luengo, "Military Engineering in Eighteenth-Century Havana and Manila: The Experience of the Seven Years War," *War in History* 24 no. 1 (2017): 4–27; Pedro Luengo, *Manila, plaza fuerte (1762–1788): Ingenieros militares entre Asia, América y Europa* (Madrid: CSIC, 2013); and Pedro Cruz Freire and Pedro Luengo, "El Caribe durante la Guerra de los Siete Años: El espionaje británico sobre las fortificaciones españolas y francesas," *Colonial Latin American Review* 28, no. 4 (2019): 556–76.

4. In this regard, it is worth highlighting the works of Emilio Roig de Leuchsering, *La dominación inglesa de La Habana* (Havana: Editorial Molina, 1929); David Syrett, *The Siege and Capture of Havana* (London: Navy Records Society, 1970); and David Greentree, *Far-Flung Gamble, Havana, 1762* (Oxford: Osprey Publishing, 2010).

5. Pedro Cruz Freire, *Silvestre Abarca: Un ingeniero militar al servicio de la monarquía hispana* (Seville: Athenaica, 2017), 167–76; Elena A. Schneider, *The Occupation of Havana: War, Trade, and Slavery in the Atlantic World* (Chapel Hill: Omohundro Institute and the University of North Carolina Press, 2018).

6. As noted in Pedro Luengo, "Portus Pulchri in Istmo Panamensis itiaccurata: Ichnographia ex prototypo Londinensi, desumta; prostat in oficina Homaniana," in *Mares fortificados: Protección y defensa de las rutas de globalización en el siglo XVIII* (Seville: Editorial Universidad de Sevilla, 2018), 94.

7. The painting titled *The Capture of Puerto Bello, 21 November 1739* is analyzed by Manuel Gámez Casado in the above-cited exhibition catalog, *Mares fortificados: Protección y defensa de las rutas de globalización en el siglo XVIII* (Seville: Editorial Universidad de Sevilla, 2018), 108.

8. One of these fans is preserved in the National Maritime Museum of Greenwich, in London. It is examined by María Mercedes Fernández Martín in the aforementioned exhibition catalog, *Mares fortificados: Protección y defensa de las rutas de globalización en el siglo XVIII* (Seville: Editorial Universidad de Sevilla, 2018), 107.

9. This character has been studied by Sarah Monks, "Our Man in Havana: Representation and Reputation in Lieutenant Philip Orsbridge's *Britannia's Triumph* (1765)," in *Conflicting Visions: War and Visual Culture in Britain and France, c. 1700–1830*, ed. John Bonehill and Geoff Quilley (Aldershot: Ashgate, 2005), 85–114.

10. This possibly refers to the Act of Parliament of November 1, 1762. Thanks to Pedro Luengo for making me aware of this reference.

11. See Monks, "Our Man in Havana," 89–92.

12. Known as *The Capture of Havana, 1762*, some of these paintings have been referenced in Pedro Cruz Freire, "The Morro Castle and the Boom Defense before the Attack and the English Battery before Morro Castle," in *Mares fortificados: Protección y defensa de*

las rutas de globalización en el siglo XVIII (Seville: Editorial Universidad de Sevilla, 2018), 115–16.

13. Library of Congress, G4924. H351. 1762.H2. Pencil, ink, and watercolor on silk. 61 × 122 cm. Acquired in 2007.

14. The most recent study of the referenced castle comes from Cruz Freire, *Silvestre Abarca*, 242–50.

15. Cruz Freire, *Silvestre Abarca*, 182–277. For more information about the construction of this castle, see Antonio Ramos Zúñiga, *La ciudad de los castillos: Fortificaciones y arte defensivo en La Habana de los siglos XVI al XIX* (Bloomington: Editorial Trafford, 2006), 191–202.

16. For more about this plan, considered as the best graphical overview of Huet's contribution to the prior proposals of Silvestre Abarca and Agustín Crame, see Cruz Freire, *Silvestre Abarca*, 267.

17. I thank Ignacio López Hernández for having informed me of the existence of this plan that is preserved in the Archivo General Militar de Madrid, Cartoteca, CUB-155/10.

18. On the view and the report developed by Knowles, see Cruz Freire, *Silvestre Abarca*, 170–71.

19. Alfredo J. Morales, "Cuba y Jamaica: Conflictos en el Caribe," in *Ingeniería e ingenieros en la América hispana, Siglos XVIII y XIX*, ed. Pedro Cruz Freire and Ignacio J. López Hernández (Seville: Editorial Universidad de Sevilla, 2017), 17–19.

20. It forms part of an ample collection that was recently published. See Alfredo J. Morales, "Cartografía de la costa y puertos de Cuba," in *Historia y globalización: Ensayos en homenaje a Alfredo Castillero Calvo*, ed. Marixa Lasso et al. (Panama City: Editora Novo Art, 2017), 81–115.

21. There is not any agreement on the number of the British assailants or on the quantity of Spanish defenders. See Freire Cruz, *Silvestre Abarca*, 172n239.

Chapter 9

1. Antonio Ramos Zúñiga, "La fortificación española en Cuba siglos XVI–XIX," *Atrio Revista de Historia del Arte*, no. 5 (1993): 49–64.

2. The rich cartography of Santiago de Cuba has been analyzed in Omar López Rodríguez, *La cartografía de Santiago de Cuba: Una fuente inagotable* (Santiago de Cuba: Oficina del Conservador de Santiago de Cuba and Junta de Andalucía, Consejería de Obras Públicas y Transportes, 2005).

3. Ramón Gutiérrez, *Fortificaciones en Iberoamérica* (Madrid: El Viso, 2005), 141–45.

4. Gutiérrez, *Fortificaciones en Iberoamérica*, 59.

5. AGI, Santo Domingo, 136.

6. Francisco Castillo Meléndez, *La defensa de la isla de Cuba en la segunda mitad del siglo XVII* (Seville: Diputación Provincial de Sevilla, 1986), 404.

7. Castillo Meléndez, *La defensa de la isla de Cuba*, 404.

8. Antonio Ramos Zúñiga, *La ciudad de los castillos: Fortificaciones y arte defensivo en La Habana de los siglos XVI al XIX* (Havana: Asociación Cubana de Amigos de los Castillos, 2004), 292, 293.

9. AGI, Santo Domingo, 66 BIS. Planta del Morro y ciudad de Santiago de Cuba. Ink drawing, 60.5 × 43.7 cm.

10. AGI, Santo Domingo, 63 Y 63 BIS. Plano de la fortificación propuesta en la ciudad de Santiago. Ink drawing, 42.2 × 29.7 cm.

11. The projects for the fortification of Grol and Dama, signed by Guil Flamaen in 1617, are of this type. See Castillo Meléndez, *La defensa de la isla de Cuba*, 407.

12. Maria Elena Orozco Melgar, "El palacio Municipal de Santiago de Cuba en la recuperación de la memoria colectiva," *Arquitectura y Urbanismo* 36, no. 2 (2015): 19–40.

13. Castillo Meléndez, *La defensa de la isla de Cuba*, 403–12.

14. Castillo Meléndez, *La defensa de la isla de Cuba*, 411.

15. The intervention in the Fort of San Francisco in the eighteenth century has been studied by Pedro Cruz Freire, "Francisco Suárez Calderín y la renovación del castillo de San Francisco de Santiago de Cuba," *Quiroga* 4 (2013): 88–93.

16. AGI, MP-Santo Domingo, 65 BIS Planta del fuerte de San Francisco (Santiago de Cuba). Drawing in black and colored ink.

17. In military architecture, a *rediente* is the line marked between two points constructed over a sloping terrain.

18. AGI, MP-Santo Domingo, 65.

19. AGI, MP-Santo Domingo, 64. San Francisco fortificado por el Maestro de Campo Don Pedro Baiona Villanueba, Gobernador de la ciudad de Cuba por su Magestad. Drawing of black ink and watercolor.

20. AGI, MP-Santo Domingo, 64 BIS. Fuerza de San Francisco hecha por el maestro de campo Don Pedro Baiona Villanueva, gobernador de Santiago de Cuba. Ink and watercolor.

21. AGI, MP-Santo Domingo, 62. Plano de la fortificación del puerto de Santiago de Cuba. Red ink. It measures 43.2 × 31.2 cm.

22. AGI, Santo Domingo, 455.

23. Castillo Meléndez, *La defensa de la isla de Cuba*, 410.

24. See note no. 15, this chapter.

25. Two of them unpublished, while the rest are reproduced in publications of Castillo Meléndez, Calderón Quijano, Orozco Melgar, and López Rodríguez. Specifically, these are the two maps of the bay of Santiago de Cuba and one of the projects signed by Juan de Císcara.

26. Jorge Galindo Díaz, *El conocimiento constructivo de los ingenieros militares del siglo XVIII* (Cali: Universidad del Valle, 2000), 113.

Chapter 10

1. *Diccionario de gobierno y legislación de Indias.* Archivo Histórico Nacional, CODICES, L.732. *Ad vocem* (dique). s/f.

2. Luis de Aponte, in office between 1724 and 1728, was the governor who intervened in this matter. For more on him, see Nicolás del Castillo Mathieu, *Los gobernadores de Cartagena de Indias (1504–1810)* (Bogotá: Academia Colombiana de Historia, 1998), 90–91.

3. Ramón Serrera notes that "a few years after the conquest of the Chibcha land having been accomplished, the Magdalena [River] had already been converted into an essential route of the country and, to some extent, a secondary route for the impoundment of cargo and passengers toward Peru through Popayán and the Kingdom of Qui-

252   Notes

to." Ramón María Serrera, *Tráfico terrestre y red vial en las Indias españolas* (Madrid: Lunwerg, 1993), 98.

4. The disembarkation and travel by land up to Cartagena took place in the ports fitted out on the river, specifically on narrow winding river gorges called *barrancas*. During the sixteenth century, numerous such places had been documented, composed of small villages, cargo warehouses, and inns for travelers' rest. The final stretch, from Mahates up to Cartagena, could be carried out on a raft that went through natural marshes and shallow channels. In that century, according to Ybot, there were several *barrancas* and pathways opened by Mateo Rodríguez (1571) or Martín Polo (1582), who repaired roads and established inns for overnight stays. Antonio Ybot León, *La arteria histórica del Nuevo Reino de Granada (Cartagena–Santa Fe, 1538–1798)* (Bogotá: Biblioteca Nacional, 1952), 137–46. José Vicente Mogollón Vélez, *El Canal del Dique, historia de un desastre ambiental* (Bogotá: El Áncora, 2013), 71–79.

5. The exposition of the city *procurador*, Bartolomé de Campusano, carried out in a letter sent to the Council of the Indies on November 2, 1588, in which he warned of the scarcity of flour and other products, emphasized the land section between the river and the city and how dangerous the crossing at the mouth was, is very expressive. For this reason, he requested the opening of a canal section between the river's *barranca* and the swamp of Matuna. Archivo General de Indias (AGI). Gobierno. Santa Fe, 62, N. 45.

6. Francisco de las Barras de Aragón, *Documentos referentes al canal de navegación construido en 1650 entre Cartagena de Indias y el Río de la Magdalena* (Madrid: Ramona Velasco, 1931), 5–8. Ybot León, *La arteria histórica del Nuevo Reino de Granada*, 154–66. Eduardo Lemaitre, *Historia general de Cartagena* (Bogotá: Banco de la República, 1983), 2: 151–64. Manuel Lucena Giraldo and Alberto Córdoba Pardo, "Ciencia y espacio colonial: Los proyectos del Canal del Dique en el siglo XVIII," in *Ciencia, vida y espacio en Iberoamérica*, ed. José Luis Peset (Madrid: Consejo Superior de Investigaciones Científicas, 1989), 2: 21–43, especially 22–24. Manuel Lucena Giraldo and Alberto Córdoba Pardo, "El Canal del Dique de Cartagena de Indias (1533–1810)," in *Antiguas obras hidráulicas en América: Actas del seminario México—1988* (Mexico City: Centro de Estudios y Experimentación de Obras Públicas, 1991), 493–503, especially 495–96. Manuel Lucerna Giraldo, "Una obra digna de Romanos: El Canal del Dique, 1650–1810," in *Obras hidráulicas en América colonial* (Madrid: Centro de Estudios y Experimentación de Obras Públicas, 1993), 105–17, especially 107–9. Mogollón Vélez, *El Canal del Dique, historia de un desastre ambiental*, 80–84. Carlos Laorden Ramos, *Obra civil en ultramar del Real Cuerpo de Ingenieros* (Madrid: Ministerio de Defensa, 2008), 1: 180–81. General works based on documentation covered by previous works include Eduardo Lemaitre, *Historia del Canal del Dique: Sus peripecias y vicisitudes* (Bogotá: Constructora Sanz, 1983). Ignacio González Tascón, *Ingeniería española en ultramar (siglos XVI–XIX)*, vol. 2 (Madrid: Centro de Estudios y Experimentación de Obras Publicas, 1992), 429–37.

7. A good example of the benefit that the canal's operability meant for the Indies fleet is in the fleet of the Marquis of Montealegre, which had to remain in the port of Cartagena for several months in 1655, a period during which he supplied himself with more than one thousand quintals of pastries at low prices, taking advantage of the good proximity of the city with the Magdalena River to transport flour. Laorden Ramos, *Obra civil en ultramar del Real Cuerpo de Ingenieros*, 1: 181.

Notes   253

8. Ybot León, *La arteria histórica del Nuevo Reino de Granada*, 190–91. In all the region's haciendas, there was an important mule hut destined for the transport of goods. The authorities always viewed the muleteers engaged in these tasks with reticence, as they were suspected of being smugglers and acting as spies for foreigners and corsairs. See María del Carmen Borrego Pla, *Cartagena de Indias: La andadura de una vida bajo la Colonia* (Bogotá: El Áncora, 2010), 109.

9. Lucerna Giraldo, "Una obra digna de Romanos: El Canal del Dique, 1650–1810," 111.

10. Lucena Giraldo and Córdoba Pardo, "Ciencia y espacio colonial: Los proyectos del Canal del Dique en el siglo XVIII," 2: 24. Lucerna Giraldo, "Una obra digna de Romanos: El Canal del Dique, 1650–1810," 108– 9.

11. Antonino Vidal Ortega, *Cartagena de Indias y la región histórica del Caribe, 1580–1640* (Seville: Consejo Superior de Investigaciones Científicas, 2002), 20–24 and 56–59. For a precise view of the relations with other Caribbean ports and regions, see 167–205.

12. A good depiction of the area around Cartagena in the colonial period can be found in Vidal Ortega, *Cartagena de Indias*, 209–13. Julián Ruiz Rivera, *Cartagena de Indias y su provincia: Una mirada a los siglos XVII y XVIII* (Bogotá: El Áncora, 2005), 231–32, stresses the sterility and the scarce productivity of the province. The choice of the placement and foundation of Cartagena in 1533 has been highlighted, based more on its optimal conditions as a port than on the ability of its surroundings to provide drinking water and sustain agriculture capable of providing food to citizens. María del Carmen Borrego Pla, "El abastecimiento de Cartagena de Indias en el siglo XVI," *Temas americanistas* 1 (1982): 1–9. A short distance away, at the Bahía del Sinú, Tolú, and Valledupar, there were optimal, rainy lands, where agriculture and livestock abounded, but the roads did not allow their convenient transport to Cartagena. Alexander O'Byrne, "El desabastecimiento de géneros agrícolas en la provincia de Cartagena de Indias a finales del período colonial," *Historia Crítica* 50 (2013): 59–78.

13. Cartagena, which became the central hub of the Caribbean region, a first-order commercial center, and a metal receiver, seems to be predestined for illicit commercial traffic, driven by its inhabitants' growing consumer needs. Vidal Ortega, *Cartagena de Indias*, 101.

14. The record, known since the times of Barras de Aragón and Ybot, has not been transcribed or analyzed in its entirety. Its essential historic milestones were cited by the referenced authors and others indicated already. AGI, Gobierno, Santa Fe, 376. Arrendamiento y apertura de boca al río Magdalena (1726–1729).

15. Among the members of the *cabildo*, the *hacedendados*, descendants of the *conquistadores* and *encomenderos*, demonstrating their ancestors' military deeds, predominated, committed to the defense of the city, its properties, and interests. Concerning the composition of Cartagena's *cabildo* at the beginning of the eighteenth century, see María del Carmen Borrego Pla, "Felipe V y Cartagena de Indias: Cabildo, crisis y desmembramiento," in *Élites urbanas en Hispanoamérica: De la conquista a la independencia* (Seville: Editorial Universidad de Sevilla, 2005), 277–92.

16. Cornejo was a general in the Windward armada. In 1717, he commanded the fleet en route to New Spain and he repeated the voyage in 1719 with the *navíos de azogue* (mercury ships). AGI, Contratación, 1290B y 1285, N. 1, R, 1, 2 y 3. In 1720, he captained

the Tierra Firme galleons. AGI, Contratación, 2400, ramo 2. 199 AGI. Gobierno, Santa Fe, 376. Arrendamiento y apertura de boca al río Magdalena (1726–1729). Carta de don Francisco Cornejo, comandante de galeones, a don Antonio Manso, presidente de la Real Audiencia de Santa Fe (1724-X-13), fols. 1r.–8v. Ybot León, *La arteria histórica del Nuevo Reino de Granada*, 327–33.

17. Beginning in 1713 with the treaty of asiento, which permitted the English to introduce enslaved Africans and certain textile pieces and foodstuffs, New Grenadian flours began to be replaced by those coming from Jamaica. The setback was complete beginning in 1778 with the new free trade law. See Jaime Jaramillo Uribe, "La economía del virreinato (1740–1810)," in *Historia económica de Colombia*, ed. José Antonio Ocampo (Bogotá: Fondo de Cultura Económica, 1988), 49–85, especially 59.

18. About the delicate, but necessary, problem of illicit commerce or contraband, which infected the entirety of Cartagena's society so much that if it were an epidemic, it would come to qualified as the region's "original sin," see Uribe, "La economía del virreinato (1740–1810)," 69–70. Lance Grahn, "Comercio y contrabando en Cartagena de Indias en el siglo XVIII," in *Cartagena de Indias en el siglo XVIII*, ed. Haroldo Calvo Stevenson and Adolfo Meisel Roca (Cartagena: Banco de la República, 2005), 19–53. Adolfo Meisel Roca, "¿Situado o contrabando?: La base económica de Cartagena de Indias y el Caribe neogranadino al final del siglo de las luces," in *Cartagena de Indias en el siglo XVIII*, ed. Haroldo Calvo Stevenson and Adolfo Meisel Roca (Cartagena: Banco de la República, 2005), 61–127, especially 88–102. José Ignacio de Pombo, *Comercio y contrabando: Cartagena de Indias* (Bogotá: Nueva Biblioteca Colombiana de Cultura, 1986). A rather complete study of the topic, focused on the first half of the eighteenth century, is that of Lance Grahn, *The Political Economy of Smuggling: Regional Informal Economies in Early Bourbon New Granada* (Boulder, CO: Westview Press, 1997), especially 27–29. For a focus on the second half of the eighteenth century, see Héctor Feliciano Ramos, *El contrabando inglés en el Caribe y Golfo de México, 1748–1778* (Seville: Diputación Provincial de Sevilla, 1990).

19. The governor and president of the Real Audiencia, he occupied the viceroy's seat in the interim between 1718 and 1719.

20. A unit of measure equal to approximately 33 inches.

21. AGI, Gobierno, Santa Fe, 374. Expediente sobre el comercio ilícito en el distrito de Santa Fe. 1720–1723. Carta del capitán don José García de Luna, defendiéndose de acusaciones (1724-IX-8), s/f.

22. Among the aristocracy, high-ranking military, moneylenders, some officials, the investment of their income in haciendas, despite their low productivity, was commonplace. Were they in the habit of keeping a large quantity of horses and goods, the benefit certainly exceeded that of agriculture and livestock. Julián Ruiz Rivera, "Cartagena de Indias en el siglo XVIII: Del dominio particular a la corrupción pública," *Boletín de Historia y Antiguedades* C, no. 856 (2013): 102–23, especially 110–11. We should keep in mind elements of high strategic value controlled by those *hacendados*, such as some of the marshes containing drinking water, especially that of Matuna, which made irrigation and even canalization to Cartagena possible, as Governor Martín de las Alas even tried in 1570, but the city budget's main objective was the monetary disbursements for

Notes 255

fortifications. Borrego Pla, "Felipe V y Cartagena de Indias: Cabildo, crisis y desmembramiento," 227.

23. AGI, Gobierno, Santa Fe, 376. Arrendamiento y apertura de boca al río Magdalena (1726–1729). Carta de don Francisco Cornejo . . . , fol. 4r.–v. This document is also cited by Barras de Aragón, *Documentos referentes al canal de navegación construido en 1650 entre Cartagena de Indias y el Río de la Magdalena*, 38–42. Ybot León, *La arteria histórica del Nuevo Reino de Granada*, 327–33.

24. AGI, Gobierno, Santa Fe, 376. Arrendamiento y apertura de boca al río Magdalena (1726–1729). Carta de don Francisco Cornejo . . . , fols. 5r.-6v. Barras de Aragón, *Documentos referentes al canal de navegación construido en 1650 entre Cartagena de Indias y el Río de la Magdalena*, 38–42. Ybot León, *La arteria histórica del Nuevo Reino de Granada*, 327–33.

25. Francisco de San Martín y La Madrid was a native of Viguera (La Rioja) and from his youth resided in Cádiz, a city connected with American commerce. In 1715, he petitioned for a royal decree of *real cédula* to move to New Spain to attend to certain business dealings. The corresponding information was made in Seville with various city merchants testifying. Among these was José de Ortigosa and Juan Manuel Pérez de Baños. AGI, Contratación, 5468, N. 2, R. 34. The presence of Juan Manuel Pérez de Baños, who had a commercial firm with his brothers, all patrons of ornate decorative items, such as *retablos* of the collegiate church of Salvador.

26. He is a native of Villa de Checa (Guadalajara) and resident of Seville, proceeding to the Province of Tierra Firme in 1713 with merchandise consigned to his name. AGI, Contratación, 5467, N. 62.

27. A type of merchant subjected to the irregular flows of metals from New Grenada's mines and also the irregular arrival of the fleets and isolated inspections. Juan Marchena Fernández, "¿Comerciantes o especuladores de metal? Las élites mercantiles de Cartagena de Indias a principios y finales del período colonial," *Memorias* 10 (2009): 32–90, for the quotation, 46–47.

28. AGI, Gobierno. Santa Fe, 376. Arrendamiento y apertura de boca al río Magdalena (1726–1729). Propuesta y condiciones de apertura del Dique (1725-III-5), fols. 5v.–8r. Ybot León, *La arteria histórica del Nuevo Reino de Granada*, 343–44.

29. Barras de Aragón, *Documentos referentes al canal de navegación construido en 1650 entre Cartagena de Indias y el Río de la Magdalena*, 42–44.

30. Ruiz Rivera, "Cartagena de Indias en el siglo XVIII," 109–13. Julian Ruiz Rivera, "Cartagena de Indias ¿Un cabildo cosmopolita o una ciudad pluriétnica?," in *El municipio indiano: Relaciones interétnicas, económicas y sociales; Homenaje a Luis Navarro García* (Seville: Editorial Universidad de Sevilla, 2009), 407–24. See also Borrego Pla, "Felipe V y Cartagena de Indias: cabildo, crisis y desmembramiento," 277–92.

31. AGI, Gobierno, Santa Fe, 376. Arrendamiento y apertura de boca al río Magdalena (1726–1729). Propuesta de mejoras y debate sobre las posturas efectuadas por los arrendatarios (1725-III-21), fols. 12r.–19v. Ybot León, *La arteria histórica del Nuevo Reino de Granada*, 347–48.

32. AGI, Gobierno, Santa Fe, 376. Arrendamiento y apertura de boca al río Magdalena (1726–1729). Representación elevada al cabildo por los diputados de capitanes de navíos mercantes (1725-IV-4), fols. 32v.–37v.

256 Notes

33. AGI, Gobierno, Santa Fe, 376. Arrendamiento y apertura de boca al río Magdalena (1726–1729). Lectura de la real provisión que dispone la puesta en circulación del canal (1725-VIII-8), fols. 61r.–64r. Also fols. 75r.–78r.

34. AGI, Gobierno, Santa Fe, 376. Escritura de contrato entre el cabildo de Cartagena entre don Francisco de San Martín y don Francisco Herranz, para aprovechar el Canal del Dique, sus pasos y balsas, fols. 138r.–165r. Ybot León, *La arteria histórica del Nuevo Reino de Granada*, 362–66.

35. AGI, Gobierno, Santa Fe, 376. Arrendamiento y apertura de boca al río Magdalena (1726–1729). Francisco de San Martín y Francisco de Herranz solicitan al gobernador de Cartagena la búsqueda de mano de obra para proceder a la apertura del nuevo cauce del Canal del Dique (1725-IX-14), fols. 178r.–180v.

36. Enrique Marco Dorta, *Cartagena de Indias: La ciudad y sus monumentos* (Seville: Escuela de Estudios Hispano-Americanos de Sevilla, 1951), 131–33, 141–52. Juan Manuel Zapatero, *Historia de las fortificaciones de Cartagena de Indias* (Madrid: Centro Iberoamericano de Cooperación y Dirección General de Relaciones Culturales del Ministerio de Asuntos Exteriores, 1979), 85–105. Juan Marchena Fernández, *La institución militar en Cartagena de Indias en el siglo XVIII* (Seville: Consejo Superior de Investigaciones Científicas, 1982), 275–90. Horacio Capel et al., *Los ingenieros militares en España: Siglo XVIII; Repertorio biográfico e inventario de su labor científica y espacial* (Barcelona: Universitat de Barcelona, 1983), 229. Manuel Gámez Casado, "Cartagena de Indias: La bahía más codiciada," in *Mares fortificados: Protección y defensa de las rutas de globalización en el siglo XVIII* (Seville: Editorial Universidad de Sevilla, 2018), 45–53.

37. Among his destinations carrying out diplomatic and reconnaissance missions, Panama, Portobelo, the Gulf of Darien, and Santa Marta are highlighted, and we should keep in mind those motivated by the project to improve el Dique, that takes it inland, to the channel of the Magdalena River. See Manuel Gámez Casado, "Ingenieros militares españoles en Nueva Granada durante el siglo XVIII: Movilidad, proyectos y expediciones," *Revista de Indias* 79, no. 277 (2019): 765–96. The willingness to travel long distances was an analogous risk of the corps of engineers, see Joan Eugeni Sánchez, "La estructura institucional de una corporación científica: El cuerpo de ingenieros militares en el siglo XVIII," in *Ciencia, vida y espacio en Iberoamérica*, ed. José Luis Peset (Madrid: Consejo Superior de Investigaciones Científicas, 1989), 2: 3–20, for the quotation, 16–17.

38. Juan Marchena Jiménez, "La primera academia de ingenieros de América," *Ejército: Revista de las armas y servicios* 447 (April 1977): 22–29. At first, he paid for it out of his own pocket, and his teachings were in line with those of the modern engineering discipline. He admitted children, cadets, officers, and interested members of the public.

39. Zapatero rated it as "representative of the bastioned fortification of baroque style." Zapatero, *Historia de las fortificaciones de Cartagena de Indias*, 86. Gámez has rejected this view of his "style," linking his work with the avant-garde Italian and French treatises from the end of the seventeenth century and the beginning of the eighteenth century. Gámez Casado, "Cartagena de Indias," 48.

40. Marchena Fernández, *La institución defensiva*, 275–82. Manuel Gámez Casado, "Ingenieros militares y arquitectura defensiva en Cartagena de Indias tras el ataque del

Barón de Pointis," in *De Sur a Sur: Intercambios artísticos y relaciones culturales* (Granada: Editorial Atrio, 2017), 179–83.

41. Pedro Luengo, "Technical Transfer and the Natural Environment: Inland canals in America in the Late Eighteenth Century," in *From Colonies to Countries in the North Caribbean: Military Engineers in the Development of Cities and Territories* (Cambridge: Cambridge Scholars Publishing, 2016), 39–54.

42. After this year, it seems that the competitiveness of the Spanish and creole merchants compared to the English ones has begun again and increased. All types of infrastructural projects received attention of the first order. See Allan Kuethe and Kenneth J. Andrien, *The Spanish Atlantic World in the Eighteenth Century: War and the Bourbon Reforms, 1713–1796* (New York: Cambridge University Press, 2014), 326– 29.

43. It consists of the plan and project of a redoubt in the form of a strong tower, with a covering of wood in which, going by Pasacaballos, "are transported all the foodstuffs to this city." Cartoteca del Centro Geográfico del Ejército. Madrid. J-T.7.C.1–36b.

44. AGI, Gobierno, Santa Fe, 376. Arrendamiento y apertura de boca al río Magdalena (1726–1729). Parecer solicitado a Juan de Herrera y Sotomayor sobre la navegabilidad del canal e inconvenientes de la apertura de la nueva boca y cauce, fols. 19r.–24r., de la cita fol. 19v. Document transcribed in Ybot León, *La arteria histórica del Nuevo Reino de Granada*, 348–53.

45. AGI, Gobierno, Santa Fe, 376. Arrendamiento y apertura de boca al río Magdalena (1726–1729). Informe solicitado a Juan de Herrera en orden a explicar y confirmar el anterior informe del mes de marzo y su viabilidad, fols. 122v.–126v. Partially transcribed in Ybot León, *La arteria histórica del Nuevo Reino de Granada*, 360–62.

46. AGI, Gobierno, Santa Fe, 376. Arrendamiento y apertura de boca al río Magdalena (1726–1729). Informe solicitado a Juan de Herrera en orden a explicar y confirmar el anterior informe del mes de marzo y su viabilidad, fol. 123r.

47. AGI, Gobierno, Santa Fe, 376. Arrendamiento y apertura de boca al río Magdalena (1726–1729). Informe solicitado a Juan de Herrera en orden a explicar y confirmar el anterior informe del mes de marzo y su viabilidad, fols. 122v.–126v; Ybot León, *La arteria histórica del Nuevo Reino de Granada*, 360–62.

48. Herrera's efforts on some locks that were never built has been highlighted by Lucena Giraldo and Córdoba Pardo, "Ciencia y espacio colonial: Los proyectos del Canal del Dique en el siglo XVIII," 25–29; Lucena Giraldo and Córdoba Pardo, "El Canal del Dique de Cartagena de Indias (1533–1810)," 496–97. Lucerna Giraldo, "Una obra digna de Romanos: El Canal del Dique, 1650–1810," 109–11. Mogollón Vélez, *El Canal del Dique, historia de un desastre ambiental*, 89–90. Laorden Ramos, *Obra civil en ultramar del Real Cuerpo de Ingenieros*, 1: 181.

49. Ibíd. s/f. Informe sobre el estado del Canal del Dique efectuado por Juan de Herrera a instancia de Francisco de San Martín y Francisco Herranz (1728-IX-18). Transcribed in Barras de Aragón, *Documentos referentes al canal de navegación construido en 1650 entre Cartagena de Indias y el Río de la Magdalena*, 47–49.

50. The studies of fluid mechanics addressed in the seventeenth and eighteenth centuries would have been used in the treatises of hydraulic engineering, which was obligatory knowledge for the majority of engineers, and frequently applied to defensive

258 Notes

structures. See Cristóbal Mateos Iguácel, "La investigación hidráulica en la Ilustración," in *Obras hidráulicas de la Ilustración* (Madrid: Centro de Estudios y Experimentación de Obras Públicas, 2014), 39–54, especially 51–54.

51. Zapatero, *Historia de las fortificaciones de Cartagena de Indias*, 92. Rodolfo Segovia Salas, "Cartagena de Indias historiografía de sus fortificaciones," in *Cartagena de Indias y su historia*, ed. Haroldo Calvo Stevenson and Adolfo Meisel Roca (Bogotá:Universidad Jorge Tadeo Lozano, 1998), 1–19. The quotation is on page 6.

52. A Habsburg Spanish infantry unit consisting of up to 3,000 men.

53. Marchena Fernández, *La institución militar*, 276.

54. Fernando Cabos Guerra and José Javier Castro Fernández, "Los ingenieros, las experiencias y los escenarios de la arquitectura militar española en el siglo XVII," in *Los ingenieros militares de la monarquía hispánica en los siglos XVII y XVIII*, ed. Alicia Cámara Muñoz (Madrid: Centro de Estudios Europa Hispánica, 2005), 71–94. The quotation is on page 91.

55. Manuel Nóvoa, "La obra pública de los ingenieros militares," in *Los ingenieros militares de la monarquía hispánica en los siglos XVII y XVIII*, ed. Alicia Cámara Muñoz (Madrid: Centro de Estudios Europa Hispánica, 2005), 183–202, especially 186–87 and 194–97; Luengo, "Technical Transfer and the Natural Environment," 41–42; Dolores Romero Muñoz, "Apuntes sobre la historia de los canales de navegación en España," in *Obras hidráulicas de la Ilustración* (Madrid: Centro de Estudios y Experimentación de Obras Públicas, 2014), 83–101.

56. Nóvoa, "La obra pública de los ingenieros militares," 194.

57. Francisco Granero Martín, "Arquitecturas del agua en el territorio: Sistemas de abastecimiento y defensa" (PhD diss., Universidad de Sevilla, 1992), 381, 384.

58. Granero Martín, "Arquitecturas del agua en el territorio," 370–80. Concerning Simon Stevin, see Ernst Crone et al., eds., *The Principal Works of Simon Stevin*, 6 vols. (Amsterdam: C. V. Swets and Zeitlinger, 1955–66). Eduard J Dijksterhuis, *Simon Stevin: Science in the Netherlands around 1600* (The Hague: Mar Tinus Nijhoff, 1970). *Simon Stevin (1548–1620): l'émergence de la nouvelle science* (Turnhout: Brepols, 2004). Jozef T. Devreese and Guido Van der Berghe, *"Magic Is No Magic": The Wonderful World of Simon Stevin* (Boston: WIT Press, 2008).

59. The following year, 1618, also in Rotterdam, the French edition was released: *Nouvelle maniere de fortification par escluses*. Both the French and the Dutch editions came from the presses of the editor Ian van Waesberghe.

60. Sebastián Fernández de Medrano, *El architecto perfecto en el arte militar* (Brussels: Editorial Maxtor, 1700), 81.

61. Stevin, *Nouvelle Maniere*, 2.

62. "Mais per telles escluses ne peuvent passer des grandes navires a masts droits, a cause de l´empeschement de la porte, & l´essieu per le quel on la guiende a mont." Stevin, *Nouvelle maniere*, 2.

63. AGI, Gobierno, Santa Fe, 376. Arrendamiento y apertura de boca al río Magdalena (1726–1729). Informe de Juan de Herrera (1725-VIII-21), fol. 123v. Cited in Ybot León, *La arteria histórica del Nuevo Reino de Granada*, 360.

64. The implementation of this wooden solution, both the floodgates and the sheet piling, is due to, as Stevin himself recognizes, the expert carpentry teachers Adrien Jans-

sen, from Rotterdam, and Cornelis Diricxen, resident of Delft. Stevin, *Nouvelle maniere*, 9–11. Regarding the sheet pilings, see Michel Steichen, *Mémoire sur la vie et les travaux de Simon Stevin* (Brussels: Van Dale, 1846), 127–33, especially 129.

65. José A. Garciá-Diego and Alexander G. Keller, *Giovanni Francesco Sitoni: Ingeniero renacentista al servicio de la Corona de España* (Madrid: Castalia, 1990), 114–18, 151–55.

66. The corresponding illustrative sheet is titled "Porte per sostener l´acqua d´alcun fiume per bisogno della navigation et altro." See Vittorio Zonca, *Novo teatro di machine et edificii per varie et sicure operationi* (Padua: Pietro Bertelli, 1607), 9–13.

67. Menno Coehoorn, *Nouvelle fortification, tant pour un terrain bas & humide, que pour un terrain sec et elevé* (The Hague: Henry van Bulderenl, 1706), 243–44.

68. Bernard Forest Bélidor, *Architecture Hydraulique seconde partie*, vol. 1 (Paris: Charles-Antoine Jombert, 1750). This volume from Bélidor's celebrated work is undoubtedly the greatest and most complete treatise about locks written up to that point. It recognizes the pioneering nature of Simon Stevin with regard to his lock projects, especially in the development of double floodgates. Miguel Sánchez Taramas, *Tratado de fortificación o arte de construir los edificios militares y civiles*, 2 vols. (Barcelona: Thomas Piferrer, 1769), 184–218. This is the Spanish translation of part of John Müller's work.

69. Lucerna Giraldo, "Una obra digna de Romanos: el Canal del Dique, 1650–1810," 112–14.

70. The system, Herrera recognizes, is the one that is practiced in Holland. See Marco Dorta, *Cartagena de Indias*, 145–47; Zapatero, *Historia de las fortificaciones de Cartagena de Indias*, 88–89.

71. Samuel Marolois, *Fortification ou architecture militaire tant offensive que defensive* (Amsterdam: Janssonius, 1627); *La seconde partie traictant de la fortification des places irregulieres*, 19–20, sheet 24, fig. 106.

72. AGI, MP-PANAMÁ, 124. "Perfil ortográphico de la Muralla que se determina hacer orillando el mar desde el Baluarte de Santa Catalina hasta el de la Cruz de la Ciudad de Cartagena. Dispuesto por S. M. y á dirección del Maestre de Campo D. Juan de Herrera y Sotomayor, Yngeniero Militar y Castellano del Castillo de S. Phelipe de Barajas por S. M. Año 1721."

Chapter 11

1. Juan Zapata Olivella, *El grito de la independencia o los mártires de Cartagena de Indias* (Cartagena de Indias: Imprenta Departamental de Bolívar, 1961), 96.

2. An effect of the attack carried out in 1697 by Baron de Pointis was the arrival of noteworthy Spanish engineers to reconstruct Cartagena's defenses, among whom Juan de Herrera y Sotomayor stands out. This event was studied by Enrique de la Matta Rodríguez, *El asalto de Pointis a Cartagena de Indias* (Seville: Consejo Superior de Investigaciones Científicas, 1979). In addition to the aforementioned publication, see also Manuel Gámez Casado, "Arquitectura defensiva e ingenieros militares en Cartagena de Indias tras el ataque del Barón de Pointis," in *De Sur a Sur: Intercambios artísticos y relaciones culturales* (Granada: Editorial Atrio, 2017), 179–83.

3. Jeremy Black, *Atlas ilustrado de la guerra* (Madrid: Akal, 1996), 146–50.

4. Juan Manuel Zapatero, "La heroica defensa de Cartagena ante el almirante in-

glés Vernon," *Revista de Historia Militar* 1 (1957): 115–78. The primary studies examining the 1741 assault of the English troops on Cartagena de Indias are Francis Rusell-Hart, "Ataques del almirante Vernon al continente americano," *Boletín de Historia y Antigüedades* 23 (1917): 76–84; Gustavo Michelsen, "Expedición de Vernon," *Boletín de Historia y Antigüedades* 19 (1932): 616–17; Guillermo Hernández de Alba, "Sir Edward Vernon y don Blas de Lezo," *Boletín de Historia y Antigüedades* 28 (1941): 468–73; Carlos Restrepo Canal, "El sitio de Cartagena por el almirante Vernon," *Boletín de Historia y Antigüedades* 28 (1941): 447–67; and José Antonio Calderón Quijano, "¿Pensó Vernon utilizar las cortinas de humo en su ataque de Cartagena de 1741?," *Revista General de Marina* 122 (1942): 651. More recent are the studies of Manuel Lucena Salmoral, "Los diarios anónimos sobre el ataque de Vernon a Cartagena existentes en Colombia: su correlación y posibles autores," *Anuario de Estudios Americanos* 30 (1973): 337–469, as well as Rafael López Guzmán and Alfonso Rafael Cabrera Cruz, "La visión del virrey Sebastián de Eslava del asedio de Cartagena de Indias en 1741: El funcionamiento de las fortificaciones," in *Ingeniería e ingenieros en la América hispana: Siglos XVIII y XIX*, ed. Pedro Cruz Freire and Ignacio J. López Hernández (Seville: Editorial Universidad de Sevilla, 2017), 49–76. Likewise, the personal diary of Vice Admiral Edward Vernon makes for interesting reading. See Edward Vernon, *Authentic Papers Relating to the Expedition against Carthagena* (London: L. Raymond, 1744).

5. The nine martyrs of Cartagena are recognized as a group of well-known leaders from Cartagena executed in 1816 on orders of the Consejo de Guerra (War Council). The Spanish Crown intended to punish the local institutions that fought against Spanish authority. See José Urueta, *Los mártires de Cartagena* (Cartagena de Indias: Antonio Araújo, 1886).

6. José Urueta, *Cartagena y sus cercanías* (Bogotá: Donaldo E. Grau, 1880), 119.

7. Archivo General de Simancas (AGS), Sección Secretaría de Estado y del Despacho de Guerra. Sign. SGU, LEG, 7236, 16. "Manuel de Anguiano: Asignación de sueldo," Madrid, Aranjuez, 7 de mayo de 1789.

8. Archivo General de Indias (AGI). Casa de la Contratación. Sign. Contratación, 5531, N. 4, R. 19. "Expediente de información y licencia de pasajero a Indias de Manuel Anguiano," Aranjuez, 7 de mayo de 1787.

9. In Servicio Geográfico del Ejército (SGE), Sign. SG-J-7-3-158. "Otro plano en la misma escala que solo comprende los recintos de plaza y arrabal," Manuel de Anguiano, Cartagena de Indias, 1 de enero de 1806. The plan's measurements are 60.2 × 80.6 cm. Ink and watercolor in green, ocher, and carmine on canvas. Signed and sealed by the author. Its scale is 1 inch per 100 *varas*.

10. Among the numerous publications that have dealt with the Spanish expeditions to Darien, see Manuel Luengo Muñoz, "Génesis de las expediciones militares al Darién en 1785–86," *Anuario de Estudios Americanos* 18 (1961): 333–416; Alfredo Castillero Calvo, *Conquista, evangelización y resistencia* (Panama City: Editora Nova Art, 2017); and Manuel Gámez Casado, "Buscando al enemigo inglés: Expediciones de guardacostas españoles al golfo del Darién, 1767–68," *Anuario de Estudios Americanos* 75 (2018): 211–36.

11. Juan Marchena Fernández, *La institución militar en Cartagena de Indias en el siglo XVIII* (Seville: Consejo Superior de Investigaciones Científicas, 1982), 452.

Notes 261

12. Ruth Meza Gutiérrez, "Prácticas sociales y control territorial del Caribe colombiano, 1750–1800: El caso del contrabando en la península de La Guajira," *Historia regional y local* 6 (2011): 39–65.

13. AGI. Audiencia de Santa Fe, Sign. Santa Fe, 952. "Relación de las maderas, clavazón, herramientas y demás efectos que necesita," Manuel de Anguiano, Cartagena de Indias, 7 de septiembre de 1805.

14. AGI. Audiencia de Santa Fe, Sign. Santa Fe, 952. "Noticia de las obras más urgentes que faltan en esta plaza," Manuel de Anguiano, Cartagena de Indias, 17 de septiembre de 1805.

15. Concerning the engineer Agustín Crame, see Horacio Capel et al., *Los ingenieros militares en España, Siglo XVIII: Repertorio biográfico e inventario de su labor científica y espacial* (Barcelona: Universitat de Barcelona, 1983), 130–32.

16. The brigadier and military engineer Agustín Crame was named "Visitador de las plazas del Mar del Norte y Seno mexicano" (*"visitador* of the places of the Northern Sea and of the Mexican heartland") by Charles III, arriving in Cartagena de Indias in 1778 to oversee its defensive works. There, he became familiar with the city's fortifications and those of Getsemaní and Bocachica overseen by Arévalo. Despite this, he focused his primary efforts on recovering the splendor of the mountain of San Lázaro, proposing a massive renovation of the castle of San Felipe de Barajas, a topic that still requires a detailed study. See Zapatero, *Historia de las fortificaciones de Cartagena*, 160–64, 198–200.

17. Zapatero, *Historia de las fortificaciones de Cartagena*, 204.

18. SGE. Sign. SG- J-7-2-84. "Plano del castillo de Sn Felipe de Barajas," Manuel de Anguiano, Cartagena de Indias, 18 de noviembre de 1801. The plan's measurements are 48.7 × 61.4 cm. Ink and watercolor in gray, ocher, and carmine on canvas. Signed and sealed by the author. Its scale is 1 inch per 100 *varas*.

19. Roberto González Arana and Edwin Monsalvo, "De la Suprema Junta de Gobierno al Estado soberano: La independencia de Cartagena de Indias (1810–1812)," *Historia Crítica* 41 (2010): 62–85. To understand the independence process in this city, see Ángel Álvarez Romero, "El consulado en el proceso de independencia de Cartagena de Indias," *Anuario de Estudios Americanos* 52 (1996): 97–121, and Catalina Jimenez, "Entre la formación de la opinión pública y la movilización: El proceso independentista de Cartagena de Indias," *Panorama* 9 (2011): 11–19.

20. Gabriel Jiménez Molinares, *Los mártires de Cartagena de Indias de 1816 ante el Consejo de Guerra y ante la historia* (Cartagena: Imprenta Departamental, 1947), 18.

21. In addition to Anguiano, those sentenced to death and known as the martyrs of Cartagena de Indias were Manuel del Castillo y Rada, Martín Amador, Pantaleón Germán Ribón, Santiago Stuart, Antonio José de Ayos, José María García de Toledo, Miguel Díaz Granados, and José María Portocarrero. See Adelaida Sourdís Najera, "El precio de la Independencia en la primera República: La población de Cartagena de Indias (1814–1816)," *Boletín de Historia y Antigüedades* 5 (2000): 103–14. The martyrs' declarations spoken during the interrogations were collected by Roberto Arrazola, *Los mártires responden* (Cartagena: Ediciones Hernández, 1973).

22. Adelaida Sourdís Najera, "El Consejo de Guerra de los Mártires de 1816," in *Cart-*

agena de Indias en la Independencia, ed. Haroldo Calvo Stevenson and Adolfo Meisel Roca (Bogotá: Banco de la República, 2011), 297–330.

23. Adelaida Sourdís Najera, "Los últimos días del gobierno español en Colombia," *Boletín de la Academia de Historia de Bogotá* 4 (2010): 67–86.

Chapter 12

1. Walter Raleigh, *History of the World* (London: Walter Stansby, 1614)

2. Juan Manuel Zapatero, *La guerra en el Caribe en el siglo XVIII* (Madrid: Servicio Histórico y Museo del Ejército, 1990).

3. AGS (Archivo General de Simancas), Estado, 6.093. Wall a Tanucci, 14 de diciembre de 1762.

4. Julio Albi de la Cuesta, *La defensa de Indias (1764–1799)* (Madrid: Instituto de Cooperación Iberoamericana, 1987).

5. John Lynch, *La España del siglo XVIII* (Barcelona: Crítica, 1999), 282.

6. Francisco Varo Montilla, "Organización militar y defensa terrestre del Virreinato de Nueva España (siglos XVIII y principios del XIX)," in *La organización de los Ejércitos*, ed. Jesús Cantera Montenegro et al. (Madrid: 2016), 1: 859–912.

7. Carlos Zamorano García, "Agustín Crame y sus planes de defensa," in *Proyección en América de los ingenieros militares, siglo XVIII*, ed. Francisco Segovia and Manuel Nóvoa (Madrid: Ministerio de Defensa, 2016), 313–29.

8. Archivo General Militar de Madrid (AGMM), Caja 1001, *Plan de defensa del reino de Nueva España por las costas colaterales comprendidas entre Alvarado y Zempoala*, Veracruz, 17 de enero de 1775.

9. AGMM, 4-1-1, *Defensa de La Habana y sus castillos por el brigadier ingeniero director D. Silvestre Abarca*. La Habana, 8 de abril de 1771.

10. Albi de la Cuesta, *La defensa de Indias*, 64–65.

11. Pedro Rodríguez Campomanes, *Discurso sobre la educación popular de los artesanos y su fomento* (Madrid: Antonio Sancha, 1774), 1: 411. The author was state counselor and director of the Royal Academy of History.

12. Jairo Eduardo Jiménez Sotero, "La Fortaleza de San Carlos y la ruta México-Veracruz durante la época colonial," *Textos ArKeopáticos* 4 (2016): 32–46.

13. José Antonio Calderón Quijano, *Fortificaciones en Nueva España* (Madrid: Gobierno del Estado de Veracruz, 1984), 182.

14. Calderón Quijano, *Fortificaciones en Nueva España*, 183. Archivo General de Indias (AGI), México, 2460. El virrey marqués de Croix al bailío Arriaga. México, 30 de enero de 1769.

15. Calderón Quijano, *Fortificaciones en Nueva España*, 186.

Chapter 13

1. Graciela Márquez, *Monopolio y comercio en América Latina, siglos XVI–XVII* (Mexico City: Centro de Estudios Económicos, El Colegio de México, 2001).

2. Aurelio Pérez Martínez, *Isla y pueblo: Un enfoque histórico geográfico de Puerto Rico* (San Juan: Cultural Puertorriqueña, 1979), and Milton Zambrano Pérez, "Los dos ataques ingleses a Puerto Rico a finales del siglo XVI en el contexto de la lucha geopolítica internacional," *Revista Amauta* 16 (July–December 2010): 49–62.

3. Sylvia-Lyn Hilton, *Las Indias en la diplomacia española, 1739–1759* (Madrid: Universidad Complutense de Madrid, 1980).

4. Nuria Hinarejos Martín, "El ingeniero Tomás ODaly en Puerto Rico," in *Actas del Congreso Internacional América: Cultura visual y relaciones artísticas* (Granada: 2015), 43–50.

5. Nuria Hinarejos Martín, "Estado de las defensas de San Juan de Puerto Rico en 1762: Informe y propuesta de Tomás O´Daly," in *Espacios y muros del barroco iberoamericano*, ed. María de los Ángeles Fernández Valle López, Carmen López Calderón, and Inmaculada Rodríguez Moya (Seville: Universidad Pablo de Olavide, 2019), 173–90.

6. *Fortificaciones, pertrechos de guerra y situados de tropa.* AGI, sig. Santo Domingo, 2501.

7. He disembarked in the city of San Juan on April 8, 1765, aboard the war frigate *El Águila*, commanded by Miguel Basabe, accompanied by three senior sergeants, eight assistants, and a lieutenant, all of whom worked with him in Cuba. He remained on the island until June 24 of that year. Thus, he stayed in Puerto Rico for only a couple of months. *Alejandro O´Reily.* AHN (Archivo Histórico Nacional), sig. OM- EXPEDIEN-TILLOS, N. 14594; *Don Alejandro O´Reilly en Comisión para Puerto Rico*, Correspondencia de Gobernadores, col. 13 (Consulted with the Centro de Investigaciones Históricas de la Universidad de Puerto Rico, Recinto de Río Piedras, Transcription Section, AGNM (Archivo General de la Nación de México, nos. 36 and 265); *Comisión a Alejandro O´Reilly para visita a Puerto Rico.* AGI, sig. Santo Domingo, 2395; *Fortificaciones, pertrechos de guerra y situados de tropa.* AGI, sig. Santo Domingo, 2501; Alejandro O'Reilly, "Memoria de Alexandro O´Reilly a S. M. sobre la isla de Puerto Rico. 1765," in *Boletín Histórico de Puerto Rico*, vol. 8, ed. Cayetano Coll y Toste (San Juan: 1921), 108–30; Ricardo Torres Reyes, "El mariscal OReilly y las defensas de San Juan, 1765–1777," *Revista Historia* 1 (1954): 3–37; Bibiano Torres Ramírez, "Alejandro O'Reilly en Cuba," *Anuario de Estudios Americanos* 24 (1967): 1357–88; and Bibiano Torres Ramírez, *Alejandro O'Reilly en las Indias* (Seville: Consejo superior de investigaciones científicas, Escuela de estudios hispano-americanos, 1969).

8. *Plano de la Plaza de San Juan de puerto Rico: Su puerᵒ y Costa desde el Boqueron de San Geronimo hasta la punta de Salinas levantado últimamente pr el Thente de Navio de la Rl. Armada Dn. Manuel Miguel de Leon, à encargo particular del Mariscal de Campo DN. Alexandro de O, Reilly, Ynspector Gl. de las Yslas de Santiago de Cuba y Sn. Juan de Puerto Rico.* AGMM (Archivo General Militar de Madrid), Cartoteca, sig. PRI-22/1; *Plano en que se manifiesta con la maior exactitud el Castillo del Morro de Sn. Juan de Puerto-Rico y todas sus inmediaciones, levantado con Plancheta y la mas escrupulosa atencion, de Orn. del Mariscal de Campo Dn. Alexandro O'Reilly.* AGMM, Cartoteca, sig. PRI-25/10. *Plano en que se demuestra con la mayor exactitud el Castillo de Sn. Xtpl. y el Frente de Tierra de Sn. Juan de Puerto Rico, con todas sus ynmediaziones, levantado con Planchea y lamas escrupulosa atención de orden del Mariscal de Campo Dn. Alexandro Ô Reylly.* AGMM, Cartoteca, sig. PRI-19/12. In Madrid's Geographic Center of the Army, several blueprints without attributed authorship (still unknown today) have been located that have certain similarities with the graphic sources kept in Madrid's General Military Archive, so it is possible to consider that they are copies of the original blueprints. *Plano en que se manifiesta con la mayor exactitud el Castillo del Morro de San Juan de Puerto-rico y todas sus inmediaciones, levantado con Plancheta y la mas escrupulosa atención, de Orden del Mariscal de Cpo. Dn. Alexandro O´Reily.* CGEM (Centro Geográfico del Ejército de Madrid), sig. Ar.J-T.4a-C.2a-65; *Plano en que se manifiesta con la mayor exactitud*

el Castillo del Morro de San Juan de Puerto-rico y todas sus inmediaciones, levantado con Plancheta y la mas escrupulosa atención, de Orden del Mariscal de Cpo. Dn. Alexandro O´Reily. CGEM, sig. Ar.J-T.4a-C.2a-65(2) y *Plano en que se demuestra con la mayor exactitud el Castillo de Sn. Christoval y el Frente de Tierra de Sn. Juan de Puerto Rico, con todas sus inmediaciones, levantado con Plancheta, y la mas escrupulosa atencion, de orden del Mariscal de Campo Dn. Alexandro O'Reilly.* CGEM, sig. Ar.J-T.4a-C.2a-68.

9. Nuria Hinarejos Martín, "La intervención del ingeniero Juan Francisco Mestre en el sistema de defensas de San Juan de Puerto Rico," in *Iberoamérica en perspectiva artística: Transferencias culturales y devocionales,* ed. Inmaculada Rodríguez Moya et al. (Castelló de la Plana: Publicacions de la Universitat Jaume, 2016), 57–72.

10. This project was accompanied by a budget valued at 26,392 *pesos,* 5 *reales,* and 27 *maravedis,* as well as with various blueprints that support the great work of Mestre as a planning engineer, since they represent several views and profiles of the defensive system built in the city so far, the state in which they were in, and the new projected defense strategies. *Proyecto de Defensa contra el desembarco de un Enemigo, desde el Puente de San Antonio, Fuerte de San Jerónimo, y Punta del Escambrón hacia la Plaza, cuyas situaciones, y defensas se señalan en el Plano que acompaña.* AGMM, Colección General de Documentos sobre Puerto Rico, sig. 4-1-7-2; *Plano de la plaza de Puerto Rico y sus inmediaciones.* AGMM, Cartoteca, sig. PRI-15/9; *Vista y Perfil de la Plaza de Puerto Rico.* AGMM, Cartoteca, sig. PRI-24/11; *Plano que manifiesta el recinto de la Plaza fortificado en la Costa del Norte que comprende el espacio qe. media entre el Fuerte de Sn. Christoval y el Castillo de Sn. Phelipe del Morro segun se demuestra.* AGMM, Cartoteca, sig. PRI-24/13; *Perfiles pertenecientes al frente de tierra.* AGMM, Cartoteca, sig. PRI-13/4; *Fortificaciones, pertrechos de guerra y situados de tropa.* AGI, sig. Santo Domingo, 2510; Horacio Capel et al., *Los ingenieros militares en España, Siglo XVIII: Repertorio biográfico e inventario de su labor científica y espacial* (Barcelona: Universitat de Barcelona, 1983), 324; Juan Manuel Zapatero, "Las fortificaciones históricas de San Juan de Puerto Rico," *Militaria Revista de Cultura Militar* 1 (1989): 141–75; Aníbal Sepúlveda Rivera, *San Juan: Historia ilustrada de su desarrollo urbano, 1508–1898* (San Juan: Carimar, 1989), 240; and Juan Manuel Zapatero, *La guerra del Caribe en el siglo XVIII* (San Juan: Instituto de Cultura Puertorriqueña, 1964), 348.

11. *Relación circunstanciada de las defensas que constituyen el frente de Tierra de la Plaza, y las Provisionales que se han construido para impedir el desembarco, desde el Puente de San Antonio, asta el Escambron; en que se complican las ventajas que pueden sacarse de dichas obras, y de los accidentes que presenta el terreno.* AGMM. Colección General de Documentos, sig. 4–1–7–1; *Proyecto de defensa contra el desembarco de un enemigo desde el puente de San Antonio, fuerte de San Jerónimo y punta del Escambrón hacia la plaza de San Juan de Puerto Rico.* AGMM. Colección General de Documentos, sig. 4-1-7-2 y *Borrador de observaciones.* AGMM, Colección General de Documentos, sig. 4-1-7-5.

12. This documentary source describes it as a well-traced continuous entrenchment. The last landing beach was Bueycabón Nuevo (modern Mar Verde), where a two-sided battery was raised as the first point of an entrenched path that ended in a narrow passageway where the defenders could easily ambush the enemy. It stretched across the San Antonio Bridge and the battery platform of Escambrón. The report states that this defensive line favored the capital's internal and external fire, as it defended the San

Jerónimo del Boquerón Fort and Olimpo from ships that might attempt to approach the northern coast. *Anteproyecto de un fuerte en el Alto del Olimpo de San Juan de Puerto Rico.* AGMM, Archidoc, sig. 5632.5.

13. Adolfo de Hostos, *Ciudad Murada (1521–1898)* (San Juan: Instituto de Cultura Puertorriqueña, 1966), 194; Bibiano Torres Ramírez, *La isla de Puerto Rico* (San Juan: Instituto de Cultura Puertorriqueña, 1968), 240; Pedro Tomás de Córdova, *Memorias gráficas, históricas, económicas y estadísticas de la isla de Puerto Rico* (San Juan: 1831), 1: 12; and *Lealtad y heroísmo en la isla de Puerto Rico 1797–1897* (San Juan: 1897).

14. *Descubridr.[i.e. Descubridor] y vigilante, Cosme de Churruca, Antonio García de Quesada.* Museo Naval de Madrid (MNM), sig. 22-A-05; *Plano de la plaza de Puerto Rico y sus inmediaciones.* AGMM, Cartoteca, sig. PRI-15/9; *Plano Geometrico del Puerto Capital de la Isla de Puerto Rico.* AGMM, Cartoteca, sig. AT-182/58 y *Plano Geométrico del Puerto Capital de Puerto Rico: construido pr. los Bergs. [i.e. Bergantines] de S. M. Descubridr.[i.e. Descubridor] y vigilante, Cosme de Churruca, Antonio García de Quesada.* Museo Naval de Madrid (MNM), sig. 22-A-05.

15. A document, dated August 22, 1882, stored in the General Military Archive of Madrid, confirms that engineer Francisco J. Zaragoza proposed building a guardhouse capable of accommodating an officer and twelve or fifteen soldiers in this first line of defense, to achieve a crossfire with the artillery set up on the bridge and battery of San Antonio, the works of which were valued at 4,140 pesos. The building's foundation had to be made of masonry reinforced with hydraulic mortar with a height of up to three meters, since it was located a few meters from the sea. The parapets facing the San Antonio Bridge must have had a thickness of 0.45 meters and arrow-slit windows strengthened with metallic plates. The opposite front had a gallery of 2.5 meters wide to facilitate the accommodation of troops and with a roof of galvanized iron covering cast iron columns. The partitions must have been made of brick to reduce costs, and the floor must have been covered with slabs from the Canary Islands. The building would be protected by the construction of several arrow slits located 1.5 meters high on the rooftop's parapets. However, it is possible that this guardhouse was never implemented because on October 20 of that year, the chief engineer Ricardo Mir and the subinspection general commander José Laguna, planned the construction of a new guard corps to be located on the right side of the first line of defense, to further protect the San Antonio Bridge. *Obras de construcción y reparación de diversos cuerpos de guardia de San Juan de Puerto Rico.* AGMM, Archidoc, sig. 5630.4; *Plan de defensas para la plaza de San Juan de Puerto Rico.* AHN, sig. Diversos colecciones, 31, N. 99 and Zapatero, *La guerra del Caribe*, 377.

16. We do not know the exact date of construction of this fortification because it is not mentioned in any graphic or documentary source analyzed for this study. However, Adolfo de Hostos states that it was erected between 1795 and 1800 and that after the 1797 British attack on the island, Mestre's labors intensified. He described it as a battery with stone parapets of just over 1,200 meters in length, protected by a bulwark at each end. Hostos, *Ciudad Murada*, 197.

17. During the 1898 war with the United States, the San Ramón barracks was built in the vicinity of the battery of the same name, but when Puerto Rico was transferred to the United States, its first line of defense was occupied by the US Navy. In 1921, the

US government leased this space to Virgil Baker, a retired lieutenant, for a period of 999 years. However, on August 26, 1929, President Herbert Hoover transferred the title and rights of several territories of San Juan to the Puerto Rican government, among these was the site leased to Baker. In October 1947, the Caribe Hilton Hotel was built at this location, although to this day the remains of the original San Ramón battery bartizan remain at the hotel's main entrance. *Anteproyecto de un fuerte en el Alto del Olimpo de San Juan de Puerto Rico.* AGMM, Archidoc, sig. 5632.5; Nicolás Cabrillana, "Las fortificaciones militares en Puerto Rico," *Revista de Indias* 27 (1967): 157–88; Héctor Andrés Negroni, *Historia militar de Puerto Rico* (Madrid: Sociedad Estatal Quinto Centenario, 1992), 192; and José E. Marull del Río, *Protegiendo la capital: Desarrollo histórico de las obras defensivas en Puerta de Tierra* (San Juan: Oficina Estatal de Conservación Histórica de Puerto Rico, 2019).

18. *Obras de derribo de murallas y ensanche de San Juan de Puerto Rico.* AGMM, Archidoc, sig. 5615.2.

19. Hostos states that it had a simpler layout than the first one. According to Torres Ramírez, it was built by the engineer Ignacio Mascaró y Homar, and his works were completed in 1788, while Andrés Negroni dates it to between 1715 and 1720. Hostos, *Ciudad Murada*, 196; Torres Ramírez, *La isla de Puerto Rico*, 241; and Negroni, *Historia militar de Puerto Rico*, 192.

20. *Obras de derribo de murallas y ensanche de San Juan de Puerto Rico.* AGMM, Archidoc, sig. 5166.10.

21. The remains of Isabel II's battery are located at the intersection of San Agustín Street and Constitution Avenue in Luis Muñoz Rivera Park.

22. In January 1896, the artillery of this second line of defense was extended with three Ordoñez howitzers of 24 centimeters in the battery of the Escambrón, and on May 22 a proposal was submitted to reinforce of the protection of said battery with two 24-centimeter cannons and have it transferred to the battery of San Ramón, the two 12-centimeter guns that were located at that time in the Escambrón and endow San Jerónimo del Boquerón fort and the Miraflores battery, with three 12-centimeter cannons, as well as build a new gunpowder storage between the first and the second line of defense, the works of which were valued at 121,350 pesos. *Se aprueba el presupuesto para construir de nuevo el puente de madera de la 2° línea de la plaza.* Archivo Histórico Nacional de Madrid, sig. Ultramar, 6346, Exp. 21; and *Obras de derribo de murallas y ensanche de San Juan de Puerto Rico.* AGMM, Archidoc, sig. 5615.2.

23. Zapatero, "Las fortificaciones históricas de San Juan," 141–75, and Nuria Hinarejos Martín, *El sistema de defensas de Puerto Rico, 1493–1898* (Madrid: Ministerio de Defensa, 2020).

24. This architectural firm built several important works on the island: the Capitol Building, the University of Puerto Rico, and the penitentiary, among others. Andrés Mignucci, *El parque Muñoz Rivera y el Tribunal Supremo de Puerto Rico* (San Juan: La Rama Judicial de Puerto Rico, 2012), 59.

25. Mignucci, *El parque Muñoz Rivera*, 72.

Chapter 14

1. Luis Navarro García, *José de Gálvez y la Comandancia General de las Provincias Internas* (Seville: Escuela de Estudios Hispanoamericanos, 1964), 160–61.

Notes

2. Bibiano Torres Ramírez, *Alejandro O'Reilly en las Indias* (Seville: Escuela de Estudios Hispanoamericanos, 1969), 100–108.

3. Torres Ramírez, *Alejandro O´Reilly en las Indias*, 127–30.

4. Gilbert C. Din, *Louisiana in 1776: A Memoria of Francisco Bouligny* (New Orleans: Collection Series, 1977), 29.

5. Francisco Bouligny, *Memoria de la Luisiana*, Madrid, August 15, 1776. Historic New Orleans Collection. MSS 171. Bouligny-Baldwin Papers, folder 44, 1978, 92 L., no pagination.

6. Bouligny, *Memoria de la Luisiana*.

7. José Montero de Pedro, *Españoles en Nueva Orleans y Luisiana* (Madrid: Ediciones de Cultura Hispánica del Centro Iberoamericano de Cooperación, 1979), 113.

8. John Francis McDermott, *The French in the Mississippi Valley* (Urbana: University of Illinois Press, 1965), 129.

9. Jerome A. Greene, *Special History Study: The Defense of New Orleans, 1718–1900* (Denver: Department of the Interior, 1982), 46–53.

10. Leoncio Cabrero, "Francisco Sabatini y la fortificación de la Luisiana," in *Trabajos y Conferencias*, vol. 2 (Madrid: Facultad de Filosofía y Letras, Universidad Complutense, 1958), 43.

11. José Miguel Morales Folguera, *Arquitectura y urbanismo hispanoamericano en Luisiana y Florida Occidental* (Málaga: Universidad de Málaga, 1987), 153.

12. Archivo General de Indias, Santo Domingo, Leg. 2.673, pp. 531–37.

13. Archivo General de Indias, Santo Domingo, Leg. 2.673, November 2, 1799.

14. Greene, *Special History Study*, 38–39.

15. Gilberto Guillemard was the most prominent and famous engineer in Spanish Louisiana. Of French origin, he came to Louisiana with O'Reilly. He held, among other positions, the functions of captain of infantry, major aide of the city of New Orleans, engineer and supervisor of the province, and cartographer and supervisor of the Commission of the Spanish Border. He was assigned to meet with the American commissioner, Andrew Ellicot, to draw the Thirty-First Parallel that would divide the Spanish and American territories according to the Treaty of San Lorenzo, or Pinckney's Treaty, in 1795. He was the designer of the most important buildings in New Orleans: the Cabildo, the Presbytery, the Cathedral of Saint Luis, a small theater, and the charity hospital.

16. Minter Wood, "Life in New Orleans in the Spanish Period," *Louisiana Historical Quarterly* 22 (1937): 45.

17. Archivo General de Indias, Mapas y Planos de Florida y Luisiana, 150 bis.

18. Archivo General de Indias, Mapas y Plano de Florida y Luisiana, 150.

19. Archivo General de Indias, Mapas y Planos de Florida y Luisiana, 216.

20. As a surveyor, Carlos Trudeau sought to measure and draw the lands of the Lower Mississippi, which would be distributed among the founders of the new cities created by Bernardo de Gálvez, many of which would be laid out by Trudeau himself. He is also the author of the plans of some of the forts of New Orleans as well as a map of the city dated to 1801. He was also the designer of the plans of two of the most important buildings: the Cathedral of Saint Luis and the Presbytery or Episcopal Palace, paid for by Andrés Almonaster and Roxas (1725–1798), a native of the Sevillian town of Mairena del Alcor.

268   Notes

21. Samuel Wilson, "Almonaster: Philanthropist and Builder in New Orleans," in *The Spanish in the Mississippi Valley, 1762–1804*, ed. John Francis McDermott (Urbana: University of Illinois Press, 1974), figs. nos. 2, 5, and 12.

22. Archivo General de Indias, Mapas y Planos de Florida y Luisiana, 219.

23. Samuel Wilson Jr., *The vieux carrè: New Orleans, Its Plan, Its Growth, Its Architecture* (New Orleans: Historic District Demonstration Study, conducted by Bureau of Governmental Research, 1968), 45–46.

24. Baron de Carondelet, *Military Report of Louisiana and West Florida*, New Orleans, November, 24, 1794, 328.

25. Víctor Collot, *Voyage dans l'Amérique septentrionale*, vol. 2 (Paris: Chez Arthus Bertrand, 1826), 126–37.

26. Translation from French to English by José Miguel Morales Folguera.

27. Joaquín de Peramás was one of the most important engineers who worked in the government of Louisiana, where he would achieve the rank of infantry captain and ordinary engineer. His most noteworthy project was the design of the city of Panzacola after the conquest of Bernardo de Gálvez.

28. Archivo General de Indias, Mapas y Planos de Florida y Luisiana, 109.

29. Archivo General de Indias, Mapas y Planos de Florida y Luisiana, 106.

30. Archivo General de Indias, Mapas y Planos de Florida y Luisiana, 108.

31. *Despatches of the Spanish Governors*. Bundle 2.354. Letter 3. Book XI, pp. 297–98.

32. Collot, *Voyage dans l'Amérique septentrionale*, 100–103.

33. Pedro José Favrot, "Colonial Forts," in Greene, *Special History Study*, 52. Parts of this chapter appear in Frank L. Owsley Jr. and Gene A. Smith, *Filibusters and Expansionists: Jeffersonian Manifest Destiny, 1800–1821* (Tuscaloosa: University of Alabama Press, 1997), and "'Our Flag was display'd within their Works': The Treaty of Ghent and the Conquest of Mobile," *Alabama Review* 52 (January 1999): 3–21.

Chapter 15

1. Frederick Merk, *Manifest Destiny and Mission in American History: A Reinterpretation* (New York: Knopf, 1963), 24.

2. Thomas Jefferson to A. Stewart, 25 January 1786, in H. A. Washington, ed., *The Writings of Thomas Jefferson*, 8 vols. (Washington, DC: Taylor and Maury, 1853), 1: 518.

3. Jefferson to John Jacob Astor, 24 May 1812, in Washington, *Writings of Thomas Jefferson*, 6: 55.

4. Jefferson to Governor James Monroe, 24 November 1801, in Andrew A. Lipscomb and Albert Ellery Bergh, eds., *The Writings of Thomas Jefferson*, 20 vols. (Washington, DC: Thomas Jefferson Memorial Association), 10: 296.

5. Garrett Ward Sheldon, *Political Philosophy of Thomas Jefferson* (Baltimore: Johns Hopkins University Press, 1991), 95; William Earl Weeks, *Adams and American Global Empire* (Lexington: University of Kentucky Press, 1992), 39.

6. Robert Middlekauf, *The Glorious Cause* (Oxford: Oxford University Press, 1982), 586–87; Samuel Flagg Bemis, *Jay's Treaty; A Study in Commerce and Diplomacy* (Knights of Columbus, 1923; reprint, New Haven, CT: Yale University Press, 1962), 23–26.

7. Albert K. Weinberg, *Manifest Destiny: A Study of Nationalist Expansion in American History* (Baltimore: Johns Hopkins University Press, 1935), 31.

Notes

8. Merrill D. Peterson, *Thomas Jefferson and the New Nation: A Biography* (New York: Oxford University Press, 1970), 746; Jefferson to William Carmichael, 27 May 1788, in Washington, *Writings of Thomas Jefferson*, 2: 398.

9. Jefferson to Thomas Mann Randolph, July 5, 1803, Thomas Jefferson Papers, Library of Congress, Washington, DC, hereinafter cited as Jefferson MSS, LC.

10. · James Madison to Jefferson, August 20, 1784, in Gaillard Hunt, ed., *The Works of James Madison* (New York: 1901), 2: 73.

11. *Annals of the Debates and Proceedings of Congress*, 7th Cong., 2nd sess., 371–74; Julius W. Pratt, *Expansionists of 1812* (Gloucester, MA: Peter Smith, 1957), 64–66.

12. Arthur Styron, *The Last of the Cocked Hats: James Monroe and the Virginia Dynasty* (Norman: University of Oklahoma Press, 1945), 284–85.

13. · Jefferson to George Washington, 2 April 1791, in Washington, *Writings of Thomas Jefferson*, 3: 235.

14. Dumas Malone, *Jefferson the President: First Term, 1801–1805* (Boston: Little, Brown, 1970), 287; "Extract from Mr. Livingston letter to Mr. Pinckney," 1803 circa May–June, James Monroe Papers, Library of Congress. Hereinafter cited as Monroe Papers, LC.

15. · James Monroe to Robert R. Livingston, 1803—May 23–June 7 (letter not sent), Monroe Papers, LC.

16. Henry Adams, *History of the United States of America during the Administrations of Thomas Jefferson and James Madison* (1891; reprint, New York: Literary Classics of the United States, 1986), 474–79.

17. Malone, *Jefferson the President: First Term*, 342–47; Jefferson's Proclamation of May 20, 1804, in James D. Richardson, ed., *A Compilation of Messages and Papers of the Presidents, 1789–1897*, 20 vols. (Washington, DC: Government Printing Office, 1896–99), 1: 357.

18. George E. Buker, *Jacksonville: Riverport-Seaport* (Columbia: University of South Carolina Press, 1992), 8–24; George Morgan, *The Life of James Monroe* (1921; reprint, New York: AMS Press, 1969), 270–71.

19. Robert W. Tucker and David C. Hendrickson, *Empire of Liberty: The Statecraft of Thomas Jefferson* (New York: Oxford University Press, 1990), 158–59.

20. Draft of a letter from Jefferson to the US Commissioners to Spain [William Carmichael and William Short], 23 March 1793, in Paul Leicester Ford, ed., *The Writings of Thomas Jefferson*, 10 vols. (New York: G. P. Putnam's Sons, 1895), 6: 206.

21. James Monroe to John Quincy Adams, 10 December 1815, in Stanislaus Murray Hamilton, *The Writings of James Monroe*, 7 vols. (New York: G. P. Putnam's Sons, 1901), 5: 381.

22. Buker, *Jacksonville*, 30–31; Jefferson to Wilson Cary Nicholas, October 25, 1805, Thomas Jefferson Papers, Manuscripts Division, Special Collections, University of Virginia Library, Charlottesville.

23. Adams, *History of the United States*, 2: 214; Joseph Burkholder Smith, *The Plot to Steal Florida: James Madison's Phony War* (New York: Arbor House, 1983), 64; James A. Padgett, ed., "Official Records of the West Florida Revolution and Republic," *Louisiana Historical Quarterly* 21 (1938): 719–21; Stanley Clisby Arthur, *The Story of the West Florida Rebellion* (St. Francisville, LA: St. Francisville Democrat, 1935), 103–7.

24. Padgett, "Official Records of the West Florida Revolution and Republic," 725–27; Arthur, *The West Florida Rebellion*, 112–15; Wanjohi Waciuma, *Intervention in the Spanish*

Floridas, 1801–1818: A Study of Jeffersonian Foreign Policy (Boston: Branden Press, 1976), 160–61; Adams, History of the United States, 214–15.

25. James Madison to Jefferson, 19 October 1810, cited in Irving Brant, James Madison: The President, 1809–1812 (New York: Bobbs-Merrill, 1956), 182–84; Arthur, The West Florida Rebellion, 130–35.

26. Brant, Madison, 184–86; James Madison, "Proclamation By the President of the United States," October 27, 1810, in Richardson, Messages of the Presidents, 2: 465–66.

27. Richardson, Messages of the Presidents, 2: 465–466; Brant, Madison, 186; Philip Coolidge Brooks, Diplomacy and the Borderlands: The Adams-Onís Treaty of 1819 (Berkeley: University of California Press, 1939), 36.

28. Spencer C. Tucker, The Jeffersonian Gunboat Navy (Columbia: University of South Carolina Press, 1993), 93–94; Isaac Joslin Cox, The West Florida Controversy, 1798–1813: A Study in American Diplomacy (1918; reprint, Gloucester, MA, 1967), 464–86.

29. Thomas Cushing to Robert Porter, December 1, 1810, Raymond and Roger Weill Collection, Historic New Orleans Collection, New Orleans, Louisiana; Robert Smith to David Holmes, December 21, 1810, Robert Smith Papers, Library of Congress, Washington, DC; John Shaw to the Secretary of the Navy, January 25, February 1, 8, 1811, Letters Received by the Secretary of the Navy: Captains' Letters, 1805–61, 1865–81 (microcopy), Reel 40: M125, Naval Records Collection of the Office of Naval Records and Library, Record Group 45, National Archives, Washington, DC (hereafter cited as M125 Captains' Letters); Tucker, Jeffersonian Gunboat Navy, 93–95.

30. Shaw to Bainbridge, June 6, 1811, Letters Received by the Secretary of the Navy: Miscellaneous Letters, 1801–84 (microcopy), Reel 22: M124, Naval Records Collection of the Office of Naval Records and Library, Record Group 45, National Archives, Washington, DC; Shaw to Secretary of the Navy, June 22, 1811, M125 Captains' Letters; Cox, The West Florida Controversy, 1798–1813, 584–85.

31. Courier of Louisiana, July 10, 1811; Shaw to Secretary of the Navy, July 26, 1811, M125 Captains' Letters; Cox, The West Florida Controversy, 1798–1813, 588–90; W. C. C. Claiborne to the Secretary of the Navy, July 9, 1811, Official Letter Books of W. C. C. Claiborne, 1801–1816, ed. Dunbar Rowland, 6 vols. (Jackson: Mississippi Department of History and Archives, 1917), 5: 298–300.

32. Julius Pratt, Expansionists of 1812, 75–76; Frank L. Owsley Jr., The Struggle for the Gulf Borderlands: The Creek War and the Battle of New Orleans (Gainesville: University Press of Florida, 1981), 21.

33. Brady to Toulmin, October 2, 1812, Toulmin to James Wilkinson, October 6, 1812, Toulmin to Cayetano Pérez, October 5, 1812, Pérez to Toulmin, October 5, 1812, all enclosures in Wilkinson to Secretary of War William Eustis, October 5, 1812, and Secretary of War John Armstrong to Wilkinson, February 16, May 27, 1813. Letters Received by the Secretary of War, Registered Series, 1801–70 (microcopy) Reel 58, M221, Record of the Office of the Secretary of War, Record Group 107 (hereafter M221), Letters Received Secretary of War: Rob W. Ord, "Memorandum Respecting Mobile," Louisiana Historical Quarterly 44 (July–October 1961): 132–33.

34. Armstrong to Wilkinson, February 16, 1813, in James Wilkinson, Memoir of My Own Times (Philadelphia, 1816), 3: 339.

Notes

35. Diego Morphy to Captain General of Cuba, March 29, 1813, Papeles Procentes de Cuba, Legajo 1836, Archivo General de Indias, Seville, Spain; James Wilkinson to John Armstrong, April, 1813, M221, Letters Received Secretary of War; James Innerarity to John Forbes, April 24, 1813, "General Wilkinson's Occupation of Mobile, April 1813," *Florida Historical Quarterly* 11 (October 1932): 88–90.

36. Benson J. Lossing, *The Pictorial Field-Book of the War of 1812* (New York: Harper and Brothers, 1869); James Wilkinson to John Armstrong, April 3, 1813, M221, Letters Received Secretary of War; Shaw to the Secretary of the Navy, April 19, 1813, M125 Captains' Letters.

37. Wilkinson to Armstrong, April 3, 1813, M221, Letters Received Secretary of War; Shaw to the Secretary of the Navy, April 19, 1813, M125 Captains' Letters; Cox, *West Florida Controversy*, 617–18; James Ripley Jacobs, *Tarnished Warrior: Major-General James Wilkinson* (New York: Macmillan, 1938), 280–81.

38. Cox, *West Florida Controversy*, 612–15.

39. Wilkinson to Cayetano Pérez, April 12, 1813, in H. S. Halbert and T. H. Ball, *The Creek War of 1813 and 1814*, ed. Frank Lawrence Owsley Jr. (1895; reprint, Tuscaloosa: University of Alabama Press, 1965), 87; Articles of Capitulation for Mobile, enclosures in Mauricio Zúñiga to Juan Ruíz Apodaca, May 2, 1813, Papeles Procentes de Cuba, Legajos 1794, Archivo General de Indias, Seville, Spain; James Innerarity to John Forbes, April 24, 1813, "Wilkinson's Occupation of Mobile," 88–90.

40. James Innerarity to John Forbes, April 24, 1813, "Wilkinson's Occupation of Mobile," 88–89.

41. Adams, *History of the United States*, 2: 1218–19; Wilkinson to Cayetano Pérez, April 12, 1813, Halbert and Ball, *The Creek War*. Articles of Capitulation for Mobile, enclosures in Mauricio Zúñiga to Juan Ruíz Apodaca, May 2, 1813, Papeles Procentes de Cuba, Legajos 1794, Archivo General de Indias, Seville, Spain.

42. Arsène Lacarrière Latour, *Historical Memoir of the War in West Florida and Louisiana in 1814–15: With an Atlas*, ed. Gene A. Smith (1816; reprint, Gainesville: University Press of Florida, 1999), 42–50. In November 1814 Andrew Jackson captured Pensacola from the Spanish, but he evacuated the city upon hearing that British forces intended to attack New Orleans. In this instance Spain occupied Pensacola at the end of the war and thus maintained control; Henry Bunbury to John Barrow, September 7, 1815, Foreign Record Office (PRO) 5/140, Public Record Office, Kew, Great Britain; Edward Nicholls to Alexander Cochrane, March 1, 1816, and Robert Spencer to Cochrane, February 17, 1816, and Cochrane to Earl of Bathurst, March 1, 1816, all in War Office 1/144, PRO. Article IX of the Treaty of Ghent promised to restore lost Indian lands to the tribes allied with Britain during the conflict, but after the war it, too, was ignored by the United States and not enforced by Great Britain.

43. James A. Carr, "The Battle of New Orleans and the Treaty of Ghent," *Diplomatic History* 3 (Summer 1979): 281; Wilbur Devereux Jones, ed., "A British View of the War of 1812 and the Peace Negotiations," *Mississippi Valley Historical Review* 45 (December 1958): 485–87.

Notes

Bibliography

Historical Sources (Pre-1900)

Adams, Henry. *History of the United States of America during the Administrations of Thomas Jefferson and James Madison*. New York: Literary Classics of the United States, 1986.

Bails, Benito. *Elementos de matemática*. Madrid: Viuda de don Joaquín Ibarra, 1779–1780.

Barón de Carondelet. *Military Report of Louisiana and West Florida*. New Orleans, 1794.

Belidor, Bernard Forest de. *La Science des Ingenieurs dans la conduite des travaux de Fortification et de Architecture civile, dediée au Roy*. The Hague: Pierre Gosse, 1754.

Benavente, Miguel. *Elementos de toda la Architectura Civil, con las mas singulares observaciones de los modernos, impresos en latin por el P. Christiano Rieger*. Madrid: 1763.

Blondel, François. *Nouvelle maniere de fortifier les places*. The Hague: Chez Arnout Leers, 1684.

Coehoorn, Menno. *Nouvelle fortification, tant pour un terrain bas & humide, que pour un terrain sec et elevé*. Wesel, Germany: 1706.

Collot, Georges-Henri-Victor. *Voyage dans l'Amérique septentrionale*, vol. 2. Paris: Chez Arthus Bertrand, 1826.

Córdova, Pedro Tomás de. *Lealtad y heroísmo en la isla de Puerto Rico 1797–1897*. Puerto Rico: 1897.

———. *Memorias gráficas, históricas, económicas y estadísticas de la isla de Puerto Rico*. Puerto Rico: 1831.

Escolano de Arrieta, Pedro. *Práctica del Consejo Real en el despacho de los negocios consultivos, instructivos y contenciosos: Con distinción de los que pertenecen al consejo pleno, ó á cada sala particular; Y las fórmulas de las cédulas, provisiones y certificaciones respectivas*. Madrid: 1796.

Fernández de Medrano, Sebastián. *El architecto perfecto en el arte militar . . .* Brussels: Lamberto Marchant, 1700.

———. *Breve tratado del ataque, y defensa de una plaza real: Y todo en verso . . .* Brussels: Lamberto Marchant, 1698.

———. *El ingeniero, primera parte de la moderna arquitectura militar*. Brussels: Lamberto Marchant, 1687.

———. *L´ingenieur pratique ou l'architecture militaire et moderne*. Brussels: Lamberto Marchant, 1696?

———. *El práctico artillero, el perfecto bombardero, y el arquitecto perfecto en el arte militar*. Brussels: Francisco Foppens, 1680.

274 Bibliography

Ford, Paul Leicester. *The Writings of Thomas Jefferson*. 10 vols. New York: G. P. Putnam's Sons, 1895.

Halbert, H. S., and T. H. Ball. *The Creek War of 1813 and 1814*. Tuscaloosa: University of Alabama Press, 1965.

Lacarrière Latour, Arsène. *Historical Memoir of the War in West Florida and Louisiana in 1814–15: With an Atlas*, 1816, edited by Gene A. Smith; reprint, Gainesville: Historic New Orleans Collection and the University Press of Florida, 1999.

Langahan. *Antigua and the Antiguans: A Full Account of the Colony and Its Inhabitants from the Time of the Caribs to the Present Day*. London: Saunders and Otley, Conduit Street, 1844.

Le Blond, Guillaume. "Fortification." In *Encyclopédie; ou, Dictionnaire raisonné des sciences, des arts et des métiers*, edited by Denis Diderot and Jean Le Rond D'Alembert. Paris: 1757.

Long, Edward. *A History of Jamaica*. London: 1774.

Lossing, Benson J. *The Pictorial Field-Book of the War of 1812*. New York: Harper and Brothers, 1869.

Lucuze, Pedro. *Principios de fortificacion, que contienen las definiciones de los terminos principales de las obras de plaza, y de campaña, con una idea de la conducta regularmente observada en el ataque y defensa de las fortalezas. Dispuestos para la instrucción de la juventud militar*. Barcelona: Thomas Piferrer, 1772.

Luffman, John. *A Brief Account of the Island of Antigua, Together with the Customs and Manners of Its Inhabitants, White as Well as Black . . . in Letters to a Friend*. London: Eighteenth Century Collections Online Print Editions, 2010 [1789].

Mandar, Charles-François. *De l'architecture des forteresses, or de l'art de fortifier les places*. Paris: Magimel, 1801.

Marolois, Samuel. *Fortification ou architecture militaire tant offensive que defensive*. Amsterdam: 1627.

McDermott, John Francis. *The Spanish in the Mississippi Valley, 1762–1804*. Urbana: University of Illinois Press, 1974.

Moreau de Saint Mery. *Description topographique, physique, civile, politique et historique de la partie francaise de l'isle Saint-Domingue*. Philadelphia: Chez l'auteur, 1798.

Müller, John, and Miguel Sánchez. *Tratado de fortificación; ó, Arte de construir los edificios militares y civiles*. Barcelona: Thomas Piferrer, 1769

Oliver, Vere Langford. *The History of the Island of Antigua, One of the Leeward Caribees in the West Indies, from the First Settlement in 1635 to the Present Time*. 3 vols. London: 1899.

Ortiz y Sanza, Joseph Francisco. *Los diez libros de Archîtectura de M. Vitrubio Polion, traducidos del Latín y comentados*. Madrid: 1787.

Pezuela, Jacobo de. *Historia de la Isla de Cuba*, vol. 2. Madrid: Carlos Bailly-Bailliere, 1868.

Raleigh, Walter. *History of the World*. London: 1614.

Richardson, James D. *A Compilation of Messages and Papers of the Presidents, 1789–1897*. 20 vols. Washington, DC: Government Printing Office, 1896–1899.

Rodriguez Campomanes, Pedro. *Discurso sobre la educación popular de los artesanos y su fomento*, vol. 1. Madrid: 1774.

Rodriguez Villa, Antonio. *Noticia biográfica de Don Sebastián Fernández de Medrano*. Madrid: Manuel G. Hernández, 1882.

Saavedra Fajardo, Diego. *Idea de un Príncipe Político Christiano he representada en cien empresas*. Munich: Nicolao Enrico, 1640.

Sánchez Taramas, Miguel. *Tratado de fortificación o arte de construir los edificios militares y civiles*. Barcelona: 1769.

Steichen, Michel. *Mémoire sur la vie et les travaux de Simon Stevin*. Brussels: 1846.

Urueta, José. *Los mártires de Cartagena*. Cartagena de Indias: 1886.

Vernon, Edward. *Authentic Papers Relating to the Expedition against Carthagena*. Londres: 1744.

Washington, H. A. *The Writings of Thomas Jefferson*. 8 vols. Washington, DC: Taylor and Maury, 1853.

Wilkinson, James. *Memoir of My Own Times*. Philadelphia: 1816.

Zonca, Vittorio. *Novo teatro di machine et edificii per varie et sicure operationi*. Padua: 1607.

Contemporary Studies

Albi de la Cuesta, Julio. *La defensa de Indias (1764–1799)*. Madrid: ICI, 1987.

Álvarez Romero, Ángel. "El consulado en el proceso de independencia de Cartagena de Indias." *Anuario de Estudios Americanos* 52 (1996): 97–121.

Angulo Íñiguez, Diego. *Planos de monumentos arquitectónicos de América y Filipinas existentes en el Archivo de Indias*. Seville: Laboratorio de arte, 1933.

Arbaiza Blanca-Soler, Silvia. "La Comisión de Arquitectura y los expedientes de ultramar en la Real Academia de Bellas Artes de San Fernando (I)." *Academia* 110–11 (2010): 89–146.

Arnal Simon, Luis. *Arquitectura y urbanismo del septentrión novohispano: Fundaciones en la Florida y el Seno Mexicano; Siglos XVI al XVIII*. Mexico City: UNAM, 2006.

Arrazola, Roberto. *Los mártires responden*. Cartagena: Ediciones Hernández, 1973.

Arthur, Stanley Clisby. *The Story of the West Florida Rebellion*. St. Francisville, LA: St. Francisville Democrat, 1935.

Baeza Martín, Ascensión. "Las argucias de la guerra: El gobernador Cagigal y el asedio inglés desde Guantánamo en 1741." *Temas Americanistas* 19 (2007): 37–51.

Bailey, Gauvin Alexander. *Architecture and Urbanism in the French Atlantic Empire: State, Church, and Society, 1604–1830*. Montreal: McGill Queen's University Press, 2018.

Barras de Aragón, Francisco de las. *Documentos referentes al canal de navegación construido en 1650 entre Cartagena de Indias y el Río de la Magdalena*. Madrid: 1931.

Bédat, Claude. *La Real Academia de Bellas Artes de San Fernando (1744–1808)*. Madrid: Imprenta de Ramona Velasco, 1989.

Bemis, Samuel. *Jay's Treaty: A Study in Commerce and Diplomacy*. New Haven, CT: Yale University Press, 1962.

Black, Jeremy. *Atlas ilustrado de la guerra*. Madrid: Tres Cantos, 1996.

———. *Maps of War: Mappinig Conflict through the Centuries*. London: Conway-Bloomsbury, 2016.

Blanco Mozo, Juan Luis. "La Cultura de Ventura Rodríguez: La biblioteca de su sobrino Manuel Martín Rodríguez." *Anuario del Departamento de Historia y Teoría del Arte* 7–8 (1995–96): 181–221.

Blanes Martín, Tamara. *Fortificaciones del Caribe*. Havana: Editorial Letras Cubanas, 2001.

———. "Historia y singularidad de una fortaleza, el Morro de Santiago de Cuba." *Arquitectura en Cuba* 377 (1998): 32–36.

Borrego Pla, María del Carmen. "El abastecimiento de Cartagena de Indias en el siglo XVI." *Temas americanistas*, no. 5 (1982): 1–9.

———. *Cartagena de Indias: La andadura de una vida bajo la Colonia.* Bogotá: El Áncora editores, 2010.

———. "Felipe V y Cartagena de Indias: Cabildo, crisis y desmembramiento." In *Élites urbanas en Hispanoamérica: De la conquista a la independencia* (2005): 277–92.

Brant, Irving. *James Madison: The President, 1809–1812.* New York: Bobbs-Merrill, 1956.

Brooks, Philip Coolidge. *Diplomacy and the Borderlands: The Adams-Onís Treaty of 1819.* Berkeley: University of California Press, 1939.

Buckley, Roger Norman. *The British Army in the West Indies: Society and the Military in the Revolutionary Age.* Gainesville: University Press of Florida, 1998.

Buisseret, David. *The Fortifications of Kingston, 1655–1914.* Kingston: Bolivar Press, 1971.

Buisseret, David, and Barrie Clark. *A Report on the Chief Monuments of: Antigua, the British Virgin Islands, the Cayman Islands, Dominica, Grenada, Montserrat, Saint Lucia, Saint Vincent, and the Turks and Caicos Islands.* Museum of Antigua, 1971.

Buker, George. *Jacksonville: Riverport-Seaport.* Columbia: University of South Carolina Press, 1992.

Cabrera Cruz, Alfonso Rafael. "El patrimonio arquitectónico y fortificaciones en Cartagena de Indias: Identidad, significado cultural y prospectiva." PhD diss., Universidad de Granada, 2018.

Cabrero, Leoncio. "Francisco Sabatini y la fortificación de la Luisiana." In *Trabajos y Conferencias.* Madrid: Facultad de Filosofía y Letras, Universidad Complutense, 1958.

Cabrillana, Nicolás. "Las fortificaciones militares en Puerto Rico." *Revista de Indias* 27 (1967): 157–88.

Cairo Hurtado, Carlos del. "Mentiras verdaderas o la topología de la guerra: Aproximación arqueológica a la cartografía colonial de Bocachica, Cartagena de Indias." *Apuntes* 26 (2013): 186–203.

Calderón Quijano, José Antonio. *Fortificaciones en Nueva España.* Seville: C.S.I.C, Escuela de estudios hispanoamericanos, 1984.

———. *Guía de los documentos, mapas y planos sobre historia de América y España Moderna en la Biblioteca Nacional de París, Museo Británico y Public Record Office de Londres.* Seville: 1962.

———. "¿Pensó Vernon utilizar las cortinas de humo en su ataque de Cartagena de 1741?" *Revista General de Marina* 72 (1942): 651–55.

———. *Visión general de las fortificaciones indianas en los distintos frentes coloniales.* Zaragoza: Academia General Militar, 1988.

Camacho Cárdenas, Enrique. "De nuevo sobre las catedrales de Santiago de Cuba." In *Temas americanistas: Historia y diversidad cultural,* edited by Sandra Olivero and José Luis Caño, 595–606. Seville: Editorial Universidad de Sevilla, 2015.

Cámara Muñoz, Alicia. *El dibujante ingeniero al servicio de la monarquía hispánica: Siglos XVI–XVIII.* Madrid: Fundación Juanelo Turriano, 2016.

———. *Los ingenieros militares de la monarquía hispánica en los siglos XVII y XVIII.* Madrid: Ministerio de Defensa and Centro de Estudios Europa Hispánica, 2005.

Bibliography

Cámara Muñoz, Alicia, and Fernando de los Cobos. *La experiencia de la monarquía española en la fortificación marítima del Mediterráneo y su proyección en el Caribe.* In *Congreso Internacional Fortificación y Frontera Marítima.* Ibiza: 2005.

Cámara Muñoz, Alicia, and Bernardo Revuelta. *Ingeniería de la Ilustración.* Madrid: Fundación Juanelo Turriano, 2015.

Cañizares-Esguerra, Jorge. *Entangled Empires: The Anglo-Iberian Atlantic, 1500–1830.* Philadelphia: University of Pennsylvania Press, 2018.

Capel Sáez, Horacio. *Los ingenieros militares en España, siglo XVIII: Repertorio biográfico e inventario de su labor científica y espacial.* Barcelona: Universidad de Barcelona, 1983.

Capel Sáez, Horacio, Joan-Eugeni Sánchez, and Omar Moncada. *De Palas a Minerva: La formación científica y la estructura institucional de los ingenieros militares en el siglo XVIII.* Barcelona: El Serbal and Consejo Superior de Investigaciones Científicas, 1988.

Cardiñanos Bardeci, Inocencio. "El arquitecto Manuel Martín Rodríguez, discípulo de Ventura Rodríguez." *Academia* 71 (1990): 411–80.

Carr, James A. "The Battle of New Orleans and the Treaty of Ghent." *Diplomatic History* 3, no. 3 (1979): 273–82.

Cartografía y relaciones históricas de Ultramar. 10 vols. Madrid: Servicio Histórico Militar and Servicio Geográfico del Ejército, 1949–96.

Castillero Calvo, Alfredo. *Portobelo y el San Lorenzo del Chagres: Perspectivas imperiales, Siglos XVI–XIX.* Panama: Editora Novo Art, 2016.

Castillero Calvo, Alfredo. *Conquista, evangelización y resistencia.* Panama: 2017.

Castillo Mathieu, Nicolás del. *Los gobernadores de Cartagena de Indias (1504–1810).* Bogotá: Academia Colombiana de Historia, 1998.

Castillo Meléndez, Francisco. *La defensa de la isla de Cuba en la segunda mitad del siglo XVII.* Seville: Excma. Diputación Prov., 1986

Castillo Oreja, Miguel Ángel, and Monica Riaza de los Mozos. "Entre el Barroco y el Neoclasicismo: La Academia de Bellas Artes de San Fernando y las últimas empresas constructivas de los Borbones en América." In *Actas del III Congreso Internacional del Barroco Americano: Territorio, arte, espacio y sociedad,* 708–24. Seville: Universidad Pablo de Olavide, 2001.

Cepeda Jiménez, José Alejandro, Camilo Andrés Montoya Pardo, and Magda Catalina Jiménez Jiménez. "Entre la formación de la opinión pública y la movilización: El proceso independentista de Cartagena de Indias." *Panorama* 9 (November 2011): 11–19.

Cerdá Crespo, Jorge. *Conflictos coloniales: La guerra de los nueve años, 1839–1748.* Alicante: Universidad de Alicante, 2010.

Céspedes del Castillo, Guillermo. *El tabaco en Nueva España.* Madrid: Real Academia de la Historia, 1992.

Cox, Isaac Joslin. *The West Florida Controversy, 1798–1813: A Study in American Diplomacy.* Gloucester, MA: P. Smith, 1967.

Crone, Ernst. *The Principal Works of Simon Stevin.* Amsterdam: C. V. Swets and Zeitlinger, 1955–66.

Cruz Freire, Pedro. "Francisco Suárez Calderín y la renovación del Castillo de San Francisco de Santiago de Cuba." *Quiroga* 4 (2013): 88–93.

—. "El hornabeque de San Diego y la conclusión del Plan de Defensa de Silvestre Abarca para la ciudad de La Habana." In *De Sur a Sur: Intercambios artísticos y relaciones culturales*, edited by Rafael López Guzmán, 165–72. Granada: Universidad de Granada, 2017.

—. *Silvestre Abarca: Un ingeniero militar al servicio de la monarquía hispana*. Seville: Athenaica, 2018.

Cruz Freire, Pedro, and Ignacio López Hernández. *Ingeniería e Ingenieros en la América Hispana: Siglos XVIII y XIX*. Seville: Universidad de Sevilla, 2017.

Cruz Freire, Pedro, and Pedro Luengo. "El Caribe durante la Guerra de los Siete Años: El espionaje británico sobre las fortificaciones españolas y francesas." *Colonial Latin American Review* 28 (2019): 556–76.

Dawdy, Shannon Lee. *Building the Devil's Empire: French Colonial New Orleans*. Chicago: University of Chicago Press, 2008.

De la Mata Rodriguez, Enrique. *El asalto de Pointis a Cartagena de Indias*. Seville: Escuela de Estudios Hispano-Americanos, 1979.

Devreese, Jozef, and Guido Van der Berghe. *"Magic Is No Magic": The Wonderful World of Simon Stevin*. Boston: WIT Press, 2008.

Díaz-Trechuelo Spinola, María Lourdes. *Arquitectura española en Filipinas (1565–1800)*. Seville: Escuela de Estudios Hispanoamericanos, 1959.

Díaz-Trechuelo Spinola, María Lourdes, Concepción Pajarón Parody, and Adolfo Rubio Gil. "El Virrey Don Juan Vicente de Güemes Pacheco, Segundo Conde de Revillagigedo." In *Los Virreyes de Nueva España en el reinado de Carlos IV*, edited by José Antonio Calderón Quijano. Seville: Consejo Superior de Investigaciones Científicas, Escuela de Estudios Hispanoamericanos, 1972.

Dijksterhuis, Eduard. *Simon Stevin: Science in the Netherlands around 1600*. The Hague: Martinus Nijhoff, 1970.

Din, Gilbert, trans. *Louisiana in 1776: A Memoria of Francisco Bouligny*. New Orleans: Louisiana Collection Series, 1977.

Donoso Anes, Rafael. "La Compañía del Asiento y la Guerra de la Oreja de Jenkins: Sus causas económicas y algunos aspectos contables relacionados." *RC-SAR* 11, no. 1 (2008): 9–40.

Dunn, Christopher Chase. *Sugar and Slaves: The Rise of the Planter Class in the English West Indies, 1624–1713*. Chapel Hill: University of North Carolina Press, 1972.

Dyde, Brian. *A History of Antigua: The Unsuspected Isle*. London: MacMillian Education, 2000.

Elkhadem, Hossam, and Wouter Bracke, eds. *Simon Stevin (1548–1620): L'émergence de la nouvelle science*. Turnhout: Brepols, 2004.

Elliot, John H. *Empires of the Atlantic World: Britain and Spain in America, 1492–1830*. New Haven, CT: Yale University Press, 2007.

Firth, Charles Harding. "The Capture of Santiago, in Cuba, by Captain Myngs, 1662." *English Historical Review* 14, no. 55 (July 1899): 536–40.

Fish, Shirley. *When Britain Ruled the Philippines, 1762–1764*. Bloomington, IN: 1st Books Library, 2003.

Felicinano Ramos, Héctor. *El contrabando inglés en el Caribe y Golfo de México, 1748–1778*. Seville: Excma. Diputación Provincial de Sevilla, 1990.

Bibliography

Fernández González, Alberto. "Trazas y proyectos para el desaparecido retablo mayor de estuco de la iglesia parroquial de Omnium Sanctorum de Sevilla." *Laboratorio de Arte*, 20 (2007): 203–28.

Fortificaciones del Caribe: Memorias de la Reunión de Expertos. Cartagena de Indias: 1996.

Fuentes Rojas, Elizabeth. *La Academia de San Carlos y los constructores del Neoclásico*. Mexico City: Escuela Nacional de Artes Plásticas, 2002.

Galindo Díaz, Jorge. *El conocimiento constructivo de los ingenieros militares del siglo XVIII*. Cali: Univerisidad del Valle, 2000.

Gámez Casado, Manuel. "Buscando al enemigo inglés: Expediciones de guardacostas españoles al golfo del Darién, 1767–1768." *Anuario de Estudios Americanos* 75, no. 1 (2018): 211–36.

———. "Ingenieros militares y arquitectura defensiva en Cartagena de Indias tras el ataque del Barón de Pointis." In *De Sur a Sur: Intercambios artísticos y relaciones culturales*, 179–83. Granada: Universidad de Granada, 2017.

———. "Ingenieros militares españoles en Nueva Granada durante el siglo XVIII: Movilidad, proyectos y expediciones." *Revista de Indias* 79, no. 277 (2019): 765–96.

García-Diego, José, and Alexander Keller. *Giovanni Francesco Sitoni: Ingeniero renacentista al servicio de la Corona de España*. Madrid: Editorial Castalia, 1990.

García Melero, José Enrique. "Arquitectura y burocracia: El proceso del proyecto en la Comisión de Arquitectura de la Academia (1786–1808)." *Espacio, Tiempo y Forma, Serie VII, Historia del arte* 4 (1991): 283–348.

———. "Nexos y mimesis academicistas: América en la Academia de Bellas Artes de San Fernando." In *Influencias artísticas entre España y América*, edited by José Enrique Melero, 261–359. Madrid: Editorial MAPFRE, 1992.

———. "Orígenes del control de los proyectos de obras públicas por la Academia de San Fernando (1768–1777)." *Espacio, Tiempo y Forma, Serie VII, Historia del arte* 11 (1998): 287–342.

Gaspar, David Barry. *Bondmen and Rebels: A Study of Master-Slave Relations in Antigua*. Durham, NC: Duke University Press, 1985.

———. "Runaways in Seventeenth-Century Antigua, West Indies." *Boletín de Estudios Lantinamericanos del Caribe* 26 (1979): 3–13.

Glassie, Henry. *Vernacular Architecture*. Bloomington: Indiana University Press, 2000.

González Arana, Roberto, and Edwin Monsalvo. "De la Suprema Junta de Gobierno al Estado soberano: La independencia de Cartagena de Indias (1810–1812)." *Historia Crítica* 41 (2010): 62–85.

González Fernández, A. "Repercusiones espaciales en la fortificación colonial en La Habana." *ERIA* 35 (1994).

González Franco, Glorinela. "Jose Antonio González Velázquez, Arquitecto del Neoclásico." *Boletín de Monumentos Históricos* 15 (1991): 30–39.

González Tascón, Ignacio. *Ingeniería española en ultramar (siglos XVI–XIX)*. Madrid: Centro de Estudios y Experimentación de Obras Publicas, 1992.

González Tascón, Ignacio, A. Vázques de la Cuenva, P. Castro Rodriguez, and A. González Santos. *Obras hidráulicas en América colonia*. Madrid: Centro de Estudios y Experimentación de Obras Publicas, 1993.

Bibliography

Gould, Elija. "Entangled Histories, Entangled Worlds: The English-Speaking Atlantic as a Spanish Periphery." *American Historical Review* 112, no. 3 (2007): 764–86.

———. *The Persistence of Empire: British Political Culture in the Age of the American Revolution.* Chapel Hill: University of North Carolina Press, 2000.

Grahn, Lance. "Comercio y contrabando en Cartagena de Indias en el siglo XVIII." In *Cartagena de Indias en el siglo XVIII*, edited by Haroldo Calvo and Adolfo Meisel Roca, 19–53. Cartagena: Banco de la República, 2005.

———. *The Political Economy of Smuggling: Regional Informal Economies in Early Bourbon New Granada.* Boulder, CO: Westview: 1997.

Granero Martín, Francisco. "Arquitecturas del agua en el territorio. Sistemas de abastecimiento y defensa." PhD diss., Universidad de Sevilla, 1992.

Greene, Jerome. *Special History Study: The Defense of New Orleans, 1718–1900.* Denver: United States Department of the Interior, 1982.

Greentree, David. *Far-Flung Gamble, Havana, 1762.* Oxford: Osprey Publishing, 2010.

Guarini, Elena Fasano. "Center and Periphery." *Journal of Modern History* 67 (1995): S74–S96.

Gutiérrez, Ramón. *Fortificaciones en Iberoamérica.* Madrid: El Viso, 2005.

Gutiérrez, Ramón, and Cristina Esteras. "La distancia entre Europa y América en la colonia: A propósito de la Catedral de Santiago de Cuba." *Cuadernos de Arte Colonial* 1 (1986): 47–63.

Gutiérrez Meza, Ruth. "Prácticas sociales y control territorial del Caribe colombiano, 1750–1800: El caso del contrabando en la península de La Guajira." *Historia regional y local* 6 (2011): 39–65.

Gywn. Julian. *An Admiral for America: Sir Peter Warren, Vice Admiral of the Red, 1703–1752.* Gainesville: University Press of Florida, 2004.

Hague, Stephen. "Historiography and the Origins of the Gentleman's House in the British Atlantic World." In *'The Mirror of Great Britain': National Identity in Seventeenth-Century British Architecture*, edited by Olivia Turner, 233–59. Reading: Spire Books, 2010.

Hämäläinen, Pekka, and Samuel Truett. "On Borderlands." *Journal of American History* 98 (2011): 338–61.

Hamilton, Stanislaus Murray. *The Writings of James Monroe.* New York: G. P. Putnam's Sons, 1901.

Hernández de Alba, Guillermo. "Sir Edward Vernon y don Blas de Lezo." *Boletín de Historia y Antigüedades* 28 (1941): 468–73.

Hernández González, Manuel. *En el vendaval de la revolución: La trayectoria vital del ingeniero venezolano José del Pozo y Sucre.* Santa Cruz de Tenerife: Idea, 2010.

Higueras, María Dolores, ed. *Cuba ilustrada: Real Comisión de Guantánamo, 1796–1802.* Barcelona: Lunwerg Editores, 1991.

Hilton, Sylvia-Lyn. *Las Indias en la diplomacia española, 1739–1759.* Madrid: Editorial de la Universidad Complutense de Madrid, 1980.

Hinarejos Martín, Nuria. "Estado de las defensas de San Juan de Puerto Rico en 1762: Informe y propuesta de Tomás O'Daly." In *III Simposio Internacional Jóvenes Investigadores del Barroco Iberoamericano 'No hay más mundo que uno': Globalización artística y cultural.* Seville: 2017.

———. "El ingeniero Tomás O'Daly en Puerto Rico." In *Actas del Congreso Internacional América: Cultura visual y relaciones artísticas*, 43–50. Granada: 2015.

———. "La intervención del ingeniero Juan Francisco Mestre en el sistema de defensas de San Juan de Puerto Rico." In *Iberoamérica en perspectiva artística: Transferencias culturales y devocionales*, 57–72. Castelló de la Plana: Universitat Jaume I, 2016.

Hostos, Adolfo de. *Ciudad Murada (1521–1898)*. Havana: 1948.

Hunt, Gaillard. *The Works of James Madison*. New York: 1901.

Jacobs, James Ripley. *Tarnished Warrior: Major-General James Wilkinson*. New York: Macmillan, 1938.

Jaramillo Uribe, Jaime. "La economía del virreinato (1740–1810)." In *Historia económica de Colombia*, edited by José Antonio Ocampo, 49–85. Bogotá: Banco de Bogotá, 1988.

Jiménez Molinares, Gabriel. *Los mártires de Cartagena de Indias de 1816 ante el Consejo de Guerra y ante la historia*. Cartagena: Imprenta Departamental, 1947.

Jiménez Sotero, Jairo Eduardo. "La Fortaleza de San Carlos y la ruta México-Veracruz durante la época colonial." *Textos ArKeopáticos* 4 (2016): 32–46.

Jiménez Verdejo, Juan Ramón. "Considerations Concerning French Urban Influence on Spanish Colonial Cities on the Island of Cuba." *Journal of Asian Architecture and Building Engineering* 2, no. 8 (2009): 334–36.

Johnson, Matthew. *Behind the Castle Gate: From Medieval to Renaissance*. London: Routledge, 2002.

Jones, Wilbur Devereux. "A British View of the War of 1812 and the Peace Negotiations." *Mississippi Valley Historical Review* 45 (1958): 481–87.

Kuethe, Allan, and Kenneth Andrien. *The Spanish Atlantic World in the Eighteenth Century: War and the Bourbon Reforms, 1713–1796*. New York: Cambridge University Press, 2014.

Laorden Ramos, Carlos. "El ejército y la fundación de ciudades en Cuba." *Revista de Historia Militar*, no. 78 (1995): 43–84.

———. *Obra civil en Ultramar del Real Cuerpo de Ingenieros*. Madrid: Minesterio de Defensa, 2008.

———. "Obras civiles en América del Arma de Ingenieros." *Revista de Historia Militar*, Número Extraordinario (special issue) 1 (2012): 137–54.

Lemaitre, Eduardo. *Historia general de Cartagena*. Bogotá: Banco de la República, 1983.

Lipscomb, Andrew, and Albert Bergh. *The Writings of Thomas Jefferson*. Washington, DC: Thomas Jefferson Memorial Association, 1903–4.

Lombardo de Ruiz, Sonia. *La ciudadela: Ideología y arquitectura del siglo XVIII*. Mexico City: UNAM, 1980.

López Guzmán, Rafael, and Alfonso Cabrera. "La visión del virrey Sebastián de Eslava del asedio de Cartagena de Indias en 1741: El funcionamiento de las fortificaciones." In *Ingeniería e Ingenieros en la América Hispana, Siglos XVIII y XIX*, edited by Pedro Cruz Friere and Ignacio López, 49–76. Seville: Editorial Universidad de Sevilla, 2017.

López Hernández, Ignacio. "La defensa de Santiago de Cuba al ataque de Vernon de 1741: Principios de fortificación para la Guerra en el Caribe." *Anuario de Estudios Americanos* 76, no. 1 (2019): 177–207.

Bibliography

López Rodríguez, Omar. *La cartografía de Santiago de Cuba: Una fuente inagotable.* Santiago de Cuba: Oficina del Conservador de Santiago de Cuba, 2005.

———. *El Castillo del Morro de Santiago de Cuba.* Havana: Editorial Pablo de la Torriente, 1997.

Lucena Giraldo, Manuel. "El Canal del Dique de Cartagena de Indias (1533–1810)." In *Antiguas obras hidráulicas en América: Actas del seminario México—1988,* 493–503. Madrid: Ministerio de Obras Publicas y Transportes, Secretaria General Tecnica, 1991.

———. "Una obra digna de Romanos: El Canal del Dique, 1650–1810." In *Obras hidráulicas en América colonial,* 105–17. Madrid: Ministerio de Obras Públicas Transportes y Medio Ambiente, 1993.

Lucena Giraldo, Manuel, and Alberto Córdoba Pardo. "Ciencia y espacio colonial: Los proyectos del Canal del Dique en el siglo XVIII." In *Ciencia, vida y espacio en Iberoamérica,* edited by José Luis Peset, 21–43. Madrid: Consejo superior de investigaciones científicas, 1989.

Lucena Salmoral, Manuel. "Los diarios anónimos sobre el ataque de Vernon a Cartagena existentes en Colombia: Su correlación y posibles autores." *Anuario de Estudios Americanos* 30 (1973): 337–469.

Luengo, Pedro. *Manila, plaza fuerte (1762–1788): Ingenieros militares entre Asia, América y Europa.* Madrid: Consejo superior de investigaciones científicas, 2013.

———. *Mares fortificados: Protección y defensa de las rutas de globalización.* Seville: Editorial Universidad de Sevilla, 2018.

———. "Military Engineering in Eighteenth-Century Havana and Manila: The Experience of the Seven Years War." *War in History* 24, no. 1 (2017): 4–27.

———. "Movilidad de los ingenieros militares en Cuba a finales del siglo XVIII." *Quiroga* 6 (2014): 36–47.

Luengo, Pedro, and Ignacio López. "Fortificaciones francesas en el Caribe frente a los ataques de la Guerra de los Siete Años." *Aldaba* 43 (2018): 273–89.

Luengo, Pedro, and Gene A. Smith. *From Colonies to Countries in the North Caribbean: Military Engineers in the Development of Cities and Territories.* Cambridge: Cambridge Scholars Publishing, 2016.

Luengo Muñoz, Manuel. "Génesis de las expediciones militares al Darién en 1785–86." *Anuario de Estudios Americanos* 43 (1961): 333–416.

Lynch, John. *La España del siglo XVIII.* Barcelona: Crítica, 1999.

Malone, Dumas. *Jefferson the President: First Term, 1801–1805.* Boston: Little, Brown, 1970.

Mañas Martínez, J. *Puertos y fortificaciones en América y Filipinas: Catálogo de la exposición.* Madrid: Ministerio de Obras Públicas y Urbanismo, 1985.

Marchena Fernández, Juan. "¿Comerciantes o especuladores de metal? Las élites mercantiles de Cartagena de Indias a principios y finales del período colonial." *Memorias* 10 (2009): 32–90.

———. *La institución militar en Cartagena de Indias en el siglo XVIII.* Seville: Escuela de Estudios Hispano-Americanos, 1982.

Marco Dorta, Enrique. *Cartagena de Indias: La ciudad y sus monumentos.* Seville: Escuela de Estudios Hispano-Americanos (CSIC), 1951.

Bibliography

283

———. "El Palacio de los Virreyes de Bogotá: Un proyecto fracasado." *Anales del Instituto de Arte Americano e Investigaciones Estéticas* 2 (1949): 88–98.

Marley, David. *Wars of the Americas: A Chronology of Armed Conflict in the New World, 1492 to the Present.* Santa Barbara, CA: ABC-CLIO, 2008.

Márquez, Graciela. *Monopolio y comercio en América Latina, siglos XVI–XVII.* Mexico City: El Colegio de México, Centro de Estudios Económico, 2001.

Marrero, Leví. *Cuba: Economía y sociedad.* Madrid: Playor, 1975.

Martín González, Juan José. "Problemática del retablo bajo Carlos III." *Fragmentos* 12–14 (1988): 32–43.

Mateos Iguácel, Cristobal. "La investigación hidráulica en la Ilustración." In *Obras hidráulicas de la Ilustración.* Madrid: 2014.

McDermott, John Francis. *The French in the Mississippi Valley.* Urbana: University of Illinois Press, 1965.

Mcneill, J. R. *Mosquito Empires: Ecology and War in the Greater Caribbean, 1620–1914.* Cambridge: Cambridge University Press, 2010.

Merk, Frederick. *Manifest Destiny and Mission in American History: A Reinterpretation.* New York: Knopf, 1963.

Michelsen, Gustavo. "Expedición de Vernon." *Boletín de Historia y Antigüedades* 19 (1932): 616–17.

Middlekauf, Robert. *The Glorious Cause.* Oxford: Oxford University Press, 1982.

Mignucci, Andrés. *El parque Muñoz Rivera y el Tribunal Supremo de Puerto Rico.* San Juan: Rama Judicial de Puerto Rico, 2012.

Mogollón Vélez, José Vicente. *El Canal del Dique, historia de un desastre ambiental.* Bogotá: El Áncora Editores, 2013.

Moncada Maya, José Omar. *El ingeniero Miguel Constanzó: Un militar ilustrado en la Nueva España del siglo XVIII.* Mexico City: UNAM, 1994.

Moncada Maya, José Omar. "El ingeniero militar Miguel Constanzó en la Real Academia de Bellas Artes de San Carlos de la Nueva España." *Scripta Nova: Revista electrónica de Geografía y Ciencias Sociales* 7 (2003).

———. *Miguel Constanzó y la Alta California: Crónica de sus viajes (1768–1770).* Mexico City: Instituto de Geografía, Universidad Nacional Autónoma de México, 2012.

Monks, Sarah. "Our Man in Havana: Representation and Reputation in Lieutenant Philip Orsbridge's Britannia'sTriumph (1765)." In *Conflicting Visions: War and Visual Culture in Britain and France, c. 1700–1830,* edited by John Bonehill and Jeoff Quilley, 85–115. Aldershot: Ashgate, 2005.

Montero de Pedro, José. *Españoles en Nueva Orleans y Luisiana.* Madrid: Ediciones de Cultura Hispánica del Centro Iberoamericano de Cooperación, 1979.

Morales, Alfredo J. "Cartografía de la costa y puertos de Cuba." *Historia y globalización: Ensayos en homenaje a Alfredo Castillero Calvo.* Panama: Editora Novo Art, 2017.

———. "Cuba y Jamaica: Conflictos en el Caribe." In *Ingeniería e Ingenieros en la América Hispana: Siglos XVIII y XIX,* edited by Pedro Cruz and Ignacio López, 13–28. Seville: Editorial Universidad de Sevilla, 2017.

Morales Folguerra, José Miguel. *Arquitectura y urbanismo hispanoamericano en Luisiana y Florida Occidental.* Málaga: Universidad de Málaga, 1987.

———. "Urbanismo hispanoamericano en el sudeste de los EE. UU. (Louisiana y Florida): La obra del malagueño Bernardo de Gálvez y Gallardo (1746–1786)." In *Actas IV Jornadas de Andalucía y América*, 119–40. Seville: Escuela de Estudios Hispanoamericanos, 1984.

Morgan, George. *The Life of James Monroe*. New York: AMS Press, 1969.

Muñoz Corbalán, Juan Miguel. *La Academia de Matemáticas de Barcelona: El legado de los ingenieros militares*. Madrid: Ministerio de Defensa; Barcelona: Novatesa, 2004.

———. "La Colección de Relieves de las Fortificaciones del Reino: Essai d'organisation du Cabinet de Plans-Reliefs en Espagne pendant le règne de Charles III." In *Actes du Colloque International sur les Plans-Reliefs au passé et au present les 23, 24, 25 avril 1990 en l'Hôtel National des Invalides*, 181–94. Paris: SEDES, 1993.

———. "El dibujante ingeniero hacia la universalidad de la dualidad arte/técnica en la cartografía militar del siglo XVIII." *Quintana: Revista do Departamento de Historia da Arte* 14 (2015): 59–79.

———. "Espionaje a contrarreloj sobre el terreno por el ingeniero del siglo XVIII." In *El ingeniero espía*, edited by Alicia Cámara Muñoz and Bernardo Revuelta Pol, 91–132. Segovia: Fundación Juanelo Turriano, 2018.

———. *Jorge Próspero Verboom: Ingeniero flamenco de la monarquía hispánica*. Madrid: Fundación Juanelo Turriano, 2015.

———. "La maqueta de Cádiz (1777–1779)." In *Milicia y Sociedad en la Baja Andalucía (Siglos XVIII y XIX): VIII Jornadas Nacionales de Historia Militar*, 889–909. Seville: Universidad de Sevilla, Cátedra "General Castaños"—Región Militar Sur, 1999.

———. "I plastici e la difesa del territorio spagnolo nel tempo di Carlo III: Fallimento e mancata assimilazione del modello francese." In *Castelli e Città Fortificate: Storia, Recupero, Valorizzazione*, edited by A. Marco and G. Tubaro, 652–58. Udine: Università degli Studi di Udine, 1991.

———. "La Real Junta de Fortificaciones de Barcelona." *Espacio, Tiempo y Forma: Revista de la Facultad de Geografía e Historia*, serie VII "Historia del Arte," 5 (1992): 351–73.

———. "*Universitas bellica*: Les Académies de Mathématiques de la couronne espagnole au XVIIIe siècle ou *Non nisi grandia canto*." In *Les savoirs de l'ingénieur militaire: Manuels, cours et cahiers d'exercices, 1751–1914. 5ème Journée d'étude organisée par Émilie d'Orgeix (INHA-Bordeaux 3), Isabelle Warmoes (Musée des Plans-Reliefs, Paris) et le Centre d'Histoire des Techniques et de l'Environnement. París, Institut National d'Histoire de l'Art, 22 octubre 2010*, 113–26. Paris: INHA, 2010.

Navarro García, Luis. *José de Gálvez y la Comandancia General de las Provincias Internas*. Seville: Escuela de Estudios Hispanoamericanos, 1964.

Negroni, Héctor Andrés. *Historia militar de Puerto Rico*. San Juan: Instituto de Cultura Puertorriqueña, 1992.

Nicholson, Desmond V. *Forts of Antigua and Barbuda*. St. John's, Antigua: Museum of Antigua and Barbuda, 1994.

O'Bryne, H. Alexander. "El desabastecimiento de géneros agrícolas en la provincia de Cartagena de Indias a finales del período colonial." *Historia Crítica*, no. 50 (2013): 59–78.

Oglesby, J. C. M. "The British Attacks on the Caracas Coast, 1743." *Mariner's Mirror* 58 (1972): 27–40.

Ojeda Pérez, Robert, Adriana Castellanos, and Sebastián Torres. "Incendio del Palacio Virreinal de Santa Fé: Resonancia histórica y patrimonial." *Módulo Arquitectura CUC* 12 (2013): 163–81.

Ord, Rob W. "Memorandum Respecting Mobile." *Louisiana Historical Quarterly* 44 (1961): 132–33.

Ordovás, Juan José. *Atlas político y militar del Reyno de Murcia*. Murcia: Mimarq, 2005.

Orozco Melgar, María Elena. "El palacio Municipal de Santiago de Cuba en la recuperación de la memoria colectiva." *Arquitectura y Urbanismo* 36, no. 2 (2015): 19–40.

Owsley, Frank Lawrence. *The Struggle for the Gulf Borderlands: The Creek War and the Battle of New Orleans*. Gainesville: University Press of Florida, 1981.

Owsley, Frank Lawrence, and Gene A. Smith. *Filibusters and Expansionists: Jeffersonian Manifest Destiny*. Tuscaloosa: University of Alabama Press, 1997.

Padgett, James A. "Official Records of the West Florida Revolution and Republic." *Louisiana Historical Quarterly* 21 (1938): 719–21.

Pares, Richard. *War and Trade in the West Indies, 1739–1763*. Oxford: Clarendon Press, 1936.

Pearce, Edward. *The Great Man: Sir Robert Walpole; Scoundrel, Genius, and Britain's First Prime Minister*. London: Cape, 2007.

Pérez de la Riva, Juan: "Inglaterra y Cuba en la primera mitad del siglo XVIII: Expedición de Vernon contra Santiago de Cuba en 1741." *Revista Bimestre Cubana* 36 (1935).

Pérez Guzmán, F. *Modo de vida de esclavos y forzados en las fortificaciones de Cuba: Siglo XVIII*, en *Anuario de estudios americanos*. 1990.

Pérez Martínez, Aurelio. *Isla y pueblo: Un enfoque histórico geográfico de Puerto Rico*. Madrid: Cultural Panamericana, 1992.

Peterson, Merrill D. *Thomas Jefferson and the New Nation: A Biography*. New York: Oxford University Press, 1970.

Pinon, Pierre: "Saint-Domingue: L'Île à villes." In *Les vilels françaises du Nouveau Monde*, edited by Laurent Vidal and Émilie d'Orgeix. Paris: Somogy éditions d'Art, 1999.

Pombo, José Ignacio de. *Comercio y contrabando: Cartagena de India*. Bogotá: Procultura, 1986.

Pratt, Julius W. *Expansionists of 1812*. Gloucester, MA: Peter Smith, 1957.

Quintana Martínez, Alicia. *La Arquitectura y los arquitectos en la Real Academia de Bellas Artes de San Fernando (1744–1774)*. Madrid: Xarait, 1983.

Ramos Zúñiga, Antonio. *La ciudad de los castillos: Fortificaciones y arte defensivo en La Habana de los siglos XVI al XIX*. Havana: Asociación Cubana de Amigos de los Castillos, 2004.

———. "La fortificación española en Cuba siglos XVI–XIX." *Atrio Revista de Historia del Arte* 5 (1993): 49–64.

Restrepo Canal, Carlos. "El sitio de Cartagena por el almirante Vernon." *Boletín de Historia y Antigüedades* 28 (1941): 447–67.

Richmond, Herbert William. *The Navy in the War of 1739–1748*, 3 vols. Cambridge: Cambridge University Press, 1920.

Rodríguez de la Flor, Fernado. "Vauban lúdico (Un grabado de Pablo Minguet e Irol, juegos de la Fortificación, Madrid, 1752)." *Boletín del Museo e Instituto Camón Aznar* 24 (1986): 115–32.

Rogers, Nicholas. *Mayhem: Post-War Crime and Violence in Britain, 1748–53*. New Haven, CT: Yale University Press, 2012.

Roig de Leuchsering, Emilio. *La dominación inglesa de La Habana*. Havana: Editorial Molina, 1929.

Rowland, Dunbar. *Official Letter Books of W. C. C. Claiborne, 1801–1816*. Jackson: Mississippi Department of History and Archives, 1917.

Ruiz Carrasco, Jesús María. "La Real Academia de San Fernando y la proyección de consistorios en los reinos andaluces (1777–1808)." *Ars Bilduma* 8 (2018): 139–58.

Ruiz Rivera, Julián. "Cartagena de Indias en el siglo XVIII: Del dominio particular a la corrupción pública." *Boletín de Historia y Antigüedades* C, no. 856 (2013): 102–23.

———. "Cartagena de Indias ¿Un cabildo cosmopolita o una ciudad pluriétnica?" In *El municipio indiano: Relaciones interétnicas, económicas y sociales: Homenaje a Luis Navarro García*, 407–24. Seville: Universidad de Sevilla, 2009.

———. *Cartagena de Indias y su provincia: Una mirada a los siglos XVII y XVIII*. Bogotá: El Áncora Editores, 2005.

Rusell-Hart, Francis. "Ataques del almirante Vernon al continente americano." *Boletín de Historia y Antigüedades* 23 (1917): 76–84.

Sambricio, Carlos. *La Arquitectura española de la Ilustración*. Madrid: Coedicion del Consejo superior de los colegios de arquitectos de España y del Instituto de estudios de administracion local, 1986.

———. "Datos sobre los discípulos y seguidores de D. Ventura Rodríguez." In *Estudios sobre Ventura Rodriguez (1717–1785)*, edited by F. Chueca Goitia. Madrid: Real Academia de Bellas Artes de San Fernando, 1985.

———. "Juan Pedro Arnal, arquitecto del siglo XVIII." *Archivo español de arte* 183 (1973): 299–328.

———. "Juan Pedro Arnal y la teoría arquitectónica en la Academia de San Fernando de Madrid." *Goya* 147 (1978): 147–57.

Sánchez, Joan Eugeni. "La estructura institucional de una corporación científica: El cuerpo de ingenieros militares en el siglo XVIII." *Ciencia, vida y espacio en Iberoamérica* 2 (1989): 3–20.

Sánchez Guerra, José. "Guantánamo in the Eye of the Hurricane." In *Guantánamo and American Empire: The Humanities Respond*, edited by E. Walicek and Jessica Adams. Cham, Switzerland: Palgrave Macmillan, 2017.

Sanz, Nuria. *Fortificaciones Americanas y la Convención del Patrimonio Mundial*. Paris: UNESCO World Heritage Centre, 2006.

Schneider, Elena A. *The Occupation of Havana: War, Trade, and Slavery in the Atlantic World*. Williamsburg, VA: Omohundro Institute of Early American History and Culture; Chapel Hill: Univerrsity of North Carolina Press, 2018.

Segovia Salas, Rodolfo. "Cartagena de Indias historiografía de sus fortificaciones." In *Cartagena de Indias y su historia*, 1–19. Bogotá: Banco de la República, 1998.

———. *El lago de piedra: La geopolítica de las fortificaciones españolas del Caribe (1586–1786)*. Bogotá: El Áncora Editores, 2013.

Sepúlveda Rivera, Aníbal. *San Juan: Historia ilustrada de su desarrollo urbano, 1508–1898*. San Juan: CARIMAR, 1989.

Serrara, Ramón María: *Tráfico terrestre y red vial en las Indias españolas*. Barcelona: Lunwerg, 1992.

Shaw, Jenny. *Everyday Life in the Early English Caribbean: Irish, Africans, and the Construction of Difference*. Athens: University of Georgia Press, 2013.

Sheldon, Garret. *Political Philosophy of Thomas Jefferson*. Baltimore: Johns Hopkins University Press, 1991.

Sheridan, Richard B. "The Formation of Caribbean Plantation Society, 1689–1748." In *The Oxford History of the British Empire: The Eighteenth Century*, edited by P. J. Marshall, 394–414. Oxford: Oxford University Press, 1998.

———. "The Rise of a Colonial Gentry: A Case Study of Antigua, 1730–1775." *Economic History Review* 13, no. 3 (1961): 342–57.

Smith, Gene A. "'Our Flag Was Displayed within Their Works': The Treaty of Ghent and the Conquest of Mobile." *Alabama Review* 52 (1999): 3–20.

Smith, Joseph Burkholder. *The Plot to Steal Florida: James Madison´s Phony War*. New York: Arbor House, 1983.

Sourdis Najera, Adelaida. "El Consejo de Guerra de los Mártires de 1816." In *Cartagena de Indias en la Independencia*, edited by Haroldo Calvo Stevenson and Adolfo Meisel Roca, 297–330. Cartagena: Banco de la República, 2011.

———. "El precio de la Independencia en la primera República: La población de Cartagena de Indias (1814–1816)." *Boletín de Historia y Antigüedades* 5 (2000): 103–14.

———. "Los últimos días del gobierno español en Colombia." *Boletín de la Academia de Historia de Bogotá* 4 (2010): 67–86.

Styron, Arthur. *The Last of the Cocked Hats: James Monroe and the Virginia Dynasty*. Norman: University of Oklahoma Press, 1945.

Syrett, David. *The Siege and Capture of Havana*. London: Navy Records Society, 1970.

Temperley, Harold. "The Cause of the War of Jenkins' Ear, 1739." *Transactions of the Royal Historical Society* 3 (1909): 197–236.

Torre Echávarri, José Ignacio de la. "Una maqueta para un rey: El estudio de fortificación de Felipe V." In *Tesoros del Museo del Ejército*, by María Jesús Rubio and Carmen García, 99–104. Madrid: Tesoros del Museo del Ejército, 2007.

Torrejón Chaves, Vicente. "Vicente Ignacio Imperial Digueri y Trejo: Ingeniero militar, marino, urbanista y arquitecto del siglo XVIII." *Espacio, Tiempo y Forma* (1989): 305–6.

Torres Ramírez, Bibiano. "Alejandro O'Reilly en Cuba." *Anuario de Estudios Americanos* 24 (1967): 1357–88.

———. *Alejandro O'Reilly en las Indias*. Seville: Escuela de Estudios Hispano-Americanos, 1969.

Torres Reyes, Ricardo. "El mariscal O'Reilly y las defensas de San Juan, 1765–1777." *Revista Historia* 1 (1954): 3–37.

Torres Sánchez, Jaime, and Luz Salazar. *Introducción a la historia de la ingeniería y de la educación en Colombia*. Bogotá: Universidad Nacional de Colombia, Facultad de Ingeniería, 2002.

Tracy, Nicholas. *Manila Ransomed: The British Assault on Manila in the Seven Years War*. Exeter: University of Exeter Press, 1995.

288 Bibliography

Tucker, Robert, and David Hendrickson. *Empire of Liberty: The Statecraft of Thomas Jefferson*. New York: Oxford University Press, 1990.

Tucker, Spencer. *The Jeffersonian Gunboat Navy*. Columbia: University of South Carolina Press, 1993.

Urrutia y Montoya, Ignacio José. *Primeros Historiadiores: Siglo XVIII*. Havana: Imagen Contemporánea, 2012.

Varo Montilla, Francisco. "Organización militar y defensa terrestre del Virreinato de Nueva España (siglos XVIII y principios del XIX)." In *La organización de los Ejércitos*, 859–912. Madrid: 2016.

Venegoni, Giovani. "De la Hermandad de la Costa a la Compañía Real de Saint Domingue: Compañías comerciales, filibusteros y administración colonial en Santo Domingo, 1684–1720." *Boletín AFEHC*, no. 58 (2013).

Vidal Ortega, Antonio. *Cartagena de Indias y la región histórica del Caribe, 1580–1640*. Seville: Escuela de Estudios Hispano-Americanos, Universidad de Sevilla, 2002.

Waciuma, Wanjohi. *Intervention in the Spanish Floridas, 1801–1818: A Study of Jeffersonian Foreign Policy*. Boston: Branden Press, 1976.

Waters, Christopher K. "Putting Forts in Their Place: The Politics of Defense in Antigua, 1670–1785." PhD diss., Syracuse University, 2018.

Waters, Ivor. *The Unfortunate Valentine Morris*. Chepstow: Chepstow Society, 1964.

Warmoes, Isabelle, Émilie D'Orgeix, and Charles Van der Heuvel. *Atlas militaires manuscrits européens (XVIe–XVIIIe siècles): Forme, contenu, contexte de réalisation et vocations; Actes des 4es journées d'étude du Musée des Plans-Reliefs. Paris, Hôtel de Croisilles. 18–19 avril 2002*. Paris: Musée des Plans-Reliefs, 2003.

Webb, Steven Saunders. *The Governors-General: The English Army and the Definition of Empire, 1569–1681*. Chapel Hill: University of North Carolina Press, 1979.

———. *Marlborough's America*. New Haven, CT: Yale University Press, 2013.

Weinberg, Albert. *Manifest Destiny: A Study of Nationalist Expansion in American History*. Baltimore: Johns Hopkins University Press, 1935.

White, Richard. *The Middle Ground: Indians, Empires, and Republics in the Great Lakes Region, 1650–1815*. Cambridge: Cambridge University Press, 1991.

Wilson, Samuel. *The vieux carré: New Orleans, Its Plan, Its Growth, Its Architecture*. New Orleans: Historic District Demonstration Study, conducted by Bureau of Governmental Research, 1968.

Wood, Minter. "Life in New Orleans in the Spanish Period." *Louisiana Historical Quarterly* 22 (1937).

Ybot León, Antonio. *La arteria histórica del Nuevo Reino de Granada (Cartagena-Santa Fe, 1538–1798)*. Bogotá: Ministerio de Educación, 1952.

Zacek, Natalie. *Settler Society in the English Leeward Islands, 1670–1776*. Cambridge: Cambridge University Press, 2010.

Zambrano Pérez, Milton. "Los dos ataques ingleses a Puerto Rico a finales del siglo XVI en el contexto de la lucha geopolítica internacional." *Revista Amauta* 16 (2010): 49–62.

Zamorano García, Carlos. "Agustín Crame y sus planes de defensa." In *Proyección en América de los ingenieros militares, siglo XVIII*, 331–29. Madrid: Ministerio de Defensa, 2016.

Zapato Olivella, Juan. *El grito de la independencia o los mártires de Cartagena de Indias.* Cartagena de Indias: 1961.

Zapatero, Juan Manuel. "Las fortificaciones históricas de San Juan de Puerto Rico." *Militaria Revista de Cultura Militar* 1 (1989): 141–75.

———. *La guerra en el Caribe.* Madrid: Servicio Histórico y Museo del Ejército, 1990.

———. "La heroica defensa de Cartagena ante el almirante inglés Vernon." *Revista de Historia Militar* 1 (1957): 115–78.

———. *Historia de las fortificaciones de Cartagena de Indias.* Madrid: Ediciones de Cultura Hispánica, 1979.

Contributors

Mónica Cejudo Collera is a professor and researcher at the Universidad Nacional Autónoma de México. She is the author of *Del Batallón al compás: Cien años de aportaciones arquitectónicas de los ingenieros militares (1821–1921)* and *La influencia del Tratado de Lupicini en la arquitectura militar en Nueva España*. She is editor of *Teoría e historia de la arquitectura: Pensar, hacer y conservar la arquitectura* and *R50 Restauración UNAM 50 Años: Medio siglo de contribuciones de la Maestría en Restauración de Monumentos*.

Pedro Cruz Freire teaches in the Department of Modern, Contemporary, American, and Art History at the Universidad de Cádiz. He is the author of *Silvestre Abarca: Un ingeniero militar al servicio de la monarquía hispana*; coauthor of *Estrategia y propaganda: Arquitectura militar en el Caribe (1689–1748)*; and editor of *Ingeniería e ingenieros en la América Hispana: Siglos XVIII y XIX*.

María Mercedes Fernández Martín is a *profesora titular* in the Department of Art History at the Universidad de Sevilla. Her research focuses on Spanish and Ibero-American art in the modern era.

Manuel Gámez Casado is a professor in the Department of Art History at the Universidad de Sevilla. He is the author of *Ingeniería militar en el Nuevo Reino de Granada: Defensa, poder y sociedad en el Caribe sur (1739–1811)*, among other titles.

Aaron Graham was a lecturer in Early Modern British Economic History at University College London. He authored *Corruption, Party, and Government in Britain, 1702–13* and *Bills of Union: Money, Empire, and Ambitions in the Mid-Eighteenth Century British Atlantic*.

Francisco Javier Herrera García is a professor in the Department of Art History at the Universidad de Sevilla. He is the author of *Fuentes para la Historia del Arte Andaluz: Noticias de Arquitectura (1700–1720)* and *El retablo sevillano durante la primera mitad del siglo XVIII*.

Nuria Hinarejos Martín is a professor in the Department of Art History at the Universidad Complutense de Madrid.

List of Contributors

Ignacio J. López Hernández is a professor of art history at the Universidad de Almería and principal investigator of the project "Modelos de Fortificación para la defensa del Caribe Occidental." He is the author of *Ingeniería e ingenieros en matanzas: Defensa y obras públicas entre 1693 y 1868* and coauthor of *Estrategia y propaganda: Arquitectura militar en el Caribe (1689–1748)*.

Pedro Luengo is associate professor in the History of Art Department at the Universidad de Sevilla. He is author of *Intramuros: Arquitectura en Manila, 1739–1762; Manila, plaza fuerte: Ingenieros militares entre Europa, América y Asia*; and *The Convents of Manila: Globalized Architecture during the Iberian Union*.

Alfredo J. Morales is an emeritus professor of the history of art at the Universidad de Sevilla. He has directed various research projects concerning the work of military engineers in the Caribbean, the Gulf of Mexico, and southeast Asia.

José Miguel Morales Folguera is a professor emeritus of the history of art at the Universidad de Málaga. He is the author of *Arquitectura y urbanismo hispanoamericano en Luisiana y Florida Occidental; Tunja: Atenas del Renacimiento en el Nuevo Reino de Granada*; and *La construcción de la sociedad utópica: El proyecto de Felipe II para Hispanoamérica (1556–1598)*.

Juan Miguel Muñoz Corbalán is an art history professor at the Universitat de Barcelona, Spain. He is the author of *Los ingenieros militares de Flandes a España, 1691–1718, La iglesia de la Ciudadela de Barcelona* and *Jorge Próspero Verboom: Ingeniero militar flamenco de la monarquía hispánica* and the editor of *La Academia de Matemáticas de Barcelona: El legado de los ingenieros militares*.

Jesús María Ruiz Carrasco is a professor of the history of art at the Universidad de Córdoba.

Germán Segura García is an instructor of Spanish military history, fortifications, and poliorcetics, and the history of armaments. He is the author of *Las fortificaciones de los Antonelli en Cuba, Siglos XVI–XVII*.

Gene Allen Smith is a professor of history at Texas Christian University and author of *The Slave's Gamble: Choosing Sides in the War of 1812*; coauthor of *In Harm's Way: A History of the American Military Experience*; and coeditor of *From Colonies to Countries in the North Caribbean: Military Legacies of the Development of Cities and Territories*.

Christopher K. Waters is the manager of the Heritage Department and archaeologist at the National Parks Authority of Antigua and Barbuda and the Antigua Naval Dockyard and Related Archaeological Sites.

Index

Page numbers in italics refer to figures.

Abanico Fort (San Juan, Puerto Rico), 189

Abarca, Silvestre, iii, 103; Havana, Cuba's fortifications and, 121

Academia de Matemáticas y Arquitectura Militar (Madrid, Spain), 135

Academia de San Carlos de Valencia, 29

Academia Militar de Matemáticas Cartaginesa, 148

academies: military engineers' training in, 13–27, 28, 41

Academy of Mathematics (Barcelona, Spain), 22; military engineers' training at, 14–19

Academy of Mathematics (Brussels), 15, 17

Acapulco, New Spain: Manila galleon and, 178

Adelantado pillbox (Santiago de Cuba), 130

Aguadores beach (Santiago de Cuba), 96

Aguadores River (Cuba), 96, 134

Aguirre, Pedro: Santiago de Cuba cathedral plans of, 32–33

Alabama River: navigation and deposit rights on, 210–11

Alicante, Spain: Luis Huet in, 102; Francisco Bouligny born in, 199

Allan, David, 49

American War for Independence (1775–83), ii, 57; Jamaica and, 46–47, 53, 107–10; Luis Huet's intelligence gathering during, 107–10

Ángel Custodio church (Havana, Cuba), 120

Anguiano, Manuel de, 148, 160–73

Anguiano, Sebastián de, 163

Anson, George, 115

Antigua: defense policy of, 58; fortifications in, 55–67, 100, 221; geography of, 56; politics of, 56–57

Antonelli, Juan Bautista, 95, 130

Apalachicola River: navigation and deposit rights on, 210–11

Aponte, Luis de: Canal del Dique (Cartagena de Indias, Nueva Granada) and, 142, 146, 147

Aranda, 10th Conde de (Pedro Pablo Abarca de Bolea y Jiménez de Urrea), 15, 21; San Carlos de Perote fort (New Spain/Mexico) and, 179

Arcos Moreno, Alonso, 95, 96, 98

Arévalo, Antonio de, 148, 157, 166, 168–69, 172; death, 162, 163

Armstrong, John, 216

Army of the Three Guarantees, 180

Aróstegui Hill (Havana, Cuba), 121, 122

Arredondo, Antonio de, 80

artillery park: at Cumberland Camp (Guantanamo Bay, Cuba), 82–83, 84; in New Orleans, Louisiana, 202

Asia (Spanish ship), 120–21

asiento de negros, 87, 175–76; smuggling and, 143–44

Bacuranao castle (near Havana, Cuba), 116, 121, 124

Bacuranao River (Cuba), 121, 122
Bails, Benito, 15
Bainbridge, Joseph, 215
Bambote, Nueva Granada, 139
Baracoa, Cuba: mapping of, 103
Barbados, 62, 116; Antigua's military supplies siphoned off to, 58; fortifications of, 81; geostrategic importance of, 69, 71; Washington House in, 69, 84
barracks master: Luis Huet as, 108–10
Barranca del Rey, Nueva Granada, 137, 139, 150
Bahamas: Old Canal of, 116; Providencia, drawing of, 110, *111*
Barranquilla, Nueva Granada: batteries in, 165
Baton Rouge, Louisiana: U.S. acquisition of, 210, 213–14, 221–22
Bayona Villanueva, Pedro, 130, 131, 134
Bayou Mardi Gras (Louisiana), 206
Bayú de San Juan (Louisiana): fort on 200, 203
Bedmar, 5th Marquis of (Isidoro de la Cueva y Benavides), 101
Belgium: Academy of Mathematics (Brussels), 15, 17; Royal Military Academy (Brussels), 101, 153. *See also* Flanders
Bélidor, Bernard Forest de, 15, 157
Belize. *See* British Honduras
Belize River, 70
Beltrán de Santa Cruz, Gabriel, 104
Benavides, Ambrosio, 187
Benítez, Carlos, 121
Bennett, Parsons & Frost, 197
Bierna y Mazo, Anselmo, 172
Black people: at Cumberland (English settlement of Guantanamo Bay), 72, 84; Pensacola defended by (1813), 217. *See also* enslaved people; Maroons
Blondel, François, 88
Bocagrande, Nueva Granada: gatehouse at, 167
Boligny, Alejandro, 221
borderlands: eighteenth-century wars and, ii–iii; as geographical concept, i

Borgoña fort (New Orleans, Louisiana), 200, 203, 204
Bouligny, Francisco: New Orleans, Louisiana's fortifications and, 199–200
Bourbon Reforms: canals and, 148; military engineers and, 101
Bowyer, John, 216, 217
Breda, Treaty of (1667), 55
brick: at Fort Charlotte (Alabama), 216; in Jamaican fortifications, 47, 48, 54; in New Orleans, Louisiana, fortifications, 200, 203, 205, 206
Bridgetown, Barbados, 71; fortifications in, 81; social organization in, 83; urban plan of, 69, 85; Washington House in, 69, 84
Briones Hoyo y Abarca, Carlos, 102
Britannia's Triumph (print series), 116
British Honduras: encampment attempts in, 68; fortifications of, 69–70; social organization in, 83
Bucareli, Antonio María, 179
Buceta, Ventura: Santiago de Cuba cathedral plans of, 32–34, 35–36
Buenos Aires, Argentina: Juan de Herrera y Sotomayor in, 148
Bueycabón Nuevo beach (Santiago de Cuba), 98
Bussa, José de, 20

Cabañas, Bay of (Cuba), 96, 98
Cádiz, Spain: Alonso Ximénez's three-dimensional recreation of, 23; Escuela de Navegación in, 72; Luis Huet in, 103; Manuel de Anguiano in, 163; Real Academia de Guardiamarinas in, 122
Cagigal, Juan Miguel, 122
Cajigal de la Vega, Francisco, 95, 96, 100; Charles Knowles's Havana visit (1756) and, 122; Edward Vernon's attack against Santiago de Cuba (1741) and, 113
Calabro, Mateo, 15, 22–23
Callao, Peru: fixed battalion in, 175
Camino Real (New Spain), 178
Campbell, John, 122

Index

Campbell v. Hall (1773), 51

Canal de Castilla (Spain), 153

Canal del Dique (Cartagena de Indias, Nueva Granada), 137–59

Canal Imperial de Aragón (Spain), 153

canals: Bourbon reforms and, 148; Canal del Dique (Cartagena de Indias, Nueva Granada), 137–59; in France, 153; in Spain, 153

Canot, Pierre Charles, 116

Canterbury, HMS, 98

Caparra, Puerto Rico: fortifications in, 186; founding of, 187

Cap-Français, Saint-Domingue: Charles Knowles's attack against (1743), 94; fortifications of, 88–89, 100; geostrategic importance of, 88, 100

Caribbean Sea: center and periphery dependence model in, i–ii; imperial competition in, 13

Carondelet, 5th Baron of (Francisco Luis Héctor): New Orleans, Louisiana's fortifications and, 200–201, 203, 205, 207–8

Carrasco, Pedro, 187

Cartagena, Spain, 102

Cartagena de Indias, Nueva Granada: Canal del Dique improvements in, 137–59; commercial importance of, 140; Edward Vernon's attack against (1741), 70–71, 85, 99, 113, 115, 162, 167–68, 169, 175–76, 187; enslaved workers trafficked in, 140, 143–44; fixed battalion in, 175; French attack against (1697), 145, 148, 174; independence movement in, 172; Manuel de Anguiano as military engineer in, 163–71; smuggling in, 140, 143–45

Casa Blanca (San Juan, Puerto Rico), 186

Casa de Dirección de la Renta (Mexico City), 37–39

Casa Yrujo, 1st Marquess of (Carlos Martínez de Irujo y Tacón), 212

Castelló, Pablo, 187

Castle of Real Fuerza (Havana, Cuba), 120

Castillo del Príncipe (Havana, Cuba), 103, 121

Castillo de San Marcos (St. Augustine, Florida), iv

Castle of San Carlos de la Cabaña. *See* La Cabaña (Havana, Cuba).

Castle of San Salvador de la Punta (Havana, Cuba), 120, 122, 123–24

Castle of San Severino (Matanzas, Cuba), 131

Castle of Santo Domingo de Atarés (Havana, Cuba), 120

Cauvet, Philippe, 91

Cejudo, Anastasio, 164

center and periphery dependence model, i–ii

Centro Estatal de Readaptación Social del Estado de Veracruz: San Carlos de Perote fort (New Spain/Mexico) as, 184

Ceuta, Spain: Luis Huet in, 102; mathematics academy at, 14, 17; troops from, 188

Chamba, Nueva Granada: battery at, 164, 165

Charles III of Spain, 22; defensive policy of, 176–78, 187; San Carlos de Perote fort (New Spain/Mexico) named for, 179

Chastenoye, Étienne Cochard de, 94

Chef Menteur pass (Louisiana), 201

Churruca, Cosme, 189

Císcara, Baltasar, 135

Císcara, Juan de: career of, 131; Santiago de Cuba's fortifications and, 95, 130–36; training of, 21, 135

Cispatá, Nueva Granada: battery in, 165

Claiborne, William C. C., 213, 214

Clifford, George, 186

Codrington, Christopher, II, 59

Codrington, Christopher, III, 59

Cofresí, Francisco Valinés, 197

Cojimar castle (near Havana, Cuba), 116, 121, 124

Collell, Francisco, 215

298   Index

Collot, Victor: on New Orleans, Louisiana's fortifications, 205–6, 207
Colombia: independence movement in, 172–73. *See also* Nueva Granada
Columbus, Christopher, 187
Commissioners of Forts and Fortifications (Jamaica), 47, 50, 52–53
comparative history: of forts, iii
Compendio de modernas fortificaciones (Císcara), 135
Constanzó, Miguel: Fábrica de Tabacos (Mexico City) plans of, 38–39
"Consulta al rey sobre la arquitectura de los Templos" (1777), 29–30
Continental Plan of Defense (Plan Continental de Defensa; 1779), 177
contraband. *See* smuggling
coquina, iv
Cornejo, Francisco: Canal del Dique (Cartagena de Indias, Nueva Granada) and, 142–43, 144–45
Cornwall, HMS, 88, 98
Corps Royal du Génie (France), 101
Corral, Miguel del, 102
corsairs. *See* piracy
Cotilla, Juan, 199
Cott, Victori M., 197
Crame, Agustín: Cartagena de Indias, Nueva Granada's fortifications and, 166, 167, 168–69; Continental Plan of Defense (1779) of, 177; Veracruz, New Spain's fortifications and, 177
Creek Indians, 217
criollos (creoles): in Spanish navy, 177
Cripplegate Battery (Antigua), 62, 65
Croix, 1st Marquis de (Carlos Francisco de Croix): San Carlos de Perote fort (New Spain/Mexico) and, 178–79
Croix, Maximiliano de la, 187
Cruillas, 1st Marquess of (Joaquín de Montserrat), 178
Cuba: English settlement of Guantanamo Bay, 68–85; Luis Huet in, 102, 104–7; social organization in, 83. *See also* Havana, Cuba; Santiago de Cuba

Cumberland (English settlement of Guantanamo Bay), 68–85, 88
Curaçao: British fleet at, during American War for Independence (1775–83), 108

Dalling, John, 53
Darien Gap, 164
defensive lines, 222–23; in Cartagena de Indias, New Granada, 157; in San Juan, Puerto Rico, 185–97
de Grand-Pré, Luis Antonio, 213
De Grasse, François Joseph Paul, Comte, 46–47
De l'architecture des forteresses, ou, De l'art de fortifier les places (Mandar), 15–16
de la Cruz battery (Cartagena de Indias, Nueva Granada), 169
De Lassus, Carlos, 213
Del Pozo Sucre, José, 106–7
Denia, Spain, 102
depopulation: of Caribbean, 99
de Quesada y Barnuevo, Juan Nepomuceno, 211
Desnaux, Carlos, 80
Devis, Nicolás: Veracruz, New Spain's fortifications and, 177
Dexter, Daniel, 214
Díaz, Porfirio, 184
Díez Navarro, Luis, 102
Drake, Francis, 113, 186
Dufresne, José, 188
Duncan, Guillermo, 104
Dutch: in American War for Independence (1775–83), 46; engineering contributions of, 154, 157; fortification policy of, 81; San Juan, Puerto Rico besieged by (1625), 186, 187; Santiago de Cuba's fortifications and, 130
Dutch West India Company, 185
El Cañuelo (San Juan, Puerto Rico), 186, 188
El Corozal, Nueva Granada, 164, 165
Eliott, George, 123
El Morro (Santiago de Cuba). *See* San

Index

Pedro de la Roca castle (Santiago de Cuba)

Encyclopédie: "fortification" entry in, 16

Encyclopédie méthodique, 16

England: fortification policy of, 81, 221; Havana, Cuba, captured by (1762), 100, 112–25, 176, 187; Guantanamo Bay (Cuba) settlement of, 68–85; military engineers' training in, 13; piracy and, 113, 186. *See also* Antigua; Jamaica; Knowles, Charles; Vernon, Edward

English Harbour, Antigua: dockyard at, 59–60

Enrico, Balduino, 186

Ensenada, 1st Marquess of (Zenón de Somodevilla y Bengoechea), 177

enslaved people: Antigua's economy and, 63; Antigua's fortifications and, 55, 58; Cartagena de Indias, Nueva Granada, traffic of, 140, 143–44; Jamaica's fortifications and, 46, 47, 48, 49–50; Treaty of Utrecht (1713) and, 87, 143–44 (see also *asiento de negros*); in West Florida, 212

Escambia River: navigation and deposit rights on, 210–11

Escambrón battery platform (San Juan, Puerto Rico), 186, 188, 189, 192, 195

Escuela de Navegación (Cádiz, Spain), 72

Eslava, Sebastián de, 175

espionage, 80–81, 222, in the English attack on Havana, Cuba (1762), 122, 123. *See also* intelligence gathering

Esquiaqui, Domingo: Santa Fé de Bogotá viceregal palace plans of, 39–40

Europa (Spanish ship), 120–21

Fábrica de Tabacos (Mexico City), 37–39

Fábrica de Tabacos (Seville, Spain), 37

Ferdinand VII of Spain, 172

Fernández, Pedro, 35

Fernández de Medrano, Sebastián, 14–15, 153, 154, 221

financing: of Antigua's fortifications, 60; of Jamaican fortifications, 50–51. *See also* taxation

Flanders, 108; Juan de Herrera y Sotomayor in, 153; locks in, 150, 152. *See also* Belgium

Flores, Salvador, 163

Flores de Aldana, Rodrigo, 130

Florida(s): as British colony, 107; geostrategic value of, 212; Juan de Císcara in, 131; U.S. acquisition of, 211–13. *See also* West Florida

Floridablanca, 1st Count of (José Moñino), 30, 37

fluvial knowledge. *See* hydrology

Fort Augusta (Jamaica), 45, 47, 48

Fort Berkeley (Antigua), 61

Fort Charles (Jamaica), 45, 46, 47, 48, 49

Fort Charlotte (Alabama), 215, 216, 217

Fort Charlotte (Antigua), 61

Fort Dauphin (Fort-Dauphin, Saint-Domingue), 89

Fort-Dauphin, Saint-Domingue, 88; fortification of, 89, 100

Fort Edward (New York), iv

Fort Hamilton (Antigua), 61, 62, 63–65

Fort Isaac (Antigua), 61

Fort James (Antigua), 62, 63–65

Fort Picolet (Saint-Domingue), 89

forts: comparative history and, iii; significance of, ii–iii. *See also specific forts*

Fort San Felipe de Barajas (Cartagena de Indias, Nueva Granada), 73, 113, 168, 170, 171; Manuel de Anguiano and, 163–71

Fort San Jago (Cartagena de Indias, Nueva Granada), 73

Fort San José (Cartagena de Indias, Nueva Granada), 70, 73

Fort San Luis de Bocachica (Cartagena de Indias, Nueva Granada), 70, 73

Fort Stoddert (Alabama), 212, 214–15, 216

Fort Ticonderoga (New York), iv

Fort William Henry (New York), iv

France: canals in, 153; Cartagena de Indias, Nueva Granada, attacked by (1697), 145, 148, 174; fortification policy of, 99; military engineers' training in, 13

French America: Jamaican fortifications

300 Index

compared to fortifications in, 54. *See also* Saint-Domingue

French and Indian War, 4. *See also* Seven Years' War (1753–64)

French West India Company: Antigua invasion by (1666), 55–56, 58

Fuerte Borbón (New Orleans, Louisiana), 201, 206, 207–8

Gálvez, Bernardo de, 110; New Orleans, Louisiana's fortifications and, 203

Gálvez, José de, 122, 163, 177, 179, 199

García de Luna, José, 144

Gardoqui, Diego de, 210

General Plan of the Engineers (1711), 101–2

Getsemaní, Nueva Granada, 164, 167, 169

Ghent, Treaty of (1814), 219

Gibraltar, 24, 108

Gonaïves, Saint-Domingue, 89

González Velázquez, Antonio: Casa de Dirección de la Renta and Fábrica de Tabacos (Mexico City) plans of, 38–39

Great Britain. *See* England

Guadalupe Victoria (José Miguel Ramón Adaucto Fernández y Félix), 180

Guanabacoa, Cuba, 123, 124

Guantánamo Bay (Cuba): English settlement of, 68–85, 88; mapping of, 103

Güemes Pacheco, Juan Vicente de, 38

Guillemard, Gilberto: New Orleans, Louisiana's fortifications and, 203

Gulf of Gonâve (Saint-Domingue): fortification of, 89

Gurtel, Carlos, 107–8

Halstead, William, 48

Havana, Cuba: Edward Vernon's attack against (1739), 71, 85; English capture of (1762), 100, 112–25, 176, 187; fixed battalion in, 175; fortifications of, 102, 129, 131, 177; Francisco Bouligny in, 199; geostrategic importance of, 129; Juan de Císcara in, 131; Juan de Herrera y Sotomayor in, 148; Luis Huet in, 103; Manila galleon in, 146

Hawk, James: English capture of Havana, Cuba (1762) depiction by, 116–25

Hermosilla, José de, 31

Hermosilla, Joseph, 187

Hermosilla, Miguel de: Santiago de Cuba cathedral plans of, 33–34, 36

Heroico Colegio Militar (Mexico): at San Carlos de Perote fort, 180

Herranz de Meñaca, Francisco: Canal del Dique (Cartagena de Indias, Nueva Granada) and, 142, 145, 152

Herrera y Sotomayor, Juan de: Canal del Dique (Cartagena de Indias, Nueva Granada) and, 137, 142, 146, 147–59, 223

Holmes, David, 213, 215–16

Hood, Samuel: visit to Havana, Cuba by (1758), 122

Hospital Real (Santiago de Cuba), 131

hospitals: in Cartagena de Indias, Nueva Granada, 163; Hospital Real (Santiago de Cuba), 131; John Müller on, 82; in New Orleans, Louisiana, 203; Royal Hospital (San Juan, Puerto Rico), 188; in Spanish Town, Jamaica, 48

Howe, William, 123

Hudson, Thomas, 116

Huet, Luis, 85, 101–11, 121, 122

hydrology: military engineers and, 137, 153–59, 223

Île-à-Vache (Saint-Domingue), 94

Imperial Digueri y Trejo, Vicente Ignacio, 103

ingeniero director, 19; Luis Huet as, 102, 103; Manuel de Anguiano as, 163

ingeniero extraordinario: Manuel de Anguiano as, 163

ingeniero jefe, 19

ingeniero ordinario, 19; Luis Huet as, 102

innovation, 222

intelligence gathering, 222; by Luis Huet, 107–10

Isabel II battery platform (San Juan, Puerto Rico), 194

Isla de León (Spain), 103

Italian peninsula, 24; locks on, 157; Luis Huet on, 102; military architectural model of, 81, 135, 186
Iturbide, Agustín de, 180

Jacmel, Saint-Domingue, 89
Jamaica: in American War for Independence (1775–83), 46–47, 53, 107–10; fortifications of, 45–54, 69, 81; geostrategic importance of, 69; Santiago de Cuba's fortification and, 130
Jay, John, 210
Jay-Gardoqui Treaty (1784), 210
Jefferson, Thomas: on Floridas, 211–14; on Manifest Destiny, 209; on Spanish possession of the Gulf South, 210
Jiménez Donoso, Juan, 157
Juárez, Benito, 183
Juraguá Chico beach (Santiago de Cuba), 96
Juraguá Grande beach (Santiago de Cuba), 96

Kelly, John, 50
Keppel, Augustus, 116
Keppel, George (3rd Earl of Albemarle), 116
Keppel, William, 116
King's Negroes (Jamaica), 48, 50
Kingston, Jamaica: classical architecture of, 84–85; fortifications of, 45, 47, 69; inhabited lots in, 72; military intelligence from, 107–8, 222; social organization in, 83, 84; urban plan of, 85
Knowles, Charles: Antigua's fortifications and, 61; attacks in Cuba and Saint-Domingue by (1748), 86–100; Havana, Cuba, visit of (1756), 122
Kress, Georg, 23

labor: on Antigua's fortifications, 58; on Jamaica's fortifications, 47, 49–50, 54. *See also* enslaved people
La Cabaña (Havana, Cuba), 120, 122, 123–24

La Chorrera castle (near Havana, Cuba), 116, 121, 122, 124
La Estrella fort (Santiago de Cuba), 94, 96, 98, 130, 131
La Guaira, Nueva Granada: Charles Knowles's attack against (1743), 87, 94, 175
Laguna, José, 192
La Lance, Louis-Joseph, 89
Lancey, Thomas F., 62
Langle, Francisco de: Cumberland investigated by, 80; Santiago de Cuba's fortification and, 95–96, 99–100
Languedoc, France: canal in, 153
La Perla battery platform (San Juan, Puerto Rico), 186
La Popa Mountain (Nueva Granada): batteries on, 164, 165, 166
La Redonda battery (Santiago de Cuba), 96
lime: in Jamaica's fortifications, 48, 48–49, 54; in New Orleans, Louisiana's fortifications, 200; in San Juan, Puerto Rico's fortifications, 188
limestone, iv
Le Blond, Guillaume, 16
Leogane, Saint-Domingue, 89; Charles Knowles's attack against (1743), 94
León, Manuel Miguel de, 187
Les Cayes, Saint-Domingue, 89
Lezo, Blas de, 113, 175
Limonta, Isidro, 95, 96
Livingston, Robert, 211–12
locks: on Canal del Dique (Cartagena de Indias, Nueva Granada), 152, 153–57; in Italy, 157; Simon Stevin on, 154
Long, Edward, 52
Los Doce Apóstoles battery (Havana, Cuba), 123
Louisiana: Baton Rouge, Louisiana, U.S. acquisition of, 210, 213–14; New Orleans, Louisiana's fortifications, 198–208
Louisiana Purchase (1803), 210; West Florida and, 211–12, 218
Lozano, Antonio, 20

Index

Lucuze, Pedro, 15, 20–21, 23, 221
Luffmann, John: on St. John's Roads (Antigua) fortification, 62
Luis Muñoz Rivera Park (San Juan, Puerto Rico), 197

MacEvan, Juan Bautista, 80
Madison, James: West Florida acquisition and, 210, 211, 214, 216, 218
Magaña, Andrés de, 131, 134
Magdalena River (Nueva Granada): flooding on, 150; significance of, 138
Mahates, Nueva Granada, 139, 140
mahogany: use in Jamaica of, 48
Málaga, Spain: Luis Huet in, 102; Manuel de Anguiano in, 163
Manchak fort (Louisiana), 200
Mandar, Charles-François, 15–16
Manifest Destiny, 209
Manila, Philippines: British capture of (1762), 115, 125, 176
Manila galleon, 178
Marianao castle (near Havana, Cuba), 121
Marianao River (Cuba), 121, 122
Mariel, Cuba: mapping of, 103
Marín, Miguel: atlas of, 21–22, 23
Marolois, Samuel, 157
Maroons: at Cumberland, 84; in Jamaica, 46; in Spanish navy, 177
Martín Rodríguez, Manuel: Santiago de Cuba cathedral plans of, 34–36
Mascaró, Manuel Agustín: Casa de Dirección de la Renta and Fábrica de Tabacos (Mexico City) plans of, 37–38
Mason, James, 116
Matamoros, Manuel, 213
Matanzas, Cuba: fortifications of, 129, 131; mapping of, 103
Mathew, William: on Antigua's geostrategic importance, 56; on Fort Hamilton (Antigua), 62
Maximilian of Mexico, 183
Mayorga, Martín: on San Carlos de Perote fort (New Spain/Mexico), 179
Mazas fort (Louisiana), 202

Melilla, Spain, 102
mestizos (mixed-race people): in Spanish navy, 177
Mestre, Juan Francisco: San Juan, Puerto Rico's fortifications and, 187, 188–92
Mexican-American War (1846–48): San Carlos de Perote fort (New Spain/Mexico) during, 180
Mexican independence movement: San Carlos de Perote fort (New Spain/Mexico) in, 180
Mexican Revolution: San Carlos de Perote fort (New Spain/Mexico) during, 184
Mexico: San Carlos de Perote fort, 174–84
Mexico City, Mexico: Casa de Dirección de la Renta plans, 37–39; Fábrica de Tabacos plans, 37–39; Real Academia de San Carlos in, 31–32
Midi, France: canal in, 153
military engineers: Bourbon reforms and, 101; fluvial knowledge and, 137, 153–59; integration into American society of, 161–62; ranks of, 19; training of, 13–27, 136, 148, 153, 221
Minguet e Yrol, Pablo, 23–24, 25
Miranda, Francisco de, 122
Miró, Esteban, 206
Mississippi River: during American War for Independence (1775–83), 107; geostrategic importance of, 209–11
Mobile, Alabama: U.S. acquisition and, 210, 214–18
Mobile Act (1804), 212
Moñino, Francisco, 33
Monroe, James, 211–12; on British acquisition of the Floridas, 213
Montalembert, Marc René de, 15
Mopox Commission (1796–1802), 68
morenos (dark-skinned people): in Spanish navy, 177
Morgan, Henry, 113
Morillo, Pablo, 172
Morris (enslaved worker in Jamaica), 48
Morro Castle (Havana, Cuba): during

Index   303

English attack (1762), *113–14*, 116, 120, 122, 123, 124

Müller, John, 15, 157, 221; influence on Cumberland Camp (Guantanamo Bay, Cuba) of, 82–83, 84–85

Muñoz Rivera, Luis, 197

Murcia, Spain: Luis Huet in, 102

Museum of Natural History (San Juan, Puerto Rico), 197

Myngs, Christopher: Santiago de Cuba attacked by (1662), 96, 130

Napoleon I of France, 198, 218

Nassau, Bahamas. *See* Providencia, Bahamas

Navacerrada, Manuel de, 187

Neptuno (Spanish ship), 120–21

New Orleans, Louisiana: fortifications of, 198–208

New Road (New Spain), 178

New York, New York: British fleet in, during American War for Independence (1775–83), 108

Nieuwe maniere van sterctebov door spilsluysen (Stevin), 154

North America: fortification historiography of, iv

Nueva Granada: independence movement in, 172–73; Santa Fé de Bogotá viceregal palace, 39–40. *See also* Cartagena de Indias, Nueva Granada

Nueva Movila fort (Louisiana), 202

Nuovo Theatro di machine (Zonca), 157

O'Daly, Thomas: San Juan, Puerto Rico's fortifications and, 187–88

Ogle, Chaloner, 87

Old Canal (Bahamas), 116

Olivares, Count-Duke of (Gaspar de Guzmán y Pimentel), 185

Oran (modern-day Algeria), 188; Manuel de Anguiano born in, 163; mathematics academy at, 14, 17, 163

Ordenanzas (1739), 16, 17–19, 22–23

Ordinances of Philip II (1573), 104, 107

Ordovás, Juan José: atlas of, 23

O'Reilly, Alejandro: New Orleans, Louisiana's fortifications and, 199, 202–3; San Juan, Puerto Rico's fortifications and, 177, 187–88, 189

Orford, HMS, 116

Orsbridge, Philip, 116

Oses de Abía, Joaquín Antonio, 35

Pacte de Famille (Third; 1761), 162, 176, 198

Pacte de Famille (1796), 185

Padilla, Pedro, 187

Pagan, Count of (Blaise Francois de Pagan), 16

Palacio, Juan Fernando de: Veracruz, New Spain's fortifications and, 177

Palacio de Chapultepec (Mexico City), 37

Palo Alto, Nueva Granada: hornwork at, 167

Panama: British attack considered against (1741), 115; Darien Gap, 164; fixed battalion in, 175. *See also* Portobelo, Panama

"*parallèle des systèmes*," 16

Paris, Treaty of (1763), 176, 198

Parke, Daniel, 59, 62

Parsons, William, 197

Pasacaballos, Nueva Granada, 139

Pasacaballos Strait (Nueva Granada), 139, 150, *151*

Pascagoula River: navigation and deposit rights on, 210–11

Patiño, José: naval reforms of, 177

Payen, Marc, 89

Pearl River: navigation and deposit rights on, 210–11

Pedrosa y Guerrero, Antonio de la, 144

Peñalver, Luis de, 204

Pensacola, Florida. *See* San Miguel de Panzacola, Florida

Peramás, Joaquín de: New Orleans, Louisiana's fortifications and, 206, 207–8

Perchet, Juan María, 201

Perdido River, 216, 218, 219; navigation and deposit rights on, 210–11

Perejil Island, 102

304 Index

Pérez, Cayetano, 217–18
Pérez, Francisco, 130
periphery: Caribbean Sea as, i–ii
Petit-Goâve, Saint-Dominique: Charles
 Knowles's attack against (1743), 94;
 fortifications of, 89, 100; founding of,
 88, 89
Philip II of Spain: Academia de
 Matemáticas y Arquitectura Militar
 (Madrid) founded by, 135; fortifications during reign of, 174; Ordinances
 of (1573), 104, 107
Philip V of Spain, 187; *docere et delectare*
 items and, 23, 24; Portobelo, Panama's
 fortifications and, 71; portrait of, 147;
 royal military engineers and, 101–2;
 Spanish navy rebuilt by, 175
piracy: Cuba and, 129–30, 132; by English,
 69, 85, 113; Nueva Granada and, 138,
 146, 150; Puerto Rico and, 186; Saint-
 Domingue and, 100
pitch pines: use in Jamaica of, 48
Plan Continental de Defensa (1779). *See*
 Continental Plan of Defense (Plan
 Continental de Defensa; 1779)
Plymouth, HMS, 98
Pocock, George, 116, 124
Pointis, Baron de (Bernard Des Jean):
 assault on Cartagena de Indias, Nueva
 Granada, by (1697), 145, 148, 174
polycentrism: in Saint-Domingue's forti-
 fications, 100
Ponce de León, Juan, 186
Porcel, Antonio, 35
Port-de-Paix, Saint-Dominique, 87
Portobelo, Panama: Edward Vernon's
 attack against (1739), 71, 85, 87, 113, 115,
 175, 187; Manila galleon in, 146; smug-
 gling in, 144
Prince's Ravelin (San Juan, Puerto Rico), 195
Princess's battery platform (San Juan,
 Puerto Rico), 189, 195
privateering: Antigua and, 63, 65; Jamaica
 and, 46; as War of Jenkins' Ear cause,
 63. *See also specific privateers*

Providencia, Bahamas: map of, 110, *111*
Puerta de Tierra region (Puerto Rico):
 defensive lines in, 188–97
Puerto Cabello, Nueva Granada: Charles
 Knowles's attack against (1743), 87
Puerto Rico: fixed battalion in, 175; San
 Juan's fortifications, 185–97

Queen Anne's War (1702–13), 13

Raleigh, Walter: on Spanish empire, 174
Real Academia de Bellas Artes de San
 Fernando (Madrid, Spain): Casa de
 Dirección de la Renta and Fábrica
 de Tabacos (Mexico City) plans and,
 37–39; Comisión de Arquitectura of,
 founded, 30; military engineers' train-
 ing at, 14, 21, 27; Real Academia de San
 Carlos (Mexico City) and, 31–32; Santa
 Fé de Bogotá viceregal palace plans
 and, 39–40 Santiago de Cuba cathe-
 dral plans and, 33–34; Spanish Amer-
 ican building projects and, 28–41;
 Spanish Corps of Military Engineers
 and, 31, 40
Real Academia de Guardiamarinas
 (Cádiz, Spain), 122
Real Academia de San Carlos (Mexico
 City), 31–32, 38
Real Cuerpo de Ingenieros (Spain). *See*
 Spanish Corps of Military Engineers
Real Junta de Fortificaciones (Madrid),
 19–20
Real Sociedad de Matemáticas (Madrid,
 Spain), 15, 21
recreation: military engineers' training
 and, 23–27
Reform War (1857–61): San Carlos de Per-
 ote fort (New Spain/Mexico) during,
 183
Regla, Cuba, 121
Rey, Juan del, 20
Reynolds, Joshua, 115, 116
Rezusta, Pascual de, 35
Ricaud de Tirgale, Balthasar, 72

Index

Roatan Island: English attack against (1742), 85; fortifications of, 70

Rocha, Nueva Granada, 139

Rock Fort (Jamaica), 45

Rojas, Cristóbal de, 14–15, 153

Royal Artillery (United Kingdom), 58

Royal Engineers (United Kingdom), 58, 60, 62

Royal Hospital (San Juan, Puerto Rico), 188

Royal Military Academy (Brussels), 101, 153

Royal Military Academy (Woolwich), 82

Ruiz y Díaz, Francisca, 163

Ryswick, Treaty of (1697), 88

Saavedra Fajardo, Diego, 24, 26–27

Sabatini, Francisco, 31; New Orleans, Louisiana's fortifications and, 201–2

Saint Charles battery (Fort-Dauphin, Saint-Domingue), 89

Saint-Domingue: Charles Knowles's attack on Saint-Louis-du-Sud (1748), 88–94, 99; fortifications of, 54, 99, 100

Saint Frederic battery (Fort-Dauphin, Saint-Domingue), 89

Saint-Louis-du-Sud, Saint-Domingue: Charles Knowles's attack on (1748), 88–94, 99; fortification of, 88, 89–91, 91–93; founding of, 89

Saint Marc, Saint-Domingue, 89

Sala, Ignacio, 102

Saldurtum, Palacios, 135

Salemas Canal (Puerto Rico), 189

Salmon, Hipólito, 107–8

San Antonio de los Baños, Cuba, 104

San Antonio Bridge (San Juan, Puerto Rico), 188, 189, 192

San Antonio bulwark (Santiago de Cuba), 134

San Antonio Canal (San Juan, Puerto Rico), 188, 189, 192

San Carlos battery (Cartagena de Indias, Nueva Granada), 169

San Carlos de Perote fort (New Spain/Mexico), 174–84

San Carlos fort (New Orleans, Louisiana), 200, 203, 205

Sánchez Taramas, Miguel, 15, 157

San Cristóbal Castle (San Juan, Puerto Rico), 186, 189, 192, 195

San Diego provisional fort (Havana, Cuba), 103

San Estanislao, Nueva Granada, 139

San Felipe del Morro Castle (San Juan, Puerto Rico), 186, 188, 195

San Felipe de Placaminas fort (New Orleans, Louisiana), 201, 206–7

San Felipe Neri tower (Havana, Cuba), 120

San Fernando fort (New Orleans, Louisiana), 201, 203, 205, 206

San Francisco castle (Santiago de Cuba), 94, 130, 132–36

San Francisco convent (Havana, Cuba), 120

San Francisco convent (Santiago de Cuba), 131

San Francisco de Paula church (Havana, Cuba), 120

San Ildefonso, Second Treaty of (1796), 185

San Ildefonso, Third Treaty of (1800), 198

San Jerónimo del Boquerón fort (San Juan, Puerto Rico), 186, 188, 192

San Juan, Puerto Rico: fortifications of, 185–97, 222

San Juan Degollado bulwark (Santiago de Cuba), 133, 134, 135

San Juan de Jaruco, Cuba: Luis Huet's urban planning for, 104–5

San Juan de Ulúa castle (Veracruz, Mexico), 177, 178; Saint-Louis-du-Sud, Saint-Domingue compared with, 89, 91

San Juan fort (New Orleans, Louisiana), 200, 201, 203, 204, 205

San Julián de los Güines, Cuba: Luis Huet's urban planning for, 105–7

San Lázaro castle (near Havana, Cuba), 121

San Lázaro fort (Cartagena de Indias, Nueva Granada), 168

San Lorenzo de Chagres, Panama: Edward Vernon's attack on (1740), 87, 175

San Luis fort (New Orleans, Louisiana), 200, 203, 204, 205

San Martín y La Madrid, Francisco: Canal del Dique (Cartagena de Indias, Nueva Granada) and, 142, 145, 152

San Maxent, Gilberto Antonio de, 207

San Miguel de Panzacola, Florida: English attack planned on (1781), 108; fortifications of, 202; map of, 109

San Pedro bulwark (Santiago de Cuba), 134, 135

San Pedro de la Roca castle (Santiago de Cuba), 94, 95–96, 98, 130, 131, 132, 134

San Ramón battery platform (San Juan, Puerto Rico), 192

Sans Souci, Haiti: social organization in, 83

Santa Anna, Antonio López de, 180

Santa Bárbara battery (Cartagena de Indias, Nueva Granada), 168, 169, 170, 171

Santa Catalina battery (Santiago de Cuba), 96, 130, 131

Santa Catalina beach (Cartagena de Indias, Nueva Granada), 166

Santa Catalina church (Santiago de Cuba), 132

Santa Catalina fortress (San Juan, Puerto Rico), 186, 188

Santa Clara bulwark (Cartagena de Indias, Nueva Granada), 166, 167

Santa Cruz bulwark (Cartagena de Indias, Nueva Granada), 166

Santa Elena battery platform (San Juan, Puerto Rico), 186

Santa Fé de Bogotá, Nueva Granada: audiencia of, on Canal del Dique (Cartagena de Indias, Nueva Granada) and, 147; viceregal palace in, 39–40

Santa Teresa battery platform (San Juan, Puerto Rico), 189

Santiago de Cuba: cathedral plans (1779) for, 32–36; Charles Knowles's attack against (1748), 98; Christopher Myngs's attack against (1662), 96, 130; Edward Vernon's attack against (1741), 71–72, 85, 96, 98, 99, 113; fortifications of, 94–98, 99–100, 129–36; founding of, 129–30

Santiago de las Vegas, Cuba, 104

Santísimo Sacramento battery (Santiago de Cuba), 95–96

Santistevan, Manuel de, 177; San Carlos de Perote fort (New Spain/Mexico) and, 179

Santo Domingo: social organization in, 83

Santo Domingo bulwark (Cartagena de Indias, Nueva Granada), 166

Santo Domingo de Atarés castle (Havana, Cuba), 120

Scheither, Johann Bernhard von, 16

seawalls: on Canal del Dique (Cartagena de Indias, Nueva Granada), 157. See also walls

Second Mexican Empire (1863–67): San Carlos de Perote fort (New Spain/ Mexico) during, 183

Second Plan for the Defense of the Caribbean (II Plan de Defensa del Caribe; 1765), 177

Serres, Dominic, 116

Seven Years' War (1753–64), ii, iv, 107, 176; Caribbean's importance in, 86; economic devastation of, 104; French defensive strategy in, 100; Havana, Cuba's capture during (1762), 112–25, 187; intelligence gathering before, 70; San Carlos de Perote fort (New Spain/ Mexico) and, 178

Shaw, John, 215, 216, 217–18

shingles: in Jamaican fortifications, 54

Simcocks, Thomas, 50

Síscara, Juan de. See Císcara, Juan de.

Sitoni, Giovanni Francesco, 157

smuggling: in Jamaica, 46; in Nueva Granada, 140, 143–45

social organization: of Cumberland Camp (Guantanamo Bay, Cuba), 83–84

Somovilla y Tejada, Juan de, 139

Soto Hill (Havana, Cuba), 120

Spain: canals in, 153; fortification policy of, 99, 221–222; Luis Huet in, 102;

military engineers' training in, 13, 221; naval development of, 177

Spanish America: fortification historiography of, iii–iv; Jamaican fortifications compared to fortifications in, 54. *See also specific regions and colonies*

Spanish-American War (1898), 186

Spanish Civil War, 184

Spanish Corps of Military Engineers, 27, 30–31; creation of, 101–2, 129; *Instrucción* (1718) for, 17, 22–23; Real Academia de Bellas Artes de San Fernando (Madrid, Spain) and, 31, 40; urban works and, 103–4

Spanish Town, Jamaica: governor's house in, 52–53; new barracks and hospital in, 48

Stevin, Simon: enclosure locks model by, 156; floodgate model by, 155; influence on Juan de Herrera y Sotomayor of, 154, 157

St. John's Roads (Antigua): fortification of, 62–65

St. Kitts, 55

stone: in Jamaican fortifications, 47, 48, 54

Suárez Calderín, Francisco: San Francisco castle (Santiago de Cuba) and, 133, 135; Santiago de Cuba cathedral plans of, 32

Sucre, Carlos, 144

sugar cultivation: in Antigua, 55, 56, 63; in Cuba, 104; in Jamaica, 47, 54

Superviela, Pedro, 20

Tackey's Revolt (1760), 46

Tajamar battery platform (San Juan, Puerto Rico), 189, *193*, 195

Tantete, José, 104

taxation: in British West Indies, 46–47, 51–52, 55

Thomas, Philemon, 213

tile: use in Jamaica of, 48

timber: in Antigua, 63; in Jamaican fortifications, 47, 48, 54

Toledo y Portugal, Juan de, 153

Tolú, Nueva Granada, 143, 150; batteries in, 164, 165

Tordesillas, Treaty of (1494), 185

Torno de los Ingleses (Louisiana), 199–200, 206

Torno de Placcamin (Louisiana), 206–7

Torres, Gabriel de, 173

training: of Juan Císcara, 135; of Juan de Herrera y Sotomayor 153; of military engineers, 13–27, 136, 148, 153, 221

Trattato delle virtù e proprietà delle acque (Sitoni), 157

Treatise containing the Practical Part of Fortification, for the use of the Royal Military Academy (Müller), 15

Trelawney, Edward: on Jamaica's fortifications, 45

Trudeau, Carlos: New Orleans, Louisiana's fortifications and, 204–5

Truxillo, Honduras: British attack against, 70

Twelve Years' Truce (1609–1621), 185

United Kingdom. *See* England

Unzaga, Luis de, 122, 203

Utrecht, Treaty of (1713), 187; *asiento de negros* and 87, 143, 175

Vaillant, Juan Bautista, 33

Valdivia, Chile: fixed battalion in, 175; Juan de Herrera y Sotomayor in, 148

Valencia, Spain, 102; Academia de San Carlos in, 29

Valparaíso, Chile: Juan de Herrera y Sotomayor in, 148

Valtellina Agreement (1609–1621), 185

Van Coehoorn, Menno, 16, 157

Vauban, Sébastien de, 16; influence on American fortifications of, iv, 14, 100, 153; influence on John Müller of, 82; Saint-Louis-du-Sud, Saint-Domingue's fortifications and, 91

Velázquez de Cuéllar, Diego, 129–30

Vendaval wall (Cádiz, Spain), 103

Index

Veracruz, New Spain: fixed battalion in, 175; fortifications of, 177–78. *See also* San Juan de Ulúa (Veracruz, Mexico)

Veracruz Road (New Spain), 178

Verboom, Isidro Próspero, 24

Verboom, Jorge Próspero, 20, 101, 136

vernacular architecture: fortifications as, 66

Vernon, Edward: Cartagena de Indias, Nueva Granada, attacked by (1741), 71, 113, 115, 162, 167–68, 169, 175–76, 187; Charles Knowles compared to, 87; Guantánamo Bay (Cuba) encampment of, 71, 99; Havana, Cuba, attacked by (1739), 71, 85; Portobelo, Panama attacked by, 71, 87, 113, 115, 175, 187; propaganda about, 115; San Lorenzo de Chagres, Panama, attacked by (1740), 87, 175; Santiago de Cuba attacked by (1741), 71–72, 85, 96, 98, 99, 113

Villalba Angulo Ponce de León, Juan de, 177

Villalobos, Juan, 134–35

Villalonga, Jorge de, 144

Vizcaína (Spanish frigate), 163

Wall, Ricardo, 176

walls: in Antigua's fortifications, 59, 61; in Saint-Domingue's fortifications, 88, 100; in Santiago de Cuba, 94. *See also* seawalls

Walpole, Robert, 87

War of 1812, 210, 216, 218–19

War of Austrian Succession. *See* War of Jenkins' Ear (1739–48)

War of Jenkins' Ear (1739–48), ii, 45, 175–76, 187; Antigua's defenses and, 63; Caribbean's importance in, 86; causes of, 87; Charles Knowles's attacks in Cuba and Saint-Domingue (1748) during, 86–100. *See also* Vernon, Edward

War of the Spanish Succession (1701–14), ii, 17, 174–75; effect on San Juan, Puerto Rico, 186–87; effect on Spanish navy of, 177

Washington, George, 71, 84, 211

Washington, Lawrence, 71–72, 84

Washington House (Bridgetown, Barbados), 69, 84

Wentworth, Thomas, 71, 83, 99; Cartagena de Indias (1741) defeat attributed to, 115

West Florida: as Spain-U.S. contention point, 211; U.S. acquisition of, 213–18, 221–22

Wilkinson, James: U.S. acquisition of Mobile, Alabama, and, 216–18

Willoughby, 6th Lord (William Willoughby), 58

Windward Passage: importance in War of Jenkins' Ear (1739–48) of, 87–88

World War II: San Carlos de Perote fort (New Spain/Mexico) during, 184

Ximénez, Alonso, 22, 23

Yucatán Peninsula: fixed battalion in, 175

Zabalda, Agustín de, 35

Zapata, Pedro de, 139

Zermeño, Martín, 20–21

Zonca, Vittorio, 157

Zúñiga, Mauricio, 217